A MATTER OF HOPE

A MATTER OF HOPE

A Theologian's Reflections
on the Thought of Karl Marx

NICHOLAS LASH

UNIVERSITY OF NOTRE DAME PRESS

Notre Dame, Indiana

University of Notre Dame Press edition 1982
Published by arrangement with
Darton, Longman and Todd Limited

Copyright © 1981 by Nicholas Lash

Library of Congress Cataloging in Publication Data

Lash, Nicholas.
  A matter of hope.

  Bibliography: p.
  Includes indexes.
  1. Marx, Karl, 1818–1883. 2. Communism and
Christianity. I. Title.
B3305.M74L28 1982   261.2'1   82-1980
ISBN 0-268-01352-7   AACR2

Printed in the United States of America

For
Donald MacKenzie MacKinnon

CONTENTS

Acknowledgements   xi

Preface   xiii

Abbreviations   xiv

PART I   PRELIMINARIES

1 Introduction   3

2 Marx: 'Early' and 'Mature'   10

3 Meanings of 'Marxism'   24

4 *The German Ideology*   36

PART II   THEMES

5 Revelation, Appearance and Reality   51

   'Veils' and 'Masks'   52

   Hegel and Marx   55

6 The Meaning of History   64

   Two Senses of 'Historicism'   64

   The Narration of Hope   68

   Prophecy and Prediction   71

7 Correctness and Truth   73

   Appearance, Reality and the 'True Individual' 73

   Locating the Question of Truth   77

8 Marx and Materialism   88

	Materialism as Social Protest	88
	Marx, Hegel and Feuerbach	93
9	Materialist Theory and Idealist Practice	105
10	Base and Superstructure	112
11	Ideology	125
12	Christian Materialism	135
	Materialism and Christian Belief	136
	Event and Interpretation	145
	Materialist Theory and Idealist Practice	149
	Conclusion	151
13	The Criticism of Religion	153
	The 'Essence of Christianity'	155
	'Man Makes Religion'	156
	Opium and Endurance	158
	The Abolition of Religion	165
	The 'Content' of Religion	167
14	Alienation and Redemption	169
	Concept and Terminology	170
	Alienation in Capital	174
	Illustrations and Analogies	176
	'Alienation' and 'Objectification': Theological Reflections	180
	'Alienation' and the Human Condition	186
	Death and Resurrection	191
15	Theory and Symbolism	195
	Art and Knowledge	196
	Sense and Thought	198
	Wealth and Poverty	201
	Religion and Theology	204

16 'Scientific' Marxism: Problems of Method 210

    Senses of 'Science' 210

    Search for a Starting-Point 216

    Science and Prediction 227

17 Utopia, Hope and Revolution 231

    Prediction, Persuasion and Preference:

    Introductory Remarks 231

    The Critique of Utopianism 234

    Utopianism and Christianity 236

    Expectation and Prediction 239

    Proletariat and Revolution 243

18 Optimism, Eschatology and the Form of the Future 250

    The 'Birth' of History 250

    Judgement and Mercy 257

    Freedom and Necessity 262

    The Organization of Freedom 273

PART III   POSTFACE

19 In Place of Conclusion 283

List of Works Cited 293

Index of Marx references 299

Index of names 301

Index of subjects 304

ACKNOWLEDGEMENTS

Thanks are due to the following for permission to reproduce extracts from copyright sources.

Lawrence & Wishart Ltd: *Collected Works* vols. IV and V by Karl Marx and Frederick Engels.

The Merlin Press Ltd: *Marx's Theory of Alienation* by István Mészáros and *The Poverty of Theory and Other Essays* by E. P. Thompson.

Penguin Books Ltd: *The First International and After: Political Writings* vol. 3 by Karl Marx (Pelican Marx Library/New Left Review 1974) pp. 37, 62, 80, 155, 213, 262, 298, 299, 337, 346, 347, 355. Edited by David Fernbach. Selection and Notes copyright © New Left Review, 1974. Introduction copyright © David Fernbach. Translation copyright © Paul Jackson, 1974. Translation copyright © David Fernbach, 1974. Translation copyright © Rosemary Sheed, 1974. *Early Writings* by Karl Marx translated by Rodney Livingstone and Gregory Benton (Pelican Marx Library/New Left Review 1975) pp. 64, 86, 110, 217, 229, 236, 239, 241, 243, 244, 245, 249, 255, 256, 257, 260, 265, 325, 328, 329, 330, 348, 351, 352, 353, 354, 355, 356, 375, 381, 389, 398, 421, 422, 423, 424, 425, 426, 430. Selections and Notes © New Left Review 1974. Translation copyright © Rodney Livingstone, 1975. Translation copyright © Gregory Benton, 1975. Translations in the Appendix copyright © Lawrence & Wishart, 1971, 1973. *Grundrisse* by Karl Marx translated by Martin Nicolaus (Pelican Marx Library/New Left Review 1973) pp. 83, 85, 88, 94, 95, 97, 99, 100, 101, 102, 103, 105, 106–7, 108, 110, 111, 164, 221, 247, 487, 488, 490, 542, 749, 639. Translation and Foreword copyright © Martin Nicolaus, 1973. *Capital* vol. I by Karl Marx translated by Ben Fowkes (Pelican Marx Library/New Left Review 1976) pp. 89, 92, 102, 103, 164, 165, 173, 178, 182, 203, 204, 217, 272, 375, 416, 618, 675, 682, 716, 718, 739, 757, 772, 799, 918, 943, 990, 1006. Translation copyright © Ben Fowkes, 1976. Appendix translation copyright © Rodney Livingstone, 1976.

Thanks are due to Random House, Inc: for permission to reproduce the following in the USA and Canada: *The First International and After: Political Writings*, vol. 3 by Karl Marx, edited by David Fernbach. Copyright © 1974 New Left Review. *Early Writings* by

PREFACE

This book has grown out of the O'Hara Lectures in the Philosophy of Religion which I gave in the University of Notre Dame in April 1980. My first thanks, therefore, go to the Department of Philosophy at Notre Dame for their kindness in inviting me to give those lectures and, especially, to the O'Hara Professor, Frederick J. Crosson, who was unsparing in his generosity to my wife and myself. We are also deeply indebted to all our other friends at Notre Dame, whose kindness and hospitality did so much to make our stay in South Bend both enjoyable and profitable. Several chapters were drafted while staying at the University of San Diego: this was an unforgettable experience and, thanks to the kindness of Dr Gary Macy and others, also a pleasant one.

I have profited greatly from the advice of several people who either heard the original lectures, or were kind enough to read various chapters in draft, especially Professors David Burrell, Stanley Hauerwas, Enda McDonagh, Ernan McMullin and Mr James Bradley.

To two people, above all, I am deeply grateful: to Professor David McLellan, of the University of Kent at Canterbury, who read the entire text, and whose detailed and thoughtful comments and suggestions gave me both help and encouragement, and to my wife, whose limitless patience during the time of preparation was further tested by having each draft of every chapter submitted to her scrutiny.

My thanks, also, to John M. Todd, a most considerate and encouraging publisher, to his staff at Darton, Longman and Todd; to the staff of the University of Notre Dame Press, and to Mrs Frances Robertson for her careful typing.

The dedication of this book to my predecessor in the Norris-Hulse chair at Cambridge is intended as a gesture, however inadequate, both of personal friendship and of gratitude for all that I have learned from him over the years. It is my hope that he will approve of the general intention underlying the work, if not of every detail of its execution.

Nicholas Lash

Cambridge
March 1981

ABBREVIATIONS

Cap I, II	K. Marx, *Capital*, vols. I and II. Penguin, 1976, 1978.
Cap III	K. Marx, *Capital*, vol. III. Lawrence and Wishart, 1959.
CW4, 5	K. Marx and F. Engels, *Collected Works*, vols. IV and V. Lawrence and Wishart, 1975, 1976.
EW	K. Marx, *Early Writings*. Penguin 1975.
FI	K. Marx, *Political Writings, III, The First International and After*. Penguin, 1974.
G	K. Marx, *Grundrisse*. Penguin, 1973.
HM	K. Marx, F. Engels, V. Lenin, *On Historical Materialism*. Moscow 1972.
KI, II, III	L. Kolakowski, *Main Currents of Marxism*. Oxford 1978. *I. The Founders* *II. The Golden Age* *III. The Breakdown*
Life	D. McLellan, *Karl Marx: His Life and Thought*. London 1973.
R1848	K. Marx, *Political Writings, I, The Revolutions of 1848*. Penguin, 1973.
SE	K. Marx, *Political Writings, II, Surveys from Exile*. Penguin, 1973.

NOTE

Full bibliographical details for other works referred to in the notes are given in the list of works cited on pp. 293–8.

PART I   PRELIMINARIES

1

INTRODUCTION

'Christianity', said Newman, 'has been long enough in the world to justify us in dealing with it as a fact in the world's history.'[1] The same, by now, can surely be said of Marxism. It would clearly be misleading to suggest that Christians have failed to attempt to 'deal with this fact', have held it as of little account. Indeed, throughout much of the 'first world', and especially in the United States, many Christians have been almost obsessively preoccupied with this 'fact', to the point (at times) of virtually defining their Christianity in terms of its opposition to 'atheistic communism'.

And yet, if we turn our attention from the practice of Christianity to the forms of reflection that constitute the disciplines of academic theology, the picture looks rather different. In spite of the fact that Marxist theorists have made significant contributions in such fields as historiography, economic and political theory, psychology, philosophy and literary criticism, a glance at even quite recent learned and influential works of biblical criticism, church history and doctrinal theology suggests that, at least in the English-speaking world, Christian theologians do not regard it as incumbent upon them to take the 'fact' of Marxist theory seriously into account. In a word: there is a curious disparity between contemporary Christianity's practical obsession with Marxism and its theoretical indifference.

This neglect is doubtless partly attributable to the implacable hostility with which Marxism and Christianity have usually confronted each other. Theologians seemed to suppose that they had little to learn from the 'enemy' (and they further curiously supposed that they knew what that 'enemy' was like without submitting him to close scrutiny)[2] and Marxist theorists returned the compliment. Thus it is that, although much has been written on Christianity from a variety of Marxist standpoints, from Kautsky[3] to Machoveč,[4]

---

1 J. H. Newman, *An Essay on the Development of Christian Doctrine*, p. 3.
2 There are, of course, exceptions, such as Gustav Wetter's massively learned study: *Dialectical Materialism: A Historical and Systematic Survey of Philosophy in the Soviet Union*.
3 K. Kautsky, *Foundations of Christianity*, tr. H. F. Mins (original first published in 1908).
4 M. Machoveč, *A Marxist Looks at Jesus*.

and although there have been numerous philosophical and sociological studies of Marx's critique of religion, there has been
surprisingly little direct and reasonably detailed discussion of
Marx's thought by professional students of Christian theology. Even
the shift of mood, in the 1960s, 'from anathema to dialogue'[5] and,
more recently, the widespread interest shown in 'liberation theology', seem to have done little to interest English and North American
theologians in Marx's own texts.[6]

This is not to say that Christian theology in the English-speaking
world has been wholly uninfluenced by Marxist thought, but only
that the influence has been, for the most part, diffuse and indirect.[7]
Thus, for example, the work of German theologians such as Jürgen
Moltmann, Johann-Baptist Metz and Wolfhart Pannenberg, and
the writings of Edward Schillebeeckx, have helped to stimulate
interest in the thought of Ernst Bloch, Max Horkheimer, T. W.
Adorno and Jürgen Habermas, all of whom stood or stand in some
sense in the Marxist tradition.[8] In contrast, however, the work of
European theologians from other countries who have either closely
studied Marx's thought (such as J.-Y. Calvez)[9] or who have been

5 Cf. R. Garaudy, *From Anathema to Dialogue*. Peter Hebblethwaite's survey of this
   shift (*The Christian-Marxist Dialogue and Beyond*) makes no mention of earlier
   attempts, such as J. Lewis, K. Polanyi, D. K. Kitchin, ed., *Christianity and the
   Social Revolution*, which appeared with an Introduction by Charles Raven, then
   Regius Professor of Divinity at Cambridge. (It must be admitted that some of
   the contributions indicate to what extent it was still a 'dialogue des sourds': cf.
   e.g. Ivan Levisky, 'Communism and Religion', pp. 262–96.) Nor does Hebblethwaite mention such significant expressions of the shift as the informed and
   balanced, if theoretically lightweight, study produced for and approved by the
   General Council of the United Church of Canada: D. Evans, *Communist Faith and
   Christian Faith*. From the same stable, cf. W. A. Luijpen, *Phenomenology and Atheism*;
   A. Miller, *The Christian Significance of Marx*.

6 Although Gustavo Gutierrez acknowledged that 'it is to a large extent due to
   Marxism's influence that theological thought . . . has begun to reflect on the
   meaning of the transformation of this world and the action of man in history'
   (*A Theology of Liberation*, p. 9), and Juan Luis Segundo, tired of 'trying to forestall
   every partisan and stupid misunderstanding', declared roundly that 'Latin American theology is certainly Marxist' in the sense that 'present-day social thought
   . . . is profoundly indebted to Marx' (*The Liberation of Theology*, p. 35), few of the
   'liberation theologians' appear closely to engage with Marx's own texts. An
   exception, from Mexico, would be José Porfirio Miranda, but his reading of the
   Bible in *Marx and the Bible* seems to me as tendentious as his reading of Marx in
   Marx Against the Marxists.

7 For the influence of Marx on Paul Tillich and Reinhold Niebuhr, cf. C. West,
   Communism and the Theologians.

8 Amongst the flood of recent studies of the 'Frankfurt School', cf. D. Held,
   Introduction to Critical Theory; M. Jay, *The Dialectical Imagination*; T. McCarthy, *The
   Critical Theory of Jürgen Habermas*. Perhaps the most thorough attempt, so far, by
   an English-speaking theologian, to engage with the German debates, is C. Davis,
   Theology and Political Society.

9 Cf. J.-Y. Calvez, *La Pensée de Karl Marx*; also H. Chambre, *De Karl Marx à Lenine
   et Mao Tsé-Toung*; R. Coste, *Analyse Marxiste et Foi Chrétienne*.

profoundly influenced by Marxist theory (such as Alfredo Fierro[10] and Giulio Girardi)[11] seems to have had little impact.

It is also worth remembering that Marxism has exerted an even more indirect and 'invisible' influence on Christian thought as one of the formative influences in the development of what might be called 'sociological awareness': the recognition that the worlds of meaning and relationship that we inhabit are social, historical constructs. Even the use, by theologians as by others, of concepts such as 'alienation' and 'ideology' owes something to the influence of the Marxist tradition, even though it may be difficult or impossible, in particular cases, to specify that 'something' with any precision.

The uncomprisingly negative character of the perceived relationship between Marxism and Christianity is reflected in the fact that such direct attention as Marxist theory in general, and Marx's own thought in particular, have received from Christian theologians has been largely apologetic in character. I would not wish to deny that apologetics, the exposition and attempted justification of patterns of Christian belief and action, has its place. But the mood of apologetics is assertive, rather than interrogative. The apologist sets out to teach rather than to learn, to prove or refute rather than to enquire, to give rather than to receive. Academic theology, on the other hand, as I understand it, is – or should be – fundamentally interrogative in character. It is the refraction, into the technically ordered realm of 'scientific' discourse (historical, literary-critical or philosophical) of that wonder, that contemplativity, which is the heart and centre of faith's relationship to its object: the mystery of God. It is not the theologian's business to tell other people what, or how, to believe. His responsibilities are critical, interpretative or clarificatory rather than declaratory. And theological discourse is never more threatened than when corrupted by its own misconceived autonomy. It follows that a theology whose basic mood has shifted, under pressure from apologetic concerns, from enquiry to assertion, is exposed to the dangerous illusion (about which we shall have more to say later) that it *possesses* its truth. This book is not a work of Christian apologetics. When I set out, I did not know what I would learn from Marx, nor what form eventual agreement or disagreement would take. I have tried, in other words, to employ the strategy recommended by the Czech theologian, Josef Hromadka, who, according to his pupil Jan Milič Lochman, was 'constantly urging us to "take Marxism seriously" '.[12]

10 Cf. A. Fierro, *The Militant Gospel*. An Althusserian Christian writing from Madrid is, indeed, a 'sign of the times'.
11 Cf., e.g., G. Girardi, *Marxism and Christianity*.
12 J. M. Lochman, *Encountering Marx*, p. 11. Lochman has summarized the argument of his little book in his contribution to J. C. Raines and T. Dean, ed., *Marxism and Radical Religion*.

But why should a Christian theologian suppose that the outcome of an attempt on his part to take Marx seriously was likely to be such as to justify the time and effort involved? This question breaks into three. Firstly, surely enough has already been written on Marx? Secondly, is there not little in Marx's own work which is of direct interest to the Christian theologian? Thirdly, even if the project be deemed worthwhile in principle, within what limits do I suppose myself competent to undertake it?

The suspicion that lies behind the first of these questions deepens when we hear Leszek Kolakowski complaining that 'The profusion of works directly or indirectly related to Marxism is such that of recent years a degree of satiety has become noticeable.'[13] The warning is timely, even if there is a certain irony in receiving it five hundred pages into the third volume of the most massive study of Marxist thought yet to have appeared in English. Nevertheless, even if a study such as this were of no direct interest or use to anybody else, it should be of *some* interest to Christians, for reasons at which I have hinted already. Christianity continues to exert powerful (even if extremely ambiguous) influence on human affairs. Anyone who doubts this must be curiously forgetful of events in Northern Ireland, Nicaragua and Poland, and of some of the forces at work in the process of electing President Ronald Reagan. For this reason alone, it would seem desirable that the enduring 'practical' influence of Christianity should be subject to continual scrutiny by a theology 'located', not in some private walled garden of ecclesiastical or supposedly purely 'religious' interests, but in that public forum in which, in our culture, concepts and beliefs, presuppositions, methods and strategies, are exposed to consideration and criticism. I am suggesting, in other words (and few theologians would dispute the suggestion, at least in principle), that the influence of Christianity on human affairs is still such as to render it dangerous (and not only for Christians) for Christian theology to be allowed to go about its business in real or imagined isolation from the forces that shape our culture and our history. And amongst these forces, Marxism occupies a significant place.

As an illustration (and it is only that), I would wish to argue that, today, forms of belief in God that have not *internally* felt the pressure, experienced the persuasiveness and power, of the dominant forms of contemporary atheism, are likely to hinder rather than to help the human quest for truth, justice and freedom. Christians are often strangely undisturbed by, and hence inadequately contest, the oppressive or destructive uses to which Christian belief sometimes continues to be put: uses which would have come as no surprise to Karl Marx.

13 *KIII*, p. 494.

With that remark, we are entering the territory indicated by my second question. It is true that Christian belief, and especially Christian theology, are matters upon which Marx had little to say that was original. But it does not follow that there is nothing of interest to the Christian theologian in those issues with which Marx *was* centrally concerned, and in the manner in which that concern was expressed.

Robert Tucker, whose study of *Philosophy and Myth in Karl Marx* has attracted widespread attention, is, I believe, justified in asserting that there is a 'redemptive idea' at the core of Marx's thought.[14] Unfortunately, Tucker's attempt to elucidate that 'core' is less than satisfactory. It is unsatisfactory, firstly, because he concentrates on the philosophical background to Marx's ideas, and on the overall 'pattern' or 'structure' of those ideas as they developed, in such a way as to distract attention from questions such as the following: however Marx may have come by his ideas, did he discover *nothing* of the way in which social processes work irrespective of our recognition that they work that way? In other words, within Tucker's framework the problem of the 'scientific' character of Marx's thought simply does not arise. I do not mean that he does not mention the matter, but it is symptomatic that his account of Marx's concept of 'science' concludes with the grossly misleading interpretative summary: 'what makes [Marxism] scientific is *nothing at all* but the fact that it is true.'[15]

In the second place, Tucker operates with an extremely simplistic typology of 'classes of mind', according to which if Marx is (as he claims) to be classified as a 'religious'[16] or 'totally committed mythic thinker'[17] (these descriptions are apparently interchangeable), he is thereby declared to have been incapable of critical philosophical or ethical reflection. This is a familiar schema: it is one according to which no committed Christian (for example) can also be a critically reflective theologian. But such crude oversimplifications of fundamental problems concerning the relations between commitment and enquiry, practice and theory, action and reflection, do not become more true merely by being frequently asserted by sociologists of religion.

I have mentioned Tucker's book because, notwithstanding these and other limitations,[18] it has the merit of indicating that it is only

---

14 Cf. R. C. Tucker, *Philosophy amd Myth in Karl Marx*, p. 24. The opening chapter of *KI* focuses on the soteriological motifs in the prehistory of Hegelian and Marxist dialectic.

15 Tucker, op. cit., p. 180, my stress.

16 Ibid., p. 22.

17 Ibid., p. 231.

18 Some of which have been trenchantly analysed by István Mészáros, *Marx's Theory of Alienation*, pp. 331–6.

through an examination of those themes which were fundamental to Marx's thought as a whole (by which I do *not* mean: as a more or less arbitrarily constructed 'system' of ideas) that the theological significance of his work can be exhibited. Thus it is that, of the fourteen chapters into which, in Part Two, I have grouped the topics chosen for consideration, only one is exclusively devoted to Marx's critique of religion.

So far as my third question is concerned, I am only too well aware of the limitations of my competence. I am not an expert either on Marx or on Marxism, and am therefore not equipped to undertake a scholarly examination either of the movement or of the thought of the man from whom the movement takes its name. I am only a Christian theologian who has sat down (the image is appropriate as a reminder that this book came into existence in the dangerous tranquillity of an academic's study) in front of a number of Marx's texts, and has tried to understand them, to learn from them and critically to confront them from the resources of my own experience and understanding.

But if my qualifications for the task are so exiguous, why undertake it? Quite simply: because (as I indicated earlier) it seemed to me to be a task which needed to be done and nobody else appeared to be doing it.

I would like to emphasize that the focus of attention in what follows is on Marx's own texts. Although I have tried to acquaint myself with some of the more influential strands in the Marxist tradition, my use of this material has been a matter of 'listening in' to Marxist debates in the hope that, by doing so, I would reduce the chances of seriously misrepresenting Marx's thought. This is a study, not of Marxisms, but of Marx. I shall be more than satisfied if I succeed in encouraging my fellow theologians to 'take Marx seriously', and if I persuade my Marxist readers that I have tried to do just this and that they – in turn – should refrain from discussing Christian theology unless they have studied its products with comparable seriousness.

It follows, I think, that any contribution which this book can make to 'Christian-Marxist dialogue' (a notion not without its difficulties, as I shall suggest in the final chapter) will be not only limited but indirect.

It also follows (and some of my Christian readers may regard this as a more serious limitation) that this is not, in any straightforward sense, a work of Christian theology. It is, rather, one individual theologian's 'reading' of Marx. For this reason, my treatment of doctrinal topics amounts to little more than an indication of the 'shape' which familiar problems appear to me to take when set in the context of a consideration of Marx's thought. Thus, for example, little or no reference will be made to the work of other theologians (although the theologically informed reader will have little difficulty in discovering where I stand on a number of issues that have engaged the attention of Christian theologians, both ancient and modern).

Because I assume that most of my readers are more likely to be 'at home' in Christian theology than in Marxian theory, I shall presuppose no greater familiarity with Marx's life and thought than can be acquired, for example, from David McLellan's little book on Marx in the Fontana Modern Masters series.[19] That book ends with some useful hints on how to set about reading Marx. McLellan suggests that, having read *The Communist Manifesto*, 'the next work to read is the first part of *The German Ideology*'.[20] I therefore propose to devote a chapter to that text. Before doing so, however, there are two other 'preliminaries' to which we must attend. The first is the problem of the continuities and discontinuities between the thought of the 'early' and the 'mature' Marx; the second is the question as to what might be meant by 'Marxism'. The reader more interested in Marx than in his commentators may prefer, at least in the first instance, to omit the next two chapters and to move immediately to Chapter Four.

19 D. McLellan, *Marx*.
20 Ibid., p. 85.

2

MARX: 'EARLY' AND 'MATURE'

When did Karl Marx become 'Marx'? The question may seem a curious one, and yet Lenin, in *Materialism and Empirio-Criticism*, referred to 1843 as the time 'when Marx was only becoming Marx, i.e. the founder of scientific socialism, the founder of *modern materialism*'.[1] More recently, the editor of an English edition of *The German Ideology* refers to it as 'the first recognisably "Marxist" work', in the sense that here, for the first time, Marx and Engels 'took their distance from Feuerbach'.[2]

The German Ideology was written between 1845 and 1846. It was thus written shortly after the 'Paris Manuscripts' of 1844, and a decade earlier than the *Grundrisse* – that massive series of seven notebooks in which Marx worked out the structure of his definitive critique of classical political economy. And yet, although written in the mid-nineteenth century, *The German Ideology* was not published until after the October Revolution: the first chapter (which I shall discuss in Chapter Four) appeared in 1924 and the full text only in 1932.[3] If we take all these considerations together it soon becomes clear that a decision to use it as a 'way in' to those aspects of Marx's thought with which I am principally concerned presupposes one of a number of possible approaches to the complex and still controversial problem of the relationship between the thought of the 'early' and the 'mature' Marx. As we shall see, discussion of this problem has been dominated by consideration, on the one hand, of the extent to which Hegelian methods, concerns and categories continued to influence Marx and, on the other, of questions concerning the sense in which Marxist theory is or is not appropriately described as 'scientific'. Both these issues, as well as others on which I shall touch in this chapter, will demand further consideration later on. For the time being, the task is simply to take our bearings.

To anyone familiar with Marx's writings it is perfectly clear that, in the course of a long career, his thought underwent several significant and profound shifts and developments. It is also clear that

1 V. I. Lenin, *Materialism and Empirio-Criticism*, p. 408, his stress.
2 C. J. Arthur, 'Introduction', K. Marx and F. Engels, *The German Ideology, Part One*, p. 4.
3 For a detailed discussion of the history of the text, cf. *CW5*, pp. 586–8.

the year 1845, which saw the production of both the *Theses on Feuerbach* and *The German Ideology*, marked a watershed in the development of his thought. Louis Althusser, whom we shall meet in a moment, has found few more trenchant and devastating critics than the historian E. P. Thompson. When Althusser and Thompson agree the occasion is so rare as to lend credibility to its content. And, according to Thompson: 'Althusser is of course right that Marx's thought came together into a *new kind of totality* in the late 1840s; and that those seminal concepts present in earlier writings, of essence and existence, of alienation, of civil and political society, are afforded new meanings within the newly-discovered context of historical materialism.'[4]

To what extent did this 'newly-discovered context', the achievement of this 'new kind of totality', constitute a radical break with what had gone before? The question is important for us, not only because most of Marx's extended discussion of religious and explicitly theological topics occurs in his pre-1845 writings, but also because many of those fundamental themes in his thought which, I shall argue, are theologically significant, are handled – in the earlier work – in a form which is more directly amenable to theological and philosophical discussion and criticism than is the case with their treatment in *Capital* and other writings of the later period.

There are those who would stress the discontinuities between the 'earlier' and the 'later' Marx to the point of denying that a study of his early writings can throw any direct or positive light on his mature thought. Thus, for example, C. J. Arthur says that 'Up to this time [the writing of *The German Ideology*] Marx and Engels would not have been considered by their contemporaries as especially different from Feuerbach or Hess – but the breakthrough represented by *The German Ideology* marks them off *finally* from their German philosophical past.'[5] Similarly, David Fernbach, the editor of the three volumes of *Political Writings* in the Pelican Marx Library, says of the Paris Manuscripts of 1844 that, although they 'certainly foreshadow Marx's future concerns . . . rather than heralding the birth of the new theory, they represent in fact Marx's last staging-post within the realm of the "German Ideology" '.[6] In other words, the author of these manuscripts is, on this view, still a neo-Hegelian humanist philosopher, a bird of a very different feather from the theorist of 'scientific' historical materialism who produced *Capital*.

Why is it that so many commentators find it so easy, and so important, to assert that there are radical discontinuities between the author of *The German Ideology*, the *Communist Manifesto* and *Cap-*

---

4 E. P. Thompson, 'An Open Letter to Leszek Kolakowski', *The Poverty of Theory and Other Essays*, p. 142, my stress.
5 Arthur, op. cit., p. 21, my stress.
6 D. Fernbach, 'Introduction', *R1848*, p. 16.

ital, on the one hand, and the young neo-Hegelian philosopher on the other?

In the first place, Marx himself, in the Preface to *A Contribution to the Critique of Political Economy*, which he published in 1859, said that in 1845 he and Engels had decided to 'set forth our conception as opposed to the ideological one of German philosophy, in fact to settle accounts with our former philosophical conscience', and that 'this intention was carried out' in *The German Ideology*.[7] Of course, the mere fact that Marx and Engels believed that a 'break' of some kind had occurred in 1845 does little to decide the issue: both continuities and discontinuities in a thinker's development are often more readily discerned by other, more 'distanced' readers of the texts than by their producers. Be that as it may, what are we to take to be the contrasting characteristics of Marx's thought before and after whatever 'break' it was that occurred in 1845? According to some commentators, Marx's 'intellectual career was divided into a pre-Marxist early philosophical period and a post-philosophical later Marxist period'.[8] This interpretation of what was involved in 'settling the account' with his 'former philosophical conscience' is only sustainable in the measure that 'philosophy' is quite arbitrarily identified with those forms of German idealism from which, from 1845 onwards, Marx sought to take his distance.

Moreover, as an interpretation of the 1859 Preface, and similar passages, any straightforward contrast between a 'philosophical' and a 'post-philosophical' Marx is necessarily misleading on account of its wholly non-dialectical character.[9] For Marx, as for Hegel, to change the world by revolution is to 'abolish' it *as it is*, in the form that it exists, before the revolution – not simply to annihilate or dispose of it. Similarly, as Karl Korsch, who was one of the first 'to rehabilitate the Hegelian element in Marxism',[10] rightly insisted: 'the abolition of philosophy did not mean for [Marx and Engels] its simple rejection'.[11] The laconic opening sentence of Kolakowski's massive study is both accurate and a neat piece of understated polemic: 'Karl Marx was a German philosopher.'[12] A slightly more plausible suggestion than that of the 'post-philosophical' mature Marx would be to the effect that, by 1859, Marx and Engels saw their work as having been 'ideological' in character

7 K. Marx, 'Preface to *A Contribution to the Critique of Political Economy*', *EW*, p. 427.
8 R. C. Tucker, *Philosophy and Myth in Karl Marx*, p. 174. Tucker, who vigorously rejects this account, instances Paul Sweezy's *The Theory of Capitalist Development* as representative of it.
9 Cf. I. Mészáros, *Marx's Theory of Alienation*, pp. 217–9.
10 D. McLellan, *Marxism After Marx*, p. 166.
11 K. Korsch, *Marxism and Philosophy*, p. 68.
12 *KI*, p. 1.

before 1845 and as now being free from this limitation. To this suggestion we shall return.

In the second place, it is important to remember that *The German Ideology* and the 'Paris Manuscripts' were not published until 1932. With the exception of the Introduction, which Kautsky published in 1903, and of which Lukács made extensive use, the *Grundrisse* 'was not subjected to thorough examination and discussion until the 1960s',[13] although it first appeared, in a limited edition, 'in Moscow in 1939–41, an unpropitious time for academic study'.[14] In other words, a whole generation of Marxist theorists inevitably approached his thought via *Capital* and, where the theoretical (or philosophical) dimension of that thought was concerned, they were obliged to derive it from Engels rather than from Marx himself. Marx and Engels were close collaborators, but Marx was not Engels and Engels was not Marx. As Colletti remarked, in the course of his polemic against the 'dialectical materialism' of Engels, Plekhanov and Lenin, 'the relationship between the "young Marx" and the "old Marx" is . . . altogether unresolvable wherever Marx's thought in his full maturity is regarded as identical with that of Engels and the entire tradition of "dialectical materialism".'[15]

That 'entire tradition' was firmly established by the time that the early writings appeared. It is thus hardly surprising that, when they did appear, the discontinuities between their content and what had come to be regarded as 'Marx's thought' should have been more immediately apparent than the equally significant continuities.

In the third place, there were political reasons why many Marxists found it necessary to distance themselves from the thought of the young German philosopher of the early 1840s. 'Towards the end of his life Marx moved nearer to the positivism then so fashionable in intellectual circles. This tendency . . . reached its apogee in Soviet textbooks on dialectical materialism.'[16] Thus, 'orthodox' Marxism has claimed for the theory of 'dialectical materialism' the status of an ultimate, 'correct', 'scientific' explanation, definitive, unarguable and unsurpassable. As such it is, without much difficulty, made to fulfil the function of legitimating existing socialist regimes. Thus, 'the sheer rigidity of official doctrine, the *rigor mortis* which had already gripped Marxism under Stalin, contributed in no small way to the cool reception which the [early] writings met with when they appeared, to the absence of any debate about them, and to the manner in which they were immediately classified and

13 *KI*, p. 236.
14 Loc. cit. Cf. M. Nicolaus, 'Foreword', *G*, p. 7.
15 L. Colletti, *Marxism and Hegel*, p. 51.
16 *Life*, p. 423.

pigeon-holed',[17] as the now uninteresting first efforts of an immature mind, as belonging to the period before Karl Marx became 'Marx'.

For over twenty years, the most influential exponent of the 'radical break' theory has been the French philosopher, Louis Althusser.[18] Since Kruschev, there had been much talk of 'liberating' Marxist thought from the rigidities of Stalinist 'dogmatism'. Communist intellectuals began to be attracted, as non-Communists had been, by the thought of the young Marx, in which 'the old philosophical themes of "freedom", "man", the "human person" and "alienation" ',[19] occupied a central place. Althusser feared that the new freedom, the new 'philosophizing' of Marx, threatened to deprive Marxist theory of specificity, coherence, unity and power. The young Marx – interrogative, exploratory, 'unscientific' – appeared to be a dangerously 'unMarxist' thinker. Therefore, if the movement of Marxism was to proceed with political effectiveness and unruffled theoretical assurance, the thought of the young Marx must be shown to be no longer of legitimate interest to Marxists.

A Western 'liberal intellectual' may be tempted to read *simply* as wholly admirable indications of creative flexibility and renewed intellectual vitality those signs which Althusser perceived as a threat. Any such reaction would, I suggest, be philosophically superficial and sociologically naive, expressive of an extremely oversimplified view of the paradoxes of human action and, especially, of the irreducible tension between commitment and enquiry, action and reflection. 'Reason', said Newman in a seminal sermon on 'Faith and Reason, Contrasted as Habits of Mind', 'analyses the grounds and motives of action: a reason is an analysis, but is not the motive itself.'[20] And he went on: 'Faith is a principle of action, and action does not allow time for minute and finished investigations. We may (if we will) think that such investigations are of high value; though, in truth, they have a tendency to blunt the practical energy of the mind, while they improve its scientific exactness.'[21] I have known very distinguished natural scientists who have gone to great lengths to prevent their students from becoming 'contaminated' by exposure to questions in the philosophy of science, lest, as a result, the 'practical energies' of their scientific enquiry become 'blunted' by the permanent puzzlement characteristic of the philosophic temperament. Obscurantism is not a virtue: it is a risk unavoidably run by any pattern of effective action. Scientific, poli-

17 L. Colletti, 'Introduction', *EW*, p. 15.
18 When reading the editorial introductions to *R1848*, *SE* and *FI*, it is worth bearing in mind that Fernbach is reading Marx through Althusserian spectacles.
19 L. Althusser, *For Marx*, p. 10.
20 J. H. Newman, *Newman's University Sermons*, introd. D. M. MacKinnon and J. D. Holmes, p. 183.
21 Ibid., p. 188.

tical and religious movements may be deprived of practical and transformative power in the measure that they succumb to the illusion that the only authentically 'rational' mode of intellectual procedure is that characteristic of the academic seminar.

I have dwelt on this point at some length in order to indicate why it is that I do not believe that the fears of Althusser and others, that an awakening interest in the thought of the young Marx would emasculate Marxist theory, can *simply* be dismissed as 'dogmatic', obscurantist or politically opportunist. And the formal validity of such consideration is unaffected by the fact that I happen to regard that which was threatened as a singularly unlovely structure of totalitarian oppression. More to our purpose, however, is the manner in which Althusser, the Marxist theoretician, responded to the threat which he perceived.

Taking over from Gaston Bachelard the concept of an 'epistemological break'[22] to characterize the radical shift from a pre-scientific world of ideas to an authentically scientific, practically effective, *knowledge* of reality,[23] he argued that such a break occurred in Marx's thought. It is Marx the scientific innovator of genius who is the father of Marxism – the political movement whose theoretical dimension is the definitive, unsurpassable *knowledge* of historical process – not the pre-scientific, ideological speculator who, we might say, died when the breakthrough into scientific knowledge occurred.

But when did this 'break' take place? In 1965, Althusser claimed that it occurred in 1845.[24] Four years later, he admitted that he had previously given 'a much too abrupt idea of this thesis [of the 'break'] in advancing the idea that it was possible to locate this rupture in 1845'.[25] He now acknowledged that there were 'traces of Hegelian influence', and hence of idealist, or ideological, pre-scientific infection, in the *Grundrisse*, in the first volume of *Capital*, indeed almost everywhere except in the 1875 *Critique of the Gotha Programme*.[26] 'At this point', says an exasperated Kolakowski, 'we begin to wonder if Marxism existed at all in Marx's day, or whether it was left to Althusser to invent it.'[27]

Even if Althusser's position is (as I believe it to be) untenable it is not, however, thus easily dismissed. The central claim that he makes, concerning the initial 'constitution' (a favourite word) of a new mode and content of scientific knowledge by Marx, from 1845

---

22 Cf. G. Bachelard, *La Formation de l'Esprit Scientifique*. On the background to Althusser's use of the concept, cf. *For Marx*, pp. 249, 257.

23 Cf., e.g., Althusser, *For Marx*, pp. 32, 167–8.

24 Cf. *For Marx*, pp. 35–7.

25 Althusser, *Lenin and Philosophy and Other Essays*, p. 90.

26 Loc. cit.

27 *KIII*, p. 486. For a less polemical comment, cf. McLellan, *Marxism after Marx*, p. 299.

onwards, cannot be falsified merely by pointing out that 'materi-alistic' (or 'scientific') 'elements' can be discerned in the thought of the young Marx, and 'idealist' (or Hegelian, or 'ideological') 'ele-ments' in his later work. It is the contrasting character of Marx's system of thought *as a whole*, before and after the break, that is in question, not this or that 'element' retrospectively isolated.[28] And I take the significance of the remarks quoted in the previous para-graph from his 1969 essay to be that we should not suppose the break to have been instantaneous: scientific revolutions are rarely like that.

According to Althusser, then, 'Marxism', as a *theory* (his preferred term for the philosophy of dialectical materialism)[29] is to be found operatively present exclusively in Marx's mature works. I say 'op-eratively present' because he admits that, even in *Capital*, the theory is not present 'in a theoretical form'.[30] Marx never wrote his own 'dialectics'. 'He talked of writing it, but never started. He never found the time.'[31] Or so he thought. In fact, *'whatever* [Marx] *may have thought* . . . the ultimate reason is that the times were not ripe.'[32] That is to say, Marxist 'science' had not yet developed sufficiently to generate Marxism's 'new practice of philosophy'.[33] (Perhaps Ko-lakowski's exasperation is justified after all: at least it begins to become clear why we need a chapter on 'meanings of Marxism'!)

Althusser is careful to point out that, even on his account, it does not follow that Marx's 'pre-scientific', 'ideological' writings are no longer of interest. Every society, including communist society, needs an ideology, 'the *lived* relation between men and their world'.[34] Marxist ideology, feeding on the thought of the young Marx, be-comes a corrosive force only when it is misunderstood as possessing scientific, explanatory power: as constituting authentic *knowledge* of reality.[35] This I take to be the drift of Althusser's remark that 'the *theoretical* effects of ideology . . . are always a threat or a hindrance to scientific knowledge'.[36]

In recent years, Althusser's distinction between Marxist 'ideolo-gy' and Marxist 'science' has been put to paradoxical use by some Christian theologians. Thus, for example, when the Peruvian theo-logian Gustavo Gutierrez speaks of 'the current vogue of interpret-

28 Cf. *For Marx*, pp. 56–7.
29 Cf. *For Marx*, p. 162.
30 Ibid., p. 174.
31 Loc. cit. Cf. L. Althusser and E. Balibar, *Reading Capital*, pp. 29–31.
32 *Lenin and Philosophy*, p. 46, his stress.
33 Ibid., p. 67.
34 *For Marx*, p. 233.
35 Cf. ibid., p. 231.
36 Ibid., p. 12, his stress.

ing Marxism in Latin-America according to Althusser',[37] he is
referring to attempts to use the distinction as a means of endorsing
Marxist explanations of the emergence, structure and transience of
capitalism (Marxist science) while rejecting Marxist atheism, which
is seen as an aspect of its ideology. I have described this use as
paradoxical because Althusser himself employed his distinction in
order to 'save the appearances' of Communism. Moreover, I am
not sure whether all the theologians who use the distinction are
prepared (as Fierro is) to pay the full price: namely, to surrender
any attempt to speak of man's *knowledge* of God.[38]

As with all other attempts to defend the theory that there is a
'radical break' between the thought of the early and the mature
Marx, Althusser's position is, for all its intellectual sophistication,
in the last resort quite untenable. It is untenable, firstly, because it
is so heavily dependent on his ultimately circular strategy of reductively identifying 'knowledge' with 'science', and of offering little
more, by way of a definition of 'science', than that which constitutes
authentic 'knowledge'. 'Althusser', says Professor McLellan,
'claimed that dialectical materialism was a science but offered no
criterion of scientificity.'[39] As a result, his form of the distinction
between 'science' and 'ideology', upon which the whole theory of
the 'radical break' depends, is, in the last resort, quite arbitrary:
although he 'seeks to escape the polarity of ideology as "false", and
science as "valid", his standpoint in fact rests upon a peculiarly
ungrounded version of such a differentiation'.[40]

As I have already indicated, there is, in Marxist thought, a long
tradition of claiming unsurpassable validity for Marxist theory.
Thus, in 1922, Lukács asserted that the 'underlying premise' of the
essays which he published as *History and Class Consciousness* was 'the
belief that in Marx's theory and method the *true method* by which to
understand society and history has *finally* been discovered'.[41] Nearly
fifty years later, in 1970, Althusser announced that we owe to Marx
'the greatest discovery of human history: the discovery that opens
for men the way to a *scientific* (materialist and dialectical) understanding of their own history as a history of the class struggle'.[42]
Five years earlier he had put it even more strongly, in referring to

37 G. Gutierrez, *A Theology of Liberation*, p. 97; cf. P. Hebblethwaite, *The Christian-
Marxist Dialogue and Beyond*, pp. 50–2.
38 Cf. A. Fierro, *The Militant Gospel*, pp. 239, 317, 354–5, 412. For some brief
comments of mine on Fierro's position, see N. L. A. Lash, 'Theory, Theology
and Ideology', pp .211–2.
39 McLellan, *Marxism after Marx*, p. 303.
40 A. Giddens, *Central Problems in Social Theory*, p. 181.
41 G. Lukács, *History and Class Consciousness*, p. xliii, his stress.
42 Althusser, *Lenin and Philosophy*, p. 7.

'that most precious of all things Marx gave us – the possibility of scientific knowledge'.[43]

Such claims are ridiculously pretentious. It is not given to any human individual to elaborate the definitive, unsurpassable, normative structure of true knowledge: not to Aristotle, not to Aquinas, not to Kant, not to Marx. In order to justify claims as grandiose as those made by Lukács, Althusser and their followers, what would be needed would be not so much an exposition of Marxist theory as a 'christology' of Marx. There are, as Max Horkheimer saw, fascinating parallels, of considerable interest to the social historian of the mid-twentieth century, between the claims made on behalf of Marxist theory by Althusser and by much 'orthodox' Marxist writing, on the one hand and, on the other, those made by neo-scholastic theologians, in the 1930s and 1940s, on behalf of 'Thomism'.[44]

Moreover, it would seem that any such claim on behalf of Marxist theory risks falling back into just that 'idealism' in contrast with which Marx elaborated his own theory of 'historical materialism'. For how could we, as agents and thinkers within the historical process, know that our cognitive strategies possessed a validity that was timeless in the sense of being incapable of future supersession? The question is baldly put, because we shall have occasion to return to it several times in the course of this study. For the time being, however, it can serve as a link with the second set of considerations which cast grave doubt upon Althusser's theory: namely, those considerations which arise from his treatment of the *Grundrisse*.

The *Grundrisse*, it has been said, 'challenges and puts to the test every serious interpretation of Marx yet conceived'.[45] It is not, according to Kolakowski, that its publication 'has altered the general picture of Marxist doctrine in any important respect, but it has upheld the view of those who believed in the continuity of Marx's philosophical inspiration, and not of those who postulated a radical breach between the anthropological theories of his youth and the economic tenets of his mature years'.[46] Far from abandoning the 'anthropological ideas of the 1840s', Marx can be observed, in the *Grundrisse*, 'attempting to translate them into economic terms'.[47] Here, in Marx's draft notebooks for *Capital*, all those themes that he is supposed to have left behind in 1845 are strikingly present: 'the parallels between religious alienation and economic alienation',[48] the tendency towards utopianism (albeit of a different sort

43 Althusser, *For Marx*, p. 241.
44 Cf. M. Horkheimer, 'Conflicting Panaceas', *The Eclipse of Reason*, pp. 58–91.
45 M. Nicolaus, 'Foreword', *G*, p. 7.
46 *KI*, p. 237.
47 *KI*, pp. 236, 237.
48 *Life*, p. 304.

from that which he systematically criticized), 'the idea of nature as (in a sense) man's body',[49] and so on. Nor is this just a matter of discovering isolated 'elements' of continuity. 'Close scrutiny of the ... [*Grundrisse*] leaves no doubt that Marx did not abandon the perspective which guided him in his early writings.'[50] Thus the *Grundrisse* helps one to appreciate that the 'central inspiration or vision' of the author of *Capital*, as of the Paris Manuscripts, remains 'man's alienation in capitalist society, and the possibility of his controlling his own destiny through communism'.[51]

The suggestion is not, of course, that the dominant themes in the early writings are handled in the same way in Marx's mature work. In order to emphasize the fundamental continuity in Marx's thought, it is not necessary to minimize the profound shifts that occurred, especially around 1845. Thus, for example, it is notorious that the *term* 'alienation' occurs relatively infrequently in the later writings.[52] But, with the *Grundrisse* as a guide, we are able to appreciate more easily than was possible on the basis of *Capital* alone that 'the specifically Marxist theory of value ... is nothing but the definitive version of the theory of alienated labour'.[53] If any concept is 'Hegelian', it is that of 'alienation'. However profound the ways in which Marx reworked the notion, at least it is clear that, in the light of the *Grundrisse*, 'the writers who have wished to minimize the influence of Hegel on Marx will have to revise their ideas'.[54]

One such writer has undoubtedly been Louis Althusser. What, then, has been his reaction to the publication of this text? He has continued to insist that *Capital* is the work 'by which Marx has to be *judged*. By it alone, and not by his still idealist "Early Works" (1841–1844); not by still very ambiguous works like *The German Ideology*, or even the *Grundrisse*'.[55] Or even the *Grundrisse*. And the grounds of this arbitrary stipulation? By now they come as little

---

49 Loc. cit. Cf. J. Plamenatz, *Karl Marx's Philosophy of Man*, pp. 71–3.

50 A. Giddens, *Capitalism and Modern Social Theory*, p. ix.

51 *Life*, p. 128.

52 By 'relatively infrequently' I do not mean, however, 'on few occasions'; on the persistence of both the term and the concept, cf. Mészáros, *Marx's Theory of Alienation*, pp. 221–7.

53 *KI*, pp. 132–3.

54 *Life*, p. 296. Although McLellan describes Rebecca Cooper's study of *The Logical Influence of Hegel on Marx* as 'under-appreciated' (*Marxism after Marx*, p. 12), he would not, I think, disagree that her central thesis that 'the connection between the Marxian and Hegelian systems is for the most part a purely external and verbal rather than an integral one' (Cooper, p. 178), can no longer be sustained. For the influence of Hegelian categories on the *Grundrisse* and, via the *Grundrisse*, on *Capital*, cf. R. Rosdolsky, *The Making of Marx's 'Capital'*. Rosdolsky, who was able to read the *Grundrisse* as early as 1948, described it in 1955 as 'a massive reference to Hegel, in particular to his *Logic*' (p. xiii). I am grateful to Dr Bernard Sharratt for drawing my attention to Rosdolsky's impressive study.

55 Althusser, *Lenin and Philosophy*, p. 71.

surprise: 'In many places in the *Grundrisse* . . . a strong Hegelian influence can be detected combined with whiffs of Feuerbachian humanism. It can be judged with some certainty that, along with *The German Ideology*, the *Grundrisse* will provide all the dubious quotations needed by idealist interpretations of Marxist theory.'[56] In order to protect the chimeric purity of 'Althusser's Marx', therefore, he resorts to the somewhat desperate expedient (from a scholarly point of view) of simply ignoring these threatening texts. With one exception.

That exception is the 1857 Introduction, beloved by Lukács and (if only because it has been available since 1903) admissible of inclusion, by an 'orthodox' Marxist-Leninist philosopher, in the 'canon' of 'Marxist' writings. To that Introduction, and especially to the few pages entitled 'The Method of Political Economy',[57] Althusser returns again and again.[58] Wherein lies its attraction for him?

At one level, the answer would seem to be that discourse is only 'scientific', only 'theoretical', in Althusser's view, in so far as its method is that of 'analysis' or 'exposition', and that this is the method of *Capital*, whereas the *Grundrisse* is presented in the 'mode of investigation'.[59] Therefore it is not 'scientific'; therefore, with the exception of those pages in the Introduction in which such methodological issues are discussed, it can be neglected by Althusser in his exposition of Marx's 'theory', as having 'disappeared in the result'.[60]

Althusser finds his warrants for restricting Marxist 'theory' to modes of 'philosophical' discourse that rigorously exclude, as 'unscientific', any serious consideration of matters of empirical, historical fact, in passages such as the following: 'It would therefore be unfeasible and wrong to let the economic categories follow one another in the same sequence as that in which they were historically decisive. . . . The point is not the historic position of the economic relations in the succession of different forms of society . . . rather, their order within modern bourgeois society.'[61] The 'two crucial pages'[62] in which Althusser attempts to demonstrate the 'absolutely decisive scope' of a 'few lucid sentences from the *Poverty of Philosophy*

56 Ibid., pp. 97–8.
57 *G*, pp. 100–8.
58 Cf. *For Marx*, pp. 182–93; *Reading Capital*, pp. 41–2, 46–7, 54, 64, 86f, 98, 114, 121–5, 168–70, 192.
59 Althusser, *Reading Capital*, p. 50, commenting on *Cap. I*, p. 102, a text which we shall consider in Chapter Sixteen.
60 Cf. *Reading Capital*, p. 50.
61 *G*, pp. 107–8.
62 E. P. Thompson, 'The Poverty of Theory: or, An Orrery of Errors', *The Poverty of Theory*, p. 334, referring to Althusser, *Reading Capital*, pp. 65–6.

and the *1857 Introduction* [to the *Grundrisse*]'[63] (in which, as Thompson persuasively argues, Marx is taking Proudhon to task for recommending a method that has striking affinities with M. Althusser's!)[64] encapsulate the essence of the structuralist idealism which Althusser presents as the essence of Marx's 'materialist' theory.

Rightly or wrongly, I regard it as unnecessary, since the appearance of Thompson's essay, 'The Poverty of Theory', to justify the charge that Althusser's theory is 'idealist' in precisely the sense that Marx relentlessly criticized. But the question remains: is there *nothing* in Marx's texts which could help to explain how so perverse a reading of them could be produced? According to Thompson, the answer is 'Yes, there is something.' 'From the outside, in the 1840s', the structure of classical political economy 'appeared to Marx as ideology, or, worse, apologetics':[65] the economic mechanisms of one particular, transient social form (bourgeois society) rationalized as the expression of unalterable 'laws of nature'. In the process of coming to grips with this structure, in meticulous detail, in order to overthrow it, Marx partially fell into the trap – during the years in which he struggled to elaborate his 'critique of political economy' – of constructing an equally non-historical 'anti-structure'. In other words, alongside those features to which I have already referred, 'what we have at the end [in the *Grundrisse*], is not the overthrow of "Political Economy" but *another* "Political Economy" '.[66]

According to Thompson, it is this 'moment of Marx's theoretical . . . immobilism',[67] especially evident in certain passages in the 1857 Introduction, which explains their fascination for Althusser. 'How far Marx himself ever became fully aware of his imprisonment [in this anti-structure] is a complex question. . . . But at least we should note that Marx, in his increasing preoccupation in his last years with anthropology, was resuming the projects of his Paris youth'.[68]

I am not competent to assess the strengths of Thompson's hypothesis, which he acknowledges to be controversial[69] (although I confess that, on my own reading of the texts, I find it persuasive).[70] I have mentioned it because it does perhaps throw *some* light on why it is that Althusser feels entitled to continue to argue for the 'radical break' thesis, to neglect that body of texts (the *Grundrisse*),

63 *Reading Capital*, p. 66.
64 Cf. the passage from Proudhon quoted and discussed by Marx in *The Poverty of Philosophy*, pp. 97, 108–10.
65 'The Poverty of Theory', p. 252.
66 Loc. cit.
67 Ibid., p. 396.
68 Ibid., p. 355.
69 Cf. ibid., p. 388, n. 57.
70 For a detailed discussion of the 1857 Introduction, cf. below, Chapter Sixteen, 'Search for a Starting-Point'.

certain features of which constitute the most convincing refutation of the thesis, and yet also feels entitled to appeal, again and again, to a handful of sentences from the Introduction to the neglected texts.

It is time to draw these remarks to a conclusion. If one wants to find out whether a particular commentator holds the view that there is a radical discontinuity, a theoretical chasm, between the thought of the 'early' and of the 'mature' Marx, or whether he believes the continuities to be at least as significant as the discontinuities, there are two simple, and closely related, tests that can be applied. In the first place, does he acknowledge the enduring centrality of the concept of 'alienation' in Marx's thought, or does he maintain that 'alienation' is a pre-Marxist notion which, except in the form of an occasional terminological gesture, is absent from the thought of the mature Marx and, as such, has no place in Marxist theory? In the second place, does he maintain that, in the thought of the mature Marx, 'Hegelian categories have been dead for a long time',[71] or does he take very seriously Lenin's ambiguous remark, jotted down in 1915 while studying Hegel's *Logic*, to the effect that because Hegel went unread, Marx was not understood for half a century?[72]

In my own judgement, however profound the shifts in Marx's method and concerns during his career, these shifts should not be exaggerated, or the theoretical positions implicit in his mature thought so abstracted from their context, as to make us lose sight of the extent to which his thought is 'best viewed as a continuing meditation on central themes first explored in 1844'.[73] This being the case, we are justified in assuming that Marx's thought *as a whole*, and not simply the thought of some youthful 'pre-Marxist' Marx, is of interest to the theologian and philosopher of religion. Consider, for example, the concept of 'alienation' which, in all its forms, and in all the situations and relationships to which it refers, is of inescapably central interest to a religion of redemption, such as Christianity, and to the theology that seeks critically to reflect on that religion.

When did Karl Marx become 'Marx', the author of 'Marxism'? If we have disposed of the idea that 'Marx' did not exist before

71 Althusser, *For Marx*, p. 200.
72 Cf. Althusser, *Lenin and Philosophy*, p. 108. As an indication of *how* ambiguous that remark is, here is Althusser's 'reading' of it: 'Lenin did not need to read Hegel in order to understand him, because he had already understood Hegel, having closely read and understood Marx' (ibid., p. 109)! This is hardly how Lenin saw the matter, if McLellan is correct in arguing that the remark 'was in fact a self-criticism' (*Marxism after Marx*, p. 108).
73 *Life*, p. 303. Cf. D. Lecompte, 'Marx Selon Althusser: La "Coupure Epistémologique" ', *Les Quatre Fleuves*, 8 (1978), pp. 90–5, a summary presentation of a full-length study.

1845 (at the earliest!), we have now to consider what might be meant by 'Marxism'.

3

MEANINGS OF 'MARXISM'

If I am concerned, in this study, not directly with actual or possible relationships between 'Christianity' and 'Marxism', but only with the significance for Christian theology of certain themes in Marx's own writings, why is this chapter necessary? Surely, any consideration of what, since Marx's time, 'Marxism' has come to mean, is irrelevant to my purpose? The project on which I am engaged would undoubtedly be more straightforward if this were the case. Unfortunately, distinctions between 'Marx's meaning' and 'the meanings of Marxism' are not so easily drawn.

Our discussion in the previous chapter has already shown that judgements concerning the continuity or discontinuity in Marx's intellectual development are influenced by, and influence in turn, judgements concerning the character and content of 'Marxism'. Thus, for example, some proponents of 'radical break' theories would insist that the thought of the 'early' Marx is not yet 'Marxist', and that 'Marxism' refers not to any and every movement or viewpoint for which warrants can be found in some, at least, of Marx's texts, but only to that movement whose structuring theory is the theory which Marx eventually elaborated – although he himself never gave it formally theoretical expression.

In more general terms, we can say that some consideration of 'the meanings of Marxism' is a necessary preliminary to a study of Marx because an individual's approach to the task of interpreting Marx's texts will be shaped and guided by his 'pre-understanding' of the meaning of Marxism. It follows, therefore, that we cannot avoid the problem simply by distinguishing between 'Marxism' – as movement or method, system or doctrine – on the one hand, and 'Marxian' methods and concepts (i.e. those that are attributable to Karl Marx) on the other, and declaring that the latter alone are our concern. Debates concerning the meaning of 'Marxism' have, as a matter of fact, regularly included discussion and disagreement concerning 'Marx's meaning'. Decisions as to what methods and concepts, beliefs and strategies, are or are not attributable to Marx are interpretative judgements, and the varieties of 'Marxism' reflect the range and variety of such interpretations.

This is not to say that, if a particular claim, or concept, or method, were agreed to be characteristically 'Marxian', it would thereby have been demonstrated, without further ado, to be authentically 'Marxist', any more than agreement that a particular claim or concept was characteristically 'biblical' or 'Pauline', for example, would constitute a sufficient reason for judging it to be, today, authentically 'Christian'. 'In one hundred years the intellectual universe has changed, and even those propositions of Marx which require neither revision nor elucidation were defined in a particular context, and very often in antagonism to particular and now-forgotten opponents; and in our new context, and in the face of new and, perhaps, more subtle objections, these propositions must be thought through and stated once again. This is a familiar historical problem. Everything must be thought through once more: every term must sit for new examinations'.[1] As a Christian theologian, I wholeheartedly endorse that description of the interpretative task. Both Marxism and Christianity have been bedevilled by unhistorical, hermeneutically naive 'fundamentalisms', and yet both traditions have contained internal resources on the basis of which such fundamentalisms can be shown to entail the denial or neglect of central features of their own constitutive convictions and strategies.

But surely, to claim that fundamentalisms are deviant forms is tacitly to assume certain criteria of what would or would not count, in either tradition, as 'authentic' or 'non-deviant' interpretations? Yes indeed. The Western liberal tradition is, today, understandably suspicious of 'orthodoxies'. And yet, however, much damage has been done, and continues to be done, to both Marxism and Christianity, by certain ways of negotiating, in practice and theory, the problem of ascertaining, recovering and maintaining the *identity* of a movement of thought and behaviour, that problem remains. If nothing counts *against* the propriety of describing a pattern of behaviour, a method or a belief, as 'Marxist' or as 'Christian', then nothing counts *in favour* of the propriety of such description.

It is worth noticing, in passing, that, just as some Christians claim that only a Christian can 'correctly' interpret the New Testament (for example), so also some Marxists claim that only a Marxist can 'correctly' interpret Marx's texts.[2] Nor are such claims necessarily as arbitrary or obscurantist as they may sometimes appear. This, however, is an issue to which we shall return in a later chapter when we consider the question of Marxism and truth.

This chapter is entitled 'meanings of Marxism', and not 'the meaning of Marxism', because it is evident that Marxism has by

---

1 E. P. Thompson, 'The Poverty of Theory', *The Poverty of Theory and Other Essays*, p. 218.
2 For a sophisticated version of this claim, cf. I. Mészáros, *Marx's Theory of Alienation*, p. 23.

now become as bewilderingly pluralistic as has Christianity. Peter Hebblethwaite, in *The Christian-Marxist Dialogue and Beyond*, lays great stress on the variety of contemporary meanings of Marxism. Unfortunately, not only does he use this as an excuse for evading the problem: ' "Marxism" thus turns out to be an extremely slippery concept which eludes grasp and definition',[3] but he attempts to make apologetic capital out of the evasion: 'For all these reasons, the Christian response to Marxism was not and could not be a simple matter. There is in Marx and Marxism something for everyone.'[4] I would prefer to suggest, not only that the variety of contemporary meanings of Marxism is by no means so extensive as to render the concept vacuous, but also that any such charge, on the part of a Christian, has a boomerang effect. Nowhere in his book does Hebblethwaite advert to the fact, let alone explore the implications of the fact, that Christianity is, today, every bit as internally diverse as is Marxism. Nor are the forms of this diversity wholly dissimilar in the two cases, as I now propose to indicate with the aid of E. P. Thompson's classification of the meanings of Marxism.

Thompson suggests a fourfold classification of 'the ideas which are offered as Marxisms'.[5] Firstly, there is 'Marxism conceived of as a self-sufficient body of doctrine, complete, internally-consistent, and fully realized in a particular set of written texts'.[6] Secondly, there is Marxism 'upheld less as doctrine than as "method" '.[7] Thirdly, there is what he describes as 'Marxism as Heritage. All human culture is a supermarket in which we may shop around as we choose, although some products are more gorgeous and more heavy than others. Karl Marx was a great man, and so was Jesus Christ; so too were Hegel, Husserl, Tolstoy and Blake. The producer of ideas may be forgotten, it is the customer who must be pleased.'[8] The fourth position is that of 'Marxism as Tradition', on which he comments: 'In choosing the term tradition I choose it with a sense of the meanings established for it within English literary criticism.'[9] (We are here, presumably, being reminded of the work of, amongst others, I. A. Richards, F. R. Leavis, Raymond Williams.)

Before commenting in detail on Thompson's classificatory scheme, it is worth noticing that it is proposed as a taxonomy of

---

3 P. Hebblethwaite, *The Christian-Marxist Dialogue and Beyond*, p. 7.
4 Loc. cit.
5 E. P. Thompson, 'An Open Letter to Leszek Kolakowski', *The Poverty of Theory*, p. 110. The prudent reader, noticing the extent of my indebtedness to some of Thompson's essays, is advised to turn to the first four chapters of Perry Anderson, *Arguments Within English Marxism*, for a critical, but not unsympathetic, assessment of Thompson's work, which takes 'The Poverty of Theory' as its focus.
6 Loc. cit.
7 Ibid., p. 112.
8 Ibid., p. 114.
9 Ibid., p. 116.

'the *ideas* which are offered as Marxisms'. It follows that such parallels as may exist, within Christianity, with the varieties of Marxism thus described, are to be sought in the variety of Christian theological approaches rather than, for example, in forms of worship and organization. In other words, 'Marxism' is here being construed in theoretical rather than in institutional terms.

It does not follow that 'structural', or at least organizational, considerations are irrelevant. Marxism (1), says Thompson, 'is normally found in some institutionalized form: since no one can prevent reality from changing in ways which the texts did not . . . anticipate, there must be not only approved texts, but approved interpretations of those texts . . . and this entails an Office, or a Priest, or . . . at least a priestly editorial board, which can signify approval and changes in the body of textual truth.'[10] Stalin's Russia is, of course, the *locus classicus* of Marxism (1), of Marxist theory degenerating from critique into the ideological rationalization of political power. The history of Marxism has been marked by the recurrent struggle between forms of Marxism (1) and the work of those groups and individuals that have sought to recover just that critical, dialectical dimension which Marxism (1) abandons – in practice, though not in self-description – for 'dogmatism' and, in so doing, abandons its historical materialism. We shall return to this theme in Chapter Nine, but even at this stage one or two illustrations may be in order.

Karl Korsch's *Marxism and Philosophy*, published in 1923, contained a sustained attack on this tendency to distort 'the revolutionary doctrine of Marxism itself into a purely theoretical critique'.[11] Later, in 1930, Korsch said of this book that it 'advanced a conception of Marxism that was quite undogmatic and anti-dogmatic, historical, and which was therefore materialist in the strictest sense of the word'.[12] More recently, much of the argument of Colletti's *Marxism and Hegel*, and especially his use of the distinction between 'dogmatism' and 'critical thought', was directed at the same target: 'Dogmatism is the presupposition of the Idea, the assumption that knowledge is already given.'[13] Again, Sartre's argument that, at the present moment, existentialism is necessary to Marxism as a reminder of certain features that have, in the course of its development, been the victim of its own internal distortions,[14] would seem to have Marxism (1) in view: 'It is *inside* the movement of Marxist thought that we discover a flaw of such a sort that despite itself Marxism tends to eliminate the questioner from his investigation

10 Ibid., p. 110.
11 K. Korsch, *Marxism and Philosophy*, p. 57.
12 Ibid., p. 92.
13 L. Colletti, *Marxism and Hegel*, p. 90.
14 J.-P. Sartre, *Search for a Method*, pp. 179–81. (This study was originally published, in 1960, as a prefatory essay to the *Critique de la Raison Dialectique*.)

and to make of the questioned the object of an absolute Knowledge.'[15] 'The open concepts of Marxism', he says, 'have closed in':[16] its concepts have become 'dictates'.[17]

One factor which, it would seem, has contributed powerfully to the development of Marxism (1) has been the insistence, which dates at least from the time of Lenin's teacher, Plekhanov, on the character of Marxism as an *integral system*. Because 'Marxism is an integral world outlook',[18] therefore any supplementation it receives from non-Marxist theoretical elements can only dilute and corrupt it. 'No attempts have yet been made', wrote Plekhanov in 1908, 'to "supplement Marx" with Thomas Aquinas. It is however quite feasible that, despite the Pope's recent encyclical against the Modernists, the Catholic world will at some time produce from its midst a thinker capable of performing this feat in the sphere of theory.'[19] The irony is multiple. Pope Pius X, to whose encyclical *Pascendi Dominici Gregis* Plekhanov refers, held a similarly 'integralist' view of Catholic doctrine, and would certainly have regarded any attempt to 'supplement' official neo-scholasticism with Karl Marx as similarly corrosive of the integrity of Christian truth.

That example is of more than anecdotal significance. The religious imagery in Thompson's description of Marxism (1), the reference to 'an Office or a Priest', was presumably intended as an echo of Kolakowski's essay, 'The Priest and the Jester',[20] since the essay in which he expounds his fourfold classificatory scheme is 'An Open Letter to Leszek Kolakowski'.[21] Nevertheless, that imagery cannot fail to be, for a Roman Catholic reader, uncomfortably provocative. In modern times, 'official' Roman Catholic thought and policy have often tended to take the form of what we might call 'Christianity (1)'. I call it 'Christianity (1)', rather than 'Catholicism (1)', because there have also been influential styles of Protestant biblicism which have similarly conceived of Christian doctrine as 'complete, internally-consistent, and fully realized in a particular set of written texts'.[22] Or again, the accounts given, in both Catholic and Protestant theology, of the relationships between 'theology' and 'philosophy', have often tended in a similarly integralist direction. A common weakness of all such systems and strategies is that the privileged text – be it the New Testament, conciliar

15 Ibid., p. 175.
16 Ibid., p. 27.
17 Ibid., p. 28.
18 G. V. Plekhanov, *Fundamental Problems of Marxism*, p. 21.
19 Ibid., p. 22. Sure enough, some years later a study appeared arguing that Aristotle, Aquinas and Marx were 'antimystical, realistic, empiricist and political' thinkers: cf. M. Reding, *Thomas von Aquin und Karl Marx*, p. 10.
20 L. Kolakowski, 'The Priest and the Jester', *Marxism and Beyond*, pp. 29–57.
21 Thompson, *The Poverty of Theory*, pp. 93–192.
22 Ibid., p. 110.

definitions, or the writings of Marx – is one-sidedly 'brought *to* the object of examination', to the problem, situation or circumstance that is under consideration.[23] Christianity (1) is as innocent of hermeneutics as Marxism (1) is, in practice, of dialectics.

'In its worst institutional expression', says Thompson, Marxism (1) 'has done man's culture injury enough. It is sufficiently discredited', even though variant forms of it continue to exhibit 'an astonishing vitality'.[24] Something similar can be said of the various forms, both Catholic and Protestant, of Christianity (1). It must immediately be added, however, that the analogy between 'Marxism (1)' and 'Christianity (1)' has its limits, especially for those of us who would wish to maintain (as I would) that Christianity is committed, in a way that Marxism is not, to the belief that a certain past event or sequence of events is of unsurpassable determinative significance for human history, and hence for our attempts to construct and interpret that history. It therefore follows that questions concerning the definitive character of the revelation in Christ, the normative character of Scripture, the logic and function of 'dogmatic statements' and the role of 'interpretative authority' in matters of Christian doctrine, may certainly not be presumed to have been negatively foreclosed with the admission that 'Christianity (1)' is as much a distortion of Christianity as 'Marxism (1)' is, in Thompson's view, of Marxism. In other words, to indict 'Christianity (1)' as distortion is by no means necessarily to endorse an 'undogmatic' conception of Christian truth. Not all uses of dogma are 'dogmatic' in the pejorative sense attributed to that term by the Marxist writers I have quoted and, more generally, in popular journalism.[25]

Our treatment of Marxism (2) can be briefer. On this account, it will be remembered, 'Marxism is upheld less as doctrine than as "method".'[26] Once again, we can trace this description at least as far back as Plekhanov: 'the materialist explanation of history was primarily of *methodological significance*'.[27] In Lukács' hands, it became a way of defending the concept of Marxist 'orthodoxy' without having recourse to Marxism (1). Even if 'recent research had disproved once and for all every one of Marx's individual theses . . . every serious "orthodox" Marxist would still be able to accept all such modern findings . . . without having to renounce his orthodoxy for a single moment. Orthodox Marxism . . . is not the "belief" in

23 Ibid., pp. 110–11.
24 Ibid., p. 111.
25 In not going further into these matters here, I am not being evasive: my present concern is simply to establish the preliminaries for a Christian study of Marx, not to write a treatise in fundamental theology. I have discussed elsewhere some of the topics touched on in these paragraphs: cf., e.g., N. L. A. Lash, *Change in Focus*; *Voices of Authority*, esp. Chaps. 3–5; *Theology on Dover Beach*, Chaps. 2, 6.
26 Thompson, op. cit., p. 112.
27 Plekhanov, op. cit., p. 43, his stress.

this or that thesis, nor the exegesis of a "sacred" book. On the contrary, orthodoxy refers exclusively to *method*.'[28] In our own day, a similar position has been upheld by Roger Garaudy: 'Marxism . . . is essentially a *methodology of historical initiative*.'[29]

Thompson expresses his respect for the work of many of 'those who associate themselves with Marxism as method'.[30] Nevertheless, he is 'not persuaded as to the adequacy of the definition'.[31] The more loose and metaphorical the sense in which 'method' is used, the more Marxism (2) turns out to be a variant of Marxism (4), which we shall discuss in its place. If, on the other hand, we attempt to specify more exactly, and in more detail, what is meant by 'Marxist method', 'we encounter, in the end, an irresolvable difficulty in distinguishing between Marx's method and some of his premises and, indeed, some of his conclusions'.[32] Thus it is that 'those who espouse the notion of Marxism as method with the most intellectual rigour are exactly those who are caught insensibly in the undertow which drags them back to Marxism (1) as doctrine.'[33] And against this tendency to *a priori* abstract construction Thompson, the historian, continues vigorously to protest.

It is not clear to me that there is, in Christian thought, a 'Christianity (2)' which corresponds, in a manner sufficiently close to be illuminating, to Marxism (2). If there is, it perhaps consists in the purely *theoretical* use to which the fashionable insistence on 'orthopraxis', rather than 'orthodoxy', is sometimes put. Merely to *define* the maintained identity of Christianity in terms of 'orthopraxis' does not, of itself, ensure that – in practice – that identity is thus maintained. Perhaps the point would be that, however admirable and justified this shift of emphasis, it brings about its own reversal in so far as it is used as yet another device by means of which to avoid exposing theological affirmation to continual corrective purification from the particularity of human action and experience. We can insist (correctly) that Christianity is not a theory but a 'way of life', a way of discipleship. But discipleship is concrete, specific: it occurs, or does not occur, in particular patterns of engagement, relationship, suffering and worship. Discipleship reflected in thought is not the same thing as merely theoretical exploration of the meaning of discipleship. It is possible to insist that Christianity is a way of life without ever, in fact, entering upon that way.

Thompson notes that Kolakowski himself once proposed a form of Marxism (3), Marxism as 'heritage', when he wrote: 'The greatest

28 G. Lukács, *History and Class Consciousness*, p. 1, his stress.
29 R. Garaudy, *From Anathema to Dialogue*, p. 64, his stress.
30 Thompson, op. cit., p. 113.
31 Loc. cit.
32 Ibid., p. 112.
33 Ibid., p. 113.

triumph of an eminent scholar comes when his achievements cease to define a separate school of thought, when they merge into the very tissues of scientific life . . . losing their disparate existence.'[34] (It seems clear that certain aspects of Marxian economics, for example, have been thus 'assimilated'.) 'In philosophy you foresaw a rather different evolution: Marxism, like Platonism, would remain as a distinct school of thought.'[35] (The extent to which this has, in fact, occurred – on which Thompson does not comment – is more problematic.)

Thompson acknowledges that 'The influence of certain ideas which perhaps originated from the Marxist tradition is certainly enormous'.[36] Nevertheless, he believes that, at least in the social sciences, Kolakowski 'greatly underestimated the capacity for capitalist society to generate and regenerate its own defensive ideological formations'.[37] In other words, in the process of 'assimilation', Marxist ideas have only too often been defused and domesticated, set to the service of a social system for which they were originally constructed as elements of a critique.

This time, the analogy with Christian thought, though severely restricted, is not without interest. It is restricted because Christianity does not take its origin from an 'eminent scholar' or original thinker, but from a life lived, a deed done, a death undergone. Nevertheless, the parallels are there. Is it not the case, for example, that many of the so-called 'Christian values' of Western society, in the actual form in which they are promoted and defended, have at best an indirect and problematic relationship to the gospel of Jesus Christ, crucified and risen? Thus, for example, the assumption that 'social order' is, in all circumstances, a Christian value to be sustained, and that conflict and struggle are disvalues to be resisted and deplored, would be an instance of such 'domestication' of the subversive element in Christianity, as indeed would be the transformation of the doctrine of the transcendence of God's Kingdom into the belief that Christianity has 'nothing to do' with politics.

Thompson's complaint against Marxism (3), however, is not simply that it is innocent of the ways in which 'assimilation' is often evidence, not of the 'influence' of Marxism, but rather of the extent to which it has been deprived of influence; he is also suspicious of the eclecticism which fosters this innocence: 'in Britain, when we

---

34 L. Kolakowski, 'Permanent and Transitory Aspects of Marxism', *Marxism and Beyond*, p. 204. Thompson (op. cit., p. 114) quotes, without reference, a slightly different version.

35 Thompson, 'An Open Letter . . .', p. 115. 'It is otherwise in the field of philosophy, taken as a discursive expression of a view of the world' (Kolakowski, 'Permanent and Transitory Aspects of Marxism', p. 204).

36 Thomson, loc. cit.

37 Loc. cit.

think of heritage . . . we surrender to inertia; we lie upon our heritage like a Dunlopillo mattress and hope that, in our slumbers, those good, dead men of history will move us forward. We are dosed with eclecticism . . . as regularly as we are dosed with librium.'[38] I think I understand: Gethsemane and Calvary, the poverty of Francis and the anger of Luther; these things do not regularly feature in the speeches of those who appeal to us to uphold 'our great Christian heritage'.

Having sketched, and indicated his objections to, his first three meanings of Marxism, Thompson proposes a fourth: Marxism as Tradition. 'The notion of tradition', he maintains, 'entails some of the advantages but avoids certain difficulties of Marxism (2).'[39] The difficulties that he has in mind arise principally from the fact that, when Marxism is defined in terms of method, 'what remains disallowed is the criticism of that method itself by criteria external to the method'. The method thus becomes not only self-validating but, as increasingly sophisticated attention is paid to its theoretical elaboration, 'the empirical controls and the empirical transfusions – leading on to the breaking and making anew of concepts – intrinsic to the method of historical materialism',[40] in fact get lost.

'If, on the other hand, we are willing to bring any and every part of Marxist thought under scrutiny – and to employ any instrument of criticism which seems legitimate (whether historical evidence, or the examination of its inner consistency, or the well-founded objections of intellectual opponents) – then we can only describe ourselves as Marxists in the fourth sense.'[41] It would be pointless to ask whether Marxism as tradition is *possible* because, as a matter of historical fact, 'This tradition exists; it has defined itself in Marx's work and in the evolution (contradictory as that is) of his ideas.'[42] The question at once arises: has not this tradition become, in fact, *so* internally diverse, so contradictory, as no longer to merit description as a single stream of tradition? We shall consider Thompson's answer in due course. At this point, however, I want to raise the very different question: does there, as matter of fact, exist that which could be described as 'Christianity (4)'? And the answer, as a matter of fact, is surely: Yes. This tradition exists; it has defined itself in the New Testament and in the evolution (contradictory as that is) of Christian theology and spirituality.

'The point is (if one affirms this tradition as one's own) less to define the tradition than to define where one stands within it.'[43]

38 Ibid., p. 116.
39 Loc. cit.
40 Ibid., p. 117.
41 Loc. cit.
42 Loc. cit.
43 Loc. cit.

This Thompson has sought to do: positively, in the description quoted at the start of the previous paragraph; negatively, in his criticisms of Marxisms (1), (2), and (3). The definition of where one stands in the tradition is demanded because, since the tradition has, as a matter of fact, 'defined itself historically and existentially . . . it contains, whether we like it or not, all those sub-traditions (the Marxisms (1) and (2)) which can claim some relevant descent from Marx's ideas'.[44] This position is not, he insists, eclecticist (and thus does not turn out to be no more than a variant of Marxism (3)). It is 'at the present time – a comfortless and strenuous one, since it must entail a definition (and definitions continually re-newed) as to where [one] stands within it',[45] and thus be a definition affirmed in *opposition* to other aspects of the tradition.

In noting the analogies between Marxism (4) and 'Christianity as Tradition', that last point is of some importance. It is common-place, nowadays, to insist that unity in faith is compatible with the most diverse pluralism in theology. But too often that pluralism is eclectically conceived, as if the most divergent and mutually incom-patible approaches to Christianity could simply coexist, in untrou-bled tranquillity, within the household of the faith. This is an illusion. The relationship between different theological approaches will often be one of tension and conflict: the position of one who seeks to stand within 'Christianity as tradition' will often be, in many respects, 'comfortless and strenuous', as he seeks, again and again, to define with accuracy and integrity where it is that he does and does not stand.

'The question arises: if a great part of Marxism (1) is politically damaging and a caricature of rational thought, and if some part of Marxism (2) is intellectually limiting and resistant to development, why should one maintain allegiance to the tradition at all?'[46] His answer is twofold: intellectually, 'one cannot be true to one's own thought in any other way'; politically, 'one can share strong political commitments with Marxists with whom one's greatest source of disagreement is nevertheless about Marxism.'[47] It is not only Marx-ists who have been known to wonder why they should maintain allegiance to the tradition in which they have hitherto sought to stand. And it seems to me that a similar twofold answer can be given by the Christian confronted with the correlative question: intellectually, I could be true to my experience and understanding in no other way; practically, it is possible to share strong religious convictions and commitments with Christians with whom one's greatest source of disagreement is nevertheless about Christianity.

44 Ibid., p. 122.
45 Loc. cit.
46 Loc. cit.
47 Loc. cit.

The essay on which I have been commenting was written in 1973. By 1978, at the end of his long essay on Althusser, Thompson said of the position sketched in the letter to Kolakowski: 'I can now see that this was an inadequate and evasive resolution. Politically, it has long been impossible for the Stalinist and anti-Stalinist positions to cohabit with each other. It is clear to me now . . . that we can no longer attach any theoretical meaning to the notion of a common tradition . . . There are *two* traditions.'[48] As between these two traditions, 'between idealist and materialist modes of thought, between Marxism as closure and a tradition, derivative from Marx, of open investigation and critique',[49] it is necessary, 'from this point forward . . . to declare one's allegiance to one or the other'.[50] (When discussing Marxism (1), I noted Thompson's tendency to assume that all doctrinal systems were necessarily 'dogmatic' in the pejorative sense: were, that is to say, 'systems of closure'. It is consonant with this unwarranted assumption that now, as in many other places in these essays, he abusively – and without offering the slightest justification – characterizes any 'system of closure' as a 'theology', and announces: 'Between theology and reason there can be no room left for negotiation'.)[51]

I do not see how even the most liberal and accommodating of Christian theologians could deny the possibility that Christians, too, may from time to time be obliged to acknowledge the occurrence of similarly fundamental splits within Christianity. And if, in recent decades, strenuous efforts have been made to heal those breaches that occurred in the past, it seems possible that new and equally fundamental 'cleavages' are occurring today, although the patterns of solidarity and division will henceforth be very differently drawn and are likely to be perceived as cultural, even political, rather than directly or immediately doctrinal in character.

My aim in this chapter has been threefold. Edward Thompson is an historian and polemicist of distinction who stands in a peculiarly English tradition of social and political radicalism. From such a source, one would hardly expect some academically cool, detached taxonomy. Nevertheless, it seems to me that the essay on which I have been commenting, although written from a highly personal (and, it would doubtless seem to many Marxists, idiosyncratic) standpoint, perceptively sketches four fundamental forms of Marxist interpretation. As such, it offers at least a provisional sketch of the meanings of Marxism.

In the second place, my own scattered reading of the writings of Marxists has persuaded me that, in the history of their interpret-

48 Thompson, 'The Poverty of Theory', p. 380.
49 Loc. cit.
50 Ibid., p. 381.
51 Loc. cit.

ation, Marx's ideas have indeed been subject to something like the twofold distortion which Thompson describes in his criticism of Marxisms (1) and (2). (At this stage, I leave open the question as to whether, and to what extent, the seeds of these distortions were sown in certain tendencies and ambiguities in Marx's own writings.)

At the beginning of this chapter, I criticized Peter Hebblethwaite for contrasting a 'Marxism' so amorphous as to elude all grasp and definition with a 'Christianity' which appeared, if only from his silence, to be more or less uniform. Therefore, thirdly, it seemed a good idea to attempt impressionistically to illustrate my conviction, not only that Marxism has more 'shape' and Christianity more variety than he indicates, but also that there are certain similarities between their respective patterns of unity and diversity. Be that as it may, we are now, I think, in a position to conclude the preliminaries by turning, at last, to Marx himself, in order to indicate something of the relationships between some of the themes that I shall discuss in Part II by noticing the way in which these themes occur in the first chapter of *The German Ideology*.

4

THE GERMAN IDEOLOGY

'The philosophers have only *interpreted* the world, in various ways; the point is to *change* it.'[1] This eleventh 'Thesis on Feuerbach', set down in the spring of 1845, has been described as 'Marx's most frequently quoted saying'.[2] It bears succinct and aphoristic witness to a conviction whose presence is already discernible in the 'Paris Manuscripts' of 1844. In these Manuscripts, we find Marx reflecting on man's alienation from the world of nature, from the work of his hands and from his fellow-men. This is hardly surprising: it merely sets him, alongside his contemporaries, in the complex tradition of post-Hegelian German philosophy.[3] And, thus expressed, it thereby also sets him alongside Feuerbach whose work, it has been said, showed Marx 'just how much of Hegel's philosophy could be swallowed by a resolute atheist unable to swallow it whole'.[4] His reading of Feuerbach, however, had never been uncritical, and already in the 1844 Manuscripts the central issue on which his thought increasingly diverged from that of Feuerbach begins to come into focus. The contradictions in the human condition cry out for resolution: but *theoretically*, philosophically, to think them through and to resolve them is only to resolve them in *thought*. The point is, however, that these contradictions need to be resolved in *fact*, in reality, and not simply in our minds: 'their resolution is for that reason by no means only a problem of knowledge, but a *real* problem of life, a problem which *philosophy* was unable to solve precisely because it treated it as a *purely* theoretical problem.'[5]

The 'Theses on Feuerbach' are 'a very brief sketch of the ideas that [Marx] and Engels elaborated a few months later in *The German Ideology*'.[6] 'It seemed to me very important', wrote Marx in a letter, 'that a work polemicizing against German philosophy and current

---

1 *EW*, p. 423.
2 *KI*, p. 88.
3 'Comme tous les penseurs qui se livrent à la tâche critique dans la période post-hégélienne, Marx fait porter son effort sur la réduction des "aliénations" ' (J.-Y. Calvez, *La Pensée de Karl Marx*, p. 27).
4 J. Plamenatz, *Karl Marx's Philosophy of Man*, p. 111.
5 'Economic and Philosophical Manuscripts', *EW*, p. 354.
6 *Life*, p. 140.

German socialism should precede my positive construction. This is necessary in order to prepare the public for the point of view of my *Economics*.[7] My intention in this chapter is purely expository: by quoting extensively from and briefly commenting on the Preface and first chapter of the text, it will be possible to indicate something of the way in which most of the themes which we shall discuss in subsequent chapters are related in Marx's thought. I have already indicated, in Chapter Two, that the selection of this text for this purpose is by no means arbitrary. McLellan has said of the first chapter of *The German Ideology*, 'one of the most central of Marx's texts',[8] that 'Marx never subsequently stated his materialist conception of history at such length and in such detail'[9] and, according to Kolakowski, 'all his later work may be regarded as a continuation and elaboration of the body of thought which was already constituted by the time of *The German Ideology*'.[10]

'Hitherto', says Marx in the opening words of the Preface, 'men have always formed wrong ideas about themselves, about what they are and what they ought to be. They have arranged their relations according to their ideas of God, of normal man, etc. The products of their brains have got out of their hands. They, the creators, have bowed down before their creations. Let us liberate them from the chimeras, the ideas, dogmas, imaginary beings under the yoke of which they are pining away. Let us revolt against this rule of concepts.'[11] It seems clear that this 'liberation', this 'revolt', must take the form of an inversion of the present state of affairs: it must be such as to enable men to arrange their *ideas* of 'God', and of 'normal man', according to their relationships, rather than the other way round. There will be no genuflection when man, the creator, has ceased to bow down before the idols he has made; idols which, in so far as they have 'got out of his hands', stand over against him as alien and alienating powers.

The German philosophers, imagining themselves to be immensely radical and subversive, have supposed that, in order to achieve such liberation, all that is necessary is to change the way that people think. These philosophers have quite failed to realize that thought is merely the shadow of reality (twelve years later, in the *Grundrisse*, Marx will characterize 'philosophical consciousness' as that for which 'conceptual thinking is the real human being, and for which the conceptual world as such is thus the only reality').[12] Hence, 'The first volume of the present publication has the aim of uncloak-

7 Quoted in *Life*, p. 143.
8 *Life*, p. 151.
9 Loc. cit.
10 *KI*, p. 177.
11 *CW5*, p. 23.
12 *G*, p. 101.

ing these sheep, who take themselves and are taken for wolves. . . .
It is its aim to ridicule and discredit the philosophic struggle with
the shadows of reality, which appeals to the dreamy and muddled
German nation.'[13]

If the project of liberating men from the 'rule of concepts', of
inverting the perceived relationship between human existence and
its reflection in thought, is 'materialist' in a sense which he will
elaborate in the next section of the text, the use of the metaphor of
'uncloaking', and the emphasis on the illusory identification of reality with its reflection, its 'shadow', contain hints of a view of historical process, and of the transformative participation in that
process in quest of truth and reality, which we shall discuss in the
following three chapters. The Preface ends with a splendid parable:
'Once upon a time a valiant fellow had the idea that men were
drowned in water only because they were possessed with the *idea of
gravity*. If they were to get this notion out of their heads, say by
avowing it to be a superstition, a religious concept, they would be
sublimely proof against any danger from water. His whole life long
he fought against the illusion of gravity, of whose harmful consequences all statistics brought him new and manifold evidence. This
valiant fellow was the type of the new revolutionary philosopher in
Germany.'[14]

The battle between the rival schools of post-Hegelian thought
was originally theological in character: most of the participants
'were interested in religion above all; and the attitude of the Prussian Government made politics an extremely dangerous subject for
debate'.[15] It was the publication of David Friedrich Strauss's *Life
of Jesus*, in 1835, four years after Hegel's death, that polarized the
debate, and it was Strauss who, in 1837, first used the labels 'Right'
and 'Left' to designate the opposing parties.[16] 'The entire body of
German philosophical criticism', says Marx, 'from Strauss to Stirner
is confined to criticism of *religious* conceptions.'[17] And he complains
that neither side 'even attempted a comprehensive criticism of the
Hegelian system':[18] they contented themselves with extracting one
side of that system and turning it against the whole. 'The Young
[or 'Left'] Hegelians are in agreement with the Old [or 'Right']
Hegelians in their belief in the rule of religion, of concepts, of a
universal principle in the existing world. Except that the one party
attacks this rule as usurpation, while the other extols it as legiti-

13 *CW5*, pp. 23–4.
14 *CW5*, p. 24.
15 *Life*, p. 31.
16 Cf. D. McLellan, *Marx Before Marxism*, pp. 35–7.
17 *CW5*, p. 29.
18 *CW5*, pp. 28–9.

mate.'[19] Marx's critique of religion is, as these passages indicate, tightly woven into the fabric of his criticism of 'idealism' in general.

The one-sidedness of both parties' criticism of Hegel is illustrated by their use, as slogans, of one half of the 'classic aphorism'[20] in the Preface to Hegel's *Philosophy of Right*: 'What is rational is actual and what is actual is rational'.[21] According to T. M. Knox, 'Hegel is not saying that what exists or is "real" is rational. . . . If we say of a statesman who accomplishes nothing that he is not a "real" statesman, then we mean by "real" what Hegel calls "actual". . . . Hegel's philosophy as a whole might be regarded as an attempt to justify his identification of rationality with actuality and vice versa, but his doctrine depends ultimately on his faith in God's providence. . . . It follows that Hegel's identification of the actual and the rational is not a plea for conservatism in politics. The actualization of God's purpose is not yet complete.'[22] It is arguable that, once the concept of 'reason' had been 'naturalized' by Marx, had been brought down from heaven to earth, he was in a position to realize the transformative, revolutionary potential of Hegel's notion of history as the actualization of reason[23] in a way that neither of the post-Hegelian parties were, precisely on account of that one-sidedness against which he protested.

The conservatives, the 'Right-Hegelians', the 'idealists', for whom 'the real is the rational', regarded the central beliefs and convictions of society or, as Marx calls them, 'the products of consciousness', as 'the true bonds of human society',[24] and sought to preserve and to strengthen them. The radicals, the 'Left-Hegelians', the 'materialists' (such as Feuerbach), for whom 'the rational is the real', did not disagree that the 'products of consciousness' were 'the true bonds of human society', but, for them, these were bonds of slavery, 'the real chains of men',[25] which they accordingly sought to shatter by the tools of rational critique.

Marx's point is that, however bitter this dispute, both parties to it assume that, in the quest for truth and freedom, the fundamental problems are problems of the imagination and the reason, of religion, theology and philosophy. The radicalism of the Left-Hegelians is, for Marx, a spurious radicalism: the 'demand to change consciousness amounts', he says, to no more than 'a demand to

---

19 *CW5*, p. 30.
20 *KI*, p. 66.
21 G. W. F. Hegel, *Philosophy of Right*, tr. T. M. Knox, p. 10.
22 Ibid., p. 302. Perhaps it would have been better, in order to avoid begging central questions in the interpretation of Hegel's theology, to have said 'divine providence' and 'divine purpose'.
23 Cf. C. Taylor, *Hegel*, pp. 422–6.
24 *CW5*, p. 30.
25 Loc. cit.

interpret the existing world in another way',[26] to knock the idea of God, or gravity, out of people's heads. Such radicalism is spurious because it never pauses to examine the concrete reality itself, reflected into that consciousness about which the battle rages, or to ask whether the quest for truth and freedom does not demand that it is the world as it exists, and not merely the forms of its reflection in thought, that needs to be changed: 'It has not occurred to any one of these philosophers to inquire into the connection of German philosophy with German reality, the connection of their criticism with their own material surroundings.'[27]

If, in the quest for truth and freedom, we set aside these sterile conflicts and seek to grasp the relation between thought and its 'material surroundings', where shall we begin? What will our 'premises' be? If we are to avoid the illusions of 'the German ideology', these premises must be, not propositions, but people: 'real individuals, their activity and the material conditions of their life'.[28] Human beings are physical organisms, aspects of nature, in relationship to the rest of nature: 'All historical writing must set out from these natural bases and their modification in the course of history through the action of man.'[29] And the history of the 'modification' of nature by human action is the history of modes of production: human beings 'begin to distinguish themselves from animals as soon as they begin to *produce* their means of subsistence. . . . By producing their means of subsistence men are indirectly producing their material life.'[30]

In these paragraphs, Marx is laying down two fundamental features of what he will call 'historical materialism'. The first, which has been called the 'most fundamental idea in *The German Ideology*',[31] an idea first sketched in the Paris Manuscripts and taken for granted in *Capital*, is that 'man produces himself through labour',[32] through physically and mentally 'working' the material conditions of his existence. The second is the insistence that, if we would attend to 'real individuals', to what they produce with their hands and minds, and to the modes of production, then we must proceed *historically*, or else we shall find ourselves suffering from the illusion that contemporary modes of production are fundamentally timeless, immutable, pertaining to the unchanging 'essence of man'. (Later we shall see that, in his economic writings, and especially in *Capital*,

26 Loc. cit.
27 Loc. cit.
28 *CW5*, p. 31.
29 Loc. cit.
30 Loc. cit.
31 C. J. Arthur, 'Introduction', K. Marx and F. Engels, *The German Ideology, Part One*, p. 21.
32 Loc. cit.

this becomes one of the central thrusts of Marx's criticism of the work of the classical, or 'bourgeois', economists.) Materialist method is thus historical method or, perhaps better, historical method is a matter of grasping the process of human action in the material world.

Marx therefore now proceeds to offer a thumbnail sketch of the history of successive modes of production, with their corresponding forms of ownership. The sketch focuses on the history of the *division of labour*, and the antagonisms to which this gives rise. Thus, for example, 'The division of labour inside a nation leads at first to the separation of industrial and commercial from agricultural labour, and hence to the separation of *town* and *country* and to the conflict of their interests.'[33]

The social historian must, however, never lose sight of the fact that 'Men are the producers of their conceptions'.[34] Instead of proceeding, as the 'ideologist' does, from the examination of concepts of 'man', or 'society', or 'the State', he must proceed empirically: 'Empirical observation must in each separate instance bring out empirically, and without any mystification and speculation, the connection of the social and political structure with production.'[35]

This insistence that, in inverting the procedure of the 'ideologist', he is, in fact, merely setting matters the right way up, leads Marx to use a notoriously unsatisfactory optical metaphor. The passage in which he does so is among the most discussed in *The German Ideology* (indeed, few passages in his entire work have received such persistent and confusing attention from his commentators): 'in all ideology men and their relations appear upside down as in a *camera obscura*. . . . In direct contrast to German philosophy which descends from heaven to earth, here it is a matter of ascending from earth to heaven. That is to say, not of setting out from what men say, imagine, conceive, nor from men as narrated, thought of, imagined, conceived, in order to arrive at men in the flesh; but setting out from real, active men, and on the basis of their real life-process demonstrating the development of the ideological reflexes and echoes of this life-process. . . . Morality, religion, metaphysics, and all the rest of ideology as well as the forms of consciousness corresponding to these, thus no longer retain the semblance of independence. They have no history, no development. . . . It is not consciousness that determines life, but life that determines consciousness.'[36] We shall have occasion to return to this passage when we come to consider the distinction between 'base' and 'superstructure'. For the moment, it is sufficient to point out that although, if

33 *CW5*, p. 32.
34 *CW5*, p. 36.
35 *CW5*, p. 35.
36 *CW5*, pp. 36–7.

we were to overlook the polemical character of this passage, it would be easy to misunderstand Marx as advocating a crudely reductionist materialism according to which modes of thought are purely epiphenomenal, any such account of his position grossly misrepresents it.

Marx's contrast between the 'empirical' character of the procedure he is recommending and the historically unreferred 'speculation' of the German ideologists leads him to draw a distinction which will have far-reaching consequences in the subsequent development of Marxist theory. 'Where speculation ends', he says, 'where real life starts, there consequently begins real, positive science [*wirkliche, positive Wissenschaft*], the expounding of the practical activity, of the practical process of development of men. Empty phrases about consciousness end, and real knowledge [*wirkliches Wissen*] has to take their place. When the reality is described, a self-sufficient philosophy loses its medium of existence.'[37] In the context, the general drift of these remarks is clear enough. 'Speculation', 'empty phrases about consciousness' are, to use an ancient distinction, at best 'opinion' and not 'knowledge'. 'Speculation', or 'ideology', may indeed be defective as knowledge, but it does not follow, in English usage, that 'real knowledge' can simply be identified with 'real science'. There are other paths towards the knowledge of reality than those which it would be appropriate to describe as 'scientific'. The German language facilitates the assumption that 'real *knowledge*' may be reductively identified with 'real *science*'.[38] This assumption has, I believe, exercized an unfortunate influence on Marxist debates concerning what might and might not constitute modes of authentic knowledge.[39]

Once philosophy ceases to be regarded as 'self-sufficient', its place can only be taken, according to Marx, 'by a summing-up of the most general results, abstractions which are derived from the observation of the historical development of men'.[40] He now proceeds to offer a selection of some of these permissible 'abstractions', focusing his selection on another aspect of the division of labour: 'Division of labour only becomes truly such from the moment when a division of material and mental labour appears. (The first form of ideologists, *priests*, is coincident.)'[41] From this moment onwards consciousness *can* really flatter itself that it is something other than consciousness of existing practice . . . from now on consciousness is in a position to emancipate itself from the world and to proceed to the formation of "pure" theory, theology, philosophy, morality,

37 *CW5*, p. 37.
38 Cf. below, p. 215.
39 Cf. below, pp. 130–1, 196–8.
40 *CW5*, p. 37.
41 Marginal note by Marx.

etc.'[42] In other words, in insisting that it is 'life that determines consciousness', not 'consciousness that determines life',[43] Marx was protesting against the view that the world of thought may legitimately be regarded as *autonomous*, an illusion that is the more easily maintained and fostered in the measure that 'mental labourers' come to occupy a distinct and privileged social role.

The grounds of his protest are, of course, practical and social, and not merely theoretical. The division between 'mental' and 'material' labour is not itself a division between social classes. It occurs *within* 'the ruling class . . . so that inside this class one part appears as the thinkers of the class . . . who make the formation of the illusion of the class about itself their chief source of livelihood'.[44] In other words, the 'mental labourers' in the ruling class enable that class, by education and other forms of social control, to perpetuate its dominance over the rest of society – a dominance that will appear to be the result of the natural order of things, or of inherited excellence, rather than of economic and political power. This seems to be the sense of the famous pronouncement: 'The ideas of the ruling class are in every epoch the ruling ideas: i.e., the class which is the ruling *material* force of society is at the same time its ruling *intellectual* force. . . . The ruling ideas are nothing more than the ideal expression of the dominant material relations, the dominant material relations grasped as ideas.'[45] Thirty years later, in 1875, Marx was to say, in an equally famous passage, that only in an 'advanced phase of communist society, when the enslaving subjugation of individuals to the division of labour, and thereby the antithesis between intellectual and physical labour, have disappeared', will it be possible for society wholly to 'cross the narrow horizon of bourgeois right and inscribe on its banner: From each according to his abilities, to each according to his needs'.[46]

If the 'ruling ideas' are, indeed, 'nothing more than . . . the dominant material relations grasped as ideas', then the dominance of one section of society over the rest will be the more easily exercized and accepted when, refracted into the realm of ideas, this dominance is presented, not simply in terms of the sovereignty of 'truth', for example, or of 'law and order', but of the sovereignty of an absolute ground of truth, law and order. 'Once the ruling ideas have been separated from the ruling individuals and, above all, from the relations which result from a given stage of the mode of production, and in this way the conclusion has been reached that history is always under the sway of ideas, it is very easy to abstract

42 *CW5*, pp. 44–5.
43 *CW5*, p. 37.
44 *CW5*, p. 60.
45 *CW5*, p. 59.
46 'Critique of the Gotha Programme', *FI*, p. 347.

from these various ideas "the Idea", the thought, etc., as the dominant force in history, and thus to consider all these separate ideas and concepts as "forms of self-determination" of the Concept developing in history.'[47] Here, with reference to what he calls 'the whole trick of proving the hegemony of the spirit in history',[48] Marx is criticizing Hegel for having 'separated' the 'ruling ideas' from the 'ruling individuals', and for having ascribed to the former autonomous and, ultimately, absolute status. It is not difficult to see how central to this debate is the question of the status and function of concepts of God.

Marx insists that there is no such thing as ' "pure" consciousness', pure thought. 'The "mind" is', he says with irony, 'from the outset afflicted with the curse of being "burdened" with matter, which here makes its appearance in the form of agitated layers of air, sounds, in short, of language. Language is as old as consciousness, language *is* practical, real consciousness . . . language, like consciousness, only arises from the need, the necessity, of intercourse with other men.'[49] Ten years later, in the *Grundrisse*, he will say: 'language itself is the product of a community, just as it is in another respect itself the presence of the community'.[50] It follows that, if the community is, in fact, rent with contradictions, class-divisions, structures of domination and alienation, then the language or languages in which the community expresses itself – in which it is, as it were, 'self-present' in the world – will be similarly distorted. The users of a language, however, are commonly unable to perceive its distortions; *a fortiori*, they are unable truthfully to perceive the contradictions and distortions in the underlying patterns of social and economic relationship. Thus it is that language, as the product, expression and presence of a distorted social situation, 'mystifies'.

Linguistic distortion, then, is the expression, not the cause, of our alienated condition. Hence the foolishness of those philosophers, those 'valiant fellows', who imagine, for example, that the mere exposure of the illusory character of religious belief is *as such* emancipatory. For the healing of our alienation a deeper transformation is required. Marx himself locates the cause of alienation in the fact that, throughout history, the specific forms of human activity, instead of being freely chosen by individual people, have been *imposed* upon them – either by an as yet untamed world of nature, or by patterns of social domination which function as if they were natural, and hence immutable, forces (which, indeed, they are frequently supposed to be). This seems to be the sense of 'naturally' in a

47 *CW5*, p. 61.
48 *CW5*, p. 62.
49 *CW5*, pp. 43–4.
50 *G*, p. 490.

passage such as the following: 'the division of labour offers us the first example of the fact that . . . as long as a cleavage exists between the particular and the common interest, as long, therefore, as activity is not voluntarily, but naturally, divided, man's own deed becomes an alien power opposed to him, which enslaves him instead of being controlled by him.'[51]

'This fixation of social activity, this consolidation of what we ourselves produce into a material power above us, growing out of our control', the power of property and of money, 'is one of the chief factors in historical development up till now.'[52] But how is that which we ourselves produce to be brought under the control of the producers, and thereby cease to be an 'alien', oppressive power? In order to understand Marx's answer to this question it is necessary to take up the reference in the previous paragraph to the 'cleavage' between 'the particular and the common interest'. The division of labour, according to Marx, 'implies the contradiction between the interest of the separate individual or the individual family and the common interest of all individuals who have intercourse with one another'.[53] The common interest 'does not exist merely in the imagination'.[54] It takes concrete shape and form in the *State*. But the State, which *appears* – to all classes – to represent or embody the common or general interest, in *fact* embodies the particular interest of the ruling class. It therefore follows that 'every class which is aiming at domination . . . must first conquer political power in order to represent its interest as the general interest.'[55]

This may be an admirable commentary on the necessities of revolutionary *Realpolitik*, but it hardly provides an answer to the question: how is human labour and the fruit of that labour to be brought under the control of its agents and thus cease to be an alienating and alien power? Or, at least, it would only provide such an answer if there were to emerge, in the course of history, a class whose particular interest in *fact* coincided with the general interest, the fundamental needs, of all members and classes of society. Paradoxically, there could only be such a class if it had, in fact, *no* 'particular' interest, nothing particular to defend, to cling on to. And the nineteenth-century industrial proletariat, in its abject poverty, its total dispossession and radical alienation, is, according to Marx, just such a class: 'Only the proletariat of the present day, who are completely shut off from all self-activity, are in a position to achieve a complete and no longer restricted self-activity, which

51 *CW5*, p. 47.
52 *CW5*, pp. 47–8.
53 *CW5*, p. 46.
54 Loc. cit.
55 *CW5*, p. 47.

consists in the appropriation of a totality of productive forces and in the development of a totality of capacities entailed by this.'[56]

The coming into existence of such a radically dispossessed and alienated class, 'a class . . . which has to bear all the burdens of society without enjoying its advantages, which is ousted from society and forced into the sharpest contradiction to all other classes',[57] is therefore one necessary condition of the definitive abolition of 'alienation' or 'estrangement'.[58] The other necessary condition is this deprivation's *alter ego*: that 'existing world of wealth and culture',[59] that 'development of productive forces'[60] on a world scale, which has been the achievement of capitalism. This, too, is 'an absolutely necessary practical premise, because without it privation, *want* is merely made general, and with *want* the struggle for necessities would begin again, and all the old filthy business would necessarily be restored.'[61]

This, briefly summarized, is Marx's analysis of the preconditions of that definitive, unsurpassable – and, as such, one is tempted to say 'eschatological' – transformation of human society which he sees as implicit in the logic of the development of capitalism. What will be the outcome or aftermath of such a revolution? Marx does not tell us; he is in the business, not of predicting the future, but of analysing current trends. Hence his warning, apparently added as an afterthought, against the utopian construction of *imagined* future states of affairs: 'Communism is for us not a *state of affairs* which is to be established, an *ideal* to which reality [will] have to adjust itself. We call communism the *real* movement which abolishes the present state of things. The conditions of this movement result from the now existing premise.'[62] Almost the only passage in which he seems, according to some of his commentators, to be predicting the character of post-revolutionary society, is a lyrical sketch of how things would be if the 'division of labour' had been abolished: 'as soon as the division of labour comes into being, each man has a particular, exclusive sphere of activity, which is forced upon him and from which he cannot escape. He is a hunter, a fisherman, a shepherd, or a critical critic, and must remain so if he does not want to lose his means of livelihood; whereas in communist society, where nobody has one exclusive sphere of activity but each can become accomplished in any branch he wishes, society regulates the general production and thus makes it possible for me to do one

56 *CW5*, p. 87.
57 *CW5*, p. 52.
58 Cf. our discussion of Marx's terminology in Chapter Fourteen.
59 *CW5*, p. 48.
60 *CW5*, p. 49.
61 Loc. cit.
62 Loc. cit.

thing today and another tomorrow, to hunt in the morning, fish in the afternoon, rear cattle in the evening, criticize after dinner, just as I have a mind, without ever becoming hunter, fisherman, shepherd or critic.'[63]

This theme, which we shall consider in due course, recurs in a much later chapter, in the course of his critique of Stirner, who had claimed that 'The organization of labour concerns only such work as can be done for me by others, such as cattle-slaughtering, ploughing, etc . . . [whereas] no one can compose your music for you, complete the sketches for your paintings, etc. No one can do Raphael's work for him'.[64] On this Marx comments: 'The exclusive concentration of artistic talent in particular individuals, and its suppression in the broad mass which is bound up with this, is a consequence of the division of labour. . . . In a communist society there are no painters but merely people who engage in painting among other activities.'[65]

Professor McLellan says of the first chapter of *The German Ideology* that it 'remains a masterpiece today for the cogency and clarity of its presentation'.[66] Some of the cogency and clarity have, I fear, inevitably been lost in my attempt so briefly to indicate the outlines of its argument. Nevertheless, it seemed appropriate to offer this summary exposition in order to provide an indication of the way in which some of the principal topics that we shall be considering in the second part of this study – the method of historical materialism, the concept of 'ideology', alienation and the criticism of religion, the 'scientific' character of Marxist theory and the extent to which it does or does not contain 'utopian' and 'eschatological' elements – hang together in Marx's thought. In so far as this sketch has served its purpose, the 'preliminaries' are now complete.

63 *CW5*, p. 47.
64 Quoted by Marx, *CW5*, p. 391.
65 *CW5*, p. 394.
66 *Life*, p. 151.

PART II THEMES

5

REVELATION, APPEARANCE AND REALITY

'A distinction is made in private life', wrote Marx in 1852, 'between what a man thinks and says of himself and what he really is and does. In historical struggles one must make a still sharper distinction between the phrases and fantasies of the parties and their real organization and real interests, between their conception of themselves and what they really are.'[1] That passage gives clear and succinct expression to one of the most pervasive themes in Marx's thought. Indeed, if one sought some single slogan which would serve as a clue to Marx's method – whether in historical, philosophical, economic or political analysis – one could do worse than propose: 'Things aren't what they seem to be'.

If, however, Marx's strategy consists in a sustained attempt to penetrate the superimposed layers of 'appearance' that disguise and obscure from view the underlying 'reality', that is only half the story. The strategy is chosen because the historical process which he seeks to understand and in which he seeks to intervene is itself a 'dialectic of appearance and reality'. It is this dialectic of appearance and reality of which I propose to treat in this chapter. I shall, for the most part, keep the discussion at a very general level because my aim is simply to offer an introductory sketch of themes and issues which will come into somewhat sharper focus in subsequent discussion of such topics as, for example, truth, 'materialism', 'ideology' and religion. My purpose in setting out, in the first part of the chapter, a catena of Marx's texts, is twofold. In the first place, I wish to indicate how pervasive is this theme of the dialectic of appearance and reality, at all periods in Marx's career and in respect of an extremely wide range of topics. In the second place, I hope that the cumulative effect of these passages, and of the recurring use in them of one or two favourite metaphors for the dialectic, will be to indicate why it is that, in conceiving of historical process, and of our grasp of that process, in terms of a dialectic of appearance and reality, Marx may be said to have been working with a secularized doctrine of revelation. The plausibility of this suggestion partly depends on one's view of the similarities and

---

1 'The Eighteenth Brumaire of Louis Bonaparte', *SE*, p. 174.

differences between Hegel's and Marx's uses of the dialectic. In the second part of the chapter, therefore, I shall tentatively enter this minefield.

'Veils' and 'Masks'

The resolution of the dialectic of appearance and reality in particular circumstances is frequently described by Marx in terms of the removal of a 'veil' or 'mask'. For a first example, we may turn to an article, written in 1844, in which he argues that revolutionary struggle for the achievement of socialism is a struggle for the transformation of society at a level more profound than that of mere political structure and organization. Nevertheless, the struggle for social change must take political form, have political 'appearance', if existing political structures, forms of the state, are to be overthrown. Hence, he concludes, 'All revolution . . . is a *political* act . . . without revolution *socialism* cannot be made possible. . . . But as soon as its *organizing functions* begin and its *goal*, its *soul* emerges, socialism throws its *political* mask aside.'[2] It is the metaphor of the 'mask' which interests us.

Three years later, in the 'Manifesto of the Communist Party', Marx and Engels declared that 'The bourgeoisie has stripped of its halo every occupation hitherto honoured and looked up to with reverent awe. It has converted the physician, the lawyer, the priest, the poet, the man of science, into its paid wage labourers. The bourgeoisie has torn away from the family its sentimental *veil*, and has reduced the family relation to a mere money relation.'[3] Degeneration? Undoubtedly; and yet, as the image of the 'veil' suggests, degeneration whose revelatory character consists in the disclosure of the possibility of the liberating overthrow of the underlying structure that is now exposed in its enhanced brutality: 'for exploitation, *veiled* by religious and political illusions, [the bourgeois] has substituted naked, shameless, direct, brutal exploitation.'[4]

In Paris, in June 1848, 'The workers were left with no choice; they had either to starve or to strike out. They answered on 22 June with the gigantic insurrection, in which the first great battle was fought between the two great classes which divide modern society. It was a fight for the preservation or destruction of the bourgeois order. The *veil* which shrouded the republic was torn asunder.'[5]

---

2 'Critical Notes on the Article "The King of Prussia and Social Reform. By a Prussian" ', *EW*, p. 420.
3 *R1848*, p. 70, my stress.
4 Loc. cit., my stress.
5 'The Class Struggles in France: 1848 to 1850', *SE*, pp. 58–9; cf. 'Eighteenth Brumaire', *SE*, p. 173.

The insurrection was violently suppressed. But failure, far from clouding the revelatory character of the event, clarified it. And so Marx comments on this failure: 'By making its burial place the birthplace of the *bourgeois republic*, the proletariat forced this republic to *appear in its pure form*, as the state whose avowed purpose it is to perpetuate the rule of capital and the slavery of labour.'[6]

In March 1855, Marx expected an economic crisis in Britain to have as its effect 'a revival of the political movements which for six years have been more or less dormant among [the working classes]. . . . The conflict between the industrial proletariat and the bourgeoisie will', he says, 'begin again at the same time as the conflict between bourgeoisie and aristocracy reaches its climax. The *mask* will then drop, which until now has *hidden* from the foreigner the *real* features of Great Britain's political physiognomy.'[7]

Many years later, in the first draft of the address which he prepared, in 1871, for the General Council of the First International, on 'The Civil War in France', Marx analysed the significance of the Paris Commune which he saw, for all its failure, as an important revolutionary model. The French republic, during that autumn of 1870, 'was impregnated with a new world. Its *real tendency, veiled* from the eyes of the world through the deceptions . . . of a pack of intriguing lawyers and word forcers, came again and again to the surface in the spasmodic movements of the Paris working classes . . . whose watchword was always the same, the *Commune!*.'[8] And the metaphor of the 'mask' returns several times in the final text of the address: the government's '*mask of imposture* was at last dropped on 28 January 1871';[9] 'The judicial functionaries were to be divested of that sham independence which had but served to *mask* their abject subserviency to all succeeding governments.'[10]

Let us now turn from political to economic uses of the language of 'appearance' and 'reality'. In 1844, in the course of his defence of Proudhon against Bauer, Marx said that 'all treatises on political economy take *private property* for granted. . . . *Proudhon* has put an end to this unconsciousness once for all. He takes the *human semblance* of the economic relations seriously and sharply opposes it to their *inhuman reality*.'[11] Over a decade later, in the *Grundrisse*, the language of 'appearance' and 'reality' continues to dominate the analysis. Here are just two examples: 'In present bourgeois society as a whole, this positing of prices and their circulation etc. *appears as the surface process*, beneath which, however, *in the depths*, entirely different

6 'Class Struggles in France', *SE*, p. 61, second stress mine.
7 'The British Constitution', *SE*, p. 284, my stress.
8 'First Draft of "The Civil War in France" ', *FI*, p. 244, first stress mine.
9 'The Civil War in France', *FI*, p. 189, my stress.
10 Ibid., p. 210, my stress.
11 'The Holy Family', *CW4*, pp. 31, 33, his stress.

processes go on';[12] 'While in the workshop of the productive process capital *appears* as proprietor and master, in respect of circulation it *appears* as dependent and determined by social connections. . . . But this circulation is a *haze* under which yet another whole world *conceals itself*, the world of the interconnections of capital.'[13]

'On the surface of bourgeois society', says Marx in *Capital*, 'the worker's wage appears as the price of labour.'[14] In other words, the contract between employer and employee *appears to be* a contract freely entered into by the contracting parties, whereby the employer buys what the worker has to sell: namely, his labour. But, if this were what was *really* happening, and if the employer paid the full price for the 'commodity' he purchased, then the profit he makes, and for which he operates, would be inexplicable. However, things are not what they seem. What the employer in *fact* purchases – and the fact is disguised by economic theory both from himself and from the worker – is the worker's labour-*power*, only a proportion of which is realized in the form of wages. Hence, said Marx, writing in 1875: 'Since Lassalle's death the scientific insight has made headway in our party that *wages are not what they appear to be*, namely the value or price of labour, but only a disguised form of the value or price of labour power.'[15] And so, to return to the text of *Capital*: 'All the notions of justice held by the worker and the capitalist, all the mystifications of the capitalist mode of production, all capitalism's illusions about freedom . . . have as their basis the *form of appearance* discussed above, *which makes the actual relation invisible*, and indeed presents to the eye the precise opposite of that relation.'[16]

That example was not chosen at random. Not only does it illustrate a central theme in Marx's economic theory, but it does so in a manner that highlights one aspect of what Calvez has called the 'double perspective' which 'dominates' the argument of *Capital*:[17] firstly, at the level of economic analysis, that which appears to be a harmonious process of production, exchange and consumption is in reality a process riddled with contradiction and exploitation; secondly, this state of affairs appears to be simply the working-out of timeless economic 'laws', but is in reality an historically particular state of affairs, the product of humanly, historically constructed patterns of social and economic organization.

So far, I have done no more than indicate the centrality of the 'dialectic of appearance and reality' in Marx's thought, and to suggest that the dialectical character of history and of its interpret-

12 *G*, p. 247, my stress.
13 *G*, p. 639, my stress.
14 *Cap. I*, p. 675.
15 'Critique of the Gotha Programme', *FI*, p. 352, my stress.
16 *Cap. I*, p. 680, my stress.
17 Cf. Calvez, *La Pensée de Karl Marx*, pp. 147–8.

ation may be said to embody, in his handling of it, a secularized doctrine of revelation. The suggestion is not that, beneath its rigorously and systematically atheist, naturalist 'appearance', the Marxian dialectic is 'really' theological. That suggestion would have been strenuously resisted by Marx himself and by those – from Lenin to Althusser – who, following in his footsteps, have seen in any weakening of the 'materialism' he sought to secure, not simply a collapse back into 'idealism', but, *thereby*, a collapse back into 'religious' or 'theological' perspectives and strategies.

According to Hegel, it is in Christianity that '*Geist*' is revealed as that which is, by nature, essentially self-revelation. Hegel saw 'in Christian theology the whole truth of speculative philosophy laid out in images'.[18] Hegel's philosophy does not 'deny the truth' of Christianity: it expresses theoretically, philosophically, that which religious discourse can only express in narrative form. Marx, taking over the 'dialectic of appearance and reality' from Hegel, sought to perform, non-theologically, tasks which, in Hegel's view, had irreducibly theological implications. In the course of this study we shall have to consider the twofold possibility, firstly, that Marx's critique of Hegel's idealism is justified but that, nevertheless, secondly, Hegel's insistence on the irreducibility of the religious dimension was *also* justified. If this were the case, then there would be an incoherence, a 'silence', in Marx's use of the dialectic which we might indicate by saying that it is sustained by an absent theology. My description of the Marxian dialectic as a secularized doctrine of revelation is intended to serve as a reminder of these possibilities.

The drift of these somewhat elliptical remarks will, I hope, become clearer as we proceed. At this point, their purpose is simply to suggest one reason why it is that any attempt to characterize the Marxian dialectic must include some consideration of the similarities and differences between Hegel and Marx. The other reason, of course, is that it was in critical reflection on Hegel and Feuerbach that Marx elaborated his version of the dialectic.

Hegel and Marx
The Phenomenology of Spirit is announced, in its Introduction, as 'an exposition of how knowledge makes it appearance'.[19] Even if the deliberate ambiguity of that phrase were not already clear from the context in which it occurs, it would soon become apparent if we asked: if this is Hegel's programme, and if Marx's programme is, on his own account, in some sense an 'inversion' of Hegel's, how is this 'inversion' to be described? As an exposition of how 'reality'

18 C. Taylor, *Hegel*, p. 211. Taylor should perhaps have said 'in Christian religious discourse', rather than 'in Christian theology'.
19 G. W. F. Hegel, *Phenomenology of Spirit*, tr. A. V. Miller (Oxford 1977), p. 49.

makes its appearance? As the achievement in 'reality' of that which only 'appears' in knowledge? Neither description captures the difference (although the latter comes nearer to it) because it is as central to Hegel's conviction as it is to Marx's that 'reality' and 'appearance', 'reality' and 'knowledge', 'life' and 'thought', are not yet and cannot yet be wholly coincident; hence the restlessness, the ceaseless movement, of history as dialectic.[20]

At every turn in the *Phenomenology*, we are presented with the dialectical contrast between 'our idea of ourselves, what we claim to be, and what we actually are'.[21] 'Le meilleur de l'effort de Hegel sera . . . une critique des prétensions du sujet à la certitude absolue de soi.'[22] But, quite apart from the fact that Marx, on account of his atheism, could not share the ultimately religious *grounds* on which Hegel was confident that 'reality' and 'appearance' would eventually be coincident, he regarded Hegel's analysis of the dialectical character of history as defective on another score: 'Hegel', said Marx in 1844, 'has merely discovered the *abstract, logical, speculative* expression of the movement of history.'[23] In view of the over-sharp contrasts which Marx sometimes draws, for polemical effect, between his position and Hegel's, it is worth noticing that he is here acknowledging that Hegel *has* 'discovered the movement of history', even if he has only done so 'abstractly', 'logically', 'speculatively'.

Let us now briefly turn to a passage from the critical notes which Marx made, in the summer of 1843, on Hegel's *Philosophy of Right*. In the section on the State (the final section of the book), Hegel has said that the social 'function assigned to any given individual is visibly mediated by circumstances, his caprice and his personal choice of his station in life'.[24] Why 'visibly'? Why not simply 'is mediated'? Because, according to him, this discernible distribution of social roles is merely the surface activity of that 'mind', that 'real idea', of which the State is the concrete embodiment and which is, as it were, organizing affairs 'invisibly', behind the scenes: he speaks of 'the real Idea . . . assigning the material of its finite reality'.[25]

Marx regards this whole account as thoroughly misleading. He insists that 'the *real* relationship is "that the assignment of the material of the State to any given individual is mediated by circumstances, his caprice and his personal choice of his station in life"'. This fact, this *real relationship* is described by speculative philosophy as *appearance*, as *phenomenon*. These circumstances, this caprice and

20 Cf. Taylor's chapter on 'Reason and History' (*Hegel*, pp. 389–427), esp. p. 426.
21 Taylor, *Hegel*, p. 148.
22 Calvez, *La Pensée de Karl Marx*, p. 25.
23 'Economic and Philosophical Manuscripts', *EW*, p. 382.
24 G. W. F. Hegel, *Philosophy of Right*, tr. T. M. Knox, p. 162.
25 Loc. cit.

this personal choice of a station in life, this *real mediation*, are merely [according to Hegel] the *appearance of a mediation* which the real Idea performs on itself and which takes place behind the scenes. . . . The ordinary empirical world is not governed by its own mind but by a mind alien to it.'[26]

From that passage a number of things begin to become clear. In the first place, we begin to see why it is that, while sharing Hegel's conviction that the process of history is a dialectic of appearance and reality, Marx should seek to 'invert' Hegel's account of that dialectic. In the second place, if human beings are governed, not by their own minds, but by an 'alien' mind (and Marx is certainly not disposed to deny this), it is important to name that 'alien mind' correctly and to locate it accurately. Hegel knows that (in the case in point) it is the State, but he misleads by speaking as if the State were the concrete embodiment of something else. What is this 'something else'? Without even attempting the impossible task of answering that question (impossible at least for one who, like myself, is baffled by the problem of how to 'read' the theological dimension of Hegel's philosophy) it is at least not difficult to see why Marx should have supposed this 'something else' to be the God of Christian belief. And here we have a clue, not only to the central role which Marx's atheism plays in his critique of philosophical idealism, but also to the reason for the frequency of the analogies which he draws between political and religious 'alienation'.

But that is, once again, to look ahead to topics of which we shall treat in later chapters. My concern, for the time being, is simply with the broad differences between Hegel's and Marx's handling of the dialectic of appearance and reality. Marx took over from Feuerbach the complaint that Hegel had inverted the correct relation of subject and predicate. 'That which in religion is the predicate', said Feuerbach, 'we must make the subject, and that which in religion is a subject we must make a predicate . . . and by this means we arrive at the truth. God suffers – suffering is the predicate – but for men, for others, not for himself. What does this mean in plain speech? Nothing else than this: to suffer for others is divine.'[27] More generally: 'the true relationship of thought to being is this: being is the subject, thought the predicate. Thought arises from being – being does not arise from thought.'[28] Or, as Marx put it: 'The crux of the matter is that Hegel everywhere makes the Idea into the subject, while the genuine, real subject, such as "political sentiment", is turned into the predicate.'[29]

26 'Critique of Hegel's Doctrine of the State', *EW*, pp. 61–2, his stress.
27 L. Feuerbach, *The Essence of Christianity* (New York, Harper Torchbooks, 1957), p. 60.
28 Feuerbach, quoted *Life*, p. 68.
29 'Critique of Hegel's Doctrine of the State', *EW*, p. 65.

Thought arises from being. It is actual, living, breathing, human beings who think thoughts: *I* have an *idea*. The ideas that I have are the objects which I, the subject, think. Our ideas have no existence, no reality, except as the objects of our thinking. Hegel (according to Feuerbach and Marx) had reversed this. He had written as if individual human beings were the objects of a centre of thought, a subject, other than themselves. In the limit, Hegel writes, according to Marx, as if human beings were objects thought by an 'alien', transcendent, absolute mind, which is itself the sole 'real' subject or agent of reality.

Marx's complaint against Hegel, far from being primarily philosophical (let alone theological), is rooted in what he sees as the social and political implications of Hegel's account. (It was, after all, on Hegel's doctrine of the *state* that he made those extensive notes in 1843.) If you start talking abstractly about 'the state' or 'society', as the subject of the sentence, then real individual men and women, in the concrete complexity of their relationships and circumstances, get flattened into expressions of this abstraction: England expects every man will do his duty. Who is 'England'?

Or consider the question of sovereignty. Sovereignty is one aspect, and only one aspect, of social existence. 'In monarchy', says Marx, 'the whole, the people, is subsumed under one of its forms of existence, the political constitution; in democracy the constitution itself appears only as *one* determining characteristic of the people, and indeed its self-determination. . . . Just as religion does not make man, but rather man makes religion, so the constitution does not make the people, but the people the constitution.'[30] To think of the constitution as making the people, rather than the people making the constitution, is to reverse subject and predicate. Hegel, in his treatment of the constitution, 'has converted into a product, a predicate of the Idea, what was properly its subject'.[31]

Constitutionally to declare that all men are equal cannot *make* men equal, although it may create a society in which it *appears* as if all men are equal. Similarly, a society in which all men are declared free, in which their freedoms are constitutionally secured, may *appear* to be a 'free society' and yet, in reality, beneath the surface, this appearance of freedom may be masking manifold structures of unfreedom. Western liberal democrats are often repelled by the Marxist's apparent lack of interest in, or hostility to, our much prized 'freedom of thought'. Our suspicion of and distaste for the practice of societies that call themselves 'socialist' may frequently be justified, but this does not exonerate us from the need to reflect on the extent to which, in our own society, 'freedom of thought' is,

30 Ibid., p. 87.
31 Ibid., p. 69.

or may be, not the reality, but only the appearance, of human freedom. Hegel himself, in his treatment of 'Freedom of Self-consciousness', insisted that 'freedom in thought' is, as such, only freedom in *thought*: it lacks 'the living reality of freedom itself'.[32] Freedom of thought that is not accompanied by freedom of effective speech and action is only the 'appearance' of freedom. In the measure that we luxuriate in our ability to 'think what we like', or to 'say what we like', unconscious of the severe limits imposed, in practice, upon our ability effectively to translate our thoughts into deeds, our words into actions, our prized freedom of thought is – in reality – an aspect of our bondage.[33] 'Like several of the early French socialists, Marx saw in the idea of freedom, as liberals used it in his day, an idea whose prime social function is to justify the egoism of the socially strong.'[34]

To confuse appearance with reality is thus to mistake what seems to be the case for what is in fact the case. But the superficial analysis which mistakenly assumes that what 'appears' to be going on is, in fact, what is 'really' going on, frequently makes the further mistake of supposing that what appears to be going on, here, today, is what in fact goes on, or at least *ought* to be going on, everywhere, at all times. It not only describes misleadingly, but it further invests its misleading descriptions with prescriptive status. Thus, in 1847, in a characteristic attack on the classical, 'bourgeois' economists, Marx wrote: 'The economists have a singular way of proceeding. For them there are only two kinds of institutions, artificial and natural [i.e. given in the natural order of things]. The institutions of feudalism are artificial institutions, those of the bourgeoisie are natural institutions. In this they resemble the theologians, who likewise establish two kinds of religion. Every religion which is not theirs is an invention of man [and hence 'artificial'], while their own is an emanation of God.'[35]

The third and final stage is to assume, not only that what appears to be the case is in fact the case; not only that what appears to be the case is what ought always to be the case; but also that what appears to be the case is *necessarily* the case. And once this stage is reached, the possibility of social change has disappeared from view. So, in *Capital*, Marx says: 'The advance of capitalist production develops a working class which by education, tradition and habit

---

32 Hegel, *Phenomenology*, p. 122.
33 Cf. Marx's discussion of the French and American declarations of 'human rights': 'On the Jewish Question', *EW*, pp. 227–34.
34 J. Plamenatz, *Karl Marx's Philosophy of Man*, p. 253.
35 Marx, *The Poverty of Philosophy*, p. 115. He later quoted this passage in a footnote to *Capital*; cf. *Cap. I*, p. 175.

looks upon the requirements of that mode of production as self-evident natural laws.'[36]

I have already mentioned that it was from Feuerbach that Marx took over the model of the 'inversion of subject and predicate' as a characterization of what seemed to both of them to be the principal weakness in Hegel's dialectic. But, by 1845, Marx had come to see that Feuerbach's critique was vitiated by its 'one-sidedness'; it remained (to use the language of the *Theses on Feuerbach*) 'contemplative': it was effectively concerned solely with *understanding* social reality and hence could not contribute to that reality's transformation. In other words, the charge may plausibly be levelled against Feuerbach that all this talk of 'appearance' masking, veiling or disguising an underlying 'reality' presupposes that 'reality' to be already simply *there* – preconstituted, finished, given – only requiring perceptive scrutiny for its unveiling. This charge cannot, however, be convincingly levelled against Marx. For him, the hidden 'reality' is the social process that is actually occurring: it is what is happening and is likely to happen; it is not simply whatever has already happened in the past. 'Marx's position involved both a rejection of Hegel, and a recovery of certain features of Hegel's philosophy that had largely evaporated in Feuerbach's "inversion". In Hegel, human beings appear as the creators of their own history, but in conditions only partly disclosed to them in terms of their own consciousness: conditions that can only be understood retrospectively. In rejecting the latter claim and in holding that social analysis (as opposed to philosophy) can discern and help to actualize immanent tendencies in contemporary social development, Marx introduced a radically new perspective into social theory.'[37]

It would be difficult for anyone to insist more strenuously on the novelty of Marx's perspective than does Louis Althusser. A comment on Althusser's account of the differences between the Hegelian and the Marxian dialectic may therefore be in order. Moreover, his account illustrates a point I made earlier concerning the way in which many Marxist thinkers presuppose the validity of Marx's assumption that a critique of Hegelian 'idealism' is, *eo ipso*, a critique of 'religious' attitudes and perspectives.

Althusser acknowledges, of course, that Marx took over the language of 'appearance' and 'reality' from Hegelian philosophy, but claims that he did so only because he was not yet able to give his own radically non-Hegelian philosophy appropriate theoretical expression.[38] He further claims that what he calls 'the empiricist notion of knowledge' was 'profoundly present in Hegelian philoso-

---

36 *Cap. I*, p. 899.
37 A. Giddens, *Central Problems in Social Theory*, p. 166.
38 Cf. L. Althusser, *Reading Capital*, p. 38.

phy'.[39] In order to understand this curious claim (which even he admits will appear 'paradoxical')[40] it is necessary to say a word about his characterization of 'religious' and 'empiricist' epistemological strategies.

'The truth of history', according to Althusser, 'cannot be read in its manifest discourse, because the text of history is not a text in which a voice (the Logos) speaks, but the inaudible and illegible notation of the effects of a structure of structures.'[41] In simpler terms, this seems to be an admirable reminder of the poverty of historical positivism: of the illusion, that is to say, that texts or monuments 'contain' their meanings in somewhat the same way that bottles contain beer. It is a reminder that historical interpretation is not a matter of passively 'gazing' at the texts, but is a process, an activity, to which the historian brings certain questions, skills, interpretative frameworks, and in which his self-understanding, and not merely his understanding of the objects of his study, is at issue.

So far, so good. But what is 'the Logos' doing there? Althusser refers to something which he calls 'the religious myth of *reading*', and to a 'religious complicity between Logos and Being'.[42] The implication seems to be that anyone who affirms that, in one particular historical event, or series of events, word and flesh, meaning and reality, 'Logos and Being', *coincided*, must necessarily be someone who presupposes the validity of 'a conception of knowledge in which all the work of knowledge is reduced in principle to the recognition of the mere relation of *vision*; in which the whole nature of its object is reduced to the mere condition of a *given*'.[43] Christians have undoubtedly often supposed that their ascription of unsurpassable significance to a particular set of events, and to the earliest texts that bear witness to and interpret those events, not only exempts them from the need continually to risk the activity of interpretation, to risk that 'performance' of Christianity which is the fundamental form of the Christian interpretation of Scripture, but also thereby insulates them from the risks and hazards of historical existence in their quest for meaning and truth. But I see no reason whatsoever to accept Althusser's quite arbitrary (and historically preposterous) implication that Christian belief *necessarily* entails subscription to some form of fundamentalism, or what he calls 'the religious phantasm of epiphanic transparency'.[44]

For the Christian believer, on Althusser's account, 'appearance'

39 Loc. cit.
40 Loc. cit.
41 *Reading Capital*, p. 17.
42 Loc. cit., his stress.
43 Ibid., p. 19, his stress.
44 Ibid., p. 35.

and 'reality' simply and unproblematically coincide. The Christian relationship to truth is not, on this account, forged in death and brokenness, in the agony in the Garden and the cry from Golgotha, but is simply a matter of the 'vision of the essence in the transparency of existence'.[45] And, according to Althusser, 'the empiricist conception of knowledge is the twin brother of . . . the religious vision.'[46] For the 'empiricist', 'Discovery should be taken in its most literal sense: removing the covering, as the husk is removed from the nut, the peel from the fruit, the veil from the girl, the truth, the god or the statue.'[47]

That mention of the 'veil' affords us a clue. Althusser is aware of the fact that it would be easy, on a superficial reading of Marx's texts, to be misled by his choice of metaphors into supposing that, for him, the dialectic of appearance and reality was merely a matter of 'uncovering' an already constituted given reality. And Althusser knows that Marx was not Feuerbach. He therefore wishes to insist that 'reading Marx' must be a process, as was Marx's own 'reading' of history and economics, not simply of 'making manifest what is latent',[48] but rather of *working up* certain 'notations' – the 'raw materials' of the interpretative process. Interpretation is therefore acknowledged to be, we might say, itself a 'mode of production'.

At this point, however, two comments are in order. In the first place, Althusser's characterization of that epistemological strategy to which he is opposed as 'empiricist' is as tendentious and misleading as is his account of Christian belief. I believe that E. P. Thompson is justified in deploring 'Althusser's continuous, wilful and theoretically-crucial confusion between "empiricism" (that is, philosophical positivism and all its kin) and the empirical mode of intellectual practice'.[49] In the second place, in the prosecution of the endless and ever-varying struggle between 'idealism' and 'realism' (or 'materialism') in philosophy and theology[50] there are, in either direction, traps set which lure the traveller towards the very path he set out to avoid. Thus Althusser, pouring scorn on the supposed passivity, contemplativity, of all conceptions of knowledge that existed before Marx, lays considerable emphasis on the fact that the pursuit of knowledge is a 'mode of production'. But the insistence that 'coming to know' something is a 'productive' or 'constructive' enterprise, and not merely a matter of 'discovering' a previously given and constituted reality, while it may serve as a useful corrective to Feuerbachian materialism, threatens to topple

45 Ibid., p. 37.
46 Loc. cit.
47 Loc. cit.
48 Ibid., p. 34.
49 E. P. Thompson, 'The Poverty of Theory', *The Poverty of Theory*, p. 202.
50 Cf. N. L. A. Lash, 'Ideology, Metaphor and Analogy'

over into a new form of absolute idealism. If this threat is to be averted, the metaphor of 'production' needs to be handled with considerable care. In particular, we need to know to what extent, and in what ways, the 'raw material'[51] on which the thinker 'works' effectively constrains and determines his productive transformation of it. We also need to know how this constraint is exercized in practice, in 'reality', and not merely in 'appearance', in the account which the individual thinker gives of his performance. I have no quarrel with Althusser's contention that 'there is no such thing as an innocent reading'.[52] All hermeneutics is an hermeneutics of suspicion: both Hegel and Marx would have agreed that, here as elsewhere, things are never quite what they seem to be.

In conclusion, our discussion of Althusser's reading of Marx has indicated the outlines of one aspect of the challenge with which the Marxian dialectic implicitly confronts Christian doctrines of divine revelation. I take it that any such doctrine articulates the conviction that our apprehension of ultimate hope is, in the last resort, *given*, and is not merely the product of human construction (the fact that, as we shall see later on, there is, in Marx's thought, a non-theological form of that conviction is a further justification for describing his use of the dialectic as embodying a secularized doctrine of revelation). I say 'in the last resort', for two reasons. Firstly, as an indication that I accept Althusser's criticism of the 'phantasm of epiphanic transparency'[53] and, by implication, of all forms of fundamentalism or of what is sometimes referred to as 'revelational positivism'. If meaning and hope are given, they are not immediately, non-mediately, given. That is to say, secondly, that the Marxian dialectic, with its emphasis on the active, practical or 'productive' character of the quest for knowledge of reality beyond the surface appearance of things, calls in question any attempt to see, in the sources and grounds of Christian hope, exceptions to the rule that, if history makes sense, it is human beings, in their conduct and reflection, who 'make' whatever sense in history there may be. The very confessional narrative that declares our hope to be – in 'reality' and despite the 'appearances' – 'received' and not merely 'invented', is itself an interpretative and, in that sense, a constructive enterprise.

51 Cf. Althusser, *Reading Capital*, p. 34.
52 Ibid., p. 14.
53 Ibid., p. 35.

6

THE MEANING OF HISTORY

Two Senses of 'Historicism'

I remarked in the previous chapter that it is axiomatic for Marx, as it was for Hegel, that, within history, 'reality' and 'appearance', 'life' and 'thought', are not and can never be wholly coincident.[1] To suppose, in any particular set of historical circumstances, that things are just what they seem to be, that how we perceive them to be is how they permanently and necessarily are, is to fall into the sort of illusion to which, for example, the classical political economists succumbed in supposing that how things appeared to be (from the standpoint of economic theory) was not only how they in fact were, but also how they permanently and necessarily were. And Marx devotes lengthy passages in his economic writings to exposing and criticizing the 'forgetfulness of history' implicit in these assumptions. There is thus a strand in Marx's thought which lends itself to the kind of 'historicist' interpretation – in the sense of a thorough-going historical relativism – which was developed by (amongst others) Karl Korsch. Commenting on Hegel's remark that 'philosophy . . . is its own time apprehended in thought',[2] and is to be understood as such, Korsch insisted that 'we must try to understand every change, development and revision of Marxist theory, since its original emergence from the philosophy of German idealism, as a necessary product of its epoch (Hegel)'.[3]

Marxism, on Korsch's account, is ' "true" only in the sense that at the present stage of history it articulates the consciousness of the "progressive" movement and is aware of that fact.'[4] When Althusser insists, with Korsch among others in mind,[5] that 'Marxism is not a historicism',[6] he finds it necessary to protect his flank by reminding us that Marx's early works are not 'Marxist' in his sense, and by acknowledging that 'the *Theses on Feuerbach* or *The German Ideology*

---

1 Cf. above, pp. 55–6.
2 G. W. F. Hegel, *Philosophy of Right*, p. 11.
3 K. Korsch, *Marxism and Philosophy*, p. 50.
4 *KIII*, p. 314.
5 Cf. L. Althusser, *Reading Capital*, pp. 120, 140.
6 Ibid., pp. 119–44.

... still reverberate profoundly with humanist and historicist echoes'.[7]

In Hegel's case, the 'historicist' strand in his thought was restrained by his conviction that even if, within the process and movement of history, 'appearance' and 'reality' never wholly coincide, the rationality or intelligibility of history was secured by the fact of their ultimate coincidence or identity. In this sense, as I suggested in Chapter Four, Hegel's philosophical programme presupposes or implies a doctrine of divine providence:[8] 'History is according to providence, and the true philosophy of history as Hegel says is a theodicy.'[9] We would not, of course, expect Marx to make any such claim. Nevertheless, if there is, in Marx's thought, that which corresponds to Hegel's conviction that history is, in the last resort, rational, and that the rationality of history is, in principle, capable of 'making its appearance' in human thought and action, then must we not say that Marx's thought contains what might be called a secularized doctrine of providence?

It may be helpful to approach this question indirectly, by briefly considering Sir Karl Popper's savage critique of Hegel and Marx in the second volume of *The Open Society and its Enemies*. In that volume, Popper accuses both Hegel and Marx of 'historicism', but his use of the term is very different from that which we have just considered. For Popper, 'historicism' is the illusion that the historical process as a whole has a shape, a significance, a direction, which, once grasped through our study of the past, may be used in the present to predict and organize the future. The final chapter of *The Open Society and its Enemies* is therefore entitled 'Has History Any Meaning?'. Popper's answer is vigorously negative: 'Historicism is out to find The Path on which mankind is destined to walk; it is out to discover The Clue to History . . . or The Meaning of History. But . . . *History has no meaning*'.[10]

Why does Popper assert this so uncompromisingly? Partly because he wants to emphasize that, when we speak about 'the history of mankind', we are not in fact speaking about the endlessly rich and complex patterns of event and relationship, achievement and failure, that constitute the concrete process of human history, but about that concrete process as abstractly, selectively mediated into our thought and imagination by the work of the historian. He is especially critical of the fact that the one aspect of the process on which historical consciousness regularly concentrates, and on which it is fed, is 'the history of political power. A concrete history of

7 Ibid., p. 121.
8 Cf. above, p. 39.
9 C. Taylor, *Hegel*, p. 389. Cf. Hegel, *Lectures on the Philosophy of World-History. Introduction: Reason in History*, tr. H. R. Nisbet, p. 42.
10 K. Popper, *The Open Society and its Enemies, Vol. II. Hegel and Marx*, p. 269.

mankind . . . would have to be . . . the history of all human hopes, struggles, and sufferings. For there is no one man more important than any other. Clearly, this concrete history cannot be written. We must make abstractions, we must neglect, select. But with this we arrive at the many histories; and among them, at that history of international crime and mass murder which has been advertised as the history of mankind.'[11]

In this passage Popper seems, at least at first sight, to be doing little more than issuing a legitimate warning against the tendency to identify one aspect of the 'appearance' of history – namely, its appearance as the process of the struggle for political power – with the total reality from which that abstraction is derived. But while the warning is legitimate inasmuch as it is certainly possible to think of works of history which approximate to Popper's caricature, is not the effectiveness of his criticism weakened by the swashbuckling indiscriminacy and generality of its formulation? Thus, for example (and I take the example because Marx is, after all, one of the two principal targets of Popper's criticism), if we read 'The Eighteenth Brumaire of Louis Bonaparte',[12] it is clear that we are reading a history of the struggle for political power, and that it is this aspect of events in France in 1851 which is of primary interest to Marx (were it otherwise, it would be difficult to describe this detailed historical study as Marx's 'most brilliant political pamphlet').[13] But I find nothing in Marx's text which would lead me to suppose that he imagined the significance of those events to be *exhausted* by their political significance. And what are we to make of Popper's peremptory assertion that 'there is no one man more important than any other'? From what point of view? To whom? Is Popper issuing an embargo against biographies? Or does he suppose that I, who have never composed a line of music, am as 'important' for the history of mankind's musical achievement as Johann Sebastian Bach? Or does he mean 'intrinsically important' and, if so, what *sort* of judgement is this and to what warrants does it appeal?

It soon becomes apparent, however, that it is not the abstraction, the selectivity – inevitable if any aspects of our past are to be mediated into present thought and imagination – that is the real target of Popper's polemic. He is protesting against the tendency to ransack the past in order to legitimate present action and future policy. And it is the theological form of this abuse of history on which he next focuses his attention.

'It is often considered a part of the Christian dogma', he writes, 'that God reveals Himself in history; that history has meaning; and that its meaning is the purpose of God. . . . I contend that this view

11 Ibid., p. 270.
12 *SE*, pp. 143–249.
13 *Life*, p. 243.

is pure idolatry and superstition.'[14] Why? Because it identifies the perceived meaning of history, the story as it is in fact told, with God's meaning and God's purpose. It thus confuses the complex whole with the narrative by which that whole is partially and selectively mediated into our thought and imagination. That is to say, it confuses the 'appearance' of history with its 'reality'. Moreover, it mistakenly identifies the fruit of this confusion with the truth of divine purpose. Such 'theistic historicism', says Popper, 'looks upon history . . . as a kind of lengthy Shakespearean play.' Thus to conceive it, and further to suppose that the author of the play is God, is 'pure blasphemy, for the play was . . . written not by God, but, under the supervision of generals and dictators, by the professors of history'.[15]

Popper next considers the Christian who counters his critique by saying: Yes, but that human history whose meaning is God's meaning for man is the history, not of power, but of weakness, not of fame, but of obscurity, not of success, but of failure. *This* is history read in the light of the cross of Christ. To such a reply, Popper has three comments to make. Firstly, he admits that, if such a history could be written, 'I should certainly not say that it is blasphemy to see the finger of God in it'.[16] However, secondly, such a history has never been and cannot now be written. The history of weakness and failure is the history of those who did *not* frame the policies, shape the language, employ the poets, chroniclers and architects of funerary monuments. It is the history of those whose hopes and fears were unattended to and unrecorded and whose deeds only figure in the narrative as the obverse of the forms of power: the vanquished and enslaved as the shadows of their lords and conquerors. It may, indeed, be a fundamental dimension of the reality of historical process, but – at least for the most part – it cannot now be mediated into historical consciousness and become the 'appearance' of history. If this is where God's providence was at work, then the workings of that providence are irretrievably hidden from our sight.

Thirdly, those Christians who thus argue that that history, whose meaning is God's meaning for man, is the history of weakness, 'of the unknown individual man; his sorrows and his joys, his suffering and death',[17] nevertheless betray their historicism when they go on to assert that *this* reality *will* become appearance: that the meek *shall* inherit the earth. According to Popper, any such 'substitution of certainty for hope, must lead to a moral futurism. "The law *cannot* be broken" '.[18] For Popper a fundamental weakness of historicism,

14 Popper, *Open Society*, p. 271.
15 Loc. cit.
16 Ibid., p. 272.
17 Loc. cit.
18 Ibid., p. 274.

in any form, consists in the fact that, by substituting certainty for hope, it denies man's moral responsibility for the construction of his future. Now it becomes clearer why he includes Marx, as well as Hegel, amongst the 'historicists'. In so far as the claim is made that the dialectic of appearance and reality eventually generates a state of affairs in which the ultimate outcome of the historical process can be predicted 'scientifically', can be non-dialectically asserted, the very ineluctability of the outcome renders the exercise of free choice both illusory and harmful. The political stance of those who know too much about that shape to which the future 'must' conform is inevitably totalitarian.

The Narration of Hope

Popper's critique of 'historicism' is, as we have seen, directed not only against Hegel and Marx, but also against some forms of the Christian doctrine of providence. It may be helpful, therefore, briefly to indicate where and how it seems to me, as a theologian, that his criticism 'bites'. The discourse of Christian faith is, as Hegel insisted, narrative in form. More specifically, it is, as the discourse of faith, of personal commitment and self-understanding, autobiographical: the Christian is the narrator of a story which he tells as *his* story, as a story in which he acknowledges himself to be a participant.[19] Christian religious discourse, as autobiographical, frequently tends to attribute an unwarranted universality to the particular forms in which, in particular circumstances, it finds expression. Convinced that the tale that we tell is truly told, Christians tend to assume that the way they tell it is the way it has ever been and is ever to be told. But, in succumbing to this illusion, they are thereby liable to the temptation to suppose that they know a great deal about the future: that their faith provides them with predictive warrants.

Another way of putting this would be to say that the Christian, as one who confesses his faith in a God who is Lord of nature and history alike, is thereby constrained to affirm that the world and its history *have* unified and unifying meaning and purpose, since they are the expression of God's purposive governance of his creation. But it is all too easy to make the move from the affirmation that history has meaning to the supposition that this meaning may be more or less straightforwardly discerned, grasped, 'read off' our individual and group experience. It is all too easy to make the move from the recognition that Christian faith necessarily finds narrative expression to the assumption that it is possible to give to that

19 On the issues discussed in this and the following paragraph, cf. N. L. A. Lash, 'Ideology, Metaphor and Analogy'; also *Theology on Dover Beach*, pp. 150–63.

narrative clear and unified form. This assumption must be mistaken because the Christian, like any autobiographer, stands in the midst of the story that he tells. As a result, the outcome of the story is unknown or, at least, is unknown in the specificity that would be required if the story were to be completed: I know that I shall die, but I do not know when or how, in what mood or in what circumstances. I therefore lack just that information which would be necessary for the complete narration of my life-story. And what is true of my individual autobiography is true of me as narrator of the story of my tribe, religious tradition, social group or nation – let alone of the 'meaning of history' as a whole. Only the dead, for whom history has ended, could write a complete autobiography, and the dead cannot write. The narrative forms of Christian faith and hope are therefore necessarily infected with provisionality. We may have grounds for hope, but we do not have warrants for specific predictions: we do not know the 'shape' of the future.

In saying this, however, have I not conceded too much to Popper, by apparently depriving Christian hope of its title to certainty? I think not, if only because Popper's distinction between 'certainty' and 'hope', by which he sets such store, is confused and misleading. He seems to suppose that the only certainty available to human beings as products and agents of history would be that associated with abstract, 'scientific' knowledge, the fruit of theoretically de-monstrated conclusions. He does not envisage the possibility of there being grounds for certainty concerning the future, grounds for unshakeable hope, that are none the less 'rational' for all that they cannot be cast into the form of specific 'scientific' predictions. Nor does he seriously consider the possibility of there being irreducibly distinct modes of knowledge. From the fact that hope is not know-ledge of the sort that can be theoretically demonstrated to be know-ledge, and that the *forms* of hope, the conceptual, symbolic and institutional forms in which hope finds expression, are necessarily provisional, it does not follow that hope is, or should suppose itself to be, less 'certain' than scientifically expressible knowledge.[20]

Another way of putting this would be to say that, in so far as hope is to be considered as a mode of knowledge of 'the meaning of history', it is hermeneutic, interpretative knowledge, and not 'explanation'. As interpretative of history, its significance and out-come, hope may indeed serve as a *guide* to future action and policy, but it cannot (as 'explanatory' knowledge could do, were it avail-able) furnish us with warrants for specific prediction or for 'control' of the outcome. This distinction between 'interpretative' and 'ex-planatory' knowledge brings us back to the discussion of Hegel and Marx, because it is similar to the distinction drawn by Charles

20 I shall discuss the concept of 'hope' in Chapters Seventeen and Eighteen.

Taylor between 'two ways in which a dialectical exposition can command our assent. There are *strict* [i.e. 'theoretical' or 'explanatory'] *dialectics*, whose starting-point is or can reasonably claim to be undeniable. And then there are *interpretative or hermeneutical dialectics*, which convince us by the overall plausibility of the interpretation they give.'[21] According to Taylor, Hegel's attempts at the former are, in the last resort, unsuccessful, whereas 'If we look at Hegel's most successful historical dialectics, the ones which are the most illuminating and convincing, we find that in fact they convince the way any good historical account does, because they "fit" well as an interpretation.'[22]

If our concern is to understand what it was that Hegel was trying to do, Taylor's use of the distinction between explanation and interpretation may obscure rather than clarify because it seems certain that Hegel would have resisted the suggestion that any such distinction between (shall we say) metaphysics and the interpretation of history was, in the last resort, legitimate. But, for that very reason, Taylor's comments are helpful. By prising apart modes of reflection that Hegel strenuously sought to unify, he reminds us that Popper's critique of 'historicism' is directed against any conflation of metaphysics and history. The question which we have to consider, however, concerns the extent to which Marx's use of the dialectic is affected by such conflationary tendencies.

Schmidt has insisted that, unlike Hegel, 'Marx did not regard the world as a whole as subject to any uniform idea which might give it meaning'.[23] Marx 'knew of no other purposes in the world than those determined by man. The world could therefore, he said, contain no more meaning than men themselves have succeeded in realizing by the organization of the conditions of their life.'[24] We are reminded of a passage in *The German Ideology* to which I drew attention in Chapter Four, in which Marx insisted that, once the critique of 'idealism' has been effectively carried through, and philosophy (or theoretical explanation) has thereby been deprived of 'self-sufficiency', its place can only be taken by 'a summing-up of the most general results, abstractions which are derived from the observation of the historical development of men'.[25] And it would seem unlikely that such summarizing abstractions could have the status of those illusorily 'scientific' predictions of future states of affairs which Popper supposes to be the characteristic and disastrous product of the 'historicist' mentality. Nevertheless, unless those interpretations of Marx's thought which see it as embodying 'the

21 Taylor, *Hegel*, p. 218, my stress.
22 Ibid., p. 217.
23 A. Schmidt, *The Concept of Nature in Marx*, p. 35.
24 Ibid., p. 37.
25 *CW5*, p. 37; cf. above, p. 42.

discovery that opens for men, the way to a scientific . . . understanding of their own history',[26] and as expressive of a confidence that man's alienation not only can but undoubtedly will be definitively overcome, are *simply* mistaken, it would still seem to be the case that that thought contains elements which go some way, at least, towards justifying Popper's suspicions.

Prophecy and Prediction

'Instead of posing as prophets', says Popper, 'we must become the makers of our fate.'[27] His principal charge against Marx is that Marx adopted the role of prophetically predicting the future, and that his predictions failed, as all such predictions must. 'The reason for his failure as a prophet', says Popper, 'lies entirely in the poverty of historicism as such.'[28]

In taking as the targets of his critique of 'historicism' not only the philosophies of Hegel and Marx, but also certain forms of the Christian doctrine of providence, Popper would seem to endorse my suggestion that Marx's thought could be said to contain a secularized form of the doctrine of providence. Where theological forms of such doctrines are concerned, I have acknowledged that Christian faith is such as to be permanently exposed to the temptation to suppose its narrative expressions to possess a descriptive specificity and completeness which, in fact, they necessarily lack. It is thereby tempted, not so much to substitute 'certainty' for 'hope', as Popper misleadingly suggests, but rather to substitute explanation for interpretation, specific prediction for the declaration of trust, and attempted control of the outcome for the courage to risk constructing its future in a darkness only partially and indirectly illuminated by the light of a hope derived from past and present experience. The cognitive stance of Christian faith in respect of the future is undeniably 'prophetic', but I see no reason to accept Popper's arbitrary assertion that the 'prophet' is one who, instead of getting on with the construction of history, stands aside to make (inevitably unsuccessful) specific predictions concerning the future. We must indeed become the makers of our fate, but it is possible that, in the execution of this task, the prophetic imagination and the hope that it embodies have an indispensable part to play.

In this chapter, unlike the previous one, I have not discussed Marx's own texts. The reason for this is that we shall treat, in later chapters, of the specific issues in respect of which Popper's accusation of 'historicism' must be tested: namely, the sense in which Marx's thought is or is not 'scientific' in character, his critique of

26 L. Althusser, *Lenin and Philosophy*, p. 7.
27 Popper, *Open Society*, p. 280.
28 Ibid., p. 193.

'utopianism', and the general problem of the status of his discourse concerning the future. We cannot know whether Marx's predictions 'failed' until we know whether, and in what sense and in what contexts, he made 'predictions' concerning the future. Nevertheless, it seemed appropriate to provide an outline of these problems at this point because, as a cluster of related issues, they arise, and should be seen to arise, from our general discussion in the previous chapter of the dialectic of appearance and reality.

7

CORRECTNESS AND TRUTH

Appearance, Reality and the 'True Individual'
'For Herr Bauer, as for Hegel', wrote Marx in the autumn of 1844, 'truth is an *automaton* that proves itself. Man must *follow* it. As in Hegel, the result of real development is nothing but the *truth proven*, i.e. brought to consciousness.'[1] Whatever be the justice of this re-mark, as a comment on Hegel, one senses Marx's impatience with any concept of truth which would render man's relationship to truth inert, passive, or merely attentive. If truth is an 'automaton that proves itself', then all that human beings can do is to wait upon it in docility, follow its course until, without significant intervention on their part, it brings itself to consciousness in their minds, language and relationships. For Marx, on the other hand, human transformative activity – agricultural, industrial, political, critical – is constitutive of man's relationship to truth: 'The question whether objective truth can be attributed to human thinking is not a question of theory but is a *practical* question. Man must prove the truth, i.e. the reality and power, the this-sidedness of his thinking in practice.'[2] We shall return to this second 'Thesis on Feuerbach' later in this chapter. By way of introduction, however, and in order to relate our discussion of Marx's concept of truth to the questions raised in the two previous chapters, let us return to the passage from the 'Eighteenth Brumaire' which we took as the starting-point for our reflections on 'appearance' and 'reality': 'A distinction is made in private life between what a man thinks and what he really is and does. In historical struggles one must make a still sharper distinction between the phrases and fantasies of the parties and their real organization and real interests, between their conception of themselves and what they really are.'[3]

In thus contrasting 'appearance' and 'reality', Marx is not sug-gesting that the appearances are simply false, that the 'phrases and fantasies of the parties' are mere lies, in contrast to the 'truth' of their 'real organization and real interests'. This cannot be true, however much 'appearance' and 'reality' diverge or conflict, if only

1 'The Holy Family', *CW4*, p. 79.
2 *EW*, p. 422.
3 *SE*, p. 174.

for the reason that the 'phrases and fantasies of the parties', their self-description or propaganda, constitute, in fact, an aspect of how it is that they actually, empirically and thus – in one sense – truly are.

Consider the case of a schizophrenic, of an individual who supposes himself to be, not John Smith of 10 Station Road, but the Emperor Napoleon. He is not 'really' Napoleon, and yet the fact that this is who he appears to himself to be is an aspect of the 'reality' that is John Smith. He is, in one sense, truly Napoleon, and this is the sense that truly constitutes his tragic untruth. From one point of view, therefore, 'what a man thinks and says of himself' is never *simply* untrue, because it constitutes an aspect of how he in fact appears to himself and presents himself to others. The tyrant who supposes himself, in all good faith, to be the benign 'little father' of his people may indeed be accepted by them at face value. Dictatorship not infrequently 'appears', to all involved, to be a more benign relationship than it 'really' is. And the benignity of appearance is, in truth, an aspect of the social relationship.

On the other hand, of course, it is also correct to say that, in so far as 'appearance' and 'reality' fail to correspond, the appearances are false. From this point of view, 'what a man thinks and says of himself' is true to the extent that self-perception and the mode of his presentation to others corresponds to the reality, to 'what he really is and does'. So far as the individual is concerned, John Smith the schizophrenic would seem to stand at one end of a spectrum at the other end of which stands the man whose self-conception and self-presentation is *identical* with what he really is and does. In this case, too, we can *distinguish* between the thought and the reality, between how the individual appears to himself and to others and the reality that he is, but there will now be no *discrepancy* between 'thought' and 'being', 'appearance' and 'reality'. The man as he is, and as he supposes himself and is supposed by others to be, will exactly correspond.

But could such an individual ever exist or have existed? This is not a question which Marx ever considered. Nor is there any reason why he should have done so, in view of his insistence on the socially constructed nature of human reality. The 'true individual' would be a member of, but could hardly be thought to pre-exist, the 'true society'. In other words, for Marx the question of the identity, the distinction without discrepancy, of appearance and reality could only arise in respect of human society as a whole. And although Marx was too realistic to suppose that a society which was, in the achieved identity of appearance and reality, wholly 'true', could ever exist within history, there are passages in his writings (which we shall consider when we come to discuss Marxian 'eschatology') in which he gives the impression of supposing that, with the 'riddle of history' resolved, 'the true resolution of the conflict between existence and being, between objectification and self-affirmation',[4] will actually occur.

From the standpoint of Christian theology, questions concerning the possibility of 'true' community, of a state of affairs in which the appearance and reality of social relations wholly coincided, would appear as questions concerning the relationship between historical communities, secular or religious, political or sacramental, and God's 'reign' or 'Kingdom'. According to the Second Vatican Council, the Church is the 'sacrament of intimate union with God, and of the unity of all mankind'.[5] However, a distinction presumably needs to be made between what Christians 'think' the Church is and what it 'really is and does'; between (to put it rather rudely) 'the phrases and fantasies' of the churches, and their 'real organization and real interests'. If 'sacrament of intimate union with God, and of the unity of all mankind' is what Christians suppose the Church 'really' to be, why is its empirical, historical 'appearance' so manifestly contradictory to this description? Alternatively, if the Vatican Council's statement is taken to be a description of what the Church, in its self-estimation, 'appears' to be, under what circumstances might its 'reality' be brought into closer conformity with the description? I am not suggesting that such questions have not received frequent and detailed attention from theologians. Of course they have. And yet Christians continue, for the most part, to talk rather too easily about the fact or possibility of 'true community', as if a situation in which the reality and appearance of social relationships wholly corresponded could be realized at almost any point in space and time, given a modicum of selflessness and goodwill.

From the point of view of the significance for Christian theology of Marx's concept of truth, what needs to be stressed is that questions concerning the 'truth' of Christian concepts of community cannot be adequately responded to merely in theory – in theological reflection. They are questions whose adequate response calls for the transformation, not only of theological description (of what Christians conceive themselves to be) but also of structures, activities and relationships (what they, as a social fact, really are). It is not true that the Church is the sacrament, or symbol, of unity for the whole human race if, in fact, it is not.

I remarked a little earlier that the question as to whether there could exist or has ever existed an *individual* in whom 'reality' and 'appearance' wholly corresponded was not one which Marx considered or could have been expected to consider. And yet this

---

4 'Economic and Philosophical Manuscripts', *EW*, p. 348.
5 *Dogmatic Constitution on the Church (Lumen Gentium)*, para. 1. Cf. W. M. Abbott, ed., *The Documents of Vatican II*, p. 15.

question is of some urgency for the Christian who wishes to affirm that, in one man, at one particular point in history, the 'flesh' exactly and unrepeatably corresponded to the 'Word'. The Christian who confesses Jesus Christ to be the Word Incarnate is affirming the identity, in this man, of fact and significance, reality and appearance. In the light of our reflections in this chapter so far (and limiting ourselves to these) a number of considerations concerning the character of such an affirmation suggest themselves.

In the first place, no such affirmation concerning the 'truth' of an individual would be possible before the end of that individual's history, before his death. In the second place, the affirmation that, in this one man, appearance and reality coincide, cannot be a merely 'impartial' or 'neutral' assertion. In affirming the truth of Jesus' self-presentation, it expresses the affirmer's trust in his truthfulness or integrity. In the third place, to affirm that, in this one man, appearance and reality wholly coincide, is to affirm the correctness or accuracy of his conception of himself. Presumably, we would not be in a position to make such an affirmation if we had no idea at all of the 'content' of Jesus' self-conception. Nevertheless, in principle, the affirmation that his 'conception of himself' was identical with 'what he really was' is purely formal: it asserts the absence of illusion in his self-understanding. In the fourth place, although I am only concerned to indicate some of the factors entailed in the affirmation that Jesus was 'true man', it must be added that, in so far as the affirmation is a *theological* judgement, it asserts that what this man really was and did, how he spoke and acted, suffered and died, is how the reality of God makes its appearance in human history. In the fifth place, all human beings, including Jesus, are social constructs: their identity is, in part, constituted by their social relationships. It follows, as I suggested earlier, that, if there could ever be a 'true' individual, he could only 'truly' be such as a member of a 'truly human' society: 'It is above all necessary to avoid once more establishing "society" as an abstraction over against the individual. The individual *is* the *social being*. His vital expression – even when it does not appear in the direct form of a *communal* expression, conceived in association with other men – is therefore an expression and confirmation of *social life*. Man's individual and species-life are not two *distinct things*.'[6] And such a truly human society has never existed, nor can it exist within the conditions of history. The affirmation that, in Jesus, reality and appearance coincide is, therefore, not only a statement about the past, but also about the future – and this in two senses. On the one hand, it

6 'Economic and Philosophical Manuscripts', *EW*, p. 350; cf. the whole section on 'Private Property and Communism' in the Third Manuscript (*EW*, pp. 345–58) and the section on 'Estranged Labour' in the First Manuscript (*EW*, pp. 322–34).

declares that, because this man has been as we affirm him to be, therefore we have grounds for hope in the production, beyond the limits of historical experience, of a truly human society. Christological statements are eschatological statements, and the eschatological transformation of the human condition is amongst their truth-conditions.[7] On the other hand, the affirmation is thereby also expressive of a commitment to work and struggle in the direction of such a transformation of social reality: were it otherwise, our confession would be infected with untruthfulness.

It is a matter of fact that Christians have affirmed and continue to affirm their belief in the coincidence, in Jesus, of 'flesh' and 'Word', fact and significance, reality and appearance. They have affirmed and continue to affirm that Jesus is 'true man'. Consideration of whether they have or could ever have adequate grounds for doing so lie outside the scope of this study. All that I have attempted to do, in the previous paragraph (the content of which will seem very jejune to my fellow-theologians), is summarily to indicate, in the light of our reflections on the dialectic of appearance and reality, something of the logic of such an affirmation.

Locating the Question of Truth

'In *The German Ideology*, as in the Paris Manuscripts, Marx refuses to concern himself with epistemological questions.'[8] That remark is misleading, because it assumes that consideration of how human beings come to knowledge of the truth, come truly to know, can appropriately be conducted in purely formal or abstract terms. It assumes, in other words, just those notions of epistemology (or of philosophy in general) whose adequacy Marx contested. 'If by their very make-up and connection', says Schmidt, 'the moments of knowledge turn out to be differently determined products of history, it follows that a formal analysis of consciousness in the Kantian sense, i.e. knowledge about knowledge, isolated from problems of *fact and content*, is no longer possible',[9] or at least, to put it more guardedly, no longer adequate. It is, after all, no coincidence that Kantian philosophy tends to suffer from just that forgetfulness of history of which Marx also accused the economic theorists of the eighteenth century. Schmidt quotes with approval a remark of Lenin's: 'Dialectics *is* the theory of knowledge of (Hegel and) Marxism.'[10]

---

7 It follows that the truthfulness of such statements is, in a sense, provisional: their 'grammar' is that not simply of assertion but also of hope, of prayer. Cf. Titus 2: 11–14.
8 *KI*, p. 175.
9 A. Schmidt, *The Concept of Nature in Marx*, pp. 111–12.
10 Quoted Schmidt, p. 112.

For Marx, the quest for truth is a quest for the coincidence of appearance and reality, of how things seem to be and how they in fact are. It would be incoherent to suppose that this quest can be pursued at the level of theory alone, or at the level of practice alone, since what is sought, in practice and in theory, is the overcoming of the discrepancies and contradictions between the two. Theory that has established for itself an illusory autonomy, that is disengaged from practical activity, is as 'unreal' as is the sort of blind or mindless activity which would, *as* mindless, not be responsible *human* action at all. When Marx castigates 'philosophy', and he often does so in apparently very anti-intellectualist terms, he is polemicizing against the illusory autonomy of theoretical discourse that supposes itself to be in no sense dependent upon, constrained by, those concrete patterns of perception, relationship, life and activity of which it is, in fact, the expression in thought, albeit the critical expression.

But if Marx had little time for what he sometimes calls 'scholasticism', he had equally little time for antitheoretical political activism. To rouse the population without giving them well thought-out and empirically justified reasons for their activity would, he maintained, be simply to deceive them. And when the young man to whom Marx addressed this rebuke countered by saying that he believed his political activity to be doing more for the common cause than theoretical analysis, conducted from the safety of an armchair, far from the world of suffering and afflicted humanity, Marx lost his temper and shouted: 'Ignorance never yet helped anybody.'[11]

The theoretical criticism of the language and thought-forms in which a society expresses itself is indispensable precisely because there is a distinction to be made between our conception of ourselves and how we really are, between how the world is and how we spontaneously, precritically, perceive it to be. In *Capital*, Marx claimed that it is 'true of all forms of appearance and their hidden reality' that 'the forms of appearance are reproduced directly and spontaneously, as current and usual modes of thought; the essential relation must first be discovered by science'.[12]

But if theoretical criticism is indispensable, it loses its way to the extent that it establishes itself in illusory autonomy in respect of practical living. And so, in the Paris Manuscripts, Marx emphasizes 'the extent to which the solution of theoretical problems is a function

---

11 McLellan (*Life*, p. 157) quotes this remark from Annenkov's *Reminiscences of Marx and Engels*. Those interested in the vicissitudes of oral tradition may find significance in the fact that the proponent of 'theoretical practice' presents it (without indicating a source) as: 'Ignorance will never be an argument' (Althusser, *Essays in Self-Criticism*, p. 113).

12 *Cap. I*, p. 682.

of practice and is mediated through practice, and the extent to which true practice is the condition of a real and positive theory'.[13] And a little earlier in the same manuscript the 'resolution' of 'theoretical antitheses' is said to be 'by no means only a problem of knowledge, but a *real* problem of life, a problem which *philosophy* was unable to solve precisely because it treated it as a *purely* theoretical problem'.[14] These passages suggest that, in these manuscripts, epistemological issues are not so much neglected as insistently *located*, situated, in the practical processes of historical existence. As Colletti has put it: 'Marxism is not . . . either pragmatism or a *Wissensoziologie* (sociology of knowledge); it is the first theory of "situated thought", but it is also a theory of thought as *truth*.'[15] Which brings us to that second 'Thesis on Feuerbach': 'The question whether objective truth can be attributed to human thinking is not a question of theory but is a *practical* question. Man must prove the truth, i.e. the reality and power, the this-sidedness of his thinking in practice. The dispute over the reality or non-reality of thinking that is isolated from practice is a purely *scholastic* question.'[16]

The problem of the connotations of the concepts of 'objectivity' and 'subjectivity' in Hegel and Marx is a quagmire into which someone who (like myself) is not steeped in the tradition of German idealism is advised not to wander. Nevertheless, in view of the widespread habit, in everyday English, of associating 'objectivity' with 'scientific' impartiality or neutrality of description, in contrast to 'merely subjective' impressions or assertions (a contrast which has overtones of the distinction between 'knowledge' and 'opinion'), it may be worth pointing out that this is not the primary sense of Marx's reference to 'objective truth'. His concern is with the circumstances in which the truthfulness of human thinking can be displayed, not merely in its internal consistency or integrity, but in its transformative intervention in the material conditions of human existence. Thus, for example, in his notes on Hegel in the last of the Paris Manuscripts, he argues that 'An objective being acts objectively, and it would not act objectively if objectivity [or 'objectness'] were not an inherent part of its essential nature. It creates and establishes only objects, because it is fundamentally *nature*.'[17]

That reference to the 'natural', nature-like, character of human,

---

13 'Economic and Philosophical Manuscripts', *EW*, p. 364.
14 Ibid., p. 354.
15 L. Colletti, *Marxism and Hegel*, p. 230.
16 *EW*, p. 422. 'This-sidedness': the metaphor does not really work in English. Perhaps 'experiential reality' would be nearer the mark. The recent Moscow edition has 'this-worldliness', which brings out the overtones, but perhaps at the cost of pressing the metaphor in too specific a direction: cf. *CW5*, p. 3.
17 *EW*, p. 389.

historical existence offers us a clue which must be followed up (although, since 'object', in this passage, has overtones of 'materiality' or 'thingness', some of the questions at issue must be postponed until, in the next chapter, we discuss the meaning of Marx's 'materialism'). On the one hand, we have noticed Colletti's denial that Marxism is a form of pragmatism. Nevertheless, the suggestion in the second Thesis that the 'power' or effectiveness of human thinking is a criterion of its truthfulness, would seem to point in a pragmatist direction. Lenin insisted, in 1913, that 'The Marxist doctrine is omnipotent because it is true',[18] rather than the other way round. And yet, when we hear him add: 'It is comprehensive and harmonious, and provides man with an integral world outlook irreconcilable with any form of superstition, reaction, or defence of bourgeois oppression',[19] we wonder with just what concept of truth he is working. On the other hand, if human thinking is 'objective' in so far as it expresses and produces man's 'naturalness', we wonder to what *constraints* the 'power' of human thoughtful activity is subject. Within what limits can man fashion himself, and his world, as he would have them be? 'The young Marx', says Charles Taylor, 'is heir to the radical Enlightenment . . . in his notion that man comes to shape nature and eventually society to his purposes'.[20] To what extent does the natural world (including the world of man, since human being is 'fundamentally nature') set insurmountable limits to this Promethean ambition?[21] The connection between the problems of pragmatism and Prometheanism can perhaps be indicated by the question: is 'truth', in Marx's view, to be defined in terms of the success of human endeavour? This question has been discussed by Kolakowski, in an essay on the concept of truth in the Paris Manuscripts.

'The end of the nineteenth century', says Kolakowski, 'gave birth to two different, though usually ill-differentiated, theories that tried to present man's practical activity as one of the principal categories of epistemological thinking.'[22] The first of these theories, which is to be found 'in the philosophical writings of Engels',[23] and which was developed by Lenin and the Leninist tradition, 'invokes the

18 V. I. Lenin, 'The Three Sources and Three Component Parts of Marxism', *HM*, p. 452.
19 Loc. cit.
20 C. Taylor, *Hegel*, p. 547.
21 In 1839, in the preliminary notes to his unpublished Dissertation, Marx declared that 'The proclamation of Prometheus . . . "I detest all the Gods" ', is philosophy's 'own profession, her own slogan against all the gods of heaven and earth who do not recognize man's self-consciousness as the highest divinity' (*Karl Marx. Early Texts*, ed. D. McLellan, p. 13).
22 L. Kolakowski, 'Karl Marx and the Classical Definition of Truth', *Marxism and Beyond*, p. 59.
23 Loc. cit.

effectiveness of human actions as a *criterion* with whose help it is possible and justifiable to *verify* the knowledge we need to undertake any sort of activity.'[24] The second theory, 'which found its classic though rather insouciant expression in the work of William James, introduces the concept of practical *usefulness* as a factor in the *definition* of truth. This usefulness is seen not as a tool for establishing the truth of man's knowledge independent of him, but as what *creates* this truth. Truth appears, therefore, to be relative to its application in daily life.'[25]

Kolakowski's case is that the theory of cognition which is to be found in 'germinal' form in the Paris Manuscripts is, firstly, radically different from that which, under the influence of Engels and Lenin, came to be regarded as the 'classical' Marxist definition of truth; and, secondly, in spite of certain affinities with Jamesian pragmatism, is also irreconcilable with this position.[26] In the 'classical' theory, truth is regarded as 'the relation between a judgement or a sentence and the reality to which it refers'.[27] Truth is thus 'independent of man's knowledge of it. Man's practical activity does not create it, but merely ascertains its occurrence.'[28] Success proves or verifies the truth of our knowledge, but does not enter into the definition of truth. In that form of the 'pragmatist' theory with which alone Kolakowski is concerned, on the other hand, 'man's practical activity has been elevated to the rank of an epistemological category'.[29] The success or failure of such activity or endeavour now enters into the very definition of truth and falsehood. And Kolakowski indicates the historical contexts in which these two theories emerged: 'If we can perceive in Engels' doctrine the symptoms of the optimistic scientism that marked European intellectual life in the last decade of the nineteenth century, we are equally entitled to consider the first pragmatists advocates of the philosophy of individual success that for so long nourished the mind of the New World in its rapid economic development.'[30]

The most important part of Kolakowski's essay, for our purpose, is the second section, the title of which – 'Nature as a Product of Man' – reminds us of the question concerning the limits of Promethean ambition with which we began. 'The whole character of a species, its species-character', says Marx, 'resides in the nature of its life-activity, and free conscious activity constitutes the species-character of man.'[31] But, from the beginning of his history, this free

24 Loc. cit.
25 Loc. cit.
26 Ibid., p. 86.
27 Ibid., p. 59.
28 Loc. cit.
29 Ibid., p. 61.
30 Ibid., pp. 62–3.
31 'Economic and Philosophical Manuscripts', *EW*, p. 328.

conscious activity, this 'life-activity' of man, 'appears to man only
as a *means* for the satisfaction of a need, the need to preserve physical
existence.'[32] Thus it is that 'the basic point of departure for all of
Marx's epistemological thought is the conviction that the relations
between man and his environment are relations between the species
and the objects of its need.'[33] The natural world, the world of things,
'exists for man only as a totality of possible satisfactions of his
needs'.[34] He 'meets' things, as it were, in struggling to 'meet' his
needs. In the measure that he succeeds in doing so, the material
that he works thus becomes part of his historically, laboriously
constituted humanity: 'nature in so far as it is not the human body
. . . is man's *inorganic body*.'[35]

However, in seeking to meet his needs, man encounters opposition
from the intractability of the materials with which he works, be
they sticks, stones or social structures, 'and all possible cognition is
man's realization of the contact between conscious man and the
external resistance he experiences'.[36] The human environment resists man's attempts to modify it to his purposes. To the extent that
he fails, to the extent that the environment, physical or social,
successfully resists man's attempts to humanize it, he 'loses himself',
becomes dehumanized in his life-activity, his work: 'it is only when
man's object becomes a *human* object or objective man that man
does not lose himself in that object.'[37] To ask how the world would
appear to 'an observer whose essence was pure thinking and whose
consciousness was defined exclusively by a disinterested cognitive
effort, is to ask a barren [or, as Marx would say, a 'scholastic']
question, for all consciousness is actually born of practical needs,
and the act of cognition itself is a tool designed to satisfy these
needs.'[38] Nature, says Marx, 'taken abstractly, for itself, and fixed
in its separation from man, is *nothing* for man.'[39] Human language,
human consciousness, is not, as it were, 'a transparent glass through
which one can contemplate the "objective" wealth of reality. It is
a set of tools we use to adapt ourselves to reality and to adapt it to
our needs.'[40]

32 *EW*, p. 325.
33 Kolakowski, art. cit., p. 63. 'This statement', however, 'loses sight of the *specific*
   character of the relation between man and nature, since this specificity is surely
   not to be sought in the existence of species-bounded, fixed needs in man, but in
   the *creating of new wants* by, and in, work as human material activity' (George
   Márkus, *Marxism and Anthropology: The Concept of "Human Essence" in the Philosophy
   of Marx*, p. 64).
34 Kolakowski, art. cit., p. 64.
35 *EW*, p. 328.
36 Kolakowski, art. cit., p. 65.
37 *EW*, p. 352.
38 Kolakowski, art. cit., pp. 64–5.
39 *EW*, p. 398.
40 Kolakowski, art. cit., p. 69.

Marx's theory of cognition, and the concept of truth implicit in it, have this in common with Jamesian pragmatism: 'both conceive of cognition as essentially functional; a tool that permits man to master the circumstances of his life, not a photographic plate that reproduces the pictures it receives'.[41] Nevertheless, Marx's position is irreconcilable with such pragmatism, for two reasons. In the first place, although man may be said to 'create' meaning and truth in the measure that he successfully humanizes the world, fashions it to meet his needs, nevertheless his is not a creation *ex nihilo*:[42] 'The worker can create nothing without *nature*, without the *sensuous external world*.'[43] And his Promethean ambition has limits, even in principle, because, at every step along the way, he does not know and has no means of telling, what fresh and perhaps insurmountable resistance he may encounter in the future. In the second place, for all the variety of forms of human experience and activity enjoyed and suffered in the course of history, there does exist, on Marx's account, something which corresponds to a classical doctrine of 'human nature': 'a totality of human properties, biological needs and social relations which can rightfully be termed immutable'.[44]

Kolakowski summarizes his account of the doctrine implicit in the Paris Manuscripts by saying that, for Marx, 'man as a cognitive being is only part of man as a whole; that that part . . . cannot be understood otherwise than as a function of a continuing dialogue between human needs and their objects. This dialogue, called work, is created by both the human species and the external world, which thus becomes accessible to man only in its humanized form.'[45] We can ask whether Marx does not set too little store by that disinterested wonder, that spirit of pure enquiry, which many have seen as one of the hallmarks of human greatness. But Marx could counter by asking whether our disinterestedness is ever, in reality, as 'pure' as it appears.

It is important to notice the form in which, on such a model of human cognition, the question of God appears. 'In practice I can only relate myself to a thing in a human way if the thing is related in a human way to man.'[46] God is a symbol of human 'lostness', of man's dehumanization, because God is, by definition, 'a thing that man cannot assimilate'.[47] There is no way in which God, humanized by man, subjected to his control, would still be God. This is why, as we shall see in a later chapter, even the *question* of God could not

41 Ibid., p. 76.
42 Cf. ibid., p. 77.
43 *EW*, p .325.
44 Kolakowski, art. cit., p. 77.
45 Ibid., pp. 86–7.
46 *EW*, p. 352.
47 Kolakowski, art. cit., p. 78.

arise, according to Marx, for a humanity which had succeeded in becoming fully human, in transcending all 'lostness'. The free man, the fully human man, in control of his environment and his destiny, would not be an atheist: he would have transcended the distinction between theism and atheism in suppressing, as unnecessary and wholly meaningless, the very question of God. Just as Marx brushes aside, as of little account, the most implacable of the resistances encountered by man, the barrier of individual mortality,[48] so also he does not consider the possibility that, not withstanding the projective, anthropomorphic character of all man's models and concepts of God, it might still be the case that man is able to relate himself 'in a human way' to God because God has related *himself* in a human way to man. But these are questions to which we shall return.

Marx's concept of truth is more complex than those proposed in either of the traditions from which Kolakowski sought to distinguish it. That complexity is indicated in a remark of Ernst Bloch's, commenting on the second 'Thesis on Feuerbach', a remark that contains echoes of both the 'pragmatic' and the 'classical Marxist' theories' of truth. 'Correctness', said Bloch, 'is not yet truth, the reflection of reality *and* the power to exert an influence upon reality. In other words, truth is not just a relationship in theory, but is wholly a *relationship in both theory and practice*.'[49] Neither Marx nor Bloch, as I understand them, is recommending us to overlook the importance of distinguishing between, on the one hand, consideration of the truth or falsity of propositions, and, on the other, our practical quest for 'the true resolution of the conflict between existence and being':[50] between need and fulfilment, vision and actuality, 'appearance' and 'reality'. If the 'truth that sets us free'[51] is not to be identified merely with correct information, neither is it to be identified merely with integrity, let alone with power. Marx's commitment to the indissolubility of theory and practice in the quest for truth does not entail any lack of concern for 'correctness': he undoubtedly cared a great deal about the correctness or accuracy of his historical and economic judgements. 'Correctness' *does matter*.[52] If, however, this distinction between what Marx would call

48 Cf. *EW*, p. 351.
49 E. Bloch, 'Changing the World, Marx's *Theses on Feuerbach*', *On Karl Marx*, p. 81. (Extracts from *Das Prinzip Hoffnung*, 1959.)
50 *EW*, p. 348.
51 Cf. John 8: 32.
52 Whether or not Korsch was justified in saying of Lenin that he 'is not primarily concerned with the *theoretical problem* of whether the materialist philosophy he propounds is true or untrue. He is concerned with the *practical question* of its use for the revolutionary struggle. . . . Lenin decides philosophical questions *only* on the basis of non-philosophical considerations and results' (*Marxism and Philosophy*, p. 113), the same charge cannot convincingly be levelled against Marx.

'theoretical' and 'practical' uses of 'true' is fundamental, what is to be gained by binding these uses as tightly together as he does (for example) in the second 'Thesis on Feuerbach'? I would like to conclude this chapter by suggesting that the character of certain Christian doctrinal assertions renders this strategy fruitful in circumstances in which Christians tend to consider the question of the truth of such assertions more or less exclusively in terms of their historical or philosophical 'correctness'. I shall take, as my sample assertion, a proposition than which few are more central to Christian belief: 'Jesus of Nazareth is risen from the dead.'

What are the truth-conditions of this proposition? What is it that must be the case for this proposition to be considered 'true'? If, in answer to such questions, we find that our immediate and spontaneous reaction is to wonder whether or not the emptiness of the tomb, or the impossibility of discovering the bones of Jesus in Palestine, or the veridical character of the Easter 'appearances', is or is not to be included in a list of such truth-conditions, then we may be unwittingly evading the challenge with which the Marxian concept of truth confronts us. We may be *assuming*, for example, that the proposition 'Jesus of Nazareth is risen from the dead' is one whose truth-conditions can be appropriately specified without reference to the hopefulness and the humanity, to both the self-conception and the 'real organization and real interests' of the group or individual affirming the proposition. I am not denying that propositions abound the truth-conditions of which may, at least for all practical purposes, be thus specified. There may be contexts in which the proposition 'Jesus of Nazareth is risen from the dead' could appropriately be considered as being logically on all fours with the proposition 'the cat sat on the mat' (uttered in circumstances in which it mattered not whose cat it was, nor whose the mat). But it certainly cannot be taken for granted that such contexts include the use of the proposition as a Christian doctrinal statement. It cannot be taken for granted because, for example, there have been those who have suggested that, as used in Christian religious discourse, the proposition 'Jesus of Nazareth is risen from the dead' is not, or at least is not in any direct or obvious sense, a proposition about *Jesus* at all, but that it is a statement embodying an announcement about the personal freedom, the new possibilities of hope for the future, to which the speaker has been brought by reflection on the purported fact and significance of the life, teaching and death of Jesus of Nazareth.

In so far as the statement 'Jesus of Nazareth is risen from the dead' is taken to be a proposition the truth-conditions of which can be appropriately specified in terms of the historical, or quasi-historical, claims that it embodies, there is a sense in which, *if* the proposition has and can be shown to have adequate historical warrants, if, that is to say, the proposition is and can be shown to be 'correct' then, wherever and by whoever it is used, its user speaks the truth, speaks truly. On the other hand, in so far as the hopefulness of the believer, the liveliness of his trust in God, is taken to be constitutive of the truth of the proposition that 'Jesus of Nazareth is risen from the dead', then the truth-conditions of this proposition will be very differently specified. (There are theologians, for example, who would maintain that the proposition could be true even if, as a matter of fact, Jesus never existed, and others who would maintain that the believer is in a position to affirm the proposition truthfully even if he knows nothing, and knows himself to know nothing, of the circumstances of Jesus' historical existence.)

My own view (which I am clearly not in a position to justify here and now) is that neither of these accounts is satisfactory. The statement 'Jesus of Nazareth is risen from the dead' is, I would maintain, undoubtedly a proposition which embodies certain historical claims concerning not only the experience of the disciples, but also the fate of him in whom they had come to trust. In so far as it is used as an assertion of Christian religious belief, however, it is *also*, as a matter of logic, a 'self-involving' utterance, expressive of the utterer's trust in God and hope for humanity: a confession of faith. It is, in Marx's sense, a 'practical' and not merely a 'theoretical' assertion, the 'reality and power' of which therefore require to be shown in practice, in transformative activity. Its truth-conditions include, although they are by no means exhaustively specified by, the absence of significant discrepancies between the 'real interests' and the self-conception (as 'Christian believers') of those who utter it. It follows that, in the measure that the 'practice' (secular as well as religious) of those who utter it contradicts the commitment and the hope which the proposition articulates then, be it ever so abstractly 'correct', it lacks truth. 'Christ is risen' is a song more truthfully sung by the victim than by the oppressor.

In our theological reflection upon Christian religious discourse, we still too often consider the question of truth too abstractly, in terms that presuppose the autonomy of the theoretical. We tend to be preoccupied with 'correctness'. This is understandable because, unless the propositions of Christian belief are 'correct', Christianity collapses into fantasy. Nevertheless, correctness is not yet truth. Whatever the difficulties attending Marx's treatment of truth, whatever its ambiguities and inconsistencies, it should at least serve to remind us of how dangerous it is to assume that, if a proposition is correct, and if its theoretical truth-conditions are fulfilled, *therefore*, wherever and in whatever circumstances we affirm it, we are speaking the truth, speaking truly.

There is one thing more to be said. The Marxian account of man's relation to truth, as I have sketched it in this chapter, calls in question the 'truthfulness' of any 'merely theoretical' relationship between Christians and the truth which they confess. However, a Christian use of Marx's concept of truth carries with it an 'inversion' of the anthropology to which, in his hands, the epistemology is subservient. Faith in Christ's resurrection from the dead commemorates, celebrates and announces the outcome of the struggle between 'need' and 'resistance'. The intensely paradoxical manner in which it does so is radically *anti*-Promethean and yet it is, nevertheless, *man* whose victory is proclaimed.

8

MARX AND MATERIALISM

According to Roger Garaudy, 'the major portion of the theoretical misunderstandings between Christians and Marxists result from the great confusion about the word "materialism" '.[1] That is, perhaps, an oversimplification, but consider the following two arguments. Firstly: Christians believe in God; Marxists do not believe in God; therefore Christianity is incompatible with Marxism. Secondly: Christians disapprove of materialism (at least in principle); Marxists are materialists; therefore it is incumbent upon Christians to disapprove of Marxism.

Not only are these two arguments, thus naively presented, extremely influential in Christian thinking, they are also frequently conflated. It is widely supposed amongst Christians that, if a man is an atheist, he is likely to be a materialist and, conversely, if a man is a materialist, he is likely to be an atheist. One certainly gets the impression, from a great deal of ecclesiastical denunciation of 'godless materialism', that the supposed 'godlessness' and the supposed 'materialism' of our society have something to do with each other. In this chapter, I propose to offer a general sketch of what I take to be the dominant sense of Marx's 'materialism', and of its relationship to Hegel's 'idealism' and Feuerbach's 'materialism'. I shall then, in Chapter Nine, suggest an account of one strand in the history of 'Marxism after Marx' which may prove useful when, in Chapter Twelve, we take up the topic of 'Christian materialism'. Because the metaphor of 'base' and 'superstructure', and the concept of 'ideology', have been central to almost all discussion of Marxist 'materialism', I shall devote two chapters (Ten and Eleven) to their consideration.

Materialism as Social Protest
In his *Introduction to Western Philosophy*, Professor Antony Flew distinguishes between 'materialism' in the sense of a 'worldliness and carnality', and 'materialism' in the sense of a 'metaphysical thesis about what there ultimately is; that all there is is, in the last

1 R. Garaudy, *From Anathema to Dialogue*, p. 61.

analysis, stuff; and that whatever is not stuff is nonsense'.[2] I propose, in this chapter, to argue that, whatever may be the case where some Marxist theorists are concerned, Marx himself was not, in either of these senses, a materialist.

When people deplore the 'materialism' of our society, what they usually have in mind is obsession with material possessions, the tendency to make the acquisition of 'things' – money, houses, cars, freezers – the criterion of human achievement. This is the 'materialism' which permits the juxtaposition, in the colour supplements of our Sunday newspapers, of illustrated documentary articles providing continual evidence of appalling destitution, suffering and oppression, with sophisticated and expensive advertisements enticing us to suppose that authentic human existence is to be characterized by lifestyles of unrestrained material luxury. If a Christian were to say that preoccupation with the acquisition of material goods for the sake of their possession and private use is one of the most eloquent symptoms of the sickness of our society, Marx would have wholeheartedly agreed. 'Private property', he remarked in the Paris Manuscripts, 'has made us so stupid and one-sided that an object is only *ours* when we have it, when it exists for us as capital or when we directly possess, eat, drink, wear, inhabit it, etc., in short, when we *use* it . . . all the physical and intellectual senses have been replaced by the simple estrangement of *all* these senses – the sense of *having*.'[3] But merely to disapprove of this obsession with 'having', with the acquisition and possession of material goods, is to indulge in sterile moralizing. If we would help change the destructive and dehumanizing way in which we relate to material reality – to the world of nature and the work of our hands – then we would be well advised to seek to *understand* the causes of our corruption. Plamenatz seems to miss the point of the passage just quoted when he describes it as 'a wholesale attack on the institution of private property as undiscriminating as Hegel's defence of it'.[4] Marx is not moralizing, not merely protesting or registering disapproval. The passage occurs in the course of a sustained attempt philosophically to grasp the character and causes of our dehumanization.

Marx once referred to *money* as 'the *pimp* between need and object'.[5] His relentless hostility to money, especially evident in the writings of his mature period, arises from the fact that, for him, money is the pure form of that alienated condition in which the empirical reality which should express our humanity, should exist

2 A. Flew, *An Introduction to Western Philosophy: Ideas and Argument from Plato to Sartre*, p. 45.
3 'Economic and Philosophical Manuscripts', *EW*, pp. 351, 352.
4 J. Plamenatz, *Karl Marx's Philosophy of Man*, p. 121.
5 *EW*, p. 375.

as the expression of our humanity and as the medium of human communication, exists as something separated from us, standing over against us, whose slaves we become (we shall discuss the theme of 'alienation' in a later chapter). We have been brought so to relate to material reality that, instead of 'things' constituting part of our language, part of the commerce of human relations, 'a relation between people takes on the character of a thing'.[6] 'Reification' is not a Marxian term – it 'owes its currency to Lukács'[7] – but it expresses an idea central to Marx's thought, and there is an authentically Marxian passion in Lukács' brilliant study of 'Reification and the Consciousness of the Proletariat'.[8] The reversal of the trend towards reification, 'the retranslation of economic objects from things back into processes, into the changing relations between men', is described by Lukács as 'the basic thought underlying [Marx's] *magnum opus*'.[9]

In the notebooks which prepared the way for that *magnum opus*, Marx argued that, under the capitalist mode of production, 'growing wealthy is an end in itself. The goal-determining activity of capital can only be that of growing wealthier, i.e. of magnification, of increasing itself.'[10] And he makes a note that he must 'develop further' what he has come to regard as the defining characteristic of the capitalist mode of production: namely, 'the *transformation of all relations into money relations*: taxes in kind into money taxes . . . military service into mercenary troops, all personal services into money services, of patriarchal, slave, serf and guild labour [that is to say, the forms of labour characteristic of the modes of production which historically preceded capitalism] into pure wage labour'.[11] And the 'further development' of which he speaks occupies, of course, a great deal of both the *Grundrisse* and of *Capital* itself.

Is there *no* substance in the widespread assumption that Marxist 'materialism' and Marxist atheism are in some way internally connected? This is a large question but, even these introductory remarks would be incomplete if they included no mention of the frequency with which, throughout his career, Marx drew analogies between religious and economic alienation, between the function of 'money' and the function of 'God'. 'Let us not look for the Jew's secret in his religion', he wrote in his 1843 article 'On the Jewish Question'; 'rather let us look for the secret of religion in the real Jew. . . . What is the secular cult of the Jew? *Haggling*. What is his

---

6 G.Lukács, *History and Class Consciousness*, p. 83.
7 *KIII*, p. 275; cf. D. McLellan, *Marxism after Marx*, p. 161.
8 *History and Class Consciousness*, pp. 83–222.
9 Ibid., p. 183.
10 *G*, p. 270.
11 *G*, p. 146, my stress.

secular God? *Money*.'[12] 'Money is the jealous god of Israel before whom no other god may stand. Money debases all the gods of mankind and turns them into commodities. . . . The god of the Jews has been secularized and become the god of the world. Exchange is the true god of the Jew. His god is nothing more than illusory exchange.'[13] These passages represent a vein which runs through Marx's writings, on the basis of which he has often been charged with anti-semitism. There is undoubtedly some substance in the charge, but the situation is more complex than might appear at first sight. In the first place, it was Moses Hess, himself – like Marx – a Jew, who first suggested to Marx 'the analogy between religious and economic alienation'.[14] According to McLellan, some of the main points in that section of 'On the Jewish Question' in which the passages just quoted occur 'were taken over almost *verbatim* from an article by Hess – who was the very opposite of an anti-semite'.[15] In the second place, we should notice Marx's claim that what we discover in Jewish commercial practice is 'the secret of religion', and not simply of Jewish religion. It is clear from the closing pages of the article that he understands this to be the 'secret' of Christianity and Judaism alike.[16]

The analogies drawn by Marx between 'God' and 'money', far from being merely decorative rhetorical flourishes, expressive of an irrational antipathy to either Jews or Christians, are intended to be taken extremely seriously. Belief in God, and the relationship to money demanded by the capitalist mode of production, are both expressive of particular aspects of human alienation, aspects between which (as we shall see in more detail in a later chapter) there is a more than accidental or coincidental connection.[17] Thus (to illustrate the way in which such connections continue to appear in his later writings), before the industrial revolution it was commercial supremacy, supremacy in trade, which produced industrial predominance (and not, as at the time of his writing, the other way round). 'Hence the preponderant role played by the colonial system at that time. It [the colonial system] was the "strange God" who perched himself side by side with the old divinities of Europe on the altar, and one fine day threw them all overboard with a shove and a kick. It proclaimed the making of profit as the ultimate and the sole purpose of mankind.'[18] 'The criticism of religion is the

---

12 *EW*, p. 236.
13 *EW*, p. 239.
14 *KI*, p. 113.
15 *Life*, p. 86.
16 Cf. *EW*, pp. 237–41.
17 D. B. McKown, *The Classical Marxist Critiques of Religion: Marx, Engels, Lenin, Kautsky*, pp. 49–50.
18 *Cap. I*, p. 918.

prerequisite of all criticism',[19] because such religious belief as survives in industrial society disguises this state of affairs, obscuring from view the God whom this society *really* worships. The overthrow of capitalism aims at the rehumanization of man's labour and social relationships. The pure form of alienated labour, the symbol of alienated humanity, is money. 'Money is . . . the god among commodities'[20] and man cannot be free until *all* fetishes, all gods, in both their religious 'appearance' and their secular 'reality', have died.

The adequacy of Marx's socio-economic analysis is not our concern. The purpose of these remarks has simply been to indicate that, whatever else it is, Marx's 'materialism' is the antithesis of that 'worldliness' which is condemned, in theory, by Christian critics of the corrupting acquisitiveness so characteristic of modern Western societies. By the same token, Marx's 'materialism' challenges such contradictions as may exist between Christianity's affirmation of the 'primacy of the spiritual' and its frequent endorsement, in practice, of the acquisitive materialism it so roundly condemns in theory.

Consider the following illustration. The inner dynamic of the capitalist mode of production demands that 'the working-day contains the full 24 hours, with the deduction of the few hours of rest without which labour-power is absolutely incapable of renewing its services. . . . Time for education, for intellectual development, for the fulfilment of social functions . . . even the rest time of Sunday (and that in a country of Sabbatarians!) – what foolishness!'[21] And to that reference to the Sunday rest Marx adds a footnote: 'In England even now in rural districts a labourer is occasionally condemned to imprisonment for desecrating the Sabbath by working in his front garden. The same man would be punished for breach of contract if he remained away from his metal, paper or glass works on Sunday, even on account of some religious foible.'[22] Which is the more 'materialist' (in the pejorative sense): a 'materialism', such as Marx's, which insists on the primacy of the concrete, of practice in respect of theory, in its quest for a society in which *all* man's capacities would, in fact, be able to develop and to flourish; or a dualism which, while imprisoning the Sunday-gardening labourer in the name of the primacy of the spiritual, yet accepts, in the next breath, the conditions of life imposed on him by the demands of the prevailing mode of production, Sundays and weekdays alike?

Marx's illustration is, happily, outdated. But is it quite certain

19 'A Contribution to the Critique of Hegel's Philosophy of Right. Introduction', *EW*, p. 243.
20 *G*, p. 221.
21 *Cap. I*, p. 375.
22 Loc. cit.

that the insistence, for example, that 'Christianity has nothing to do with politics', does not frequently express a similar dualism, with its concomitant toleration of contradictions between the affirmation, in principle, of the 'primacy of the spiritual', and the operation of economic and social structures in which, in practice, the divinity of money goes unchallenged?

Marx, Hegel and Feuerbach
When, in quest of the meaning of Marx's 'materialism', we turn to Professor Flew's alternative description in terms of a 'metaphysical thesis about what there ultimately is, that all there is is, in the last analysis, stuff; and that whatever is not stuff is nonsense',[23] the situation becomes more complex, for at least two reasons. In the first place, although Marx was never a 'materialist' in this sense because he was never, in this sense, a metaphysician, there have been plenty of people throughout the history of Marxism who have supposed (especially under the influence of Engels) that some such doctrine is implied by, or can be extracted from, Marx's texts. In the second place, in view of the polemical, rhetorical, occasional character of so much of Marx's writing, textual warrants can be found for a wide variety of differing and often incompatible theoretical positions. Marx was an original, imaginative and restless thinker. His was the type of mind which readily invites the accusation, from hostile critics, of 'inconsistency', while too many admirers, impatient of complexity and lacking his intellectual vitality, have sought to 'reduce' the richness of his thought to some simply expressible theoretical or systematized 'essence'. It is, I believe, perfectly possible to affirm the fundamental consistency of Marx's thought without denying, on the one hand, that there are, in that thought, important contradictions or unresolved tensions and without claiming, on the other hand, that that consistency is such as to be patient of exhaustive expression in theoretically systematized form. Where this question of 'consistency' or 'coherence' is concerned, I have long been struck by the similarities (which have never been explored) between Marx's thought – and the fate it has undergone at the hands of friend and foe alike – and the thought of his contemporary, John Henry Newman, and its subsequent history. Some remarks I made a number of years ago, concerning attempts to construct a systematically unified synthesis of Newman's thought, can be applied, without significant qualification, to Karl Marx: 'The range of topics which engaged his attention, the fact that he nearly always approached them from the standpoint of the controversialist, writing to meet a specific need, his preference for detailed

23 Flew, *Introduction to Western Philosophy*, p. 45.

concrete description and his corresponding mistrust of sheerly theoretical analysis; these and other factors combine to make it more or
less inevitable that any attempt at such a synthesis will be at best
a pale, "notional" shadow, and at worst a serious distortion of the
original.'[24] To be misled by the surface of the text into losing sight
of the *interrogative* character of Newman's thought is to miss its
essential strength.[25] Similarly, Sartre has said of 'living Marxism'
that it is '*heuristic*; its principles and its prior knowledge appear as
regulative in relation to its concrete research'[26]

It is worth remarking (and the remark will serve to bring us back,
after this detour, to the specific problems with which this chapter
is concerned) that any abdication of this heuristic stance in favour
of some supposed achievement of knowledge in pure theoretical
transparency, a shift from solutions *sought* to solutions achieved –
and achieved merely in theory, would have been, on his own
account, a shift from 'materialism' to 'idealism'. It may be true that
'towards the end of his life Marx moved nearer to the positivism
then so fashionable in intellectual circles',[27] thereby facilitating the
emergence of that 'trend which presented Marxism as a philosophical world-view or *Weltanschauung* consisting of objective laws and
particularly laws of the dialectical movement of matter taken in a
metaphysical sense as the basic constituent of reality'.[28] Nevertheless, I believe that the most that can be said is that he moved
towards a position at which a path was opened up which he himself
did not take. In a word, I do not believe that Marx ever fundamentally abandoned the stance informally expressed in *The German
Ideology*'s characterization of materialist theory in terms of 'a
summing-up of the most general results, abstractions which are
derived from the observation of the historical development of men'.[29]

It will be noticed that, in the previous paragraph, two distinct
meanings of 'materialism' have begun to emerge. The first would
be a metaphysical, or ontological, doctrine concerning the fundamental constituents of reality. The second would refer less to doctrine than to method. It is, I think, important to keep this distinction
in mind even if, as we indicated in Chapter Three, attempts to
sustain it are not without their difficulties.[30]

24 N. L. A. Lash, 'Second Thoughts on Walgrave's "Newman" ', *Downside Review*,
   Vol. 87 (1969), p. 340.
25 Cf. N. L. A. Lash, 'Introduction' to J. H. Newman, *An Essay in Aid of a Grammar
   of Assent*, p. 2.
26 J.-P. Sartre, *Search for a Method*, p. 26, my stress.
27 *Life*, p. 423.
28 Loc. cit.
29 *CW5*, p. 37. For a further comment on this passage, in the context of the general
   problem of the relations between the 'scientific' and 'philosophical' aspects of
   Marx's thought, cf. below, p. 227.
30 Cf. above, p. 30.

In the third of the 'Theses on Feuerbach', Marx observed that 'The [Feuerbachian] materialist doctrine concerning the changing of circumstances and upbringing forgets that circumstances are changed by men and that it is essential to educate the educator himself. . . . The coincidence of the changing of circumstances and of human activity or self-changing can be conceived and rationally understood only as *revolutionary practice*'.[31] This thesis, according to Ernst Bloch, 'describes the priority of economic existence in a far from vulgar-materialist way, for it allows human consciousness the most "real" of all places in the "conditions" or "circumstances" by putting it within the external world that it has helped to construct.'[32] 'Vulgar-materialism' would be the kind of mechanistic reductionism which attributes to human consciousness a purely epiphenomenal status, and which accordingly construes in an inflexibly literal manner such aphorisms as: 'It is not consciousness that determines life, but life that determines consciousness'.[33]

Such statements, which abound in Marx's writings, are not to be taken as denials of the effectiveness and irreducible reality of human consciousness, but rather as warnings issued against the assumption that the world of thought is autonomous, unshaped and unaffected by the concrete circumstances in which it finds expression. And when this warning is issued in language such as the following: 'The abstraction or idea . . . is nothing more than the theoretical expression of those material relations which are their lord and master',[34] we are reminded of the need to take into account the extent to which Marx's 'materialism' was worked out in critical contrast to Hegel's 'idealism'.

One of the most famous passages in which Marx stated the difference between his method and Hegel's is the 1873 'Postface' to the second edition of *Capital*. There he said: 'My dialectical method is, in its foundations, not only different from the Hegelian, but exactly opposite to it. For Hegel, the process of thinking, which he even transforms into an independent subject, under the name of "the Idea", is the creator of the real world, and the real world is only the external appearance of the idea. With me the reverse is true: the ideal is nothing but the material world reflected in the mind of man, and translated into forms of thought.'[35] Man makes his world as he struggles to meet his needs in the material circumstances of his existence. The 'process of thinking' arises from the process of work and is to be predicated exclusively of human subjects: it does not pre-exist human activity as an 'independent subject

31 *EW*, p. 422.
32 E. Bloch, *On Karl Marx*, p. 70.
33 *CW5*, p. 37.
34 *G*, p. 164.
35 *Cap. I*, p. 102.

. . . the creator of the real world'. In other words, there are undoubtedly connections to be made, connections that we have already
glimpsed in the first section of this chapter, between Marx's 'materialism' and his atheism. As Calvez puts it: 'l'histoire, estime
Marx, n'est pas le mouvement de la manifestation de l'esprit-sujet
souverainement libre, mais un dur combat de l'homme au sein de
la nature pour accéder à une situation de sujet qui lui est encore
refusée.'[36] Therefore, one of the questions which we shall have to
consider in Chapter Twelve is: in what sense is belief in God
incompatible with a 'materialist' account of the relationships that
obtain between human thought and activity and the circumstances
of human existence?

Later in the Postface, Marx acknowledges that 'the mystification
which the dialectic suffers in Hegel's hands by no means prevents
him from being the first to present its general forms of motion in a
comprehensive and conscious manner. With him it is standing on
its head. It must be inverted, in order to discover the rational kernel
within the mystical shell.'[37] As Althusser has pointed out, the clash
of metaphors in that last sentence does not make the interpretation
of the passage any easier.[38] Are we being invited to stand Hegel's
dialectic 'on its head', or to discard Hegel's 'mystical' (or religious?)
language, retaining only the 'rational kernel' of his thought, his
grasp of the 'general forms of motion' of the dialectic of history?
Whatever the intended force of the metaphor of 'inversion', it is not
immediately apparent that the 'inversion' of the Hegelian dialectic
and its 'demythologization' would be identical operations.

As a first step, I suggest that we should give full weight to Marx's
admission that Hegel was, indeed, the first thinker to present the
'general forms of motion' of the dialectic of history 'in a comprehensive and conscious manner'. If we take this acknowledgement
seriously, it seems likely that Marx's claim that his method is
'exactly opposite' to Hegel's is to be construed as a piece of polemic
the exaggerated nature of which is reinforced by the metaphor of
'inversion'. In the second place, many of Marx's accounts of his
relationship to Hegel are complicated by the fact that we are, as it
were, seeing Hegel 'filtered' through the distorting glass of the
'one-sidedness' of left-Hegelian idealism. In the third place, *Feuerbach*'s 'materialism', with which Marx for a time identified himself,
was in some fairly straightforward sense an 'inversion' of this left-
Hegelian idealism.

In order to pursue these suggestions, I would now like to turn to
a passage in *The Holy Family*, Marx's diatribe against certain of the
left-Hegelians, written nearly thirty years before the Postface to

36 J.-Y. Calvez, *La Pensée de Karl Marx*, p. 69.
37 *Cap. I*, p. 103.
38 Cf. L. Althusser, *For Marx*, pp. 89–94.

Capital. In the *Phenomenology*, says Marx, Hegel 'substitutes *self-consciousness* for *man*, the *most varied* manifestations of human reality appear only as *definite* forms, as *determinations of self-consciousness*. . . . In Hegel's *Phänomenologie* the *material, sensuously perceptible, objective* foundations of the various estranged forms of human self-consciousness are allowed to *remain*.'[39] In other words, because Hegel regards the process of history as the working-out of the history of Mind, or Spirit, he contents himself with attempting to *understand* how things have come to be as they are. He does not go on from here to seek to change the way that things are. Hence, Marx continues, 'The whole destructive work results in the *most conservative philosophy* because it thinks it has overcome the *objective world* . . . by transforming it into a "Thing of Thought", a mere *determinateness of self-consciousness*. . . . [Hegel] stands the world on its head and can therefore *in his head* also dissolve all limitations. . . . The whole of the *Phänomenologie* is intended to prove that *self-consciousness* is the *only reality* and *all reality* . . . the Critical Critic [Bauer, following Hegel] – the theologian *ex professo* – cannot by any means entertain the thought that there is a world in which *consciousness* and *being* are distinct; a world which continues to exist when I merely abolish its existence in thought.'[40]

The first thing to notice about this passage is that, far from being reductionist, it insists on the distinction between 'consciousness' and 'being'. It is precisely because this distinction is irreducible that the purely speculative activities of Bauer and his colleagues can achieve nothing, can change nothing. All that they can do (we are reminded of the 'valiant fellow' in the Preface to *The German Ideology*) is to think and speak differently, leaving the world as it is. To any such purely speculative idealism Marx's 'materialism' is vigorously opposed. But to describe *this* opposition as an 'inversion' would be misleading. Not only does Marx's insistence on the priority of action in respect of reflection, of 'being' in respect of 'consciousness', not carry with it any endorsement of mindless activism, but any straight 'inversion' of Bauer would be as forgetful of historical process as Bauer's own speculative idealism. And it is precisely the understanding of history as dialectical process which Marx sees as the hallmark of Hegel's greatness. Thus it is that, shortly after the long passage just quoted, Marx says that 'it goes without saying that whereas Hegel's *Phänomenologie*, in spite of its speculative original sin, gives in many instances the elements of a true description of human relations. . . . [Bauer and his colleagues] provided only an empty caricature.'[41]

In that passage, as in the acknowledgement that Hegel does

39 *CW4*, p. 192.
40 *CW4*, pp. 192–3.
41 *CW4*, p. 193.

indeed present 'the general forms of motion' of the dialectic of history 'in a comprehensive and conscious manner',[42] we see once again how misleading is the metaphor of 'inversion'. Not the least of the reasons why Marx found it so difficult to disentangle his own thought from that of Hegel (and his tendency to overdramatize the contrasts between them is perhaps an index of this difficulty) is that he recognized 'how much Hegel's philosophy of history anticipates historical materialism'.[43] Thus, for example, when we hear Hegel saying that 'Freedom in thought has only *pure thought* as its truth, a truth lacking the fullness of life,'[44] it is as important to recognize that Marx would have agreed with this as it is to bear in mind the very different conclusions that they would have drawn: Hegel supposing that there was little more to be done than to wait upon the appearance of that fullness of life in due time; Marx supposing that we should cast around to explore the circumstances in which the material conditions could be so transformed as to make that fullness of life a real possibility.

Although subsequent developments in Marx's thought would introduce important distinctions and qualifications, it seems to me that the broad outlines of Marx's debt to and distance from Hegel are succinctly stated in the Paris Manuscripts: 'The importance of Hegel's *Phenomenology* . . . lies in the fact that Hegel conceives the self-creation of man as a process, objectification as loss of object (*Entgegenständlichung*), as alienation and as supersession of this alienation; that he therefore grasps the nature of *labour* and conceives objective man – true, because real man – as the result of his *own* labour . . . [nevertheless] the only labour Hegel knows and recognizes is *abstract mental* labour.'[45] Ernst Bloch has said of this passage that 'there is no better testimony to the importance of Hegel's *Phenomenology* (which Feuerbach never really understood).'[46] To the differences between Marx's 'materialism' and that of Feuerbach we must, therefore, now briefly turn.

The assertion that 'the ideal is nothing but the material world reflected in the mind of man, and translated into forms of thought',[47] although made by Marx nearly thirty years after the 'break' with Feuerbach, could nevertheless just as well have been made by Feuerbach. To concentrate on such aphoristic expressions, therefore, would be to lose sight of the fact that, as the 'Theses on

42 *Cap. I*, p. 103.
43 C. Taylor, *Hegel*, p. 157, commenting on the analysis of 'work' in the dialectic of master and slave in the *Phenomenology*.
44 Hegel, *Phenomenology*, p. 122.
45 'Economic and Philosophical Manuscripts', *EW* pp. 385–6; cf. Mészáros, *Marx's Theory of Alienation*, p. 88.
46 Bloch, *On Karl Marx*, p. 67.
47 *Cap. I*, p. 102.

Feuerbach' clearly indicate, Marx thought out his position in critical contrast not only to Hegelian 'idealism', but also to the 'materialism' of Feuerbach. And because he believed that he had gone beyond the opposition between Hegel and Feuerbach, rescuing the truth from both their positions, we sometimes find Marx seeking for a 'label' which would differentiate his position from *both* of theirs. 'Here we see', he wrote in 1844, 'how consistent materialism or humanism differs from both [Hegelian] idealism and [Feuerbachian] materialism and is at the same time their unifying truth. We also see that only naturalism is capable of comprehending the process of world history.'[48] In the light of the subsequent history of Marxist thought it is permissible, if pointless, to wish that Marx had continued to use the term 'naturalism', rather than 'materialism', to describe his position!

'Feuerbach's great achievement' according to Marx, 'was to have founded *true materialism* and *real science* by making the social relation of "man to man" the basic principle of his theory.'[49] Marx welcomed Feuerbach's empiricism: '*Sense perception* (see Feuerbach) must be the basis of all science.'[50] Unfortunately, in Feuerbach's hands that empiricism or 'materialism' was as 'one-sided' as the left-Hegelian speculative idealism from which it differentiated itself: Feuerbach, in *The Essence of Christianity*, regarded 'the theoretical attitude as the only genuinely human attitude.'[51] This 'one-sidedness' of Feuerbach is neatly captured in a passage in *The Holy Family* (a passage which indicates, therefore, the lines along which the 'break' with Feuerbach will occur in the following year): 'just as *Feuerbach* is the representative of *materialism* coinciding with *humanism* in the *theoretical* domain, French and English *socialism* and *communism* represent *materialism* coinciding with humanism in the *practical* domain'.[52] In view of the extent to which Marxist thinkers tend confusingly to identify the entire empiricist tradition with 'positivism', it is worth pointing out that that passage occurs in the course of a fascinating and appreciative sketch of the history of 'materialism' in France and England: 'Materialism is the *natural-born* son of *Great Britain*. . . . The real progenitor of *English materialism* and all *modern experimental* science is *Bacon*.'[53]

In Marx's assessment of Feuerbach we can see the scope and limits of the metaphor of 'inversion'. Feuerbach had 'inverted' Hegel's 'inversion' of 'subject' and 'predicate' with his reaffirmation of the primacy of human experience. In other words, Feuerbach's

48 *EW*, p. 389.
49 *EW*, p. 381.
50 *EW*, p. 355.
51 'Theses on Feuerbach', *EW*, p. 421.
52 *CW4*, p. 125.
53 *CW4*, pp. 127, 128.

'materialism' consisted, above all, in his insistence that it is *man* and not 'mind' that is the subject of human life and consciousness. This 'materialism' was nevertheless, according to Marx, 'one-sided' inasmuch as it relegated man to the status of 'observer' or 'contemplator' of his world, thus failing to carry through central features of Hegel's dialectic. The world of nature, in Feuerbach's account, still stood 'over against' man's conscious subjectivity. He had thus failed to overcome the fundamental dualism between man and nature, and hence between the history of man and the history of that natural world of which man is a product and an aspect, and in which he lives and works and thinks.[54]

So long as these dualisms are sustained, our understanding of human history will tend to be 'idealist'[55] in taking no account of the fact that human existence is an aspect of natural existence, and hence in its failure to derive its descriptions and explanations from the natural, material circumstances of human behaviour and activity.[56] Similarly, our anthropology, our understanding of the 'nature' of man, will be misleadingly abstract in its failure to take account of the fact that forms of human existence are *historical* products. Thus it is that Lukács accuses Feuerbach of replacing 'an abstract concept (God) by the equally abstract one of "species" '.[57] The other side of the coin is that, so long as these dualisms are sustained, our natural-scientific conceptions will tend to be 'idealist' in taking no account of the fact that such descriptions are derived from man's interaction with the material with which he works, and hence that these descriptions are socially mediated historical products. In his attempt to transcend these dualisms, 'Marx admitted no absolute division between nature and society, and hence no fundamental methodological distinction between the natural sciences and historical science'.[58] '*Industry*', he argued in the Paris Manuscripts, 'is the *real* historical relationship of nature, and hence of natural science, to man'.[59] Once this is understood, 'natural science will lose its abstractly material, or rather idealist, orientation, and become the basis of a *human* science, just as it has already become – though in

54 Thus, commenting on the first 'Thesis on Feuerbach' and on 'the parallel passage in the *The German Ideology*', Lobkowicz says that 'Marx accuses the author of the *Essence of Christianity* of overlooking the fact that virtually everything which man may contemplate today has been generated by human activities in the past' (N. Lobkowicz, *Theory and Practice, History of a Concept from Aristotle to Marx*, pp. 423–4).

55 At least in the sense, interchangeable with 'abstractly material', in which Marx uses the term in the passage from *EW*, p. 355, quoted below.

56 'The writers of history have so far paid very little attention to the development of material production, which is the basis of all social life, and therefore of all real history' (*Cap. I*, p. 286).

57 G. Lukács, *Political Writings, 1919–1929*, p. 208.

58 A. Schmidt, *The Concept of Nature in Marx*, p. 49.

59 *EW*, p. 355.

an estranged form – the basis of actual human life. . . . History itself
is a *real* part of *natural history* and of nature's becoming man. Natural
science will in time subsume the science of man just as the science
of man will subsume natural science: there will be *one* science.'[60]

For over a hundred years, that programme or vision – and its
negation – have been central to debates concerning the relationship
between the natural and the human sciences.[61] But these methodological issues are not our immediate concern. It is more to our
purpose to consider to what extent Marx's historical materialism,
and his insistence on the dialectical character of the relationship
between human existence and other natural processes, entail or
presuppose a philosophical materialism such as would satisfy Flew's
light-hearted definition. To put it very simply: fundamental dualisms of mind and matter can be opposed either by an 'absolute
idealism' which affirms that, in the last resort, reality is attributable
only to 'mind' or 'spirit', or by what we might call an 'absolute
materialism' which affirms that, in the last resort, 'all there is is
stuff'. It is clear that Marx was not a monist of the former variety.
But, in spite of my denials, and of the fact that Marx would have
refused to discuss the matter in these terms, is it certain that his
historical materialism and his insistence on the 'naturality' of man
do not presuppose or entail some form of monistic 'absolute materialism'? This would at least be one way of reading Schmidt's claim
that 'for Marx a naturalistic materialism constitutes the concealed
precondition for a theory of society'.[62]

Our suspicions are further aroused when we find Marx describing
his 'standpoint' as being one 'from which the development of the
economic formation of society is viewed as a process of natural
history'.[63] Lenin, for one, would seem to be reading this passage
monistically when he argues that 'only the *reduction* of social relations
to productive relations and of the latter to the level of productive
forces, provided a firm basis for the conception that the development
of formations of society is a process of natural history. And it goes
without saying that without such a view there can be no social sci-

60 Loc. cit.
61 For discussion of these debates in the context of fundamental issues in theological
   method, cf. the first two parts of W. Pannenberg, *Theology and the Philosophy of
   Science*.
62 Schmidt, op. cit., p. 21. The account that I am offering of the relationship
   between 'man' and 'nature' in Marx's thought seems to square with that provided
   by Mészáros, *Marx's Theory of Alienation*, pp. 81–4. It may therefore be worth
   pointing out that, when Mészáros insists that Marx *is* a 'monist' (cf. pp. 84–7),
   he is contrasting his position with Feuerbach's 'dualism', and not suggesting that
   Marx supposed that 'all there is is stuff'.
63 *Cap. I*, p. 92.

ence.'[64] But there are at least two reasons why we should hesitate before jumping to conclusions.

In the first place, there is surely a touch of irony in that passage from *Capital*? Were there not, Marx's standpoint would be as un-dialectical as that of the classical political economists against whom he is writing.[65] In the second place, Lenin himself goes on to insist that 'materialism in history has never claimed to explain everything, but merely to indicate the "only scientific", to use Marx's expression (*Capital*), method of explaining history.'[66] My own judgement, for what it is worth, is that 'materialism', for Marx, refers principally to the dependence of consciousness on social, material conditions, and that his understanding of that dependence neither presupposes nor entails any form of monistic 'materialism'. It is 'not the abstract nature of matter, but the concrete nature of social practice [that] is the true subject and basis of [Marx's] materialist theory.'[67] And, with that reference to 'social practice' we are brought back once more to Marx's critique of Feuerbach.

If it is true that Feuerbach's 'materialism' failed to overcome the dualism between man and nature and thus, at a fundamental level, between 'subject' and 'object', between thought and reality, it is also true that this dualism cannot be overcome *merely in thought*. In a passage which we discussed in the previous chapter,[68] Marx insists that the resolution of the '*theoretical* antitheses' between 'subjectivism and objectivism, spiritualism and materialism', is 'by no means only a problem of knowledge, but a *real* problem of life, a problem which *philosophy* was unable to solve precisely because it treated it as a *purely* theoretical problem'.[69] And so the first 'Thesis on Feuerbach' begins: 'The chief defect of all hitherto existing materialism (that of Feuerbach included) is that the thing, reality, sensuousness, is conceived only in the form of the *object or of contemplation*, but not as *sensuous human activity, practice*, not subjectively.'[70]

If Marx is a 'materialist' in contradistinction to Hegel's 'ideal-ism', in insisting that it is *men*, products of their nature and their history, and not 'mind' that are the subjects of human life and

64 V. I. Lenin, 'What the "Friends of the People" Are and How they Fight the Social-Democrats', *HM*. p. 319, my stress. Cf. Lenin's whole discussion on pp. 313ff; the passage from *Capital* is quoted on p. 315.

65 E. P. Thompson makes a good case for this view, in criticizing Althusser's use of this and similar passages: cf. *The Poverty of Theory*, p. 340.

66 Lenin, op. cit., p. 323. On this passage, and on Marx's discussion of the need for a natural history of 'the productive organs of man in society', similar to Darwin's history of 'the formation of the organs of plants and animals' (*Cap. I*, p. 494), cf. Schmidt, *The Concept of Nature*, pp. 44–5. On Marx and Darwin, cf. *Life*, pp. 423–4.

67 Schmidt, *The Concept of Nature*, p. 40.

68 Cf. above, p. 79.

69 'Economic and Philosophical Manuscripts', *EW*, p. 354.

70 *EW*, p. 421.

consciousness, he is nevertheless, in his insistence that man's fundamental relationship to reality is to be sought in the transformative character of human *labour*, of man's 'practical' activity, and not in 'contemplation', a 'materialist' of a very different kind from Feuerbach.[71] Man is part of material reality (even if he is not 'only' that), and it is in 'working' that reality of which he is part, with his hands and his eyes, his muscles and his mind, that he is able to *become himself* in reality and reflection, in life and in thought. Moreover, this process of man's becoming, socially and individually, in practice and in theory, is the process of human history. Therefore Marx's 'materialism' is an 'historical materialism'. That is his own name for it, and if it later came to be called '*dialectical* materialism' we should remember that the term originated, not with Marx, but with Joseph Dietzgen,[72] and that it was applied to Marx's thought, not by Marx himself, but by Engels,[73] in whose hands it rapidly acquired cosmological and, indeed, metaphysical connotations.

Several times in the course of this chapter, I have indicated the presence of theological (or, rather, anti-theological) motifs in Marx's critique of Hegelian idealism. By way of conclusion, I would like to illustrate this theme once more from a passage in Marx's diatribe against what he came to regard as Proudhon's impoverished Hegelianism. 'Economists explain how production takes place in the above-mentioned relations [the relations of bourgeois production], but what they do not explain is how these relations themselves are produced, that is, the historical movement which gave them birth. M. Proudhon, taking these relations for principles, categories, abstract thoughts, has merely to put into *order* these thoughts, which are to be found alphabetically arranged at the end of every treatise on political economy. The economist's material is the active, energetic life of man; M. Proudhon's material is the dogmas of the economist. But the moment we cease to pursue the historical movement of production relations, of which the categories are but the theoretical expression, the moment we want to see in these categories no more than ideas, spontaneous thoughts, independent of real relations, we are forced to attribute the origin of these thoughts to the movement of pure reason. How does pure, eternal, impersonal reason give rise to these thoughts? How does it proceed in order to produce them?'[74]

The theological overtones of that reference to 'eternal reason' are not accidental, as is clear from their recurring presence in a letter,

---

71 The details of Marx's respective debts to Hegel and Feuerbach are complex and controversial: cf. Lukács, *Political Writings*, pp. 181–223; Schmidt, *The Concept of Nature*, pp. 19–61.
72 Cf. D. McLellan, *Marxism after Marx*, p. 11.
73 Cf. L. Colletti, 'Introduction', *EW*, p. 10.
74 Marx, *The Poverty of Philosophy*, p. 98.

discussing Proudhon's views, which Marx wrote in the December of the previous year (1846): 'Why does M. Proudhon talk about God, about universal reason. . . . Why does he resort to feeble Hegelianism to make himself appear like a bold thinker?'; [75] Proudhon's history 'is not history but trite Hegelian trash, it is not profane history – history of man – but sacred history – history of ideas';[76] on Proudhon's account it is 'the men of learning that make history, the men who know how to purloin God's secret thoughts.'[77]

Recalling the distinction that I drew earlier, between 'materialism' as method and 'materialism' as doctrine, or ontology, it would seem that, in Marx's view, the possibility of a 'Christian materialism' is excluded on two counts. Methodologically, theological language, language that refers to a God who is the creator and providential sustainer – the 'first cause' – of nature and history, is necessarily language that 'idealistically' inverts 'subject' and 'predicate'. Ontologically, belief in God is incompatible with a naturalism which takes for granted that the 'natural' (including the human) exhausts the totality of actual and possible objects of action and discourse. On both counts, Marx shared the widespread Christian assumption, with which we began, that Christianity is incompatible with Marxist 'materialism'. We shall discuss, in Chapters Twelve and Thirteen, the extent to which this twofold assumption is justified. Before doing so, however, there are three other matters that should be considered: the circumstances in which 'materialist' theory may become 'idealist' in practice; the metaphor of 'base' and 'superstructure'; and the concept of 'ideology'.

75 Ibid., p. 174.
76 Ibid., p. 177.
77 Ibid., p. 185.

9

MATERIALIST THEORY AND IDEALIST PRACTICE

This book is a series of reflections, not on Marxism, but on the thought of Karl Marx. Nevertheless, our discussion in the previous chapter demands that we glance at certain post-Marxian developments in Marxism, in order to provide a framework for consideration of questions such as the following. Firstly, is it possible for a theory of man and society to be impeccably 'materialist' (in Marx's sense) in its formulations – that is to say, in theory – while yet becoming, in practice, 'idealist'? Secondly, if so, in what circumstances is such a shift likely to occur? These questions are important for us because, even if we were to succeed in showing that the discourse of Christian faith and theology is by no means as obviously or necessarily 'idealist' in *principle* as Marx supposed, it could still be the case that Christian discourse betrayed its 'idealism' in *practice*, in the uses to which, in particular historical and social circumstances, it was put. The issues at stake here are closely connected with those upon which we touched in the final pages of Chapter Seven, concerning the truth-conditions of doctrinal statements.

In view of Marx's hostility to 'idealism', and his insistence that, whatever the nature of the task upon which we are engaged – be it 'practical' in some straightforward sense, or be it some form of that aspect of human practice which is theoretical reflection – the only appropriate and adequate standpoint is 'materialist', it is as surprising (at least at first sight) as it is interesting, that there should have arisen a chorus of voices, many of them coming from within the Marxist tradition, charging the mainstream development of 'orthodox' Marxism, from Lenin and Lukács to Stalin and Althusser, with 'idealism'.

Thus, for example, we have already encountered E. P. Thompson's charge that Althusser's structuralist Marxism, with its attempt to filter out of 'scientific' theory any consideration of matters of empirical, historical fact, is thoroughly 'idealist' in character.[1] Althusser, for his part, pours scorn on those Marxist thinkers such as Colletti, Gramsci and Sartre, whose position he describes as 'his-

---

1 Cf. above, p. 21.

toricist', for supposing that 'the mere idea of a theoretically autonomous philosophy . . . i.e. one which is distinct from the science of
history, tips Marxism back into metaphysics',[2] and hence, in Marxist terminology, into idealism. The charge to which Althusser refers
is not one that has arisen only in the last few years. In 1935, in an
essay entitled 'Why I am a Marxist', Karl Korsch complained that
'Again and again so-called "orthodox" Marxists have relapsed into
the "abstract" and "metaphysical" way of thinking which Marx
himself – after Hegel – had most emphatically denied'.[3] However,
let us turn to two of Althusser's targets: to Colletti and Sartre.

Much of Colletti's *Marxism and Hegel* is devoted to a sustained
attack on those who are 'in the camp of "dialectical materialism" '.[4]
These include Engels, Plekhanov, Lenin and Lukács. What they
'never consider', according to Colletti, is the possibility that ' "dialectical materialism" is simply an idealism unaware of its own
nature'.[5] And it is unaware of its own nature because it has ceased
to be 'critical' and become 'dogmatic'. In *The German Ideology*, 'The
opposite natures of *dogmatism* and *critical thought* . . . are clearly
specified. Dogmatism is the presupposition of the Idea, the assumption that knowledge is already *given*.'[6] The outlines of the
charge now begin to become clear: Marxism, at least in the hands
of some of its most distinguished and influential exponents, has
ceased to be a programme of discovery, of the quest for truth
through transformative activity and critical reflection; it has become
the exposition and defence of an already given and constituted body
of knowledge.

Sartre's accusation is strikingly similar. Not long after the October Revolution, he says in a telling phrase, 'Marxism stopped'.[7]
The Party leaders 'feared that the free process of truth . . . would
break the unity of combat'.[8] As a consequence, there occurred a
'separation of theory and practice [which] resulted in transforming
the latter into an empiricism without principles; the former into a
pure, fixed knowledge'.[9]

Sartre distinguishes 'the idealism of the Right' from 'the idealism
of the Left . . . the former merits its name by the *content* of its
concepts, and the latter by the *use* which today it makes of its
concepts'.[10] This distinction between 'content' and 'use' is clearly

2 L. Althusser, *Reading Capital*, p. 137; cf. whole chapter, 'Marxism is not a Historicism', pp. 119–44.
3 K. Korsch, *Three Essays on Marxism*, pp. 61–2.
4 L. Colletti, *Marxism and Hegel*, p. 57.
5 Ibid., p. 61.
6 Ibid., p. 90.
7 J.-P. Sartre, *Search for a Method*, p. 21.
8 Ibid., p. 22.
9 Loc. cit., my stress.
10 Ibid., p. 29.

another form of the distinction, which we touched upon in the previous chapter, between 'doctrine' and 'method'. If the primacy of human experience and activity in respect of theoretical reflection on or ordering of that experience is central to Marx's 'materialism', must we not say of a state of affairs in which this primacy is merely asserted in *theory*, and is not executed or exhibited in *practice*, that it has – in fact although not in intention – once again 'inverted' the 'subject' and 'predicate' and thereby relapsed into a form of idealism? This seems, at any rate, to be Sartre's suggestion. According to Lukács (who on this, as on so many issues, can be appealed to by both sides), Hegel's 'enormous intellectual achievement consisted in making theory and history dialectically relative to each other', but he 'was never able to advance to a real unity of theory and practice'.[11] Marx's 'materialism' was an attempt to make that further 'advance', but the criticism, by Colletti and Sartre, of certain influential strands in the development of Marxism, reminds us that, if the unity of theory and practice is a *dialectical* unity, it can never become a permanent *achievement*: it always remains a *task*. To put it another way: it follows from the dialectical nature of the relationship between theory and practice that the 'reality' of Marxism may, in certain situations, contradict its materialist 'appearance', and that there can be no purely theoretical safeguards against such an occurrence.

Marxism today, says Sartre, 'no longer *knows* anything. Its concepts are *dictates*; its goal is no longer to increase what it knows but to be itself constituted *a priori* as an absolute knowledge.'[12] Thus it is that a central theme in Sartre's programme for the reformation of Marxism, for the recovery of its own original and originating strategic impulse, is the need for Marxist thought to rediscover its interrogative or *heuristic* character: 'living Marxism is heuristic; its principles and its prior knowledge appear as regulative in relation to its concrete research.'[13] The paradox here is one with which any student of the history of Christian theology should be familiar. Marxism, in order to be true to itself, must retain the character of a *'docta ignorantia'*. In the measure that it supposes that 'knowledge is already *given*', it 'no longer *knows* anything'. Knowledge of the truth, on a dialectical account of the relation between practice and theory, experience and reflection, is never a *possession*, but is always at once a task and a responsibility.

When man's relationship to truth is conceived in heuristic terms, when our prior knowledge appears as regulative in relation to our concrete research, then the specific, the concretely particular, is of paramount importance. Seriously to *enquire* is always, as any his-

11 G. Lukács, *Political Writings*, p. 221.
12 Sartre, *Search for a Method*, p. 28; cf. p. 35.
13 Ibid., p. 28; cf. pp. 113, 135.

torian or scientist knows, to enquire about something *particular*. Thus it is, according to Sartre, that, in the state into which 'official' Marxist thought has fallen today, existentialism is indispensable as a corrective, because existentialism is concerned, above all, to 'affirm the specificity of the historical *event* . . . for almost a hundred years now, Marxists have tended not to attach much importance to the event . . . today the fact – like the person – tends to become more and more symbolic'.[14] A fact that appears *only* to have significance as an 'instance' of some general 'law' is not likely to be considered in its unique and unrepeatable specificity. 'Valéry is a petit bourgeois intellectual – no doubt about it. But not every petit bourgeois intellectual is Valéry. The heuristic inadequacy of contemporary Marxism is contained in these two sentences.'[15] Sartre's point is by no means only of importance as a reminder to the historian. It is not only the dead, but also the living, who may find themselves treated as mere 'symbols', as instances of general laws or as members of a class (and that phrase may be read in either logical or political terms).

When Sartre claims that 'The materiality of fact is of no interest to these idealists; only its symbolic implications count in their eyes. In other words, Stalinist Marxists are blind to events',[16] I am reminded of a remark of Donald MacKinnon's, commenting not on Stalinism but on certain contemporary trends in Christian theology: 'It is the fault of the idealist always to seek escape from the authority of the tragic, to avoid reckoning with the burden of inescapable fact.'[17]

The suggestion so far is that a 'materialism', such as Marx's, which affirms not only the primacy of the practical, of man's transformative activity in 'working' the circumstances of his existence, but which thereby also affirms the dialectical character of the relation between action and reflection, collapses back into 'idealism' in its *use* of its theory in the measure that those who endorse the theory suppose themselves to be in *possession* of 'true knowledge'. In answer to our first question, then, it does indeed seem possible for a theory of man and society to remain impeccably 'materialist' in its content while yet becoming 'idealist' in its use.

My second question was: in what circumstances is such a shift, or 'inversion', likely to occur? If the first question was philosophical in character, this second question would seem rather to be historical or sociological. In search of an answer, therefore, I shall turn to Kolakowski's account of the crucial role played by Lenin's doctrine

14 Ibid., p. 124.
15 Ibid., p. 56.
16 Ibid., p. 126.
17 D. M. MacKinnon, 'The Conflict Between Realism and Idealism', *Explorations in Theology, 5,* p. 164.

of the 'party' in the transformation of Marxism. I do not think that
the fact that Kolakowski has, in recent years, moved ever further
away from the Marxist tradition in which he once stood, rendering
his assessment of that tradition increasingly polemical in tone and
negative in content, deprives this illustration of validity. I offer it
simply as an indication of the kind of circumstances in which the
shift from 'critical thought' to 'dogmatism' (in Colletti's sense) is
likely to occur.

In the *Manifesto of the Communist Party*, Marx and Engels had
asked: 'In what relations do the Communists stand to the proletar-
ians as a whole?'.[18] Their answer was that 'The Communists . . .
are on the one hand, practically the most advanced and resolute
section of the working-class parties of every country, that section
which pushes forward all others; on the other hand, theoretically,
they have over the great mass of the proletariat the advantage of
clearly understanding the lines of march, the conditions, and the
ultimate general results of the proletarian movement.'[19] According
to Kolakowski, Lenin's doctrine of the party embodied a number
of important departures from this description: 'What was new in
Lenin's thought was not the idea of the party as a vanguard, leading
the working class and imbuing it with socialist consciousness. The
novelty consisted, in the first place, in his statement that the spontaneous working-class movement must have a bourgeois consciousness, since it could not develop a socialist one, and no other kind
existed. . . . This is supplemented by a second inference: the
working-class movement in the true sense of the term, i.e. a political
revolutionary movement, is defined not by being a movement of
workers but by possessing the right ideology, i.e. the Marxist one,
which is "proletarian" by definition.'[20] In these developments are
sown the seeds of 'Lenin's conviction that the party, by virtue of its
scientific knowledge of society, is the one legitimate source of political initiative. This later became the principle of the Soviet State.'[21]

The most sophisticated theoretical expression of this aspect of
Leninism is probably Lukács' essay on 'Class Consciousness', in
which he argued that 'class consciousness consists in fact of the
appropriate and rational reactions "imputed" (*zugerechnet*) to a particular position in the process of production. This consciousness is,
therefore, neither the sum nor the average of what is thought or felt
by the single individuals who make up the class.'[22] That was written
in 1920. In the following year, in an essay on 'The Marxism of Rosa
Luxemburg', Lukács firmly insisted that 'the form taken by the

18 *R1848*, p. 79.
19 *R1848*, pp. 79–80.
20 *KII*, p. 389.
21 *KII*, p. 391; cf. p. 396.
22 G. Lukács, *History and Class Consciousness*, p. 51.

class consciousness of the proletariat is the *Party* ... the Party is assigned the sublime role of *bearer of the class consciousness of the proletariat and the conscience of its historical vocation*.[23]

Max Scheler once outlined a typology of 'formal modes of thought, determined by class'.[24] The members of the Frankfurt School castigated his sketch as 'astonishingly naive', on account of the way in which it 'statically' opposed two modes of thought in a manner that was 'crude and undifferentiated', lacking 'any historical consciousness'.[25] From the standpoint of sociological theory, these criticisms seem to me to be justified. Nevertheless, if we take Scheler's contrasts, not as possessing any theoretical rigour or historical adequacy, but simply as impressionistic hints at the sociological dimension of the sort of shifts in consciousness that we are considering, then they are not, I think, lacking in suggestiveness. Here are some extracts from Scheler's classificatory scheme: 'The contemplation of becoming – lower class; the contemplation of being – upper class. . . . Realism (the world predominantly as "resistance") – lower class; idealism – upper class (the world predominantly as the "realm of ideas"). . . . Materialism – lower class; spiritualism – upper class. . . . Optimistic view of the future and looking back pessimistically to the past – lower class; pessimistic view of the future and optimistic view of the past – upper class.'[26]

Scheler's attempted distribution of these 'modes of thought' between social classes may, indeed, be highly questionable. Nevertheless, in the light of my earlier remarks, his scheme does, I think, help us to construct something like the following answer to my second question. If the shift from 'materialism' to 'idealism' is likely to occur in *theory* in the measure that the proponents of a 'materialist' method, or theory, or philosophy, illusorily suppose themselves now to be in definitive *possession* of 'the truth' concerning man and society, the circumstances in which such a shift is likely to occur in *practice* will be those in which the 'materialism' in question becomes the ideology of a group wielding social and political *power*. What was once a set of critical instruments now fulfils the function of legitimating an existing social institution.

Where Marxism is concerned, the seeds of such a shift were sown, theoretically, in the increasingly confident 'scientism' of Marx's later years (and especially in the writings of Engels); they were harvested, in practice, when Marxism became – in Russia and elsewhere – not so much a critique of the existing state of affairs as its justification.

In this chapter, we may seem to have wandered excessively far

23 Ibid., p. 41, his stress.
24 M. Scheler, *Problems of a Sociology of Knowledge*, p. 169.
25 Frankfurt Institute for Social Research, *Aspects of Sociology*, pp. 195–6.
26 Scheler, op. cit., pp. 169–70.

from Marx's own texts. Nevertheless, I hope that this excursus may help us when we come to consider the extent to which Marx's assumption, that Christianity is necessarily and in principle 'idealistic', is justified.

BASE AND SUPERSTRUCTURE

'It is not consciousness that determines life, but life that determines consciousness.'[1] I have already suggested on more than one occasion that such phrases, which contrast alternative accounts of the relationship between 'life' and 'thought', are not to be taken as denials of the effectiveness and irreducible reality of human consciousness, but rather as warnings issued against the assumption that the world of thought is autonomous, unshaped and unaffected by the concrete circumstances in which it finds expression. Behind the deceptive simplicity of such expressions there hovers the metaphor of 'inversion', and we have already seen, in Chapter Eight, how misleading this metaphor is as a description of the relationship between Marxian 'materialism' and Hegelian 'idealism'.

There are few more unsatisfactory uses of this metaphor than that which occurs, in *The German Ideology*, a few lines before the sentence with which we began: 'Men are the producers of their conceptions, ideas, etc., that is, real, active men, as they are conditioned by a definite development of their productive forces and of the intercourse corresponding to these, up to its furthest forms. . . . If in all ideology men and their circumstances appear upside-down as in a *camera obscura*, this phenomenon arises just as much from their historical life-process as the inversion of objects on the retina does from their physical life-process.'[2] We shall consider Marx's concept of 'ideology' in the following chapter. In the present context, it seems reasonable to suppose that the concept refers primarily to idealist philosophy: to 'the German ideology'. If this is correct, then Marx seems to be suggesting that, under the determining influence of a particular mode of production, and of the social relations which correspond to that mode, it is inevitable and 'natural' that people should see things 'upside-down': that they should spontaneously and naturally *assume* 'ideas' rather than socio-economic circumstances to be the driving-force of the historical process.

1 *CW5*, p. 37.
2 *CW5*, p. 36; cf. above, p. 41. For discussion of these pages from *The German Ideology*, cf. A. Giddens, *Capitalism and Modern Social Theory*, pp. 208–9; J. Plamenatz, *Karl Marx's Philosophy of Man*, pp. 211ff; M. Seliger, *The Marxist Conception of Ideology*, pp. 32–3; R. Williams, *Marxism and Literature*, p. 58.

This is a plausible interpretation, but it is not without its difficulties. How literally are we supposed to take the optical analogy? If it really is the case that the phenomenon of idealist 'inversion' arises *just as much* from a particular set of historical circumstances as does the inversion of the image on the retina from a particular set of physical circumstances (the structure of the eye), then Marx's own ability to 'rectify' his vision becomes difficult to explain. If, on the other hand, the optical analogy is only intended to act as a reminder of how difficult it is for us to think otherwise than we are conditioned, by circumstances and upbringing, to do, then surely some other analogy might have served his purpose less misleadingly? I am suggesting, firstly, that Marx's choices of metaphor often offer unnecessary ammunition to critics who suspect him of mechanistic reductionism; and, secondly, that even if he can, in fact, be cleared of this charge without too much difficulty, we are still left with the need to consider questions such as the following: in what sense does life 'determine' consciousness? Are the transactions between life and consciousness *simply* 'one-way'? Is it possible to indicate more precisely what might be meant by 'consciousness' and what by 'life'? In considering these questions, this chapter will serve as a bridge passage between Chapter Eight and the consideration of Marx's concept of 'ideology'. As a focus for the discussion I have chosen the metaphor of 'base' and 'superstructure', of which Raymond Williams has written: 'In the transition from Marx to Marxism, and in the development of mainstream Marxism itself, the proposition of the determining base and the determined superstructure has been commonly held to be the key to Marxist cultural analysis.'[3]

In the *Communist Manifesto*, Marx and Engels listed a number of 'reproaches' commonly made against communism by the bourgeoisie: that communism is destructive of property, freedom, law, culture, the family, and so on. Their countercharge was that, in each case, bourgeois criticism presupposed the eternal or 'natural' validity of those particular forms of these values or institutions which have emerged as a result of a specific mode of production: 'The selfish misconception that induces you to transform into eternal laws of nature and of reason the social forms springing from your present mode of production and form of property . . . this misconception you share with every ruling class that has preceded you.'[4] As a result, 'The charges against communism made from a religious, a philosophical, and, generally, from an ideological standpoint, are not deserving of serious attention.'[5] And they asked, with heavy irony: 'Does it require deep intuition to comprehend that

3 Williams, op. cit., p. 75.
4 *R1848*, p. 83.
5 *R1848*, p. 85.

man's ideas, views and conceptions, in one word, man's consciousness, changes with every change in the conditions of his material
existence, in his social relations and in his social life? What else
does the history of ideas prove, than that intellectual production
changes its character in proportion as material production is
changed? The ruling ideas of each age have been the ideas of its
ruling class.'[6] As polemic, this is good, vigorous stuff. And a glance
at the way in which, even today, Christians frequently conduct their
defence of the family, of 'human rights', or of private property,
suggest that this is by no means of 'merely historical' interest. Thus,
for example, the defence of 'Christian values' is often conducted in
apparent forgetfulness of the extent to which our understanding and
estimation of values and institutions is, in the concrete, a product
of our social history – and hence is suspect of embodying unawares
particular social interests. Particular conceptions of the family, or
of 'human rights', or whatever, may indeed be defensible on theological as well as on other grounds. But no form of that defence
merits 'serious attention' which uncritically supposes such conceptions to embody some transculturally, timelessly valid set of infer-
ences from scriptural or doctrinal premises. On the other hand,
precisely on account of its polemical character, the passage from
the *Communist Manifesto* minimizes to 'the point of caricature the
role of ideas in society',[7] and would therefore be an extremely
dubious basis from which to construct a 'materialist' theory of
cultural analysis.

Our metaphor first turns up in a passage written four years later.[8]
It occurs in the same paragraph in the *Eighteenth Brumaire* as the
passage which we took as the starting-point for our discussion of
the dialectic of appearance and reality:[9] 'A whole superstructure of
different and specifically formed feelings, illusions, modes of thought
and views of life arises on the basis of the different forms of property,
of the social conditions of existence. The whole class creates and
forms these out of its material foundations and the corresponding
social relations.'[10] Here, the 'superstructure' is 'the whole "ideology" of the class: its "form of consciousness"; its constitutive ways
of seeing itself in the world.'[11] In terms of the metaphor, however,
that from which this superstructure arises is not clearly indicated:
we are merely told that it arises 'on the basis of' the different forms
of property and of the social conditions of existence.

6 Loc. cit.
7 *Life*, p. 183.
8 But notice the reference in *The German Ideology* to 'naturally derived and traditional
   relations, e.g. family and political relations, together with their entire ideological
   superstructure' (*CW5*, pp. 372–3).
9 Cf. above, p. 51.
10 *SE*, p. 173.
11 Williams, *Marxism and Literature* , p. 76.

The metaphor occurs in a more developed form in a passage in the 1859 Preface to Marx's *A Contribution to the Critique of Political Economy*, a text which has been described as 'as succinct an account of the materialist conception of history as Marx ever produced'.[12] The passage, which is sufficently important to merit quoting at some length, is 'commonly taken' to be the source of 'the proposition of the determining base and the determined superstructure'.[13] Marx's study of Hegel's *Philosophy of Right* led him, he tells us, 'to the conclusion that neither legal relations nor political forms could be comprehended whether by themselves or on the basis of a so-called general development of the human mind, but that on the contrary they originate in the material conditions of life, the totality of which Hegel, following the example of English and French thinkers of the eighteenth century, embraces within the term "civil society"; that the anatomy of this civil society, however, has to be sought in political economy. . . . The general conclusion at which I arrived and which, once reached, became the guiding principle of my studies can be summarized as follows. In the social production of their existence, men inevitably enter into definite relations, which are independent of their will, namely relations of production appropriate to a given stage in the development of their material forces of production. The totality of these relations of production constitutes the economic structure of society, the real foundation, on which arises a legal and political superstructure and to which correspond definite forms of social consciousness. The mode of production of material life conditions the general process of social, political and intellectual life. It is not the consciousness of men that determines their existence, but their social existence that determines their consciousness. At a certain stage of development, the material productive forces of society come into conflict with the existing relations of production. . . . From forms of development of the productive forces these relations turn into their fetters. Then begins an era of social revolution. The changes in the economic foundation lead sooner or later to the transformation of the whole immense superstructure. In studying such transformations it is always necessary to distinguish between the material transformation of the economic conditions of production, which can be determined with the precision of natural science, and the legal, political, religious, artistic or philosophic – in short, ideological forms in which men become conscious of this conflict and fight it out. Just as one does not judge an individual by what he thinks about himself, so one cannot judge such a period of transformation by its consciousness, but, on the contrary, this consciousness must be explained from the contradic-

---

12 *Life*, p. 308.
13 Williams, op. cit., p. 75.

tions of material life, from the conflict existing between the social forces of production and the relations of production.'[14]

Both terms of the metaphor are now more clearly specified. There is a 'foundation' which consists of the 'relations of production': the relations between slave-owner and slave, capitalist and hired hand, or whatever. On this foundation of property relations and the social division of labour there arises 'the whole immense superstructure' of 'legal, political, religious, artistic or philosophic' forms. Marx's distinction between the 'forces of production' and the 'relations of production' should already alert us to the inadequacy of any 'vulgar-materialist' or mechanistically reductionist interpretation of the passage. The simple – and significant – fact is that the 'material forces of production' are not amongst the factors whose relationships the metaphor is designed directly to illuminate. It is the *relations* of production which constitute the 'foundation' or 'base'. In other words, the metaphor indicates, firstly, an irreducible distinction and, secondly, a structure of dependence, between different (and sometimes contradictory) aspects of *human relationship*. Both 'base' and 'superstructure' are relational terms, descriptive of patterns of social relationship. The account is 'materialist' inasmuch as Marx argues that it is the 'base', the economic relations obtaining in practice, which 'determine' or 'condition' the 'social relations' – legal, political, religious, artistic or philosophical – rather than the other way round.

The analogy of the individual confuses at least as much as it clarifies, on account of the ambivalence of the notion of 'consciousness'. It may be important to distinguish 'what a man thinks and says of himself' from 'what he really is and does',[15] but it would be confusing to suggest that what he really is and does he is and does 'unconsciously'. People do not usually work in their sleep: the relations of production are relations that obtain between conscious individuals. The point is, of course, that the 'form' in which these relations are mediated into consciousness are distinct from them, in principle, and may be in conflict with them in fact. The way in which we think and speak about what we are doing may bear little resemblance to whatever it is that we are 'really' up to; but it does not follow that we are really doing it unconsciously. The distinction between 'life' and 'consciousness', between 'social existence' and forms of social consciousness is, however indispensable and however fruitful if handled with care, always liable to mislead.

More generally, Marx cannot be absolved of all responsibility for the clouds of abstract and highly schematic theory which have been

14 *EW*, pp. 425–6. 'In the history of human thought there are few texts that have aroused such controversy, disagreement and conflicts of interpretation as this one' (*KI*, p. 336). We have been warned.

15 *SE*, p. 174.

spun out of his metaphor, because it is a singularly inapt metaphor
for the processes he sought to describe. These are, as the passage
as a whole makes clear, historical processes, and if there is one thing
that historical process – with its ceaselessly shifting patterns of
harmony and conflict, freedom and dependence, community and
anarchy – is *not*, it is a *building*. The relationship between the
'foundation' of a building and the 'superstructure' that 'arises' from
it is rigid, fixed and complete. Armed with this disastrous metaphor,
Marxist theories have, firstly, tended to lose sight of its *metaphorical*
character and hence to suppose its terms to be patient of clear and
uniform theoretical definition and, secondly, have taken those terms
to indicate watertight categories or areas of activity, between which
patterns of temporal or causal connection have been woven with
increasing implausibility.[16] In 'serious intellectual circles', complains Thompson, 'the argument about basis/superstructure goes *on
and on and on*. . . . A whole continent of discourse is being developed
. . . which rests, not upon the solid globe of historical evidence, but
on the precarious point of a strained metaphor.'[17] Elsewhere,
Thompson insists that 'the dialectic of social change cannot be fixed
in any metaphor that excludes human attributes';[18] no analogy
derived from any other area than historical analysis itself 'can have
any more than a limited, illustrative, metaphoric value (and often,
as with basis and superstructure, a static and damaging one)'.[19]

Notwithstanding the limitations of this most influential of Marx's
metaphors, we can still use it as a framework in which to raise three
specific issues concerning the relationship between 'social existence'
in general and particular forms of 'consciousness': the problem of
how we are to understand the contention that life 'determines' or
'conditions' consciousness; the apparent *narrowness* of the 'base' in
Marx's account; and the question of the extent to which Marx
supposed transactions between the elements of the 'base' and those
of the 'superstructure' to be simply 'one-way'.

According to Raymond Williams, 'No problem in Marxist cultural theory is more difficult than that of "determination" '.[20] And
he warns us that while 'A Marxism without some concept of determination is in effect worthless'[21] (by which I take him to mean that,
without some such concept, any 'historical materialism' would be
radically incoherent), 'A Marxism with many of the concepts of

---

16 Cf. Williams, op. cit., p. 78.
17 E. P. Thompson, 'An open Letter to Leszek Kolakowski', *The Poverty of Theory*,
    p. 120. Thompson's geographical metaphor is polemical; the target is Althusser:
    cf., e.g., *For Marx*, p. 14.
18 Thompson, 'The Pecularities of the English', *The Poverty of Theory*, p. 79.
19 Thompson, 'The Poverty of Theory', *The Poverty of Theory*, p. 276.
20 Williams, *Marxism and Literature*, p. 83.
21 Loc. cit.

determination it now has is quite radically disabled'.[22] Beginning
with the German text and English translations of the 1859 Preface,
in order to indicate the linguistic complexity of the problem, he
then distinguishes between being 'determined' in the sense of being
powerless in respect of iron laws or powerful external agencies (a
sense frequently evoked in the Marxist tradition, especially in some
of its more 'scientific' forms, but one that hardly seems demanded
or even invited by any of the passages we have so far considered)
and being 'determined' or 'determinate' in the sense of being set
within certain objective limits. Marx, he reminds us, repeatedly
used the concept in this sense: 'New social relations, and the new
kinds of activity that are possible through them, may be imagined
but cannot be achieved unless the determining limits of a particular
mode of production are surpassed in practice, by actual social
change.'[23] It is because consciousness is 'determined', in this sense,
that there are, at any particular time or place, only a limited number
of 'ideological forms' – be they legal, political, religious or philosophical – that we are, in practice, able seriously to entertain as
available options, and even fewer that can, without 'structural'
change or a transformation of the 'base', be given social, institutional expression in such a way as to correspond to, and not to
contradict, the 'reality' of our situation. (There are issues here to
which we shall return when we come to consider Marx's critique of
'utopianism'.)

If this is a plausible interpretation of part, at least, of what Marx
meant by 'determination', I can see no reason why any Christian
theologian should object to the assertion that it is, in this sense,
'social existence that determines [our] consciousness'. To say this
is not to deny, of course, that many theologians continue to operate
with presuppositions concerning the relations between 'life' and
'consciousness' that are considerably more 'abstract' or 'idealist'. I
have myself had the experience of having the modest suggestion
that, in certain circumstances, social and political change may be
a necessary precondition for an adequate understanding of the New
Testament,[24] received with a mixture of puzzlement and incredulity.

Marx's concept of 'determination' cannot be exhaustively covered
by Williams' second definition because, as he himself notes, the
sense of being set within certain objective limits too easily collapses
back into a quietism – similar to that presupposed in his first
definition – which would be quite alien to Marx's thought. As an
instance he cites a letter of Engels (which we shall consider in more
detail later on) in which the latter said that 'the historical event'

22 Loc. cit. Cf. R. Williams, 'Base and Superstructure in Marxist Cultural Theory',
   New Left Review (1973), pp. 3–16.
23 Marxism and Literature, p. 86.
24 Cf. Lash, Theology on Dover Beach, p. 76.

may 'be viewed as the product of a power which works as a whole unconsciously and without volition'.[25] Here, surely, we are back – not only behind Marx but also behind Feuerbach – into a world in which 'subject' and 'predicate' are 'inverted': a world in which it is no longer men who, in 'working' the materials of their existence, 'make history' by making themselves, but rather a mythical 'power' called 'History' which makes men. According to Williams, if we are to avoid such quietism, and the 'idealism' of which it is an expression, we have to go beyond the definitions of 'determination' so far offered, and remember that 'determination is never only the setting of limits; it is also the exertion of pressures'.[26] The objective limits within which we are set, the 'resistance' that we encounter, not only define the boundaries of action but, in doing so, call from us that resolution, that 'determination' to *endure*, in work and suffering, in the hope that these limits may thereby be transcended, which is the hallmark of authentically *human* participation in natural and historical processes. Are there not, in this cluster of meanings, reminders for a theological tradition which, in disciplining its own tendency to speculative self-indulgence, has not only insisted that the God of Christian belief is a God who, if I may so put it, disbarred idolatry by the self-destruction of his own image, but of whom it is affirmed that, in his practical recognition of the tightest of limits, in Gethsemane and on Calvary, and not in any idealistic or 'utopian' forgetfulness of them, he *thereby* exerted definitive pressure, 'determined' the course and outcome of human history?[27] The doctrine of the Cross has received a bewildering variety of interpretations in the course of Christian history but, if we read it, as we must, as a commentary on the events of Christ's passion, it is not obviously capable of being legitimately interpreted – whether in the practice of Christian living or in theological reflection – *either* in fatalist (and in *that* sense 'determinist') terms, *or* as an idealist evasion of the constraints and objective limits of the material circumstances of our existence.

Our second question concerns Marx's apparently excessive restriction of the 'base' to *economic* relations: to the 'relations of production'. If we bear in mind, once again, the *metaphorical* character of the model of 'base' and 'superstructure', and refrain from treating it as a summary statement of some putatively exhaustive theory of social and historical explanation, then this restriction is neither as surprising nor as damaging as may appear at first sight. It is not surprising because, for all the range of his interests, Marx's primary

25 F. Engels, letter to J. Bloch, 21 September 1890 (*HM*, p. 295). Cf. Williams, op. cit., p. 86.
26 Williams, op. cit., p. 87.
27 I am here drawing on remarks made elsewhere: cf. N. L. A. Lash, 'Theory, Theology and Ideology', pp. 221–2.

concern is with the analysis of one particular mode of production: that of nineteenth-century capitalism. Within that mode of production, those 'forces of production' (to which the 'base', the 'relations of production', correspond, albeit conflictually) which especially required his attention were, not only economic but also, more specifically, industrial. This is clear, as early as the Paris Manuscripts, from a passage that we have come across already: '*Industry* is the *real* historical relationship of nature, and hence of natural science, to man. . . . Hence natural science has already become – though in an *estranged* form – the basis [note that] of actual human life.'[28]

Any suggestion that Marx supposed 'industrial' activity to *exhaust* man's 'real relationship' to nature would, I think, be quite unwarranted. He never, so far as I know, attempted an exhaustive classification of the 'relations of production' but, on his own account, these must include *all* those 'definite relations' into which we 'inevitably enter', 'independent of [our] will', in 'the social production of [our] existence'.[29] I have argued that 'materialism', for Marx, refers above all to the dependence of consciousness on social, material conditions.[30] His insistence that socio-economic relations exercise a more profound, more fundamental, more 'basic' influence on the historical process than do legal structures, philosophical approaches or systems of religious belief, was intended to counter the prevailing contrary assumption that the 'realm of ideas' – legal, philosophical, political or religious – was wholly independent of the material social processes above which it, as it were, floated in serene autonomy. It is thus not surprising that, especially when armed with the unhelpfully rigid metaphor of base and superstructure, his counter-assertions should have tended to fall into the trap of simply reversing (or 'inverting') the dualism he sought to transcend.[31] If an historian, or a sociologist, or a theologian, wished, from their particular interpretative standpoint, to argue that specifically economic 'relations of production' do not exhaust those 'definite relations' into which we 'inevitably enter' independent of our will, they would find plenty of passages indicating that Marx was on their side. Nor would such a broadening of the 'base' entail the suppression of the distinction between social relations and the 'forms' in which those relations are mediated into consciousness: the distinction between 'base' and 'superstructure' or, let us rather say, between 'life' and 'consciousness', would only cease to be necessary in a situation in which 'reality' and 'appearance' wholly coincided. And we may agree with Marx (and Hegel) that there is every reason

28 'Economic and Philosophical Manuscripts', *EW,* p. 355; cf. above, pp. 100–1.
29 Preface to 'A Contribution to the Critique of Political Economy', *EW*, p. 425.
30 Cf. above, p. 102.
31 Cf. Williams, op. cit., pp. 90–4.

to suppose that, within the historical process, such a situation can never occur.

Finally: to what extent did Marx suppose the transactions between the elements of the 'base' and those of the 'superstructure' to be simply one-way? In the history of Marxist theory, a crucial text here is the letter which Engels wrote to J. Bloch in September 1890: 'According to the materialist conception of history, the *ultimately* determining element in history is the production and reproduction of real life. More than this neither Marx nor I have ever asserted. . . . The economic situation is the basis, but the various elements of the superstructure . . . also exercise their influence upon the course of the historical struggles and in many cases preponderate in determining their *form*. . . . There is an interaction of all these elements.'[32] Engels goes on to insist that 'We make our history ourselves', but that we do so 'under very definite assumptions and conditions. Among these the economic ones are ultimately decisive.'[33] The constraints to which we are subject, the resistance or objective limits that we encounter are, 'in the last resort, economic'.[34] 'Marx and I are ourselves partly to blame for the fact that the younger people sometimes lay more stress on the economic side than is due to it. We had to emphasize the main principle *vis-à-vis* our adversaries, who denied it, and we had not always the time, the place or the opportunity to give their due to the other elements involved in the interaction.'[35] In the history of commentaries on this letter, and on those features of Engels' thought which it illustrates, the key phrases have been those which refer to the 'interaction' of base and superstructure and to the determination by economic factors 'in the last resort'.

According to Kolakowski, if historical materialism is 'interpreted rigidly, it conflicts with the elementary demands of rationality; if loosely, it is a mere truism. The traditional way out of this unhappy dilemma is, of course, the qualification "in the last resort"; but Engels never explained precisely what he meant by this.'[36] But in what sense could he have been expected to do so? It is clear, from Kolakowski's later discussion of Plekhanov, that his principal target is that strand in the Marxist tradition which has attempted to construct an exhaustive, monistic explanation of history: 'Plekhanov, like many Marxists, wishes to maintain his belief in a single principle accounting for the whole of history, but not to part company with common sense which tells us that events are due in

32 *HM*, p. 294.
33 Loc. cit.
34 *HM*, p. 295.
35 *HM*, pp. 295–6. Cf. also Engels' letter to F. Mehring, 14 July 1893 (*HM*, pp. 303–5).
36 *KI*, p. 364.

general to a variety of concurrent causes. Hence the numerous reservations which are meant to attenuate the rigour of "monistic" explanation, but in fact destroy it, as the vague expression "in the last resort" finally loses its meaning when we also speak of "interaction".'[37] Whatever may be the case where 'many Marxists' are concerned, I have already indictated my own belief that Marx's 'materialism', his insistence on the dependence of consciousness on material conditions, neither prcsupposes nor entails any such 'monistic' metaphysic.[38]

Kolakowski is a philosopher. He shows little interest in attempting to understand, in all their complexity, particular historical events. Marx, on the other hand, is usually at his best when attempting to come to grips with concrete particulars – be they historical events or economic formations. If, in his sketches (such as the 1859 Preface) of the heuristic framework within which he pursued his investigations, he tended to exaggerate 'the economic side', and to understate the social and historical influence of ideas this is, as Engels indicated, in large measure due to the pressures of debate. For similar reasons Engels, in turn, in his formulation of historical materialism, tended to *under*emphasize 'the role of the economic factor. This was partly because he was writing to Marxists who had run into difficulties by applying to history too simplistic an interpretation of Marx, and was thus trying to combat the trenchant criticism being directed by non-Marxists at the crude version of the theory then available.'[39] We can agree with E. P. Thompson who, finding himself in rare partial agreement with Althusser,[40] remarks that Engels 'has not offered a solution to the problem, but restated it in new terms'.[41] Nevertheless, the problem that Engels has posed – that of the role of human agency in historical process – is 'very critical' and, 'despite deficiencies, the general tendency of [Engels'] meditation is helpful'.[42]

It is time to draw this discussion to a close. Is Marx's 'historical materialism' a 'theory' which, in its attempt to give an account of the 'laws' governing historical process, betrays its true nature as an 'historicist' conflation of history and metaphysics?[43] Were there not passages in Marx's texts which lent support to this view, it is difficult to see how it could ever have won widespread acceptance as the 'orthodox' interpretation of his meaning. Nevertheless, having

37 *KII*, p. 342.
38 Cf. above, p. 102.
39 D. McLellan, *Marxism after Marx*, p. 14.
40 Althusser analyses the letter to Bloch at somewhat tedious length in *For Marx*, pp. 117–28.
41 Thompson, *The Poverty of Theory*, p. 279.
42 Ibid., p. 280.
43 Cf. above, pp. 70–1.

regard to Marx's performance as a whole, I can only repeat that I find this interpretation most unconvincing. What Marx sought for, and what he sketched in passages such as the 1859 preface, was a *model* (rather than a 'theory') of historical process. It was a model the structure of which (misleadingly pictured in the metaphor of 'base' and 'superstructure') was designed to prevent the student of social formations from succumbing to the temptation of supposing that 'ideological forms' lead an autonomous existence, unshaped and uninfluenced by the 'relations of production'. It was, at the very least, an insistent reminder of the 'objective limits' within which those forms are set, by the structure of which they are shaped, and in respect to which their relationship may often be 'contradictory' or conflictual.

Marx's 'materialism', as I have interpreted it in these chapters, constitutes a twofold challenge to Christian religious and theological discourse and behaviour. In the first place, Christianity is concerned with the transformation of man by divine grace. It is about 're-demption' and 'salvation'. And it is undoubtedly the case that much contemporary Christian preaching and belief supposes such transformation to be, at most, a transformation of individual consciousness, rather than of the material conditions of human existence. And yet the scope for healing, for 'salvation',[44] for the achievement of 'love' and 'freedom', that is available to those individuals caught (whether as agents or victims) in inherently conflictual and oppressive structures is at best partial and at worst illusory. This is neither to deny the occurrence, nor to discount the symbolic significance, of individual instances of that remarkable and unexpected 'humanness' known as sanctity. It is merely to insist that the gospel proclaims, beyond the sporadic emergence of individual excellence, of lights that shine in the darkness, the redemption not merely of consciousness but of the world.[45]

In the second place, much Christian theological writing continues to presuppose an autonomy of 'ideas' in relation to 'institutions', of 'thought' in relation to 'life', of beliefs in relation to circumstances, which Marx was amongst the first of major European thinkers radically to call in question. Fear of 'reductionism' seems sometimes to inhibit theologians (and not only theologians!) from giving appropriate consideration to the role played by material conditions, by the 'relations of production', in determining those ideas and belief-systems to whose history and interpretation it is their business to attend.

These are only hints. In order to develop them further we need to ask: what does Marx mean by 'ideology', and in what circum-

---

44 Cf. N. L. A. Lash, *Theology on Dover Beach*, pp. 138–42.
45 Cf. the discussion of 'Event and Interpretation' in Chapter Twelve.

stances are religious and theological discourse appropriately described as 'merely' ideological?

11

IDEOLOGY

We have seen that, in the 1859 Preface to *A Contribution to the Critique of Political Economy*, Marx listed, amongst those 'definite forms of social consciousness' which 'correspond' to particular determinations of the 'legal and political superstructure',[1] 'religious, artistic' and 'philosophic' forms and that he classified all five of these 'forms' of consciousness as 'ideological'.[2] In this chapter I propose to discuss two questions: firstly, what does Marx mean by 'ideology'? secondly, in what sense and in what circumstances is Christian discourse appropriately described as 'ideological'?[3]

A number of factors combine to make this discussion somewhat complex. In the first place, there arises, in the meanings of the concept which Marx inherited,[4] in his own use of it and in its subsequent history, the problem of the relationship between ideology and error. In the second place, there is the distinct but connected question of the relationship between 'ideology' and 'science'. In the third place, many of Marx's critics belabour him for what they regard as the radically inconsistent, even contradictory, character of his uses of 'ideology'. Many of these critics overreach themselves. Seliger, for example, is so concerned to demonstrate the self-contradictory character of Marx's use of the notion[5] that his treatment of it is even less satisfactory, as exposition, than that of Plamenatz, whom Seliger rightly criticizes for erroneously asserting that Marx (rather than Engels) described ideology as 'false consciousness', without adducing 'a single reference to any Marxian text'.[6] In the fourth place, any discussion of the sense in which

---

1 *EW*, p. 425.
2 Cf. *EW*, p. 426.
3 I have taken some of the material in this chapter from N. L. A. Lash, 'Theory, Theology and Ideology'.
4 On which, cf. K. Mannheim, *Ideology and Utopia*, pp. 63–6; M. Seliger, *The Marxist Conception of Ideology*, pp. 13–9.
5 Cf. Seliger, op. cit., p. 27.
6 Seliger, op. cit., p. 31. Having asserted that 'Ideology is sometimes called "false consciousness" ', Plamenatz piles confusion upon confusion (to use his own description of Marx's treatment of ideology: cf. *Karl Marx's Philosophy of Man*, p. 86), by adding, with impressive imprecision: 'which implies that it is only a

Christian discourse is appropriately described as 'ideological' is complicated by the fact that the ways in which we 'hear' the term are filtered through the bewildering variety of its post-Marxian uses. Today, at least, it is clearly a mistake to assume 'that somehow the term "ideology", being an abstract singular, must – ultimately, in the last instance – denote a single idea, or concept'.[7]

The German Ideology is a good place to start, if only because the first chapter 'is in fact the only part of Marx's writings where the notion of ideology is discussed at any length'.[8] In that work, the uses of 'ideology' are, without exception, polemical and pejorative. Nevertheless, in spite of references to, for example, 'ideological delusion',[9] Marx nowhere simply identifies ideology with error or untruth. As we would expect from the title and target of the work, 'ideological' consciousness is, throughout, taken to be identical with 'idealism'. Thus, for example, he speaks of an 'imaginary rising above the world' as 'the ideological expression of the impotence of philosophers in face of the world'.[10] In a passage which reminds us of the charge that 'in all ideology men and their relations appear upside-down as in a *camera obscura*',[11] he says: 'It is to be noted here, as in general with ideologists, that they inevitably put the thing upside-down and regard their ideology both as the creative force and as the aim of all social relations, whereas it is only an expression and symptom of these relations.'[12] In brief, the charge against the 'German ideologists' is that 'It has not occurred to any one of these philosophers to inquire into the connection of German philosophy with German reality, the connection of their criticism with their own material surroundings'.[13] From this failure arise all 'the illusions of philosophy, the ideological, speculative expression of reality divorced from its empirical basis'.[14] That it is not only *German* idealism but idealist consciousness in general which is, in this sense, 'ideological', is indicated in a passage which Marx drafted, and then deleted (perhaps because it contained a distractingly lengthy discussion of Hegel) from the Preface: 'There is no specific difference between German idealism and the ideology of all the other nations. The latter too regards the world as dominated by ideas, ideas and

---

part of consciousness' (p. 217, my stress). Seliger's reference is to the same assertion where it occurs in Plamenatz's earlier study of *Ideology*.

7 B. Wicker, 'Marxist Science and Christian Theology', *New Blackfriars*, Vol. 58 (1977), p. 89.

8 A. Giddens, *Central Problems in Social Theory*, p. 167.

9 *CW5*, p. 180.

10 *CW5*, p. 379.

11 *CW5*, p. 36; cf. above, pp. 41, 112ff.

12 *CW5*, p. 420; cf. p. 460.

13 *CW5*, p. 30.

14 *CW5*, p. 282; cf. p. 456.

concepts as the determining principles.'[15] It is clear that, so far as this use of the concept is concerned, the charge that Christian discourse is 'ideological' is identical with the charge that it is 'idealist' in character.

However, already in *The German Ideology*, there are hints of a more general use of the term. Once the transposition has been effected from an 'idealist' to a 'materialist' way of thinking, 'Morality, religion, metaphysics, and all the rest of ideology as well as the forms of consciousness corresponding to these . . . no longer retain the semblance of independence'.[16] We are not told whether such 'forms of consciousness' and the varieties of discourse in which they find expression will survive, once they have lost 'the semblance of independence', nor indeed whether, in so far as they do survive, they are still to be characterized as, in some sense, 'ideological'. But neither possibility is explicitly excluded.

The situation becomes clearer when we turn, once again, to the 1859 Preface. Here, as we have seen, *all* forms of social consciousness (or, at least, all those that are listed) are described as 'ideological'.[17] In so far as the concept of 'ideology' is taken, as in this passage, to refer to all elements of the 'superstructure', it does not carry, at least in the abstract, any pejorative connotations. This 'neutral' use of the concept was developed by Lenin: 'Since there can be no talk of an independent ideology formulated by the working classes themselves in the process of their movement, the *only* choice is – either bourgeois or socialist ideology. There is no middle course (for mankind has not created a "third" ideology, and, moreover, in a society torn by class antagonisms there can never be a non-class or an above-class ideology).'[18] Lenin is here using the concept neutrally, or descriptively, to argue that there cannot be, in practice, any such thing as a 'neutral ideology', any more than there could, for example, be a neutral social class. We are reminded of the fact that if, in the 1859 Preface, Marx classified all forms of social consciousness as 'ideological', he also observed that it was in these 'ideological forms' that 'men become conscious of [social] conflict and fight it out'.[19]

I am suggesting, in other words, that there is, in Marx's writings, a use of the concept which is neutral or descriptive in principle, and which acquires its pejorative overtones on account of the specific contexts and social formations to which it is applied. Thus, for example, he refers, in *Capital*, to 'the capitalist and his ideologist,

---

15 *CW5*, p. 24.
16 *CW5*, pp. 36–7.
17 Preface to 'A Contribution to the Critique of Political Economy', *EW*, p. 426.
18 V. I. Lenin, 'What is to be Done?', *HM*, p. 390.
19 *EW*, p. 426.

the political economist'.[20] The work of the political economist is, we may say, 'ideological' in three senses. In the first place, as one who seeks to understand and explain capitalism, he operates in the realm of theory, of ideas, those structures and relationships which the capitalist operates in the realm of practice. In the second place, because the manner in which he does so is, in his particular case, 'idealist' (he supposes the capitalist mode of production to be, not a particular, mutable, product of history, but the expression and embodiment of 'eternal' economic verities), his work is 'ideological' in the sense in which the concept is used in *The German Ideology*.

In a situation of actual or potential social conflict, however, capitalism's claim to be simply 'the way things are' is increasingly challenged. It now becomes, and is increasingly perceived to have become, merely *one* way in which things might be: a way which is perceived to embody, not the 'general interest', but the interests of a specific, dominant social group. In such a situation, the work of the political economist becomes 'ideological' in a third sense. His function shifts from being, or apparently being, that of providing theoretical *explanation* to that of providing theoretical *justification* for particular social interests and a particular state of affairs. The 'scientist' has now become, possibly quite unwittingly, an 'apologist'. This seems to be the sense of Marx's reference, in 'The Class Struggles in France', to 'the *ideological* representatives and spokesmen of the classes mentioned, their scholars, lawyers, doctors etc., in a word, their so-called *authorities*'.[21]

It is this third and most concrete sense of 'ideology' as referring, not merely to the elements of the 'superstructure' in general or in the abstract, and not merely to the explanatory, interpretative or socially-constitutive function of these elements, but to the apologetic use to which they are put in situations of social conflict, which accounts for the polemical vigour of much of Marx's language. Thus, for example, he refers in *Capital* to 'the practical agents of capitalist production and their ideological word-spinners'.[22] More trenchantly still: in France in 1849, certain sections of the middle class looked to the working class to 'convert science from an instrument of class rule into a popular force', and to 'convert the men of science themselves from the panderers to class prejudice . . . and allies of capital into free agents of thought'.[23] And, in the 'Eighteenth Brumaire', he says of 'the general relationship between the *political and literary representatives* of a class and the class which they repre-

---

20 *Cap. I*, p. 718.
21 *SE*, p. 37.
22 *Cap. I*, p. 757.
23 'First Draft of "The Civil War in France" ', *FI*, p. 259.

sent',[24] that 'their minds are restricted by the same barriers which [the class] fails to overcome in real life'.[25]

Let us recapitulate. In its most general sense, a sense which is largely implicit in Marx's use and is more explicitly developed by Lenin, the concept of ideology refers to 'the general process of the production of meanings and ideas'[26] within a particular social formation or social class. If Marx usually, though not invariably, employs the term pejoratively, this is due to a series of further specifications to which he submitted it in the course of mounting his critique of the 'scientific', absolutist, ahistorical pretensions of bourgeois political economy.[27] The first such specification arose from his insistence that 'ideas are social products, which cannot be understood by the philosopher who stands outside history'.[28] The thought of those who suppose otherwise – be they philosophers, theologians, economists, lawyers or politicians – is 'ideological'. A second specification arose from Marx's preoccupation with the class-structure of society. Not only do social circumstances condition social consciousness, but the particular circumstances of nineteenth-century Europe, according to Marx, were those of societies locked in class conflict (even if that conflict had not, for the most part, yet become explicit). 'Fundamental to Marx's "materialism" ', says Anthony Giddens, are 'the links which are drawn between *class structure* and ideology.'[29] The class struggle is not only invisible to most members of all classes, but its invisibility is the result of the effective dissemination, as the accepted language and '*Weltanschauung*' of a society, of the ideas and beliefs of whatever group wields economic power in that society. Hence, in the quest for the 'reality' underlying the 'appearance', the 'critique of ideology' is an indispensable feature of the quest for truth. And if Marx's fire is directed most heavily at 'bourgeois' or 'capitalist' ideology, this is not because capitalist patterns of language and thought are, for some obscure reason, 'more ideological' than those of other forms of social and economic organization (except in so far as they have the specific characteristic of being 'idealist'), but because, in the social formations with which he was concerned, the structure of economic power and dominance was, in fact, capitalist.

There are, undoubtedly, inconsistencies and ambiguities in Marx's use of the concept of ideology. The extent to which these inconsistencies appear fundamentally to threaten the coherence of his treatment will partly depend on whether or not we expect to

24 *SE*, p. 177.
25 *SE*, p. 176.
26 R. Williams, *Marxism and Literature*, p. 55.
27 Cf. A. W. Gouldner, *The Dialectic of Ideology and Technology* (London 1976), p. 8.
28 A. Giddens, *Capitalism and Modern Social Theory*, p. 209.
29 Loc. cit.

find, or suppose that we ought to be able to find, in his writings, the elements of a fully elaborated '*theory* of ideology'. I do not believe that Marx had any such theory, but I have tried to indicate that, nevertheless, his uses of the concept are not thereby deprived of coherence. Seliger is perfectly correct in saying that 'Marx did not use "ideology" according to a uniform definition, and the term itself did not occupy a central position in his work'.[30] But the moral that I would draw from this is that 'ideology', in Marx's writings, is not so much a theoretical concept as a variable pointer to a cluster of related problems his discussion of which (as with his discussion of 'idealism' and 'materialism' in general) is heavily impregnated with metaphorical usage of uneven quality.

It is clear that, on Marx's account, although 'ideology' is by no means simply to be equated with error or illusion, nevertheless ideological discourse expresses, in practice, a cognitively distorted and impoverished grasp of reality. Some comments are therefore in order concerning the distinction which he sometimes draws between 'ideology' and 'science'. 'Where speculation ends', he says in *The German Ideology*, 'where real life starts, there consequently begins real, positive science, the expounding of the practical activity, of the practical process of development of men. Empty phrases about consciousness end, and real knowledge has to take their place.'[31] As I said when introducing this passage in Chapter Four, the general drift of these remarks is clear enough. However, from the fact that 'speculation', or 'ideology', is at best 'opinion', and is defective as 'knowledge', it does not follow that 'real knowledge' may be identified with 'real science'.[32] This confusion (which, in Marx's case, seems to stem from a failure to distinguish between ideology in the sense of 'form of consciousness' and ideology in the sense of 'idealism') persists to our own day. Thus, when Althusser insists that 'a "pure" science only exists on condition that it continually frees itself from the ideology which occupies it, haunts it, or lies in wait for it',[33] he appears to be reminding us not only of the irreducible tension between 'scientific' discourse and other modes of knowledge, but also of the heightening of that tension which results from the recognition that scientific discourse never wholly 'escapes' from the concrete particularity of the ordinary language of social relationshps and 'common-sense' perception. Nevertheless, the manner in which he sets up this regulative ideal of scientific 'purity' seems to carry the unwarranted implication that only 'scientific' discourse constitutes a mode of *knowledge*. Thus, for example, he announces that 'ideology as a system of representations, is distinguished from

30 Seliger, *The Marxist Conception of Ideology*, p. 26.
31 *CW5*, p. 37.
32 Cf. above, p. 42.
33 L. Althusser, *For Marx*, p. 170.

science in that in it the practico-social function is more important than the theoretical function (*function as knowledge*)'.[34]

Any such restrictive identification of 'science' with 'real knowledge' (and I turned to Althusser only because his work represents, on this point at least, a powerful development of seeds sown in Marx's writings) must certainly be disallowed, and for at least two reasons. In the first place, any such distinction arbitrarily excludes from the range of modes of knowledge first-order, pre-reflexive modes of cognition. To follow Marx, and Althusser, in restricting 'real knowledge' to 'scientific' or theoretical apprehension is to deny that most people know the vast majority of the things that they not unreasonably suppose themselves to know. But the housewife *does* 'know' the price of butter and most of us may legitimately claim to 'know', albeit imperfectly, our friends. 'There is', says Mannheim, 'a type of knowledge . . . whose first assumption is the fact that we come to know our associates only in living and acting with them.'[35] In other words, the undoubted occurrence of that 'personal knowledge' which is the fruit of shared life, work and activity, constitutes a second reason for disallowing any reductive identification of 'knowledge' with *theoretical* knowledge, with 'science'. I am not suggesting that Marx denied the truthfulness, the 'reality and power', of either of these modes of knowledge, but only that, in *The German Ideology*, the contrast between 'ideology' and 'science' is drawn in a thoroughly misleading manner which was to have considerable repercussions in the subsequent history of Marxist theory.

In the light of this sketch of Marx's uses of the concept of ideology, let me now turn to my second question: in what sense and in what circumstances is Christian discourse appropriately described as 'ideological'? Both the practice of faith (including its symbolic expression in ritual) and theoretical reflection on the past history and present forms of that practice are, in all circumstances, 'ideological' in the sense that they are aspects of social consciousness, 'superstructural' forms, social products. The 'problem' of ideology arises, in the first instance, however, not from the fact that our ideas are social products, but from our 'forgetfulness' of this fact. We tend to be forgetful both of the objective limits that 'determine' our perception of our circumstances and of the extent to which the way we think, and perceive, and argue, reflects underlying patterns of

34 Ibid., p. 231, my stress. Commenting on his treatment of *The German Ideology*, Althusser later (1974) appeared to acknowledge the legitimacy of some of the criticisms that had been made of his handling of the distinction between 'science' and 'ideology': cf. 'Science and Ideology', *Essays in Self-Criticism*, pp. 119–25. It is, however, difficult to know quite what to make of his retractions. As Thompson remarks, they are either marginal and heavily qualified or 'so large that, if taken seriously, they call in question the earlier work *in toto*' (*The Poverty of Theory*, p. 391).

35 Mannheim, *Ideology and Utopia*, pp. 150–1.

social division and dominance. The struggle for the accurate 'description' of reality[36] thus becomes an aspect of the struggle for social change. The symbolic forms in which we express our social relations constitute, at one and the same time, the form of our freedom and a threat to that freedom. The fragile identity and security achieved by social legitimation, whether religious or secular, is a form of freedom from insecurity, meaninglessness and anarchy. But, in so far as we claim for such partial and particular achievements of freedom a universality and absoluteness which they do not, in fact, possess (and such a claim may be made either practically, through the exercise of power, or theoretically), we mistake 'appearance' for 'reality' and render these achievements forms of unfreedom and oppression.[37] In other words, it is as true for religious as for other social institutions that the discourse in which we express or articulate our situation can also serve to disguise, from ourselves and from others, the reality of that situation. If Christian discourse is not to become idolatrous, it must be permanently inconoclastic. The continual 'critique of ideology' is as necessary for the truthfulness and 'reality' of religious behaviour and language as for all other aspects of social consciousness.

In other words, if it is true that legal or political systems (without which no society can exist or function) may, while *appearing* to represent the general interest, in *fact* only represent the interests of a particular group, the same is true of the symbol systems of Christianity. Similarly, if it is true that economic or anthropological theory may appear to express 'universal' truths while in fact only reflecting the features of an historically specific situation, the same is true of Christian theology. This is one way, for example, of describing the ambivalence that unavoidably attends the celebration of the Eucharist and the theology of the Church. Christians do not possess any mechanisms or devices that could in principle preserve their forms of discourse, whether religious or theological, from degenerating into 'instruments of class rule'. At this level, the question as to whether the practice of faith and theological reflection are 'ideological' is one that cannot be answered in the abstract, but only by the critical examination of particular instances.

I see no reason, therefore, for denying that, so long as conflictual patterns of social existence endure, the truthfulness of Christianity is permanently threatened by 'ideological distortion'. But I should wish to argue that it follows from this that theological enquiry should include the attempted critique of its own ideological elements. In view of the fact, firstly, that Marx regarded it as axiomatic that religous belief did not and could not constitute a mode of 'real

36 Cf. *CW5*, p. 37.
37 Cf. Lash, *Theology on Dover Beach*, pp. 142–7.

knowledge' and that, secondly, he supposed all theology to be
necessarily 'ideological' (in the sense of 'idealist'), he would have
dismissed as ridiculous the suggestion that theological reflection on
religious illusion could itself contribute to the critique of ideology.
I am here touching on issues which we shall discuss in the following
two chapters but, even at this stage, there are two comments that
are in order.

In the first place, I have drawn attention to Marx's misleading
tendency to contrast 'ideology' with 'science' on the basis of a
reductive identification of 'real knowledge' with theoretical or 'scientific' knowledge, and I have insisted that our knowledge of other
persons is not less real for being 'practical' rather than 'theoretical'
in character. Our self-knowledge and our knowledge of other persons is 'ideological' in the sense that it is 'conditioned' or 'determined' by our historical and social circumstances: the stock of
imaginative, conceptual and evaluative resources that are, *in practice*,
available to us is exceedingly limited. It follows that our knowledge
of God (if such knowledge there be) is similarly determined. In this
sense Christian belief, as the thematization or categorial expression
of faith's dark knowledge of the mystery of God is, like other social
expressions of personal knowledge, 'ideological'. It is ideological in
the further sense that, in religious matters as in secular, we tend to
be 'forgetful' of the limits to which our knowledge is subject. But to
concede that religious belief is, in both senses, 'ideological', is by
no means indiscriminately to admit its false or illusory character.
Whether or not human experience is experience of God, and hence
personal or 'experiential' knowledge of God (whatever the conceptual and symbolic forms, theistic or other, in which such experiential
knowledge is categorically 'objectified') is, in terms of our discussion
so far, quite certainly an *open* question.

In the second place, in so far as 'ideology' *is* defined in contradistinction from 'theory', then those primary modes of discourse
which are constitutive of Christian religious practice are undoubtedly 'ideological', for their characteristic form is not theoretical, but
narrative, self-involving, autobiographical. The Christian believer
is a story-teller, and the story that he tells is of a process in which
he acknowledges himself to be a participant. And if it is true that
the tale that he tells is, like any autobiography, threatened with
illusion and distortion, it is also true that only in the telling of the
tale does the process of human, historical existence achieve conscious expression. The telling of the tale is certainly not a sufficient
condition of Christian truthfulness (any more than the production
of any people's sagas is a sufficient condition of the truthfulness of
their self-perception) but it is a necessary condition. The task of
theology, as critical reflection on religious practice, is to elucidate
the truth-conditions of the tale and thus to contribute to the assess-

ment of the truthfulness of its telling. If we take 'rationality' to be 'the capacity to make problematic what had hitherto been treated as given',[38] then there will be objective limits, in practice, to the extent and the manner in which either the theologian or (for example) the social 'scientist' can hope to fulfil their critical responsibilities. But I see no reason (other than prejudice) for supposing that, in principle, the theologian's rationality is any more circumscribed or inhibited than that of the social scientist.

Implied in my distinction between religious practice and theological reflection is the claim that, in so far as there are irreducibly distinct (though interdependent) forms of social consciousness – 'legal, political, religious, artistic and philosophic',[39] for example – there are also formally distinct (though interdependent) modes of theoretical criticism. Whether or not a single 'human science' (let alone a unified science of man and nature)[40] is an ideal, it is most certainly not a fact. In other words, my claim concerning the unsurpassable pluralism of modes of criticism embodies a plea for the relative autonomy of theological enquiry *vis-à-vis* other modes of reflective discourse. Clearly it is not possible here even to begin to substantiate such a claim. It is sufficient to recognize that the question as to whether or not such a claim is justifiable is, once again, at least an open question.

38 Gouldner, op. cit., p. 49.
39 Cf. *EW*, p. 426.
40 Cf. above, pp. 100–1.

12

CHRISTIAN MATERIALISM

Lenin's *Materialism and Empirio-Criticism* is, philosophically, an unsophisticated work. Conceptual precision was not, however, its author's principal concern: 'The basic conception in the book was that two philosophical schools confronted each other: materialism and idealism. The slightest concession to idealism would objectively give aid and succour to the bourgeoisie by ending up in fideism and religion.'[1] Thus it is that Lenin's unmasking of the 'stupid claim' of Mach, Avenarius and others 'to have "risen above" materialism and idealism',[2] is set in the context of an examination of 'the relation between Machism and religion'.[3] 'The connection of idealism with political reaction is most clearly shown by the fact, which Lenin regards as obvious, that all forms of idealism and, particularly, epistemological subjectivism are buttresses of religious faith.'[4] Lenin's crude simplicities are a caricature of Marx's thought on these matters. Nevertheless, as with any caricature, they highlight features of the original. The connections between 'religion' and 'idealism' are as insistently and as confidently made by Marx as by Lenin. Both Marx and Lenin would have regarded the very title of this chapter as dangerous, mystifying nonsense.

Some of the components of Marx's assumption that religious and theological discourse are necessarily 'idealist' in character have been indicated in the previous four chapters. In this chapter, I want to pause in my exposition of central themes in Marx's thought in order to offer some reflections on this assumption. From some points of view, these reflections are premature: we have not yet discussed Marx's critique of religion (and hence the specific form of his atheism), his concept of 'alienation', or his observations on the future and destiny of man. It may nevertheless be helpful, even at this stage, to consider some of the senses in which Christian religion and theology might, in principle, be said to be 'materialist' rather than 'idealist' in character, and also the circumstances in which it would,

---

1 D. McLellan, *Marxism after Marx*, pp. 106–7. Cf. V. I. Lenin, *Materialism and Empirio-Criticism*, pp. 406–20.
2 Lenin, op. cit., p. 414.
3 Ibid., p. 406.
4 *KII*, p. 452.

in practice, be appropriate thus to describe them. The distinction is important because Marx not only believed that, as a matter of fact, the history of Christianity was a history of complicity between theology and ideologies of social dominance, but that this complicity was inevitable in view of the necessarily 'idealist' character of all theological discourse.

Materialism and Christian Belief

There are, undoubtedly, forms of 'materialism' that are incompatible with Christianity. Amongst these I would include both those mentioned by Professor Flew.[5] In view of the fact, however, that – as I argued in Chapter Eight – Marx was not a 'materialist' in either of these senses, they need not detain us for long. I do not believe that Christianity is compatible either with a metaphysical monism which asserts that, in the last report, 'all that is is stuff', or – in principle – with that form of 'worldliness' which Marx described as the deification of money. I say 'in principle', because the 'God' whom we worship is the ultimate object of our trust and, in order to discover where it is that Christians, or anyone else, ultimately place their trust, it is insufficient merely to *ask* them: there is, individually and socially, a distinction to be made between self-description and actuality, between the account that we give and 'our real organization and real interests',[6] between 'appearance' and 'reality'. Whether or not I 'really' believe in God or, put it another way, what 'God' it is in whom I really believe, is something that I can never with complete assurance know.

If Marx's 'materialism' neither expressed nor entailed a metaphysical monism, an 'absolute materialism', it was nevertheless 'naturalistic' in the sense that he took it for granted that the 'natural' – including the human, and hence such human products as images and ideas – exhausts the totality of actual and possible objects of action and discourse. From this point of view, Marxian materialism, considered as a theoretical doctrine, is undoubtedly incompatible with belief in the reality of a God who is other than, and not reducible to the status of, a product of human thought and imagination. Marx was an atheist. But is belief in the reality of such a God compatible with the conviction that all that occurs, in nature and history, is explicable, in so far as it is explicable at all, without direct reference to the reality or agency of God? If it is, then there would seem to be at least a *prima facie* case for supposing that 'religious materialism' is not necessarily a contradiction in terms. That there are no insuperable logical difficulties inherent in such a

5 Cf. above, pp. 88–9.
6 *SE*, p. 174.

position is suggested, for example, by the phenomenon of deism, at least some forms of which would seem to be thoroughly 'materialist' in character. However, in view of the fact that it is just these forms of deistic belief which tend, in the uses to which they are put, to amount to what is nowadays often called 'practical atheism', they would have been seen by Marx as encouraging evidence of the erosion of religious belief.[7] As such, they would have been of little interest to him; nor need they further concern us.

Questions concerning the compatibility of belief in the reality of God with the conviction that all that occurs is explicable without direct reference to the reality or agency of God are not, of course questions that admit of any simple or straightforward answer. Or, at least, they do not so admit when the God in question is one of whom it is said that he is 'the Father of our Lord Jesus Christ', who has 'sent his Spirit into our hearts'. They are highly complex questions, central to a whole range of issues that have, in one form or another, preoccupied Christian theologians for centuries: issues concerning the senses in which the concept of God may or may not function as an element in causal explanations; issues concerning the meaning of 'divine action', of 'acts of God', of 'divine intervention', revelation and miracle. For Marx, of course, such questions do not and cannot arise. But, given that such questions necessarily arise for the Christian believer, do they necessarily do so in a manner which demands, either in practice or in theory, in behaviour or in description, an 'idealist' rather than a 'materialist' response? We shall fill this question in, render it less abstract, as we proceed; in the meantime, the following two sets of considerations may help us to get our bearings.

In the first place, Christian belief in God is clearly incompatible with 'materialism', in Marx's sense, in so far as it leads the believer to suppose that the appropriate stance in respect of the future is simply to wait and see what happens: to wait and see what God does next. Such a stance (the political form of which would be probably 'reactionary' and certainly not 'revolutionary') presupposes that divine agency is to be considered as in some sense an *alternative* to natural or human agency. And if there have been some Christians who have supposed such 'historical quietism' to be an appropriate expression of their faith – at least in relation to certain aspects of their existence, such as ill-health – there have been others who have supposed that what happens in the future depends upon what human beings do, and upon the 'resistance' they encounter from natural and social forces, and who have further supposed such conviction to be quite compatible with their trust in divine agency:

7 'For materialists, deism is but an easy-going way of getting rid of religion' (Karl Marx, *The Holy Family* [*CW4*, p. 129]).

in grace and providence. From the standpoint of Christian theology, it is not irrelevant to point out that Jesus' behaviour, in his journey to Jerusalem, in Gethsemane and on Calvary, although expressing an acceptance of his fate, was yet hardly a form of 'historical quietism'. He acted out his unswerving trust in his Father in a manner which indicated that he supposed there to be that which, if it was to be achieved, had to be done by him.

In the second place, Christian belief is clearly incompatible with 'materialism' in Marx's sense (and, for that matter, with Hegelian idealism also) in so far as it leads the believer to suppose that there are, or can be, events or situations in which the experience of God is *unmediated*. There are Christians whose accounts of divine inspiration, of revelation, of miracle, and even of faith and conversion, seem to presuppose the possibility of such unmediated experience of God. There are others, however, who would insist that the God of Christian belief can only 'appear' in natural and historical events as the unfathomable and hidden mystery which those events exemplify and signify; that there cannot be any question of 'pure' and unmediated theophany. That is to say: there cannot be any experience, any event, any series of events, any individual, or any institution, such that the only correct account of it would be that it expressed the mystery of God. The recognition of God's 'appearing' in natural and historical events is expressed in language which thus interprets those events. But the religious interpretation of an event is no more a substitute for, or competing alternative to, such natural or historical interpretations of the event as may be available than is, for example, its interpretation in poetry. Natural or historical explanations may constitute the 'only scientific' explanations that are available,[8] but it does not follow that religious or poetic interpretations contribute nothing to our knowledge or true understanding of the event. Nor, from the fact that religious interpretation is not 'scientific', does it necessarily follow that it is 'idealist' in character.[9]

In other words, if there are Christians whose religious attitudes and theological descriptions presuppose that divine agency is to be considered an alternative or a complement to human and natural agency, there are also Christians whose religious attitudes and theological descriptions presuppose that there is no single 'logic of action' capable of encompassing the human and the divine, and that it can therefore be said – quite simply, and without prejudice to the dependence of nature and history on divine grace – that it is human beings, products of their nature and history, and not anything else, who are the subjects of all action and all consciousness. If we allow

8 Cf. above, p. 102.
9 Cf. above, pp. 130–3.

that 'idealism' and 'materialism' may be contrasted as comprehensively as they were, for example, by Lenin, then the former approach would seem to be 'idealist', and the latter 'materialist' in character. It follows that the debate between 'idealism' and 'materialism' is and has long been *internal* to Christian theology – a possibility of which Marxist theorists, partly as a result of their ignorance of such theology, regularly fail to take account. In order to develop this suggestion (my remarks so far have been little more than a preliminary impressionistic skirmish) we must now consider, somewhat more exactly, why it is that Marx supposed that *all* theological discourse was, in the last resort, necessarily 'idealist' in character and function.

We have seen that the 'materialism' of both Feuerbach and Marx was initially formulated as a critique of Hegel's 'inversion' of 'subject' and 'predicate'. The central thrust of such a materialism is the insistence that it is human beings, and not 'mind' or 'reason', who are the subjects of action and discourse. Inasmuch as 'mind' or 'reason' is an aspect, but only an aspect, of human reality, idealism is criticized for its *abstractness*, for mistaking the part for the whole, and for hypostatizing the abstraction, thus making it appear that it is 'mind' and not men, thoughts and not people, that make history. It is instructive to notice that Colletti, in the discussion of Hegel which introduces his polemic against Marxist (post-Marxian) 'dialectical materialism', never questions the assumption that polarities such as 'infinite-finite', 'ideal-real', 'thought-thing', or 'God-world', are more or less interchangeable.[10] Thus, for example, while criticizing Hegel for 'taking reason, not as an attribute and property of the natural being that is man, but as God, *Logos*, Christian Spirit',[11] he does not pause to consider whether the theological dimension of Hegel's philosophy is, from the standpoint of the history of Christianity, unusual or eccentric. Quite the contrary: 'Here', says Colletti, 'is the really decisive point: the substantification of reason *as a consequence of the Christian posture*, i.e. as a consequence of the equation of reason with spirit and therefore with God. . . . This *Christian posture* is the real pivotal point of all Hegel's thought'.[12]

Colletti shows little interest in or familiarity with the history of Christian theology. He contents himself with gesturing references to something called 'the Platonic-Christian tradition', a defining characteristic of which is its *'negative* conception of the sensate or finite particular'.[13] On Hegel's dictum, in *The Science of Logic*, that 'The idealism of philosophy consists in nothing else than in recog-

---

10 Cf. L. Colletti, *Marxism and Hegel*, pp. 7–27.
11 Colletti, op. cit., p. 32.
12 Ibid., pp. 32, 33, my stress.
13 Ibid., p. 34; cf. pp. 14, 17.

nizing that the finite has no veritable being',[14] Colletti comments: 'The subsequent elucidation, in which Hegel extends the identity of philosophy and idealism to the identity of idealism and religion, *idealism and Christianity*, follows logically and comes as no surprise.'[15]

Marx took over, unexamined, this identification of Christianity and 'idealism', with its consequent suppression of the reality and significance of concrete individuals. And he did so, not out of absent-mindedness, but because this identification illuminated certain features of bourgeois society: of a social formation whose 'ideology' was 'idealist'.[16] Thus Colletti maintains that the 'intuition of the connection between Christianity and bourgeois "civil society" . . . is the focal problem for Hegel and Marx'.[17] 'Those institutions of the bourgeois world which Hegel regards as the realization of God and therefore as the sensuous incarnations of the supra-sensible . . . appear to Marx in the same light. . . . The difference is only [!] that whereas Hegel sees the actualization of God in the supra-sensible's becoming sensate, Marx (who obviously reasons in a way that goes beyond the Christian horizon) sees a process whereby *forces alienated and estranged* from mankind become present and real, beginning with capital and the State themselves.'[18] And he quotes Marx's *Theories of Surplus Value*: 'Christianity is . . . the special religion of capital. In both it is only man in the abstract who counts. . . . In the one case, all depends on whether or not he has faith, in the other, on whether or not he has credit.'[19] In the light of such connections, it is not surprising that 'The theme of the link between bourgeois society and Christianity is the leitmotiv . . . of all [Marx's] early writings',[20] and that 'the link between capitalism and Christianity is a constant and reiterated theme in Marx's work'.[21]

I have been following Colletti because he accurately highlights the grounds of Marx's conviction that Christian theological discourse is inherently idealist and hence that the complicity between Christianity and capitalism is rooted in the logic of both systems and is not something which merely happened to be the case in particular social and historical circumstances. In other words, it follows from Marx's understanding of the 'grammar' of all theological discourse that there could never be a form of Christianity which

14 G. W. F. Hegel, *Science of Logic*, tr. A. V. Miller, p. 154.
15 Colletti, op. cit., p. 7, his stress.
16 Cf. above, p. 112.
17 Colletti, op. cit., p. 266.
18 Ibid., pp. 270–1, his stress.
19 Marx, *Theories of Surplus Value*, tr. J. Cohen and S. W. Ryazanskaya, Vol. iii, p. 448; quoted Colletti, *Marxism and Hegel*, p. 27. And notice Colletti's reference to 'the "abstract man" of Christianity' (p. 276).
20 Colletti, op. cit., p. 272.
21 Loc. cit.

was anti-capitalist and yet authentically Christian. (Many capitalists, of course, have supposed the same thing!)

What are we to make of all this? To begin with, it must be
admitted that if, as Marx and most Marxists assume, Feuerbach's
account of the logic of religious and theological discourse is correct;
if, in other words, 'God' is and can only be the name for a symbolic
projection of certain features (positive or negative) of human experience (and this is something which we shall discuss in the following chapter); then the characterization of the concept of God as
an abstraction is entirely justified. In other words, if Feuerbach's
account of the reference of theological discourse is correct, then all
theological propositions – propositions of which 'God' is the subject
– need to be 'stood on their feet again' and re-expressed as propositions of which the subject is humanity and not (with an eye to
Marx's criticism of Feuerbach) simply 'humanity' in the abstract,
but specific, concrete individual human beings and social formations. If, however, we suppose that of which Christians seek to
speak when they speak of 'God' to be the eternal creative and
transformative mystery on which all nature and all history is radically dependent; if, in other words, the term 'God' does have concrete reference (even if we can never demonstrate this to be the
case); then how can the reality of God 'appear' in our language?
Or, to put it another way, can the reality of God appear in our
language in a way that does not, in fact, ineluctably lead to just
that depreciation of the reality and significance of concrete particulars against which Marx protested? If there is God, how can we so
think and speak of God as yet to treat with appropriate seriousness
the limits and capacities, the achievements and the failures, the
slavery and the freedom, of human beings?

This is, I shall suggest, both a theoretical and a practical problem.
It is a problem that concerns not only the possibility of appropriate
speech about God but also the uses to which such speech is put,
the functions it is made to serve. And the first thing to be said, I
believe, is that any form of Christian belief, or any system of Christian theology, which supposes itself to be in possession of ready-
made theoretical 'solutions' to this twofold dilemma has thereby
demonstrated its 'idealist' character. A theology that cannot conceive the possibility of its categories being broken, its language
rendered incoherent, thereby declares its conviction that 'theory' is
primary in respect of 'practice', reflection in respect of experience.

Consider, for example, the implications of our discussion, in
Chapter Ten, of the 'determination' of consciousness. 'If', says E.
P. Thompson, 'we are to employ the (difficult) notion that social
being determines social consciousness, how are we to suppose that
this is so? . . . What we mean is that changes take place which give
rise to changed *experience*: and that this experience is *determining*, in

the sense that it exerts pressure upon existent social consciousness, proposes new questions, and affords much of the material which the more elaborated intellectual exercises are about.'[22] Now, if it is true that much late seventeenth- and eighteenth-century theology was 'idealist' in the sense that it sought to protect its utterances and arguments from the corrosive consequences of the 'pressure' exerted by changing circumstances; that it sought to proceed by 'proof' rather than by risking permanent enquiry; it is also true that the history of Protestant theology since Schleiermacher, and of Catholic theology since the Modernist crisis, has been a history of continual and varied attempts to re-establish that primacy of experience which was characteristic of the best efforts of both patristic and medieval theology.

But what do we mean by 'experience'? It is, after all, not only possible for a theology to appeal to the primacy of experience, of faith, work, prayer and suffering, in a highly abstract manner; it is also possible for the range of experience to which appeal is made to be excessively narrow. For a theology that sought to be, in Marx's sense, 'materialist', it would be necessary for it to attend, at least in principle, to the whole range of 'social being', and not simply to supposedly 'religious' or 'spiritual' aspects of human life and ex- perience. This being said, however, there seems no reason why historical theology, for example, should not be 'materialist' in char- acter. It does, after all, as Kolakowski has said, make 'an essential difference . . . whether the history of Christianity is presented as an intellectual struggle about dogmas and interpretations of doctrine, or whether these are regarded as the manifestation of the life of Christian communities subject to all manner of historical contin- gency and to the social conflicts of successive ages'.[23] In the light of our discussion in Chapters Ten and Eleven, we might add that although there is a danger that the latter approach to historical theology will be 'reductionist' in character, it need not necessarily be so. The 'relative autonomy' of the 'superstructure' is no more, and no less, of a problem for the history of theology than for the history of science, law, politics or art.

It is time to return to the fundamental problem: namely, the possibility of discourse concerning God and his relationship to man which does not idealistically 'invert' the 'subject' and 'predicate' of historical action. Neither Marx nor (it would seem) Colletti devoted much time or energy to the study of Christian theology. They both take for granted the representative character of Hegelian theology. In view of the fact that the intellectual climate in which Marx worked was saturated with such theology, this assumption is more

22 E. P. Thompson, *The Poverty of Theory*, p. 200.
23 *KII*, p. 369.

excusable in his case than in that of his followers. Nevertheless, it needs to be questioned. More precisely, we need to question the assumption that the characteristic 'posture' of Christian theology consists in nothing else than the recognition that the finite has no veritable being.[24] For Hegel, according to Colletti, 'the problem of philosophy is the *realization* of idealism, the realization of the Idea or the infinite, the Christian *Logos*'.[25] If this is a philosophy of incarnation, the only incarnation that it knows negates, rather than affirms, the reality and autonomy of particular flesh. In so far as the Word becomes flesh, the flesh ceases to enjoy reality and autonomy: 'In Hegel's original conception . . . the world was negated in order to give way to the immanentization of God.'[26] From the point of view of Marx's critique of Hegel, it matters little that this 'negation' is subsumption into the Idea, rather than mere annihilation. There is no denying that Christianity, in its thought and in its patterns of behaviour, in its theology, preaching and organization, has frequently denied the 'true being' of the finite, has depreciated the particularities of the flesh, in a manner that justifies this aspect of the Marxian critique. But what is completely absent from Marx's writings is any hint of a recognition that this is only part of the story: that centuries of strenuous and by no means wholly unsuccessful effort have been devoted to elucidating the conviction that 'the autonomy of the creature does not grow in inverse but in direct proportion to the degree of the creature's dependence on, and belonging to, God'.[27] Marx never wavered in his conviction that 'The more man puts into God, the less he retains within himself'.[28]

At the heart of the Christian faith is the conviction that God has expressed himself concretely in our history, has become part of the form and meaning and texture of that history, as a man. The logic of the language in which such conviction is articulated is necessarily paradoxical, firstly, because the manner of the fulfilment of its truth-conditions is necessarily unknown to us and, secondly, because this conviction concerns not only past occurrence but also future fulfilment: christological language speaks of one man who died, but it does so in the context of eschatological hope concerning the outcome of that human future for the construction of which we acknowledge, in the employment of such language, our responsibility to work. The hope articulated in christological confession may be unfounded or illusory, but it is a hope that declares not the

---

24 Cf. above, pp. 139–40.
25 Colletti, op. cit., p. 267.
26 Ibid., p. 80.
27 K. Rahner, 'Thoughts on the Possibility of Belief Today', *Theological Investigations*, *Vol. V*, tr. K.-H. Kruger, p. 12.
28 'Economic and Philosophical Manuscripts', *EW*, p. 324.

negation but the affirmation, not the denial but the establishment of authentic humanity.

The assertion that Jesus Christ is 'truly God and truly man' is not, grammatically, a description of any kind of *process*, whether historical or metahistorical (whatever that would mean). It is not a narrative statement. Nevertheless, because the language of Christology purports to interpret human history, it is inevitable that it will include statements in narrative form. And amongst the most ancient and influential narrative expressions of Christian faith is the assertion that 'the Word became flesh'. And immediately our worst suspicions are aroused. Surely, if ever there was an 'idealist' statement, an inversion of subject and predicate, this is it? But the author of the Fourth Gospel was not an Hegelian philosopher. 'The Word became flesh' is not a description of historical process but a celebration of divine grace. If we wished to give the doctrine narrative expression in the form of an *historical* statement, a description of historical process, that statement might be: the flesh became Word. Human history produced, from its own resources (which are, not *alternative* to divine resources – to the resources of grace – but their contingent, empirical form), the individual in whom the mystery of God and his promise is historically actualized, disclosed, shown, spoken. In *every* birth the flesh becomes word: a child cries. And the birth, or becoming, or 'historical production' of the Christ is no exception. But in *that* child's cry, and its consummation in the cry on the cross, there is uttered by man, in human flesh, the reality and mystery of God. The 'materialist' assertion that 'the flesh became Word' does not contradict the assertion that 'the Word became flesh', but gives it historical expression.

The peculiar difficulty of Christian theological discourse arises from the fact that there is no common 'logical space' occupied jointly by both God and man. There is no class of which both God and man are mutually exclusive members. It follows that the only logic appropriate to theological discourse would be, if I may so put it, a 'broken' logic. But we do not possess such a tool. In so far as we speak of God and man in the same breath, we are obliged to do so in sentences the form of which suggests that we have to choose: either (with Hegel) 'God' as subject, and human existence as predicate, or (with Feuerbach) 'man' as subject and God as predicated abstraction. In reality the dilemma is unreal. In 'appearance' – in the form of our language – it is unavoidable. Therefore, the only course open to us (and it is a course which has been adopted, in a variety of ways, from the beginning of Christianity) is to proceed dialectically: to acknowledge that there is no one proposition, or set of propositions, in which the consciousness of faith can 'settle'. Our positive religious assertions are in need of continual corrective negation or critical purification.

What are the parameters within which this purification, this disciplining of religious exuberance takes place? They are, or should be, if our Christian discourse is not to become 'idealist' in character, the concrete and specific circumstances in which we work and suffer, for it is these circumstances which 'determine' our discourse. A theology which supposed itself entitled to 'freewheel', unconstrained by the actual circumstances of our existence, would justify E. P. Thompson's unfriendly reference to 'the difference between a mature intellectual discipline and a merely-ideological formation (theology, astrology, some parts of bourgeois sociology and of orthodox Stalinist Marxism)', a difference which consists in the former's submission to appropriately rigorous empirical 'procedures and controls'.[29]

One more comment, before taking the argument a step further. The Christian theologian works within a tradition of action and discourse: he cannot arbitrarily select his symbols. God has no proper name, no name that we could properly employ, but amongst the richest and most ancient of the names that the theologian inherits from the past are those which, under the cultural pressure of the tradition of German idealism, are best calculated to distort theological consciousness. Thus, for example, the recommendation that the mystery of God be 'named' as 'Spirit' or 'Word' carries with it the insidious suggestion that God relates to man more immediately in the realm of the 'ideal' than the 'real', more immediately in the imagined clarity of 'mind' than in the obscure turbulence of 'matter'. As a result, naming God as 'Word' or 'Spirit' may tempt us to seek him in the illusory security of the 'idea'; it may, in other words, tempt us to suppose that our relationship with God is to be theoretically rather than practically secured: that it is in argument rather than in action, prayer, relationship and suffering, that we come to know God. Rationalism is always 'idealist' in character.

Event and Interpretation

Christian religious and theological discourse purport to interpret human history; of that there can be no doubt, irrespective of whether Christian interpretation is – either necessarily or contingently, either in principle or as a matter of empirical fact – 'idealist' or 'materialist' in character. If the assumption (shared by Feuerbach and Marx, and central to their characterization of Christianity as necessarily idealist) that the concept of God has and can only have abstract, 'ideal' reference is, as a matter of fact, unwarranted; if, that is to say, the question at issue as between Christian theism and

---

29 Thompson, op. cit., p. 204; cf. pp. 216, 225.

Feuerbachian atheism is to be regarded as an *open* question; we would still be left with the possibility that Christianity, as interpretative of historical events and circumstances, is *only* interpretative and not transformative. If this were the case, then however 'materialist' the Christian perception of the 'determination' of 'social consciousness' by 'social being', and however 'materialist' the grammar of its historical discourse, 'Christian materialism' would still be no more than a 'contemplative' materialism, a way of looking at the world rather than a way of changing it. 'Christian materialism' in *this* sense would thus be fully exposed to Marx's critique of Feuerbach.[30]

Consider the doctrine of redemption. A form of Christianity from which the proclamation of the fact and possibility of man's redemption had been evacuated is unthinkable: however difficult it may be to specify the 'essence' of Christianity, the doctrine of redemption undoubtedly pertains to that essence. Christianity is a religion of redemption. And to speak of man as in process of being 'redeemed' is to speak of man as in process of being in *some* sense 'transformed'. But is the 'transformation' of which the doctrine of redemption speaks a transformation of 'consciousness' or a transformation of 'circumstances'? And if it is both, then under what conditions might these two aspects of the transformation of man be made to coincide? If these questions echo Marx's third 'Thesis on Feuerbach',[31] they also remind us of long-standing debates between 'objective' and 'subjective' theories of atonement, debates which illustrate the unending 'conflict between realism and idealism' in Christian theology.[32]

In order to clarify matters, it may be helpful to return, once again, to Hegel. According to J. N. Findlay, 'Hegel's philosophy is essentially a philosophy of redemption.'[33] As such, it is an interpretation of human history in terms of its redemption. It would, however, be misleading to describe it as 'merely' an interpretation, as if the philosopher stood outside, was wholly external to, the process he sought to articulate. For Hegel, philosophy, as knowledge of redemption, itself contributes to the achievement of that which it knows; philosophy, interpreting history in redemptive terms, is itself a constitutive factor in the redemptive process. As Kolakowski puts it: 'Hegel is not writing *about* the Mind: he is writing the Mind's autobiography.'[34] Nevertheless, it is, in the last resort, consciousness

---

30 Cf. especially the first and fifth of the 'Theses on Feuerbach', *EW*, pp. 421–2.
31 Cf. *EW*, p. 422.
32 Cf. D. M. MacKinnon, 'The Conflict Between Realism and Idealism', *Explorations in Theology, 5*, pp. 151–65, esp. pp. 157–9, 164–5.
33 J. N. Findlay, 'Foreword' to G. W. F. Hegel, *Phenomenology of Spirit*, p. xxvii.
34 *KI*, p. 60.

and consciousness alone that both redeems and is redeemed, transforms and is transformed. Hegel is an idealist.

Christian theology interprets history in redemptive terms. And it
is not difficult to present Christian theology as a narrative, symbolic
correlate of philosophical knowledge. Christian theology can thus
be said to be at one and the same time a redemptive interpretation
of history and a constituent factor in the process of redemption. It
follows that, if the Christian religion is reducible to theology or to
the consciousness of faith, then Christianity may be said to be a
religion of redemption, but only in the sense that it articulates, *in*
consciousness, the redemptive transformation of the human mind.

In the section on 'Revealed Religion' in the *Phenomenology*, Hegel
says of the circumstances in which 'absolute Spirit has given itself
implicitly the shape of self-consciousness, and therefore has also given
it for its *consciousness*', that 'this now appears as the *belief of the world*
that Spirit is *immediately present* as a self-conscious Being, i.e. as an
actual man . . . this self-consciousness is not imagination, but is *actual*
in the believer'.[35] And he adds: 'This incarnation of the divine
being, or the fact that it essentially and directly has the shape of
self-consciousness, is the simple content of the absolute religion.'[36]
Both the form and content of 'absolute religion' are here presented
as modes of consciousness. The emphasis is, throughout, on incarnation and belief in incarnation as modifications of consciousness,
rather than on incarnation as a transformation of 'circumstances',
as an event or occurrence distinct in principle from the categories
of its interpretation.

I began this section by acknowledging that Christian religious
and theological discourse purport to interpret human history. I now
wish to suggest that a form of Christianity which confined itself to
interpretative activity would either be 'idealist' in character or, by
laying all the emphasis on the transformation of *consciousness*, would
leave untouched that dualism of life and thought, of (material)
circumstances and self-transformation which Marx criticized in
Feuerbach. In other words, all talk of Christianity as an 'interpretation' of history tends either towards 'idealism' or towards Feuerbachian 'one-sidedness'. History demands not merely to be
interpreted, but to be changed. And it is not only our consciousness
that needs to be changed, but the circumstances in which that
consciousness finds expression. Christianity is not redemptive if it
merely interprets. And Christianity is only 'one-sidedly' – and
hence, in the last resort, impotently – transformative if it limits the
scope of its transformative activity to the form or content of consciousness. The world is not redeemed, *all* things are not made

35 Hegel, *Phenomenology*, p. 458, his stress.
36 Ibid., p. 459.

new,[37] either if we merely interpret the history of the world in redemptive terms, or if the only redemptive transformation that we seek to effect is a transformation of consciousness. It is our circumstances and not simply our states of mind, the bondage of the body and not simply the bondage of the will, that cry out for redemptive transformation. Only a form of Christian life and activity which contributed, in fact, to the liberating transformation of the material circumstances of human existence, a form of Christianity in which growth in faith, hope and charity (the aspects of 'human activity or self-changing' known to theology as conversion by God's redeeming grace) 'coincided', in socially transformative practice, with 'the changing of circumstances',[38] could be said to be 'materialist' in Marx's sense.[39] Conversely, it would be difficult to withhold the epithet 'materialist' from a form of Christianity which thus contributed in fact, and which saw itself in its theology of redemption as thus contributing, to the liberation of mankind.

The extent to which Christianity has, in different ways and in different situations, taken such form is for the historian of Christianity to decide. The question is an empirical one. Marx was not a church historian. It was not the history of Christianity, but its dominant contemporary forms, which were of interest to him. Unfortunately, his criticism of Christianity as *necessarily* 'idealist' did not sufficiently conform to his own criteria of materialist method. He did not proceed by 'empirical observation . . . in each separate instance',[40] but supposed himself entitled, on the basis of philosophical considerations concerning the 'abstract' character of theological discourse, and of his experience of one particular historical form of Christianity, to make general assertions concerning the necessarily idealist nature and ideological social functions of Christianity. My concern, therefore, in this as in the previous section, has been to suggest that the conflict between 'idealism' and 'materialism' is and has long been *internal* to Christian religious practice and to the theology which informs that practice. And, as in the previous section, I have not attempted to disguise my personal conviction that it is the 'materialist' rather than the 'idealist' forms of Christianity which conform most closely to the demands of obedience to the gospel.

---

37 Cf. Revelation 21:5.
38 *EW*, p. 422.
39 The extent to which the scope of such redemptive transformation is, within the historical process, bounded by unsurpassable constraints (as the fact of individual and social mortality would suggest), and the implications of such limitation for the theory and practice of 'revolution', are matters that we shall consider in a later chapter.
40 *CW5*, p. 35.

Materialist Theory and Idealist Practice

If Marx was correct in supposing that Christian theology has often been 'idealist' in character, that it has often inverted the 'subject' and 'predicate' of historical action in such a way as to deprive the 'finite' of 'veritable being', thus diminishing or threatening the autonomy and freedom of men and women, he was incorrect in supposing such 'idealism' to be a necessary consequence of the logic of religious belief. Similarly, if he was correct in supposing that Christianity had often shown itself to be, in practice, an aspect of the ideological legitimation of structures of social dominance, he was incorrect in supposing that it necessarily exercised this social function. The situation is complicated by the fact that it is possible for a theory of God, man and society to be 'materialist' in its formulation (in its insistence, for example, that it is human beings, and not 'mind' or 'ideas', that are the subjects of historical action) while yet betraying its 'idealism' in the uses to which the theory is put. By way of conclusion, therefore, I would like briefly to indicate the implications for Christian life and thought of the problems that we discussed in Chapter Nine. The suggestion will be, as it was in that chapter, that ideas used as instruments of power transform the quest for truth into the attempted retention of private property.

Christianity is especially vulnerable to the emergence of contradictions between the 'materialism' of its theoretical insistence on the primacy of experience and the 'idealism' of the use to which such theory is put, on account of its conviction that one particular historical event – a word once spoken, a deed once done, a life once lived, in our distant past – is of definitive and unsurpassable significance. Armed with this conviction, Christian hope, Christian trust in the fidelity of a God who has irrevocably declared himself to be 'with' man, 'on man's side', only too easily gives way to the illusory assumption that Christians now *possess* the truth, that 'knowledge is already *given*'.[41] The Christian relationship to truth ceases to be exploratory, interrogative, trustful, vulnerable to circumstance and experience. Its theology becomes a 'system of *closure* . . . self-sufficient, self-validating, self-extrapolating'.[42]

And yet it is not the *givenness* of knowledge that is the problem, so much as our habit of mistaking the nature of a gift: of supposing that 'an object is only ours . . . when we directly possess' it.[43] Knowledge of God, like knowledge of other persons, is indeed donated rather than invented, received rather than constructed. In

---

41 Colletti, *Marxism and Hegel*, p. 90; cf. above, p. 106.
42 E. P. Thompson, *The Poverty of Theory*, p. 359, on the fate of 'Marxism' as a 'finite conceptual system'. In the same passage he remarks: 'In disallowing empirical enquiry, the mind is confined for ever within the compound of the mind' (loc. cit.).
43 *EW*, p. 351.

human relationships, to transmute donation into possession is to exploit the other person, to deny his humanity, his transcendence, by treating him as a commodity at our disposal. In the relation of faith, to transmute donation into possession is to deny the divinity, the transcendence, of God by treating his truth as a commodity at our disposal. In both cases, the alchemy which seeks to transform gift and giver alike into private property dehumanizes the alchemist.

A form of Christianity which supposes itself to be in possession of the truth tends inexorably to absolutize the particular linguistic, ritual and institutional forms in which truth has found expression in the past. Changes in circumstance and experience which call in question inherited forms and categories are perceived as a threat to that truth which we suppose ourselves to possess. Idealism, as the absolutization of 'abstractions', of particular aspects, forms and expressions of truth, is socially reactionary and religiously idolatrous.

On a dialectical account of the relation between practice and theory, experience and reflection, knowledge of the truth – whether knowledge of God, knowledge of man or knowledge of nature – is never a possession, but is always a relationship, a task and a responsibility. The knowledge to which Christian faith lays claim is the knowledge (which forms the substance of its hope) that human beings are enabled by the creative and transformative grace of God to perform that task and to shoulder that responsibility. In many circumstances there is no darker knowledge than this certainty that despair is unjustified.

Finally, if the shift from 'materialism' to 'idealism', in the uses to which theology is put, occurs in the measure that Christians suppose themselves to be in *possession* of the truth concerning God, man and society, the circumstances in which such a shift is likely to occur will be those in which theological discourse becomes the ideology of a group wielding social and political power. As an instrument of power, theology ceases to exercise a critical role, and comes instead to fulfil the function of legitimating existing social institutions.[44]

There are two distinct but related contexts in which theological discourse is liable thus to abdicate its critical responsibilities. On the one hand, if Marx incorrectly assumed that the complicity between Christian theology and ideologies of social dominance was inevitable, he was perfectly correct in observing that such complicity had been a depressingly frequent feature of Christian history. There is, however, a distinction to be drawn. It is no criticism of Christian theology, in principle, that – along with legal, political, artistic and philosophical 'ideological forms' – it should be found to exercise a socially integrative function. Social existence without symbolic in-

44 Cf. above, p. 110.

tegration and, in *that* sense, without 'ideology', is impossible. The ideological function of Christian theology only contradicts the universalist and redemptive character of the gospel in so far as, under the guise of representing the 'general interest' (God's promise for mankind) it serves, in fact, merely to legitimate the particular interests of a specific, dominant social group.[45] It is difficult to imagine a more profound misuse of a message proclaiming good news to the poor, release to the captives, and liberty to the oppressed,[46] than that it should serve, in practice, to legitimate structures of social dominance.

On the other hand, the corruption of theology by power can occur, not only in the context of its general social role, but also, more narrowly, within the life and organization of the believing community. Church leaders have a responsibility to foster the protection of the identity of the movement in which they hold office. They have a responsibility to ensure that, in their churches, it is the gospel of Jesus Christ, and not some other message, that is proclaimed, embodied and borne witness to. But, in the measure that their authority equips them with power, they will be tempted to suppose themselves to be the one legitimate source of practical and theological initiative,[47] and to construe all challenges to their power as threats not only to their authority but to the authority of the gospel.

These are familiar themes. Nevertheless, they serve to remind us that when the language of Christian belief becomes 'idealist' in 'the *use* which . . . it makes of its concepts',[48] this form of 'idealism' is recognizable *as* a misuse on ancient, familiar and widely accepted criteria of Christian truthfulness. Perhaps we could say that the tension between 'constantinianism', 'priestly power' and the prophetic criticism of institutional distortions, is yet another indication of the extent to which the conflict between 'idealism' and 'materialism' is and has long been *internal* to Christianity.

Conclusion

Thirty years ago, the distinguished Christian philosopher Michael Foster remarked that 'Christianity is itself opposed to idealism, and it seems to me that the Christian should agree with almost all the criticism which the Marxist brings against idealism'.[49] In the light of our discussion of the range of meanings of 'materialism' and

45 Cf. above, pp. 128, 132.
46 Cf. Luke 4: 18.
47 Cf. above, p. 109.
48 J.-P. Sartre, *Search for a Method*, p. 29.
49 M. B. Foster, 'Historical Materialism', *Christian Faith and Communist Faith*, ed. D. M. MacKinnon, p. 90.

'idealism' in Marx's writings, in Chapters Eight, Ten and Eleven, that judgement appears to be a considerable oversimplification. Nevertheless, in this chapter I have tried to suggest some of the senses in which, contrary to the assumptions of most Marxists and indeed most Christians, the concept of 'Christian materialism' is neither as novel nor as eccentric as it might appear to be.

I have also hinted at the extent to which Marx's conviction that Christian discourse was necessarily 'idealist' in character and in social function was grounded in a particular understanding of the nature of religious belief and theological language. We must now move on, therefore, to consider, in rather more detail, Marx's critique of religion.

13

THE CRITICISM OF RELIGION

It may seem surprising that, in a study of Marx's thought by a
Christian theologian, Marx's critique of religion should receive only
cursory treatment at a fairly late stage in the proceedings. There
are, however, a number of reasons for this. In the first place, this
book would never have been written had I not been convinced that
the most basic questions which Marx puts to the practice of Christianity, and to the reflection on that practice which is Christian
theology, arise from his treatment of those themes which are discussed in previous and subsequent chapters, rather than from his
explicit consideration of religious belief and practice. In the second
place, we have already discussed some aspects of Marx's view of
Christianity (such as his claim that it is necessarily 'idealist') and
there are others that we shall consider in due course. In the third
place, Marx's writings, except in the earliest period, contain very
little direct engagement with religious or explicitly theological issues. Much of what he has to say about religion in general, and
Christianity in particular, is 'ill-informed',[1] and very little of it is
original.

Although 'Marx's writings have their initial source in the critique
of religion as formulated by . . . Feuerbach'[2] and others, his attention soon shifted elsewhere. While he continued to regard religion
as important in *practice* inasmuch as 'the purely spiritual compen-
sation it afforded men detracted from efforts at material better-
ment',[3] he came to regard it as *theoretically* uninteresting because 'its
true nature had been fully exposed . . . by his colleagues – particularly by Feuerbach. It was only a secondary phenomenon and,
being dependent on socio-economic circumstances, merited no independent criticism.'[4] Thus, in 1843, in his 'Contribution to the
Critique of Hegel's Philosophy of Right', he said: 'For Germany,
the criticism of religion has been essentially completed, and the
criticism of religion is the prerequisite [*Voraussetzung*] of all criti-

---

1 Cf. D. B. McKown, *The Classical Marxist Critiques of Religion*, p. 6.
2 A. Giddens, *Capitalism and Modern Social Theory*, p. 205.
3 *Life*, p. 89.
4 Loc. cit.

cism.'[5] A year earlier, he had written to Ruge: 'Religion has no content of its own and lives not from heaven but from earth, and falls of itself with the dissolution of the inverted reality whose theory it is.'[6]

In this chapter, I intend to lead the discussion towards a consideration of Marx's conviction that, because 'religion has no content of its own', therefore, uniquely amongst the 'ideological forms' that constitute the social 'superstructure', religious belief and practice would – in a classless, non-alienated society – lack any post-revolutionary correlate. There is, however, one preliminary question to be considered: namely, was Marx an atheist because he accepted the account of theistic beliefs offered by Feuerbach and Bauer?

Put thus, the question might imply that they helped Marx to become an atheist. But there is a sense in which Marx, unlike Engels, never having been a religious believer, did not need to 'become' an atheist. Lobkowicz's reference to 'the complete lack [in Marx] of what one might call "religious experience" ',[7] may be unhelpfully imprecise and, to that extent, 'misleading',[8] but even McKown acknowledges Marx's 'fragmentary religious involvement' and admits that he passed from 'an "extremely cerebral 'Christianity' to the atheism of the Young Hegelians" swiftly, if not so smoothly as Lobkowicz would have it'.[9] There is, so far as I know, no evidence that the adoption, at an early age, of an explicitly atheistic standpoint, was, for Marx, in any sense a *costly* process. Even if, as we shall see, his criticism of religion was more sensitive, less crudely uncomprehending, than Lenin's, the only 'religion' that he, personally, ever embraced, seems to have been exclusively an affair of the head: no biographer of Marx would need to devote so much as a paragraph to his 'spirituality', or to the experience of prayer. Perhaps we could say that Feuerbach and others helped

5 *EW*, p. 423.

6 Quoted *Life*, p. 58. Feuerbach used similar language: 'Religion has no material exclusively of its own' (*The Essence of Christianity*, p. 22). According to Zvi Rosen, however, who argues that the influence of Feuerbach on Marx has been overestimated, and that of Bruno Bauer underestimated, every phrase in the sentence quoted in the text is of 'characteristically Bauerian origin' (*Bruno Bauer and Karl Marx*, p. 138). A similar case to Rosen's is vigorously argued for by K. L. Clarkson and D. J. Hawkin, 'Marx on Religion: The Influence of Bruno Bauer and Ludwig Feuerbach on his Thought and its Implications for the Christian-Marxist Dialogue', *Scottish Journal of Theology*, Vol. 36 (1978), pp. 535–55. For a more 'old-fashioned' view of Feuerbach's influence on Marx's atheism, cf. B. Romeyer, 'L'Athéisme Marxiste', *Archives de Philosophie*, Vol. 15 (1939), pp. 293–353.

7 N. Lobkowicz, 'Karl Marx's Attitude Toward Religion', *The Review of Politics*, Vol. 26 (1964), p. 328.

8 Cf. McKown, op. cit., p. 15.

9 Ibid., p. 16. The quotation is from Lobkowicz, art. cit., p. 330.

Marx to make in his head a move that he never needed to make in his heart.

The 'Essence of Christianity'

The incompatibility of religious faith and 'scientific' knowledge, which has come to be regarded as axiomatic in Marxist theory, has its roots in Feuerbach's account of Christianity (behind which hovers the shadow of Hegel's treatment of the relationship between 'religion' and 'philosophy'). According to Feuerbach, religious faith expresses in images anthropological convictions the appropriate theoretical or philosophical form of which is necessarily atheistic. 'Thus Christ, as the consciousness of love, is the consciousness of the species. . . . [But] when there arises the consciousness of the species as a species, the idea of humanity as a whole, Christ disappears, without, however, his true nature disappearing; for he was the substitute for the consciousness of the species, the image under which it was made present to the people.'[10] The images of God, or of Christ, that form the content of religious faith, are thus the imaginative preconceptual projections of human self-understanding: 'The essence of religion is the immediate, involuntary, unconscious contemplation of the human nature as another, a distinct nature.'[11] To retain these images, once reason has awakened and, even worse, to affirm the reality of their referent as other than humanity itself, is at one and the same time to deny reality to the human and to act as a brake on authentically human, rational development. 'When the heavenly life is a truth, the earthly life is a lie; when imagination is all, reality is nothing.'[12]

Defining culture as 'the exaltation of the individual above his subjectivity to objective universal ideas',[13] Feuerbach asked: 'Did Christianity conquer a single philosopher, historian or poet of the classical period? The philosophers who went over to Christianity, were feeble, contemptible philosophers. . . . The decline of culture was identical with the victory of Christianity.'[14] It is somewhat ironic that this élitist assessment of the culturally regressive nature of Christianity will become, in Marx's hands, the doctrine that Christianity is necessarily politically reactionary.

'God', for Feuerbach, 'is the idea which supplies the lack of theory . . . he is the night of theory.'[15] It follows, according to him, that the enterprise of Christian *theology*, as the attempt to give theoretical

---

10 Feuerbach, *The Essence of Christianity*, p. 269.
11 Ibid., p. 213.
12 Ibid., p. 161.
13 Ibid., p. 132.
14 Loc. cit.
15 Ibid., p. 193.

expression to the content of religious faith is, as it were, a series of
category mistakes. 'When this projected image of human nature
[i.e. God as entertained in the religious imagination] is made an
object of reflection, of theology, it becomes an inexhaustible mine
of falsehoods, illusions, contradictions, and sophism.'[16]

Feuerbach's grasp of the history of Christianity is as fragmentary
as it is distorted by his theoretical preconceptions. The dialectic, or
tension, between the spontaneity of living faith and the tentativity
of critical reflection, between 'faith' and 'reason', between (in Newman's sense) 'religion' and 'theology', is presented as if the latter
pole of the dialectic were, historically, a late arrival. Thus, only
someone amazingly ignorant of the Neoplatonism of the Fathers,
and of the apophaticism that is so striking a feature of much medieval theology and spirituality, could assert that 'The theory that
God cannot be defined, and consequently cannot be known by man,
is . . . the offspring of recent times, a product of modern unbelief'.[17]
In other words, Feuerbach takes it for granted that the affirmation
of the incomprehensibility of God is an expression of the practical
atheism of the eighteenth century: an indication that God 'has no
longer any interest for the intellect'.[18]

All the themes that I have touched upon are present in Marx's
account of religious belief and practice, either as background assumptions or as explicit features of his own critique. They are
present, however, with a difference. Feuerbach's answer to the question: 'Why should religion disappear?' would seem to allow for 'the
abolition of religion independently of the social revolution, simply
in terms of the progress of science'.[19] Although, as we shall see, this
rationalist position is not wholly absent from Marx's thought (and
re-emerges, powerfully, in Engels), it is subordinate to his more
fundamental conviction that the abolition of religion demands, as
a necessary and sufficient condition, the transformation of those
social conditions which, under capitalism, foster its survival. As
Lobkowicz puts it: whereas 'Feuerbach and the Left Hegelians
viewed religion simply as wrong ideology . . . Marx considered it as
the reflection of a wrong world.'[20]

'Man Makes Religion'

The best-known of Marx's comments on religion are to be found in
the opening section of the 'Contribution to the Critique of Hegel's
Philosophy of Right'. 'The foundation of irreligious criticism', says

16 Ibid., pp. 213–4.
17 Ibid., p. 14.
18 Ibid., p. 15.
19 Lobkowicz, art. cit., p. 327.
20 Ibid., p. 321.

Marx, is: '*Man makes religion*, religion does not make man.'[21] We are back in the familiar territory of 'inverting' the 'inversion' of 'subject and predicate'. The Feuerbachian overtones of the next sentence are clear: 'Religion is indeed the self-consciousness and self-esteem of man who has either not yet won through to himself or has already lost himself again.'[22] Inasmuch as man is thus 'self-lost', self-estranged or, shall we say, 'alienated', religion expresses what is truly the human condition. But, by mislocating the sources of our alienation, religion contributes to the estrangement which it expresses, deflecting us from the task of coming to grips, in practice and in theory, with the real causes of human bondage.

'This state and this society produce religion', he continues, 'which is an inverted consciousness of the world, because they are an inverted world. . . . The struggle against religion is therefore indirectly the struggle against that world whose spiritual aroma is religion.'[23] Over twenty years later, in *Capital*, Marx will say the same thing more straightforwardly, less rhetorically: 'The religious reflections of the real world can . . . vanish only when the practical relations of everyday life between man and man, and man and nature, generally present themselves to him in a transparent and rational form.'[24]

The first thing to be said about such passages is that they echo certain perennial themes in mainstream Christian theology. In a world in which all men, in unrestricted brotherhood, experienced in *fact* − and not just in hope or ambition − full communion of life and love, there would be no need for, and hence no place for, symbolic and dramatic expressions of human community. In a world in which appearance and reality, fact and project, fully coincided, there would be no place for the celebration of sacraments. Symbolic, sacramental celebration is celebration of that which is not yet fully in fact, but only (at most) incipiently, in hope and in promise, the case. When what Marx himself called the 'total redemption of humanity'[25] has been achieved, when all forms of alienation have been superseded, then human existence will not require those structures of mediation that are, at present, indispensable. Thus, to anticipate an analogy which we shall discuss in more detail later on: just as man's relationship to man, his social existence, will not require objectification in the structure of the state, so also his religious existence, his relationship to God, will not require objectification in religious symbols, images and con-

21 *EW*, p. 244.
22 Loc. cit.
23 Loc. cit.
24 *Cap. I*, p. 173.
25 *EW*, p. 256.

cepts. There will be no place for the 'temple', for the human phenomenon of religion, when we know as we are known.

In a word, Christian theology has traditionally acknowledged
that, in the Kingdom of God, there will be no place for those
mediating structures of sign and symbol which constitute the human
phenomenon of religion. This acknowledgement implies (and
Christians have all too often lost sight of this implication) that
Christianity is inherently iconoclastic, suspicious of its own anthropomorphism, because the mistaken identification of the image for
the reality, the sign for the signified, the Church for the Kingdom,
is the fundamental form of idolatry.

The question to Marx (and to the Christian) is: in what sense,
and within what limits, is the realization of the state of affairs which
he prospects as the necessary and sufficient condition of 'the abolition of religion' – a state of affairs in which 'the practical relations
of everyday life . . . present themselves to man in a transparent and
rational form'[26] – an *intra-historical project?* This form of the question
about the realization of truth, about the coincidence of 'appearance'
and 'reality', raises questions concerning Marx's eschatology which
we shall consider in a later chapter.

And the question to the Christian (and to Marx) is: in so far as
Christianity deploys, in practice and in theory, its iconoclastic resources, does it not necessarily exercise a subversive rather than a
legitimatory role in respect of all absolutizations of particular historical mediations – whether social or ecclesial, political or sacramental? This is, in fact, three questions: a question to the theologian
concerning what is in principle the case; a question to the historian
concerning the extent to which this subversive or critical dimension
of Christianity has found, in fact, significant practical and theoretical expression; and a question to the social scientist concerning the
'material conditions' under which this aspect of Christianity is likely
to prove capable of effective deployment.

Opium and Endurance

Let me now return to the text of the 1843 article on Hegel. '*Religious*
suffering is at one and the same time the *expression* of real suffering
and a protest against real suffering. Religion is the sigh of the
oppressed creature, the heart of a heartless world and the soul of
soulless conditions. It is the *opium* of the people. The abolition of
religion as the *illusory* happiness of the people is the demand for
their *real* happiness. . . . The criticism of religion is therefore in
embryo the *criticism of that vale of tears* of which religion is the *halo.*'[27]

26 *Cap. I*, p. 173.
27 *EW*, p. 244. On the background to the 'opium' metaphor, cf. Rosen, op. cit.,
   pp. 140–1.

The extent to which this passage expresses a sensitive, if partial, recognition of the social function exercised by religion in certain circumstances can be highlighted by comparing it with Lenin's paraphrase, written in 1905: 'Religion is opium for the people. Religion is a sort of spiritual booze, in which the slaves of capital drown their human image, their demand for a life more or less worthy of man.'[28]

The contrast between the two passages arises partly from the fact that Lenin's attention is focused on capitalism and its 'religious ideologists' disseminating the 'booze' to tranquillize the enslaved people, whereas Marx concentrates not on the oppressor but on the oppressed (hence the shift from 'opium *of*' to 'opium *for*' the people). But Lenin's version is also less sophisticated in its failure to appreciate that religion, as described by Marx, *is* 'a protest against real suffering'. Because it is (as Marx believes) a protest grounded in illusion, therefore it distracts from the struggle to overthrow the causes of suffering. Nevertheless, the religious protest is not characterized in Marx's version, as it is in Lenin's, as *mere* distraction. However unsatisfactory and illusory its form, it *is*, for Marx, 'the sigh of the oppressed creature, the heart of a heartless world'. Thus, for example, Kautsky's account of the role played by religious associations in the Roman Empire at the time of the birth of Christianity is far closer to Marx than to Lenin: 'The only societies that maintained themselves under the Empire were religious ones, but it would be taking a mistaken view of them to let the religious form ... obscure the social content underlying all these associations which gave them their strength: the desire for a solution to the hopeless existing conditions, for higher forms of society, for close co-operation and mutual support on the part of individuals lost in their isolation who drew new joy and courage from their coming together for high purposes.'[29]

Shortly after the passage from which I have quoted already, Lenin insists that 'under no circumstances ought we to fall into the error of posing the religious question in an abstract, idealist fashion, as an "intellectual" question unconnected with the class struggle. ... It would be bourgeois narrow-mindedness to forget that the yoke of religion that weighs upon mankind is *merely* a product and reflection of the economic yoke within society.'[30] It may well be the case that, in social situations marked by class conflict, the forms of religion do indeed 'reflect' the interests of the conflicting parties, and that it would therefore be a mistake to consider the meaning or truth of religious beliefs in idealistic forgetfulness of this fact. It does not follow, however – as Lenin as-

28 V. I. Lenin, 'Socialism and Religion', *HM*, p. 411.
29 K. Kautsky, *Foundations of Christianity*, p. 137.
30 Lenin, op. cit., pp. 413, 414, my stress.

sumes without argument – that the truth-content of religious forms is exhausted by the circumstances they 'reflect' and the social functions which they serve. In other words, Lenin's 'merely', which makes explicit one of Marx's major presuppositions, serves as a reminder that, just as Marx (as we saw in the previous chapter) illegitimately generalized his accusation that Christianity is 'idealist' in character, so also his lack of *theoretical* interest in religion led him illegitimately to assume *both* that he was entitled to move from a critique of the function of religion in 'this state' and 'this society' to a general account of the social function of Christianity *and* that it could be taken for granted that the interest and significance of Christianity has been exhausted once it has been perceived that it expresses and 'reflects' underlying social disorders.

Lenin's image of the 'yoke' echoes an image which Marx used in the same passage in the 1843 article: 'Criticism', he said, 'has plucked the imaginary flowers on the chain not in order that man shall continue to bear the chain but so that he shall throw off the chain and pluck the living flower. . . . It is therefore the *task of history*, once the *other-world of truth* has vanished, to establish the *truth of this world*. . . . Thus the criticism of heaven turns into criticism of earth, the *criticism of religion* into the *criticism of law* and the *criticism of theology* into the *criticism of politics*.'[31]

There can be little doubt that Christianity has sometimes served the function of social 'yoke', to keep the potentially turbulent 'lower orders' in their place, or that the produce of the 'garden of the soul' has sometimes served to decorate the chains of human bondage. Lenin's choice of metaphor is evidence of his assumption that the image of God is *necessarily* that of an 'alien', oppressive being, the 'reflection' of earthly tyranny – whether natural or social. As Marx's interest shifts from the 'anthropology' of his early writings to the more determinate critique of political economy, his assumptions concerning that which images of God 'reflect' move, we might say, from a position close to Feuerbach's to one indistinguishable from Lenin's. Even if we grant, however, that the images of God that find readiest acceptance will be images that 'reflect' the prevailing natural or social conditions – and thus that, in the measure that human beings *are* at the mercy of alien forces, their images of God will frequently tend to 'reflect' this fact – only on a rigorously deterministic account of the relationship between social being and social consciousness could the possibility be excluded that such imagery may be subjected to criticism. I have already argued, in Chapter Ten, that Marx's account is not deterministic in this sense (and indeed, if it were, his own critical activity would be quite inexplicable). But while Marx recognized the necessity for political

31 *EW*, pp. 244–5.

and economic criticism of such images of the divine, under the influence of Feuerbach he never seriously considered the possibility that oppressive anthropomorphism allows not only of political but also of *theological* criticism. And yet it is just this possibility that must be insisted on by a Christian affirmation of faith in a God who, radically transcending all symbols and images, is yet the enabling heart of human action and possibility. A form of Christianity insistently critical of its own anthropomorphism calls for a theology that is, at least implicitly, critical of the material and social conditions which generate and foster such anthropomorphism. We have already touched on this topic earlier in this chapter, and I shall return to it in Chapter Fourteen.

If we now turn to Marx's acknowledgement that '*Religious* suffering is at one and the same time the *expression* of real suffering and a protest against real suffering',[32] it is important to ask: what forms of 'protest' are appropriate in different circumstances? Thus, for example, in situations in which the means lie to hand to alleviate 'real suffering' – by political action, agricultural or educational development, or the deployment of medical skills and resources, for example – Christian hope should serve as a stimulant, and not as a narcotic. There will often, as a result, be a struggle between conflicting forms of Christian belief, a struggle which reflects, even if it does not 'merely' reflect, the underlying conflict of particular social interests. It is not, I think, completely unrealistic to expect that Christian hope, as the 'form' (in Kautsky's sense) of social action, may sometimes moderate the violence of such conflicts.

There are situations, however (and we shall see, when we come to discuss Marx's critique of 'utopianism', that he was well aware of the fact) in which the means whereby particular forms of suffering might be alleviated are not to hand. What are the forms of 'protest' appropriate in *such* circumstances? Both the Christian and the Marxist would agree that, in such circumstances, despair is inappropriate: it is, however explicable, an abdication of the dignity and responsibility of human existence. Whereas, however, the only alternative that is open to the atheist is a stoic 'acceptance' of the inevitable (and the forms of such stoicism are often impressive in their dignity and heroism), the Christian believer may find in the resources of his faith the possibility, not simply of enduring the unendurable, but of protesting in hope against circumstances that are beyond his alteration. The paradigm of faith, in such circumstances, is the language and behaviour of Jesus in Gethsemane and on Calvary. And it may not be simply *assumed* that such 'protest' lacks efficacy.

The early article of Marx on which I have been commenting at

32 *EW*, p. 244.

no point constitutes an argument for atheism. In its characterization of the religious protest as 'illusory' it presupposes the truth of atheism. And central to the structure of that presupposition, as it functions in these passages, is the conviction that 'religion has no content of its own'. We are now in a position, therefore, to consider that claim in somewhat more detail.

The letter in which the phrase occurs was written early in Marx's career. Nevertheless, I do not think that it is improper to subject it to fairly close scrutiny, because it expresses an attitude towards religion which underwent no significant subsequent change or development. In this letter, Marx is justifying to Ruge his recent actions as editor of the *Rheinische Zeitung*. Breaking definitively with Bruno Bauer and his Left-Hegelian colleagues, Marx was now refusing to publish their eclectic, utopian, speculative left-wing effusions. Having been sent 'heaps of scrawls pregnant with world revolutions and empty of thought . . . I declared', he said, 'that I considered the smuggling of communist and socialist ideas into casual theatre reviews was unsuitable, indeed immoral, and a very different and more fundamental treatment of communism was required if it was going to be discussed at all. I then asked that religion be criticized more through a criticism of the political situation, than that the political situation be criticized through religion.'[33] The editor has decided, in other words, that it is time for the paper to come clean, and to cease protecting its flank (against the authorities) by masking political radicalism in cultural and theological criticism. The approach he proposes to adopt is, after all, 'more suited to the manner of a newspaper and the education of the public, because religion has no content of its own and lives not from heaven but from earth, and falls of itself with the dissolution of the inverted reality whose theory it is.'[34]

Could not the same shift in tactics have been similarly justified in respect, for example, of artistic and literary criticism? Could not Marx have said of art and literature that they 'have no content of their own', in the sense that artistic and literary forms, expressive of aspects of human attitude and relationship, have their 'content' not in themselves but in those patterns of social reality and conflict which they 'reflect'?

I am suggesting, in other words, that if we accept, in its broad outlines, the relationship between 'subject' and 'predicate' argued for by Marx's 'historical materialism'; if, that is to say, we endorse his insistence on the primacy of 'social being' in respect of 'social consciousness'; then it is true of a number of elements of the 'superstructure', and by no means only of religion, that they 'have no

33 Quoted *Life*, p. 58.
34 Loc. cit.

content of their own' in the sense that they 'reflect' more fundamental features of social reality. And if the danger of such a model is, as we shall suggest in Chapter Fifteen, that it risks underestimating the 'relative autonomy' of art, literature or religion, it would still seem perfectly reasonable to argue (as Marx does in the letter) that the critical analysis of social situations demands, at least in certain circumstances, 'more fundamental treatment' than is likely to be provided by artistic, literary or theological criticism.

If this were all that Marx was saying, or implying, then it is difficult to see why a Christian should wish to quarrel with his claim that 'religion has no content of its own'. It is, after all, perfectly evident that, in every period and in every place, particular forms of Christianity – literary, ritual, conceptual or organizational – have been forms expressive of human hope, fear, relationship and conflict. Perhaps we can say that the 'content' of religious symbolism, as of artistic and literary symbolism, is to be found not 'in itself', but in the human reality which it expresses.

In fact, however, Marx is saying something more than this. In order to put our finger on this 'something more', we need to consider why it is that he supposes that, of all the 'ideological forms' that constitute the social 'superstructure', religion alone is destined *simply* to disappear in a post-revolutionary situation in which all alienation will have been healed, all bondage broken. He does not, after all, suppose that, in such a society, there will be nothing that corresponds to law, polity or philosophy even if, in some cases, there is, in Althusser's phrase, 'a shift of their functions to neighbouring forms'.[35] He does, however, suppose that, in such a society, the *state* will have been 'abolished'. That is the clue which we now need to follow up.

We need not delay long on the question as to whether the state will, as it were, naturally 'wither away', or whether it needs to be directly 'abolished'. Marx himself preferred the latter expression,[36] whereas there are several passages in which Engels opts firmly for the former.[37] Lenin, for his part, commented sharply on the political danger of replacing 'abolition' by the more gradualist notion of 'withering'[38] but, in a passage written in 1917, he did speak of *democracy* withering away: 'Only in communist society, when the resistance of the capitalists has been completely crushed . . . will democracy begin to *wither away*, owing to the simple fact that, freed from capitalist slavery . . . people will gradually *become accustomed* to

---

35 L. Althusser, *For Marx*, p. 232.
36 Cf. McLellan, *Marxism after Marx*, p. 16.
37 E.g., 'The state is not "abolished", *it withers away*' (*Anti-Dühring*, p. 363); 'The state is not "abolished". *It dies out*' ('Socialism: Utopian and Scientific', *HM*, p. 194).
38 Cf. 'The State and Revolution', *HM*, p. 534.

observing the elementary rules of social intercourse that have been
known for centuries and repeated for thousands of years in all
copy-book maxims . . . without force, without coercion, without
subordination.'[39] That passage brings out clearly the extent to which
the biological metaphor of 'withering away' expresses, as the concept of 'abolition' does not, the writer's confidence in the naturalness, and hence the inevitability, of the process. Similarly, the
answer given to the correlative question: will *religion* 'wither away',
or is it to be 'abolished'? will partly depend upon the presence or
absence of a similar confidence. And there is little doubt that Marx
was quite confident that religion *would* 'wither away', would 'fall of
itself'.

Turning now to the wider question of the disappearance of the
state (whether by 'withering' or by 'abolition') we find Marx insisting, in 1844, that once the transitional phase of the revolution
is complete, communism will 'throw its *political* mask aside'.[40] That
is to say: although in the course of the revolutionary struggle,
communism cannot fail but *appear* to represent yet another partial,
particular social interest, once the revolution is successfully
achieved, its appearance will correspond to its reality, as the expression of the *general* interest of society at large. Similarly, three years
later, in answer to the question as to whether, 'after the fall of the
old society there will be a new class domination culminating in a
new political power?', he says: 'No. . . . The working class, in the
course of development, will substitute for the old civil society an
association which will exclude classes and their antagonism, and
there will be no more political power properly so-called, since political power is precisely the official expression of antagonism in civil
society. . . . It is only in an order of things in which there are no
more classes and class antagonisms that *social evolutions* will cease to
be *political revolutions*.'[41] This is the sense of his remark, the following
year, that, after the revolution, 'public power will lose its political
character'.[42]

The general picture that emerges from these texts is as follows.
In societies torn by conflict, social existence takes the form of a
struggle between competing interests. This struggle for power is the
political struggle, and the institutional expression of political dominance is the *state*. Because, after the revolution is fully achieved,
there will be no conflicting interest-groups, therefore social existence
will not be 'political' existence, 'properly so-called', and, specifi-

39 Ibid., p. 568, his stress.
40 'Critical Notes on the Article "The King of Prussia and Social Reform. By a
    Prussian" ', *EW*, p. 420.
41 *The Poverty of Philosophy*, pp. 169–70.
42 'Manifesto of the Communist Party', *R1848*, p. 87.

cally, there will be no place for that institution – the state – through which political power and domination are exercised.

It is true that, in 1875, Marx insisted on the need to provide a 'scientific' answer to such questions as: 'What transformation will the state undergo in a communist society? In other words, what social functions will remain that are analogous to the present functions of the state?'[43] The history of Marxism might have been rather different had Marx himself sought seriously to meet that need. Instead, he contented himself with general expressions of confidence concerning the future. As Engels put it in the *Anti-Dühring*: 'When ultimately the state becomes the real representative of the whole of society, it renders itself superfluous. As soon as there is no social class to be held in subjection any longer . . . there is nothing more to repress, nothing necessitating a special repressive force, the state.'[44]

The Abolition of Religion

Drawing on a brief passage in *The German Ideology*, McKown has suggested that, in that work, Marx acknowledges the existence, in primitive man, of a 'natural religion', characterized by the awe which men and animals experience in the face of nature, 'which first appears to man as a completely alien, all-powerful and unassailable force'.[45] In view of the fact that the bases of natural and social religion are distinct – the one being 'an animal response to natural forces, the other . . . a reflection in consciousness of contradictions in socio-economic life'[46] – McKown argues that, in order to be consistent, Marx would 'have had to recognize that religion will not necessarily wither and die just because a classless society abolishes [social] contradictions'.[47] The suggestion is an interesting one, but Marx could surely have met the objection, in Feuerbachian terms, by arguing that, once the material conditions had allowed the emergence of human rationality, man's attitude to natural forces would cease to be that of impotent, 'religious' awe.

A more serious objection to Marx's cavalier assumption that religion would disappear without trace in a classless society is that proposed by Alfred Schmidt. According to Schmidt, 'Marx was too hasty in drawing [the] conclusion' that 'when man's social being becomes rational in itself . . . the desires which lay hidden in religion in reified form are then satisfied'.[48] Only the future, 'the realized

43 'Critique of the Gotha Programme', *FI*, p. 355.
44 *Anti-Dühring*, p. 363.
45 *CW5*, p. 44; cf. McKown, *The Classical Marxist Critiques of Religion*, p. 23.
46 McKown, op. cit., p. 29.
47 Loc. cit.
48 A. Schmidt, *The Concept of Nature in Marx*, p. 141.

utopia can decide, in its *practice*, whether the intellectual constructions [Marx] denounced as ideological are mere appearances which will vanish along with the false society, or whether religion is absolutely posited by the being of man, as Christian apologetics would have us believe. As long as a truly human order has not been established, Christianity . . . will preserve, in whatever mystificatory form, the memory that the essence of man has not been exhausted by its modes of appearance in history so far.'[49] If Marx saw no need to exercise the caution in his judgements which Schmidt enjoins, this was only partly because of his lack of interest in the subject. It was also partly due to the fact that he believed Christianity (the only form of religion which engaged his attention) to give expression in fantasy to those structures of dominative and repressive force which are the instruments of political power in a divided society. My reason for including in this chapter a discussion of Marx's views on the disappearance of the state is that, at least from 1845 onwards,[50] Marx took it for granted that 'God' was simply the fantasy-image of the repressive force of the state. *Therefore* it could be taken for granted that, once the state has been 'abolished' or has 'withered away', the question of God simply does not and cannot arise. Hence the frequency of the analogies which he draws, and which we shall discuss in the following chapter, between political and religious 'alienation'.[51]

'Religion has no content of its own.' I have already acknowledged that there is a more than trivial sense in which this is true, but that this fact of itself no more entitles us to suppose that religion will therefore eventually disappear than does the recognition that forms of art and literature at present 'reflect' our social divisions entitle us to suppose that there will be no art or literature in an ideal future society. In other words, I believe that Lobkowicz is correct in asserting that the grounds of Marx's conviction that religion alone, of the 'ideological forms', will disappear without trace after the revolution are twofold: in addition to a social explanation of existing forms of religion there is also present – if less explicitly than in Feuerbach and Engels – the assumption that religion is due to disappear because it is, quite simply, *erroneous*.[52]

Thus, for example, if there is, as McKown suggests, the hint of

49 Ibid., pp. 141–2.
50 Cf. the reference, in *The German Ideology*, to the 'intervention and restraint' exercised 'by the illusory "general" interest in the form of the state' (*CW5*, p. 47).
51 'Marx's criticism of Hegel's theory of the State is . . . in the last resort a transference of Feuerbach's anthropologism into the political and social field; just as Feuerbach, in the field of religion, had seen in the idea of God an alienation of human nature, so Marx, in the social field, sees in the State an alienation of the collective nature of society, of social man' (G. A. Wetter, *Dialectical Materialism*, p. 22). Hegel himself had sown the seeds of the analogy: cf. *Phenomenology*, p. 325.
52 Cf. Lobkowicz, 'Karl Marx's Attitude Toward Religion', pp. 325–8.

a distinction, in *The German Ideology*, between 'natural' and 'social' religion, and if the disappearance of the latter will be achieved by the removal of its socio-economic causes, the disappearance of the former will be achieved by the progress of science. As Engels said: 'Religion arose in very primitive times from erroneous, primitive conceptions of men about their own nature and external nature surrounding them.'[53] 'All religion', said Engels again, 'is nothing but the fantastic reflection in men's minds of those external forces which dominate their daily life, a reflection in which terrestrial forces assume the form of supernatural ones.'[54] Here, Engels is closer to Marx's general position. If scientific and technological development tame the forces of nature, so that they no longer 'dominate' human existence, the abolition of the *state* is the abolition of those *social* 'external forces which dominate their daily life'. Therefore, after the revolution, 'religion will vanish . . . for the simple reason that there will be nothing left to reflect'.[55]

The 'Content' of Religion

Might it not be suggested, however, from a Christian standpoint, that if 'religion has no content of its own' in the sense indicated, there is nevertheless another sense in which it *does* have a content of its own, and that this content is the mystery of God? This would, I suggest, be an exceedingly dangerous way of attempting to meet Marx's critique. Christian belief and practice do, indeed, simultaneously refer to the mystery of man and the mystery of God. But they do so symbolically, by referring to that which they do not and cannot 'contain'. Sacramental language and practice point beyond themselves to the human, historical reality which they symbolically express or 'reflect'. The obedience of faith and the language of belief do not 'contain' their objects, but point beyond themselves to objects that are not directly expressible. I am suggesting, in other words, that if, on the one hand, in reference to the reality of the human, the assumption that religion *does* have a 'content of its own' too easily leads to just that distraction from practical activity which Marx deplored, so also, on the other hand, in reference to the reality of God, the assumption that religion has a 'content of its own' too easily leads to idolatry and superstition, for it is of the essence of idolatry and superstition to suppose that God is comprehensible

---

53 F. Engels, 'Ludwig Feuerbach and the End of Classical German Philosophy', *HM*, p. 234.
54 Engels, *Anti-Dühring*, p. 410.
55 Ibid., p. 412. Or, as Bakunin put it, in 1871: 'There is not, there cannot be, a State without religion . . . whenever a chief of State speaks of God . . . be sure that he is getting ready to shear once more his people-flock' (*God and the State*, p. 84).

and tractable. Christianity is permanently threatened by a twofold 'fetishism' in respect of its own symbols. Hence, once again, the indispensability of that negative, apophatic, agnostic dimension which has, in fact, been a recurrent feature of the history of Christian theology and spirituality.

It must be admitted, however, that, in our own time, it is this very feature of Christianity which is frequently overlooked, not only in 'popular' religion but also in much academic theology. If it is true that Christian belief and practice 'have no content of their own' – that they point beyond themselves in the twofold manner that I have suggested – then, in so far as it is also true that, in our society, both believers and non-believers alike have in large measure lost sight of this fact, we may well find that there is no 'name' for God (and perhaps especially the name 'God') which it is possible to use without continual misunderstanding. But it does not follow that the reality of that which we cannot appropriately name is not there to be experienced – not in 'religion' alone, for religion has no content of its own – but in the givenness of all responsibly appropriated human experience; to be responded to in the attentiveness and darkness of a contemplation that refuses to 'fetishize' its symbols; and to be reflectively considered in the broken and paradoxical language of critical theology. At least it seems certain that a mode of belief, or of theological enquiry, which proceeded as if it were *ever* possible to name God without misgivings concerning the appropriateness of the language employed would have abandoned the quest for God, given religion a 'content of its own', and thereby collapsed into idolatry.

'Man makes religion, religion does not make man.'[56] Marx was quite evidently correct. But he was *incorrect* in supposing that it may be assumed without argument that the proposition 'religion does not make man' is identical with the proposition 'God does not make man'. 'Man' is indeed the 'subject' and 'religion' the 'predicate', but it may not be assumed without argument that the question of the reality of God therefore simply does not and cannot arise. Or, to put it in interrogative form: from the fact that 'man makes religion', does it necessarily follow that the religion he makes is *simply* a projective construction, rather than a structure of discovery? Did not Marx far too readily assume that, after Feuerbach, 'the criticism of religion has been essentially completed'? In order to continue the discussion along these lines, it is now necessary, for reasons that have already been hinted at, to consider the theme of 'alienation'.

56 *EW*, p. 244.

14

ALIENATION AND REDEMPTION

The status of the concept of 'alienation' is, as we saw in Chapter Two, central to debates concerning the fundamental continuity or lack of continuity between the thought of the early and the 'mature' Marx.[1] Calvez goes so far as to say that the argument of *Capital* 'n'est autre chose qu'une théorie de l'aliénation fondamentale',[2] and, in support of his contention, he draws attention to the (ambivalent) influence on that argument of both Hegel's *Phenomenology* and the *Logic*. Although few Marxists would, I imagine, endorse Calvez's claim without qualification, there are Marxist thinkers who insist, as strenuously as any 'liberal humanist', on the enduring centrality of the concept of alienation in Marx's thought. Thus, for example, Istvan Mészáros not only asserts that 'The key concept of [the Paris] Manuscripts is the concept of alienation',[3] but argues, in support of the contention that 'the concept of alienation became the central concept of Marx's whole theory',[4] that 'Marx's critique of capitalistic alienation and reification' is 'the *basic* idea of the Marxian system'.[5]

In view of the interdependence, in Marx's thought, of the various themes that I have selected for discussion in this study, it is not surprising that we have already come across the notion of 'alienation' more than once. So far, however, my references to both 'alienation' and its 'supersession' have lacked precision and specificity. In this chapter, therefore, I propose to discuss Marx's concept of alienation in order to bring into somewhat sharper focus a number of questions upon which I have already touched in other contexts. After an introductory sketch of the Marxian concept, and a brief discussion of terminology, I shall illustrate Marx's use of the concept. Some consideration of his analogies between political, economic and religious alienation will enable us to raise, once again, the question of God; and I shall conclude by offering some general theological reflections on the theme.

---

1 Cf. above, p. 22.
2 J.-Y. Calvez, *La Pensée de Karl Marx*, p. 186.
3 I. Mészáros, *Marx's Theory of Alienation*, p. 11.
4 Ibid., p. 233.
5 Ibid., p. 93.

Before getting under way, there is a phrase of Mészáros' to which it may be useful to draw attention in order to indicate why I have entitled this chapter 'Alienation and Redemption'. 'The key to understanding Marx's theory of alienation', according to Mészáros, 'is his concept of "*Aufhebung*" [or "transcendence"], and not the other way round.'[6] In other words, the weight of Marx's interest lay not in understanding alienation considered as a 'fundamental dimension of history', or as an irreducible tension 'necessarily inherent in the very nature of "human self-consciousness" ',[7] but in understanding and contributing to the realization of that process whereby the distortions and dehumanizations produced by an historically specific mode of production (namely capitalism) might be 'transcended', overcome, or dialectically resolved, in concrete social and political fact. His interest was, in other words, 'practical', and not merely theoretical. In the language of theology, the process whereby man's 'self-estrangement', his 'self-lostness', his 'alienation', is overcome or 'transcended' is the process of man's redemption: hence the title of this chapter. We shall therefore have to consider the connections that might obtain between 'transcendence' as process, and 'transcendence' as the ontological condition of the possibility of that process; between 'redemption' and the question of the redeemer; between the historical action of God and his eternal being. It also follows, as we shall see, that consideration of the circumstances in which man's alienation might be definitively transcended or superseded raises questions concerning the form, content and grounds of hope for the future – questions which we shall consider in more detail in Chapters Seventeen and Eighteen.

Concept and Terminology

Marx's concept of 'alienation', as presented in the section on alienated labour in the Paris Manuscripts, 'has four main aspects'.[8] In the first place, man is alienated from *nature*, which is also to say that he is alienated from the products of his labour. In the second place, man is alienated from *himself as worker*: his labour 'does not offer satisfaction to him in and by itself, but only by the act of selling it to someone else'.[9] In the actual conditions under which man in capitalist society works and produces, it is not only the product, but also the process of production, that is estranged from

6 Ibid., p. 20.
7 Ibid., pp. 243, 244. The first phrase quoted is from Hegel, against whom Mészáros conducts a sustained polemic, and the second from Jean Hyppolite: cf. J. Hyppolite, *Etudes sur Marx et Hegel*, pp. 101–2.
8 Mészáros, op. cit., p. 14. For a reasonably lucid discussion of these four aspects, cf. B. Ollman, *Alienation: Marx's Conception of Man in Capitalist Society*, pp. 136–52.
9 Mészáros, op. cit., p. 14.

the producer. In the third place, this twofold alienation of man from that which he produces, and from the process of its production, constitutes an estrangement of man from his humanity, his human nature: man is self-estranged. 'Estranged labour therefore turns *man's species-being* . . . into a being *alien* to him and a *means* of his *individual existence.* It estranges man from his own body, from nature as it exists outside him, from his spiritual essence [*Wesen*], his *human* essence.'[10] In the fourth place, man is alienated not only from his product, from the process of production, and from his own nature, but he is also thereby alienated from his fellow human beings: 'What is true of man's relationship to his labour, to the product of his labour and to himself, is also true of his relationship to other men, and to the labour and the object of the labour of other men.'[11]

The opening section of Mészáros' chapter on the 'Origins of the Concept of Alienation',[12] a concept which, he says, 'belongs to a vast and complex problematics, with a long history of its own',[13] is misleading. The section has the appearance of being an historical sketch of the concept, from the Old Testament to the present day. In fact, it consists of little more than a series of glosses on Marx's polemical pamphlet *On The Jewish Question.* For our purpose, there are in fact only two features of the history of the concept, before Marx, that need to be borne in mind.

In the first place, the term 'alienation' is, in its origins, a legal term reflecting an economic fact: I make something of mine over to another, *ad alium.* If I make a chair, I can give it to you, or sell it to you. As Marx puts it, in *Capital*: 'Things are in themselves external to man, and therefore alienable.'[14] But, if I can 'alienate' the chair that I make by making it over to another, are there not aspects of my work, my life, my relationships that are not thus 'alienable'? In what circumstances could I 'make over to another' my activity, my imagination, my wife? According to Marx, it is the characteristic of capitalism to have rendered *each and every aspect* of human existence 'alienable'. 'There came a time', he says, 'when everything men had considered as inalienable became an object of exchange, of traffic, and could be alienated.'[15] Thus, when he says that 'Selling is the practice of alienation',[16] Marx refers to that

---

10 'Economic and Philosophical Manuscripts', *EW*, p. 329.
11 *EW*, p. 330; cf. Mészáros, op. cit., p. 15.
12 Mészáros, op. cit., pp. 28–33.
13 Ibid., p. 27.
14 *Cap. I*, p. 182. According to Rotenstreich, however, there existed 'even in classical antiquity', alongside this 'basic juridical meaning', another connotation: a reference to the loss of control characteristic of ecstasy or insanity; and he notes the importance, in this context, of Hegel's discussion of Plotinus: cf. N. Rotenstreich, *Basic Problems of Marx's Philosophy*, pp. 145, 150.
15 Marx, *The Poverty of Philosophy*, p. 28.
16 *EW*, p. 241.

specific state of affairs, namely capitalism, which is characterized by 'the universal extension of "saleability" (i.e. the transformation of *everything* into commodity)'.[17]

In the second place, therefore, it is tempting to assume that, if the 'alienated' condition of man under capitalism consists in the reduction of his product, his production, his human existence, and his relationships, to the status of 'objects', of 'things' to be negotiated, to be bought and sold, then the 'transcendence' of alienation would consist in the overcoming of all 'objectification', all 'thing-hood'. According to Marx, however, this establishment of the identity of 'object' and 'subject', this absorption of 'thing-hood' into subjectivity, of nature into mind, was precisely the misconceived project of Hegelian idealism.

In 1967, Lukács criticized the interpretation that he had offered, in 1923, of Marx's theory of alienation, on the grounds that, in that original edition of *History and Class Consciousness*, he had failed to differentiate the Hegelian from the Marxian doctrine. 'It is in Hegel that we first encounter alienation as the fundamental problem of the place of man in the world and *vis-à-vis* the world. However, in the term alienation he includes every type of objectification. . . . *History and Class Consciousness* follows Hegel in that it too equates alienation with objectification [*Vergegenständlichung*] (to use the term employed by Marx in the *Economic-Philosophical Manuscripts*).'[18] And Colletti quotes a 1962 statement by Lukács in which the latter again criticizes *History and Class Consciousness* on the grounds that, ' "throughout the basic line of argument reification (alienation, estrangement)" – *Verdinglichung* (*Entäusserung, Entfremdung*) – was "identified, as in Hegel, with objectivity" '.[19]

In fact, as Lukács acknowledged when he read the Paris Manuscripts in 1930 (before their publication), the difference between Marx's concept and Hegel's is there brought out quite clearly.[20] Thus, for example, in that section of the Manuscripts which contains the fourfold distinction with which we began,[21] Marx says: 'Let us now take a closer look at *objectification*, at the production of the worker, and the *estrangement*, the *loss* of the object, of his product, that this entails.'[22] If we add: 'that this entails under the specific circumstances that obtain under capitalism', the difference between the Hegelian and the Marxian concepts – a difference at least *emergent* in these Manuscripts, if not yet fully developed – becomes apparent. For Marx, productive labour – and hence the 'objectifi-

17 Mészáros, *Marx's Theory of Alienation*, p. 35, my stress.
18 G. Lukács, *History and Class Consciousness*, pp. xxiii–xxiv.
19 L. Colletti, *Marxism and Hegel*, p. 176.
20 Cf. Lukács, op. cit., p. xxxvi.
21 I.e., *EW*, pp. 322–34.
22 *EW*, p. 325.

cation' of human nature, in the sense that the worker puts something of himself into his work, his product – is an absolute, a transculturally invariant feature of human existence, 'because the human mode of existence is inconceivable without the transformation of nature accomplished by productive activity'.[23] But not all 'objectification' is 'alienation' in Marx's sense. It may be that I necessarily put something of myself into my work, but it is not necessarily the case that something of myself thereby 'gets lost' in the process. Mészáros neatly captures the thrust of Marx's concentration on historically specific modes of productive activity when he says that 'the self-evident truth . . . "man must *produce* if he is not to die" ' is not to be taken as equivalent to the proposition ' "man must exchange and barter if he is not to die" '.[24]

Before turning to Marx's own texts, it is necessary to add a word on his terminology (and, in doing so, I rely on those who are more closely familiar with the German sources than I am myself). In Marx's German, three principal terms 'are used to render "alienation" or "estrangement" '.[25] Of these, '*Veräusserung*', which 'occurs only rarely',[26] means the practice or activity of alienation through *selling*. The two terms that occur most frequently, '*Entäusserung*' and '*Entfremdung*' can usually be taken as interchangeable.[27] According to Mészáros, 'When the accent is on "externalization" or "objectification", Marx uses the term "*Entäusserung*" . . . whereas "*Entfremdung*" is used when the author's intention is to emphasize the fact that man is being *opposed* by a *hostile* power of his own making.'[28] Thus the translators of the *Early Writings* render '*Entfremdung*' as 'estrangement',[29] and no particular significance need be attached to the fact that whereas C. J. Arthur's edition of a much-discussed passage in *The German Ideology* renders '*Entfremdung*' as 'alienation',[30] the Moscow edition has 'estrangement'.[31] In what follows, therefore, I do not believe that I shall be distorting Marx's meaning in using 'alienation' and 'estrangement' interchangeably unless the context indicates that a distinction is being drawn between the two concepts.

---

23 Mészáros, op. cit., p. 79.
24 Ibid., p. 90.
25 Ibid., p. 313
26 Benton, 'Glossary', *EW*, p. 430; cf. Mészáros, p. 313.
27 Cf. *Life*, p. 110; A. Giddens, *Capitalism and Modern Social Theory*, p. 12.
28 Mészáros, op. cit., p. 313.
29 Cf. *EW*, p. 430.
30 C. J. Arthur, ed., *The German Ideology*, p. 56.
31 *CW5*, p. 48. Cf. Mészáros' refutation of the claim that this passage justifies the contention that 'the notion of alienation "drops out" from the later writings of Marx' (op. cit., p. 218).

Alienation in Capital

Turning now to Marx's own texts, we shall begin with the first volume of *Capital*, in order to illustrate the enduring centrality (amply documented by Mészáros)[32] of the concept of alienation in Marx's thought. There are passages, such as that from which we quoted earlier, in which the concept still strongly echoes its original legal sense: 'Things are in themselves external to man, and therefore alienable. In order that this alienation [*Veräusserung*] may be reciprocal, it is only necessary for men to agree tacitly to treat each other as the private owners of those alienable things, and, precisely for that reason, as persons who are independent of each other.'[33] Even here, we can detect other questions lurking beneath the surface of the argument – what are the dangers inherent in men treating each other as 'the private owners of alienable things'? what threats to human relationships are implicit in states of affairs in which the perceived economic relations presuppose that persons are 'independent of each other'? – and, as Marx's analysis becomes more determinate, as he penetrates successive layers of 'appearance' in quest of the underlying economic 'reality', the focus sharpens.

'Up to this point', he says, 'we have considered only one economic relation between men, a relation between owners of commodities in which they appropriate the produce of the labour of others by alienating [*entfremden*] the produce of their own labour.'[34] 'Gold is, in the hands of every commodity-owner, his own commodity divested [*entäussert*] of its original shape by being alienated [*veräussert*].'[35] Gold is, in other words, the alien form of the alienated product.

Nor is it only the product that is thus alienated, but also the process of its production. In the capitalist mode of production, the worker 'must constantly treat his labour-power as his own property, his own commodity, and he can do this only by placing it at the disposal of the buyer, i.e. handing it over to the buyer for him to consume, for a definite period of time, temporarily. In this way he manages to alienate [*veräussern*] his labour-power and to avoid renouncing his rights of ownership over it.'[36] Furthermore, if the owner of money is 'to find labour-power in the market as a commodity', the worker, 'instead of being able to sell commodities in which his labour has been objectified, must rather be compelled to offer for sale as a commodity that very labour-power which exists only in his living body.'[37] The direction in which this argument

32 Cf. *Marx's Theory of Alienation*, pp. 222–6.
33 *Cap. I*, p. 182; cf. pp. 178, 199–200.
34 *Cap. I*, p. 203.
35 *Cap. I*, p. 204.
36 *Cap. I*, p. 217.
37 *Cap. I*, p. 272; cf. pp. 277–8.

points is, by now, familiar; the worker, in making over his labour-power is, as it were, tearing himself apart, *losing* part of himself in the conditions of his labour. It is clear, in other words, that the first two aspects of the concept of alienation, as Marx sketched it in the Paris Manuscripts, have survived in *Capital*. The third aspect – man's alienation from 'his spiritual essence, his *human* essence',[38] appears in passages which treat of the division of labour; 'within the capitalist system all methods for raising the social productivity of labour are put into effect at the cost of the individual worker . . . they distort the worker into a fragment of a man, they degrade him to the level of an appendage to a machine . . . they alienate [*entfremden*] from him the intellectual potentialities of the labour process in the same proportion as science is incorporated in it as an independent power.'[39] And, in view of Marx's insistence on the irreducibly conflictual character of the relationship between the 'owner of money' and the worker, it is hardly necessary to add that the fourth aspect – man's alienation from his fellow human beings – continues to be central to his analysis.

Not only does the worker 'make over' something of his to another; not only does he do so in circumstances which amount to a dimi-nution of identity, a tearing apart or self-estrangement, and an estrangement from his fellow human beings; in the manner in which he does so, his own self-product, his work, ceases to be an expression of his human reality and becomes an alien power over his life. The machine, from being an extension of his mind and arm, becomes his master and he its slave (that metaphor is intended to serve as a reminder of the abiding influence, on Marx's theory of 'alienation' and its 'transcendence', of Hegel's account, in the *Phenomenology*, of the dialectic of master and slave – a text which we shall consider when we discuss, in Chapter Seventeen, Marx's theory of revolution).

Thus, for example, Marx argues that because, before the worker enters the process of production, 'his own labour has already been alienated [*entfremdet*] from him . . . it now, in the course of the process, constantly objectifies itself so that it becomes a product alien to him [*fremder Produkt*]. . . . Therefore the worker constantly produces objective wealth, in the form of capital, an alien power that dominates and exploits him.'[40] And again, in an unpublished draft probably written between 1863 and 1866,[41] Marx says that 'work can only be wage-labour when its *own* material conditions confront it . . . as *alien, autonomous powers* . . . the first process, the sale and purchase of labour-power, presupposes that the means of

38 *EW*, p. 329.
39 *Cap. I*, p. 799.
40 *Cap. I*, p. 716.
41 Cf. *Cap. I*, p. 943.

production and subsistence have become autonomous objects confronting the worker, i.e. it presupposes the *personification* of the means of production.'[42]

Illustrations and Analogies

In the passages that we have so far considered, there are already – in the references to dominative, personified, 'alien powers' – hints of the analogies between political, economic and religious alienation which Marx continued to draw long after he had lost interest in the 'head-on' critique of religion, believing the job to have been done.[43]

In the article which he wrote, in 1843, *On the Jewish Question*,[44] Marx argued that the political emancipation of religion – the separation of Church and state – did not, as some supposed that it would, liberate men from religious illusion, as the experience of the 'North American states' showed.[45] And why not? Because the political emancipation of religion left untouched the problem of the state. Therefore, he said, 'The question of the relationship of *political* emancipation to *religion* becomes for us the question of the relationship of *political* emancipation to *human* emancipation.'[46] His target in this article was Bruno Bauer, against whom he returned to the attack in the following year: 'Having confused political emancipation with human emancipation, he had to be consistent and confuse the *political means* of emancipation with the *human means*.'[47] Marx realizes that 'the practical supersession of alienation is inconceivable in terms of politics alone, in view of the fact that politics is only a *partial* aspect of the totality of social processes'.[48] The fundamental problem is said to be that of 'human' alienation, but what this might mean is not yet specified. What is missing in these passages, in other words, is the recognition that that dimension of social reality which is 'universal', and not 'partial', is the *economic*.[49] In the measure that this insight gathers strength, from 1844 onwards, it is with economic alienation that analogies with religion, the 'pure form' of alienation, are increasingly drawn.

Two of Marx's most detailed examinations of the theme of alienation are to be found in the Paris Manuscripts of 1844, which we have already considered, and in the notes which he made, the same

---

42 *Cap. I*, p. 1006.
43 For some instances of such analogies, other than those discussed in this section, cf. e.g., *EW*, pp. 91–2, 99, 153, 323; *FI*, pp. 155, 306–8, 328, 332.
44 *EW*, pp. 212–41.
45 Cf. *EW*, p. 217.
46 *EW*, p. 217; cf. pp. 226, 233.
47 'The Holy Family', *CW4*, p. 95.
48 Mészáros, *Marx's Theory of Alienation*, p. 75.
49 Cf. ibid., p. 75.

year, on James Mill's *Elements of Political Economy*.[50] It is 'the nature of money' as 'the *medium* of exchange', that 'the *mediating function* or movement . . . by means of which the products of man mutually complement each other, is *estranged* and becomes the property of a *material thing* external to man, viz. money. . . . Through this *alien mediator* man gazes at his will, his activity, his relation to others as at a power independent of them and of himself – instead of man himself being the mediator for man. His slavery then reaches a climax. It is obvious that this *mediator* must become a *veritable God* since the mediator is the *real* power over that with which he mediates me.'[51] This passage is of some interest because of its interweaving of echoes of Hegel's dialectic of master and slave with a christological analogy (shaped, surely, by Feuerbach's Christology)[52] which is spelt out in more detail in the following paragraph of Marx's text. Some years later, in the *Grundrisse*, this analogy is taken up again: 'Thus, in the religious sphere, Christ, the mediator between God and humanity – a mere instrument of circulation between the two – becomes their unity, God-man, and, as such, becomes more important than God; the saints more important than Christ; the pope more important than the saints.'[53]

The historian of Christianity is familiar with the tendency, in popular Christianity, to 'fetishize' (to use a metaphor we shall come across in a moment) the mediatorship of Christ: to make of 'Christ' a being neither human nor divine, but – as it were – a 'cosmic amalgam'. And when the Christ is thus conceived, as an 'alien mediator', the result has been (as Marx recognized) at once to depreciate the human and obliterate the divine. Similarly, the historian of Christianity is familiar with the tendency, especially in popular Catholicism, to 'fetishize' the saints, or the papacy (to take Marx's examples; the correlate, in popular Protestantism, would be the 'fetishizing' of the Bible). But although such (ultimately idolatrous) distortions of Christianity have rarely been long left in undisputed possession of the field; although they have provoked critical protest from within the Christian tradition; the practical efficacy of such protest has frequently been diminished by its failure to take into consideration the socio-economic circumstances that generate or foster such distortions. In other words (and this is an issue on which we have touched already, and to which we shall return) theological criticism that is not, at the same time, socio-economic criticism, is inadequately grounded. There are modes of Christian belief and practice that are recognizable, from within the Christian tradition, as expressive of and contributive to, man's alienation

50 *EW*, pp. 259–78.
51 *EW*, p. 260.
52 Cf. above, p. 155.
53 *G*, p. 332; cf. *Cap. I*, p. 907.

from God and from his fellow man. But the fundamental issue is not the religious symbolism in which such alienation is expressed, but the '*human* alienation' of which such symbolism is an expression.

Where the Christian parts company with Marx, however, is at the latter's assumption that *all* use of religious symbolism is necessarily expressive of and contributive to the various aspects of human alienation. The only concept of God that Marx ever entertained was of a God of whom it is true that, in Feuerbach's words, 'To enrich God, man must become poor; that God may be all, man must be nothing. . . . The impoverishing of the real world and the enriching of God is one act.'[54] Confronted by the Feuerbachian rhetoric, and its Marxian derivatives, the Christian may wish to protest: but have we not always insisted that, to enrich man, God became poor; that the enriching of the real world and the impoverishing of God was one act? Is not the acknowledgement of the presence of God in Jesus' death on Calvary the celebration of the abolition, by God, of that 'God' in whom Marx supposed that Christians necessarily believed? And yet such protests, however correct in principle, too easily enable the Christian to evade the force of Marx's critique. Of what 'impoverishment' and what 'enrichment' are we speaking? If it is true that '*gloria Dei vivens homo*', where are the groups and individuals who have in fact been brought alive, whose alienation from their products, their humanity, their fellow human beings, has in fact been 'transcended' by the enabling power of a transcendent God? These questions, however, are premature. Before considering them, we must first look at a few more typical passages in which Marx draws analogies between political, economic and religious alienation.

In 1843, in his *Critique of Hegel's Doctrine of the State*, Marx said that the question as to whether sovereignty resided in the people or in the monarch was liable to obscure the fact that we are here dealing with 'two *wholly opposed conceptions of sovereignty*, of which one can come into being only in the *monarch* and the other only in the *people*. It is analogous to the question, whether God or man is sovereign. One of the two must be false, even though an existing falsehood.'[55] The following year, in the Paris Manuscripts: 'A *being* sees himself as independent only when he stands on his own feet, and he only stands on his own feet when he owes his *existence* to himself. A man who lives by the grace of another regards himself as a dependent being.'[56]

When we turn to *Capital*, the analogies are, as we would expect,

54 Feuerbach, *The Essence of Christianity*, pp. 26, 73.
55 *EW*, p. 86.
56 *EW*, p. 356. For a nuanced but excessively long-winded analysis of this passage, cf. G. M.-M. Cottier, *L'Athéisme du Jeune Marx. Ses Origines Hégeliennes*, pp. 342–61.

economic rather than political. 'The mysterious character of the commodity-form consists . . . simply in the fact that the commodity reflects the social characteristics of men's own labour as objective characteristics of the products of labour themselves . . . the commodity-form . . . is nothing but the definite social relation between men themselves which assumes here, for them, the fantastic form of a relation between things. In order, therefore, to find an analogy we must take flight into the misty realm of religion. There the products of the human brain appear as autonomous figures endowed with a life of their own, which enter into relations both with each other and with the human race. So it is in the world of commodities with the products of men's hands. I call this the fetishism which attaches itself to the products of labour as soon as they are produced as commodities.'[57] Later on, the point is more succinctly put: 'Just as man is governed, in religion, by the products of his own brain, so, in capitalist production, he is governed by the products of his own hand.'[58] And, in the unpublished draft from which I quoted earlier: 'The rule of the capitalist over the worker is the rule of things over man . . . of the product over the producer. . . . Thus at the level of material production, of the life-process in the realm of the social . . . we find the *same* situation that we find in *religion* at the ideological level, namely the inversion of subject into object and *vice versa*.'[59] Historically, according to Marx, this 'antagonistic stage cannot be avoided, any more than it is possible for man to avoid the stage in which his spiritual energies are given a religious definition as powers independent of himself. What we are confronted by here is the *alienation* [*Entfremdung*] of man from his own labour.'[60]

Can the employment of religious and theological analogies, throughout Marx's career, *simply* be attributed to the fact that he considered religion to be 'le *type* même de l'aliénation'?[61] I think not. I have quoted these passages at some length because they indicate, cumulatively, a sense in which Calvez is correct in saying that 'le problème religieux . . . est toujours présent'[62] in Marx's thought. These analogies do, undoubtedly, have illustrative value, inasmuch as religious belief, lacking any real object, gives symbolic expression to man's alienation in a 'pure' form, uncomplicated by actuality. Commodities and, in particular, money, do – after all – exist, whereas God (in Marx's view) quite certainly does not. Therefore, the alienation of man from his own labour, and from his fellow

57 *Cap. I*, pp. 164–5.
58 *Cap. I*, p. 772.
59 *Cap. I*, p. 990.
60 Loc. cit.
61 Calvez, *La Pensée de Karl Marx*, p. 44.
62 Ibid., p. 46.

men, his subservience to the 'alien power' of 'things', of his own
products – whether machines, commodities or oppressive social
structures – can be illuminated by analogies drawn from that sphere
(namely, religion) in which the 'objects' under discussion are, in his
view, *manifestly* human products that have, as he puts it, come to
live a life of their own and, in so doing, have contributed to man's
enslavement.

And yet there is, I believe, more to it than this. 'For Marx, like
Sartre', says Schmidt, 'the non-existence of a "sense-giving" God
is the only guarantee of the possibility of the freedom of man.'[63]
Marx *needs* that guarantee if he is to sustain the conviction that
human alienation *can* be 'transcended', that a state of affairs can
responsibly (and not merely as a matter of wishful thinking) be
prospected and worked for in which man will 'owe his *existence* to
himself' and will thereby cease to be 'a dependent being'.[64] In a
word: the Promethean strand in Marx's anthropology necessitated
the suppression of the question of God. 'The criticism of religion'
said Marx in 1843, 'ends with the doctrine that for man the supreme
being is man, and thus with the categorical imperative to overthrow
all conditions in which man is a debased, enslaved, neglected and
contemptible being.'[65] In view of the fact that this is a very early
text, we should not perhaps make too much of the uncomfortably
rhetorical abstractness of the assertion that 'for man the supreme
being is man'. And yet, it is in order to ask: in what circumstances,
and in what sense, and within what limits, and on what grounds,
does Marx suppose that the forms of alienation that he diagnoses
can be 'transcended' or overcome?

'Alienation' and 'Objectification': Theological Reflections
In the previous paragraph I have begun to hint at some of the
questions which arise, for the Christian theologian, from a consideration of Marx's use of the concept of alienation. These questions
can be grouped under three heads, to each of which I will now
devote a section of this chapter: questions concerning Christian
'objectifications' of the mystery of God; questions concerning the
extent to which 'alienation' is a permanent feature of the 'human
condition'; and the question of death.

Marx was clearly not wrong in supposing that, amongst those
images of God which have been socially influential in Christian
history, the image of God as 'Lord' or '*Kyrios*', as the 'Power' before
whose majesty sinful man must abase himself in abject humility, is

---

63 A. Schmidt, *The Concept of Nature in Marx*, p. 37.
64 *EW*, p. 356.
65 'A Contribution to the Critique of Hegel's Philosophy of Right. Introduction',
     EW, p. 251.

of particular interest and significance. Nor was he wrong in supposing that there are links to be discerned between the use of such images of God and the particular forms of social structure and political dominance in which they find widespread acceptance. Moreover (as we remarked in Chapter Twelve), if, as Marx and most Marxists assume, Feuerbach's account of the logic of religious and theological discourse is correct; if 'God' is and can only be the name for a symbolic expression of certain features of human experience; then the characterization of such discourse as expressive of human alienation, of man's subservience to 'the products of his own brain',[66] is entirely justified.

But, if there is God; if religious language and imagery do in fact refer – however inappropriately and misleadingly – to that which resists assimilation or reduction to particular features of human, historical experience; if, in other words, Marx's 'naturalism' is in fact unwarranted;[67] then the situation is somewhat more complicated.

It is not, according to Marx, the 'objectification' of the products of labour, as such, or of economic exchange, as such, which 'alienates' the process and products of the work of men's hands, but the dominance exercised by products and relations that, in the form of 'things', have come to be endowed 'with a life of their own', and have thus acquired the status of 'alien powers'. Similarly, it is not the 'objectification' of the products of man's religious 'work', of his response to and adoration of God, as such, or the 'objectification' of the commerce between God and man, as such, which 'alienates', but the dominance exercised by religious images and symbols that have come to be endowed 'with a life of their own', and have thus acquired the status of 'alien powers'.

It is not God who is an 'alien power', but those human products that are symbols of God as an 'alien power'. If there is God, then the assumption that all 'objectification' of God, or of the relations between God and man, necessarily alienates is an instance of the confusion between 'objectification' and 'alienation' which Lukács characterized as Hegel's position in contrast to Marx's. If there is God, and if man is humanly and consciously to treat of God, to acknowledge him in faith and praise, then the 'objectification' of God is unavoidable and is, in principle, unobjectionable. What is needed, therefore, is some principle of discrimination between appropriate and inappropriate, 'alienating' and 'non-alienating', objectifications of the mystery of the divine.

If we reflect, from the standpoint of Christian theology, on the distinction between 'objectification' and 'alienation', a number of

---

66 *Cap. I*, p. 772.
67 Cf. above, p. 136.

observations suggest themselves. In the first place, God is indeed 'other' than man, but not everything that is 'other' than man is 'alien' to him or 'alienates' him. Christianity does indeed speak of the 'power' of God, of the effectiveness of divine action, but, in declaring the cross to be the privileged locus of the exercise of divine power, it refuses to identify effectiveness with force. Both man and nature are indeed radically dependent on the grace, or 'power', of that 'other' that is God. In relation to the reality and sovereignty of God, however, Marx's observation that 'A man who lives by the grace of another regards himself as a dependent being'[68] is more ambiguous than he appreciated, for his Prometheanism prevented him from considering the possibility that it could be true of man's relationship to God, and hence of other relationships in *virtue* of that relationship to God, that the autonomy and independence of the creature grow in direct and not in inverse proportion to the creature's dependence.[69]

If, as I have argued earlier, our relationship to God is never unmediated,[70] the possibility arises that that independence of the creature which grows in direct proportion to its dependence on God finds expression in a corresponding transformation of the meaning of 'dependence' and 'independence' in social relationships. In circumstances in which we are alienated from our fellow human beings (and hence from God), dependence on another can only take the form of subservience. In the measure that such alienation is transcended, however, it would become possible for human beings to experience their 'greatest wealth – the *other* man – as need'.[71]

Marx's assertion that 'A man who lives by the grace of another regards himself as a dependent being' assumes all 'dependence' to be alienatory, and thereby risks perpetuating the mistaken identification of 'objectification' with 'alienation'. Moreover, just as Marx's use of the concept of 'dependence' is (in contrast to his use of the concept of 'need') strangely undialectical, so also his use of the concept of 'grace' suffers from the same defect. If God is, and can only be, an 'alien power', then indeed his 'graciousness' – the 'benevolence' of *le roi soleil* to his subjects – can only perpetuate our alienation. But not all 'graciousness', human or divine, is thus corrupted. From the standpoint of an account of man's relationship to God, such as that which I have briefly sketched, the 'transcendence' of alienation, the establishment of human freedom and autonomy, would be the expression, and not the antithesis, of man's dependence on a transcendent God. And, from the same standpoint, the possibility would emerge of the 'transcendence' of our alienation

68 *EW*, p. 356.
69 Cf. K. Rahner, *Theological Investigations, V*, p. 12.
70 Cf. above, p. 138.
71 *EW*, p. 356.

from each other being the expression, and not the antithesis, of mutual need and dependence.

In the second place, in the measure that human beings are in fact at the mercy of 'alien powers', natural or social, then, as we remarked in the previous chapter, the images of God that find readiest acceptance will be those which reflect the prevailing natural and social conditions. These will therefore be images that express and contribute to man's alienation. However, a form of Christianity which acknowledges God's radical transcendence of nature and history, which refuses to *identify* God with particular objectifications of the divine in symbol, sacrament and ecclesial organization, will be a form of Christianity in which theological activity concentrates on the task of critically purifying its own anthropomorphisms. Such a theology will thereby embody (albeit often indirectly) a critique of the natural and social conditions which generate and foster alienatory anthropomorphism. Moreover, if such criticism is to be effective, Christianity cannot rest content with a merely theoretical criticism of these conditions. To be effective, and not inappropriately 'abstract', it must indicate and stimulate those forms of practical activity which would seek to transform the conditions and thus to 'transcend' the particular forms of alienation.

I am suggesting, in other words, that a form of Christian faith recognizant of God's radical transcendence will be a form of faith that embodies an implicit or explicit criticism of structures of alienation and domination. As Horkheimer put it: 'The concept of God was for a long time the place where the idea was kept alive that there are other norms besides those to which nature and society give expression in their operation. . . . But the more Christianity brought God's rule into harmony with events in the world, the more the meaning of religion became perverted. . . . Christianity lost its function of expressing the ideal, to the extent that it became the bed-fellow of the state.'[72]

In the third place, I have remarked on the need for some principle of discrimination between appropriate and inappropriate 'objectifications' of the mystery of God. But if God, as radically transcendent, is, as has been insisted again and again in the history of Christianity, unknown and unknowable; if God, as radically transcendent, is incapable of appropriate description in human language or appropriate embodiment in human action; then how could any such principle possibly be established? Is it not inevitably the case that the establishment of any such principle is not only impossible but that, as a result, such criticism as we make of particular anthropomorphisms, of particular objectifications of the mystery of God – practical or theoretical, linguistic or institutional – will be

72 M. Horkheimer, *Critical Theory*, p. 129.

grounded, not in the character of God, but in our historically constructed conceptions of what does and does not constitute authentic
humanity? And even if such conceptions are all that we have by
which to measure the needs and capacities of man, on what possible
grounds could it be supposed that they could constitute an appropriate 'measure' of God?

If there is God, then the only conceivable alternative to this state
of affairs would be a situation in which God himself had established,
in human history, such a principle of discrimination. That he has
done so is the heart and centre of the Christian confession of faith.
And the form in which he has done so, according to that confession,
is not that of the intrusion into history of some abstract principle,
or absolute value, but rather that of a particular event and particular action, a particular product of nature and history, a particular
human individual whose history, work and fate is perceived to
constitute such a principle of discrimination.

In the light of our discussion, in the previous chapter, of Marx's
critique of religion, we can approach the same conclusion from a
somewhat different direction. Marx is correct in supposing that
'God' is indeed made by man, made in man's image. But, because
Marx's attention was elsewhere, and because he only considered
these matters in so far as they provided him with convenient illustrations of those aspects of alienation which were his primary concern, he offered excessively generalized and insufficiently
discriminating answers to the question: in what image of man does
man make 'God' (or, as I would prefer to say, does man objectify
the mystery of God)?

It may, indeed, sometimes be the case, or be at least partially the
case that, as Marx (and, after him, Durkheim) supposed, man
makes 'God' in the image of 'society' as contrasted with, as opposed
to, the individual. But the image in which man makes 'God' may
also be (as Feuerbach recognized) an image, not of an 'alien power',
but of man's hopes and visions for his destiny and self-achievement.
Moreover, as much popular iconography would seem to suggest,
the images in which man makes 'God' may also be images of aspects
of human nature which are, under the prevailing social and cultural
conditions, repressed – and in *that* sense 'alienated' (consider, for
example, the image of 'gentle Jesus, meek and mild', as the projection of a society fearful of sentiment).

The question which the Christian will wish to ask is: if it is true
that 'God' is made in man's image, how might man be made in the
image of *God*? This is the dilemma which we encountered earlier,
and it is incapable of resolution unless we have reason to suppose,
firstly, that God enables man to make man in God's image and,
secondly, that we have at our disposal resources which would guide
us in the execution of the project; unless, in other words, there exists

in human history an image of God which, as 'appropriate' both to the character of God and the needs of man, alienates man neither from God nor from his own nature.

In the fourth place, if it is true that there is no common 'logical space' occupied jointly by both God and man, then the only form in which God can be linguistically 'objectified', can 'appear' in our language, is as that which is other than God. 'God' is not God: to identify 'God' with God is to 'fetishize' the concept of God. We may seek to define 'God', but we cannot define God. There is therefore a sense in which it is true that, in order to use my conditional phrase, 'if there is God', I have not got to suppose that I know what I mean when I use it. I have only to suppose that the concept of God has reference, even if I cannot make sense of that reference. (For those who prefer an older terminology, this is perhaps another way of saying that there is at least a 'notional' distinction between God's 'esse' and his 'essentia'.) But then why continue to use the term 'God' at all? Because the decision of Christian belief is a decision to stand in a particular tradition of interpretative action and discourse, and there seems no other way of speaking of that which Jesus is perceived to express and exemplify than to continue to situate the metaphor of Jesus' 'Father' in the context of that broader complex of metaphors and analogies that is the history of the manifold uses of the concept of God.

To put it another way: there is no common 'logical space' jointly occupied by both God and man because there is no common 'ontological space' jointly occupied by both God and man. If God is to be historically 'objectified', is to 'appear' in history, he can only do so as that which is not God: as man. According to Kolakowski, the 'philosophical prospect . . . displayed in the work of Marx' entailed 'the rejection of all solutions that involve man realizing himself by the actualization, or at the command, of an antecedent absolute Being.'[73] I have been trying to sketch an account of Christian belief which entails neither the acceptance nor the rejection of such solutions because it refuses to accept their shared presupposition: namely, that here *is* both logical and ontological space jointly occupied by God and man. If there is, then indeed either Hegel or Marx is correct, and *either* 'God' or 'man' must, in the last analysis be 'abolished'.

But does not the Christian confession that Jesus Christ is 'truly God and truly man' declare him to be an instance of that which I have insisted is an impossibility: namely (to continue my metaphor), an instance of the joint occupation of *his* 'space' by both God and man, both divinity and humanity? Yes, indeed; but it is not always sufficiently appreciated that to make this move is thereby to put our

73 *KI*, p. 80.

concepts of both divinity and humanity, of both 'God' and 'man', back into the melting-pot. The christological confession does not affirm the mysterious conjunction of two 'knowns'. The problems of Christology, of human history – man's making of man – read as the history of God's agency, do not reside simply in the conjunction ('divine *and* human') but also in both of its terms. Christianity seeks to speak of God in terms of man, and not 'man' in the abstract, but *this* man, who lived and died in Palestine. Similarly, Christianity seeks to speak of man in terms of God, and not 'God' in the abstract, but *this* God, this 'Father of Our Lord Jesus Christ', whose power and transcendence are displayed in the action and suffering, the history and death, of Jesus of Nazareth.

To those of my readers who are Christian theologians, the last few paragraphs will seem excessively jejune and oversimplified. To those who are more at home in Marxist theory, they will seem dangerously abstract and at least potentially 'mystifying'. Whether, and to what extent, and in what circumstances, Jesus' life, character and action can be, or have been shown to be, capable of functioning as a principle of discrimination in the Christian project of contributing to man's making of man in the image of God: these are questions which demand, and sometimes receive, sustained attention from exegetes, historians, theologians and social scientists. My only concern has been to indicate how the Christian project, or some aspects of that project, might be characterized in the light of Marx's critique of religious alienation.

'Alienation' and the Human Condition

The concept of 'alienation' remained central to Marx's thought throughout his career. Nevertheless, that concept undoubtedly received more detailed and more 'philosophical' treatment in the early than in the later writings. It is therefore not entirely surprising that, when those early writings were published, they attracted much attention from non-Marxist philosophers and theologians, as well as from Marxist thinkers seeking to free Marxist theory from the straitjacket of Stalinist orthodoxy.[74] In the process, however, the concept of 'alienation' was not infrequently treated in an excessively abstract, *a priori*, non-historical, 'idealist' manner.

This is the background against which Marxist writers insist that 'For Marx and Marxists, alienation is not a moral but an historical category';[75] that 'Alienation always arises as the *result* of something (it is not a "human condition") and it is always alienation or estrangement *from* something';[76] that ' "Alienation" is an eminently

---

74 Cf. above, pp. 13–4.
75 R. Garaudy, *Marxism in the Twentieth Century*, p. 122.
76 Benton, 'Glossary', *EW*, p. 429.

historical concept'.[77] When such writers declare that 'Marx had nothing to do with abstract "humanism" ',[78] I take them to be making two distinct but related claims.

On the one hand, they are insisting that, when confronted by a specific state of affairs in which human beings are alienated from the products of their labour and are, in the process of production, estranged from their own humanity and from their fellow human beings, it is quite inadequate to protest, in the name of some abstract ideal of 'humanity', that things 'ought' to be otherwise. Marx, says Mészáros, 'opposed right from the outset . . . the illusions of *abstract universality* as a *mere postulate*, an impotent "ought" '.[79]

On the other hand, the Marxist opposition to 'abstract humanism' arises from the suspicion that claims that 'it has ever been so', that men have always, in one way or another, been estranged in their labour and in their relationships, may be used as a cynical (or 'realistic') justification for the maintenance of the *status quo*: an expression of the futility of seeking to work for the 'transcending' of particular forms and aspects of alienation. Let us briefly consider these two issues in turn.

'The central feature of Marx's theory of alienation is the assertion of the historically necessary supersession of capitalism by socialism freed from all the abstract moral postulates which we can find in the writings of his immediate predecessors. The ground of his assertion was not simply the recognition of the unbearable dehumanizing effects of alienation . . . but the profound understanding of the objective ontological [i.e. 'natural'] foundation of the processes that remained veiled from his predecessors.'[80] The general thrust of that passage is clear enough: Marx believed that his analysis of capitalism had enabled him to uncover the contradictions inherent in the capitalist mode of production, contradictions which would inevitably bring about the 'transcendence' of capitalism, and hence the 'transcendence' of those aspects of alienation (such as, e.g., the universalization of the commodity form) which are its specific expressions and consequences. Nevertheless, there are two features of Mészáros' argument that call for comment.

On the one hand, his claim that 'The ground of [Marx's] assertion was not *simply* the recognition of the unbearable dehumanizing effects of alienation',[81] implies the admission that there is an *element* of moral protest in Marx's critique of alienation. It is a protest against dehumanization made in the name of humanity: 'the standpoint' of Marx's 'human science' is 'the ideal of non-alienated

77 Mészáros, *Marx's Theory of Alienation*, p. 36.
78 Ibid., p. 33.
79 Loc. cit.
80 Ibid., pp. 63–4.
81 Ibid., p. 63, my stress.

man'.[82] But whence is that image of non-alienated man, of this negation of the negation, derived? The answer, presumably, is: from that history of man's making of man in which we are situated. Only active engagement in that history – in the practical process of working for its construction, and the theoretical process of seeking critically to understand its historical formation – can disclose the needs and capacities of man.

On the other hand, Mészáros' comments on the 'necessity' or 'inevitability' of the 'transcendence' of capitalism lead him uncomfortably close to interpreting Marx's position as 'historicist', in the Popperian sense.[83] For example, what concept of 'necessity' is at work in his claim that 'Marx's line of reasoning establishes "*Aufhebung*" (the transcendence of alientation) as a concept denoting *ontological necessity*)'?[84] We might say of a plant that was dying, or a house whose bricks and mortar were crumbling, that the death of the plant or the collapse of the house were 'ontologically necessary' in the sense of being inevitable. But what model or models of social processes, of processes in which the conscious intervention of human agents plays a significant part, would justify or facilitate the predication of this sort of 'necessity' or 'inevitability' to the outcome of such processes? Mészáros is very sensitive to the charge of historicism, and insists on the essential *openness* of Marx's thought to the unpredictability of the future.[85] His position seems to be that Marx, while affirming the inevitability of the transcendence or supersession of the capitalist system, and in that sense predicting its abolition, did not suppose that it was possible to predict the specific form or shape of the outcome. This is a convincing reading of Marx; some of the issues that it raises (such as the concept of 'determination') we have considered already, and others (such as the sense in which Marx did or did not suppose his analyses to have predictive force) we shall consider in later chapters. For the time being, I simply wish to indicate the extent to which Christian doctrines of redemption, of human transformation by divine grace, are confronted by similar difficulties.

The Christian doctrine of redemption has taken many forms, but all of them have in common the declaration of the victory of divine grace over the condition of sin. Shifting the idiom, we can say that the doctrine of redemption proclaims the 'transcendence' of man's alienation from God, from nature, and from his fellow-man. To the extent that man is alienated from nature, from his work, his humanity and his fellow human beings, he is thereby alienated from God. It makes no sense to speak of man at peace with God and at

82 Ibid., p. 101.
83 Cf. Chapter Six.
84 Mészáros, op. cit., p. 113.
85 Cf. ibid., pp. 114–19.

enmity with man. Nor does it make sense to speak of man estranged from God and reconciled (in 'reality' and not merely in 'appearance') with his own humanity and with his fellow human beings.

Christianity proclaims the fact of God's effective, transformative love for his creation as the ground of possibility for the 'transcendence' of the manifold forms of alienation. The proclamation of this fact and the affirmation of this possibility have often been given extremely abstract, non-historical expression. Thus, on the one hand, the 'commandment of love' – the declaration of the responsibility to work for the achievement of that 'transcendence' of sin which is, by God's grace, man's capacity and destiny – has frequently found expression in the form of an abstract, 'impotent "ought" '. On the other hand, that ideal of the 'human', of man made in God's image, in the name of which the commandment of love is issued, has often been derived less from the specific configurations of the action and suffering of Jesus – the historical 'appearance' of God's transcendent love – than from socially conditioned, theoretical, ahistorical conceptions of 'human nature'.

In so far as Christian ethical discourse is, in either of these senses 'impotent' and 'abstract', it can only benefit from being subjected to Marxist criticism. Thus, for example, if Christian ethical practice and discourse are to avoid 'mystification', they must be specified, rendered determinate, in the analysis and resolution of specific situations and circumstances, specific dimensions of human sinfulness, individual and social.

I am suggesting, in other words, that 'sin' is an historical, and not *merely* a moral category, and that both 'sin' and 'redemption' should accordingly be construed as 'eminently historical concepts'. That this possibility exists arises from the fact that the 'premises' of the doctrine of redemption and of the ethical practice and discourse which that doctrine enjoins are not propositions, but persons, 'real individuals, their activity, and the material conditions of their life'.[86] The 'first premises' of the Christian doctrine of redemption, and hence the 'foundational axioms' of the Christian ethic, are the actions, suffering and circumstances of him in whose following Christian discipleship consists.

If the Marxian moral protest is registered in the name of a conception of the human, of 'non-alienated man', derived from the practical process of working for the 'transcendence' of alienation and the theoretical process of seeking critically to understand the historical circumstances of its occurrence, the Christian moral protest is, or should be, registered in the name of a conception of the human derived from the practical process of the 'following of Christ', and the theoretical process of seeking critically to interpret

86 *CW5*, p. 31.

the history of sin and redemption in the light of the action and suffering of the crucified.

Moreover, if Marx's confidence that the specific aspects of alienation which he examined could and would be 'transcended' was empirically warranted and yet did not entail the belief that he could predict the form or shape of a social situation in which such transcendence had been achieved, something similar needs to be said of the grounds and content of Christian hope. But these are issues to which we shall return.

Let us now turn to the second of the two issues mentioned at the start of this section: namely, 'reactionary' uses of the contention that 'alienation' is a permanent feature of the human condition. According to Mészáros, 'In the twentieth century Marx could not be ignored any longer. The best way to neutralize his intellectual impact was, therefore, an existentialist interpretation of his thought which consisted basically in the mystification of the historically specific – anticapitalist – conception of alienation.'[87] Marx did not 'look upon alienation as a "fundamental dimension of history", but as the central issue of a given *phase* of history'.[88]

I have no doubt that any account of Marx's theory of alienation which failed to put the emphasis where Marx placed it: on 'a given phase of history', on the critique of capitalism, would be grossly misleading. Nevertheless, Mészáros' account is misleading in the other direction. When Marx says that, 'like slave labour, like serf labour, hired labour is but a transitory and inferior form, destined to disappear before associated labour plying its toil with a willing hand, a ready mind, and a joyous heart',[89] we are surely entitled to assume not only that 'alienated' labour has been a characteristic of *pre*-capitalist modes of production, but also that labour will *cease* to be 'alienated' with the 'abolition' of capitalism. Similarly, when Marx declares that 'The history of all hitherto existing society is the history of class struggle',[90] we are surely entitled to assume that man's alienation from his fellow-men has been a general feature of pre-capitalist societies. And Marx undoubtedly supposed that, with the abolition of capitalism, the class-struggle would be definitively superseded. That is why he could describe the historical task of the proletariat as being that of 'the *total redemption of humanity*'.[91]

One of the most striking features of Mészáros' interpretation of

87 Mészáros, op. cit., pp. 242–3.
88 Ibid., p. 243.
89 'Inaugural Address of the International Working Men's Association', *FI*, p. 80; cf. *FI*, pp. 213, 253, 254, 256 (these passages are from the text and first draft of 'The Civil War in France').
90 'Manifesto of the Communist Party', *R1848*, p. 67.
91 'A Contribution to the Critique of Hegel's Philosophy of Right. Introduction', *EW*, p. 256, his stress.

Marx's thought is the almost complete absence of any reference to 'revolution'. And yet, as we shall see in a later chapter, this concept is central to Marx's account of the process whereby capitalism would be 'transcended'. When we are told that 'only the Marxian concept of education' – education, please note, not revolution – 'can offer a way out of the contemporary social crisis',[92] we are a long way from Marx's own texts. This is not to say that, as an analysis of current needs and circumstances, Mészáros' contention is necessarily incorrect. It is only to say that he is disingenuous in offering an interpretation of Marx's thought which obscures the extent to which Marx himself believed, firstly, that the history of all known social formations up to and including capitalism, had been a history of alienation and, secondly, that with the revolutionary supersession of capitalism at least those aspects of alienation on which he concentrated his attention would be definitively abolished.

I have been rapidly touching on issues which we shall consider in more detail in later chapters because, without some mention of them, our treatment of the theme of 'alienation' would have been seriously incomplete. If we bear in mind the four aspects of alienation discussed at the beginning of this chapter, I suggest that, at least where the known past of mankind is concerned (omitting, therefore, the problem of Marx's language concerning the future), he supposed that alienation *was* a permanent feature of the human condition in the sense that, in all known social formations, human beings had been, in different ways, alienated from the process and products of labour, from their humanity and from their fellow-men.

Sin, or alienation, never occurs in the abstract. Man's estrangement from God, from nature and from his fellow-man, only occurs in specific, historically variable forms. From the fact that alienation *is* a permanent feature of the human condition it would be as illegitimate to infer that *therefore* its specific contemporary forms do not demand theoretical criticism and practical 'supersession' as it would be to infer, from the fact that physical sickness is a permanent feature of the human condition, that therefore we can dispense with attempts to diagnose and to treat specific diseases.

Death and Resurrection
In the Paris Manuscripts, Marx speaks of the 'entire movement of history' creating a state of affairs which he describes as 'the *genuine* resolution of the conflict between man and nature, and between man and man, the true resolution of the conflict between existence and being . . . between freedom and necessity, between individual

---

92 Mészáros, op. cit., p. 24.

and species'.[93] Commenting on this passage, Mészáros says that it needs qualification (on the basis of other aspects of Marx's thought); specifically: 'Man's freedom from natural necessity must always remain a relative achievement, however high a degree it may reach.'[94]

The qualification is important, but the abstract generality of its formulation obscures from view one of the great 'silences' in Marxian and Marxist theory: the absence of serious consideration of the implications, for any account of the 'transcendence' of alienation, of the fact of individual and social mortality. By 'social mortality' I intend to refer to the fact that the history of the species, and not merely the history of the individual, is bounded by the insurmountable barrier of death. And for us who live in the late twentieth century, under the shadows of thermonuclear war and the finitude of earth's natural resources, that barrier may by no means be considered merely a distant threat that can, for all practical purposes, be ignored.

'Human freedom', says Mészáros, 'is not the transcendence of the limitations (specific character) of human nature but a *coincidence* with them.'[95] This reminder may be an important corrective to unrealizable, utopian dreams, but it leaves unanswered the question as to whether, in the last analysis, that freedom for which we struggle is not simply coincident with our mortality. Perhaps it is, but at least the question is a question of fact. The Christian doctrine of redemption proclaims not only the possibility, for man graced by God, of the 'transcending' of man's alienation from his fellows (though it does affirm, in the face of all 'mystifying' abstractions about 'love', that the cost of love is crucifixion); it also proclaims the 'transcending' of the 'limitation' of mortality: the resurrection of the dead. Whether or not the hope engendered by this proclamation is false or illusory, Christianity does at least purport to deal with death. Or, rather, it asserts that death is dealt with, in fact, by the human form of God's fidelity.

'For the idealist', says Marx, 'every movement designed to transform the world exists only in the head of some chosen being, and the fate of the world depends on whether this head, which is endowed with all wisdom as its own private property, is or is not mortally wounded by some realistic stone before it has had time to make its revelation.'[96] That which we call the 'work' of Christ did not consist in the execution of a programme of material construction (though he was a carpenter). But neither did that 'work' consist in the elaboration of a programme for the transformation of the world

93 *EW*, p. 348.
94 Mészáros, op. cit., p. 155.
95 Ibid., p. 162.
96 *CW5*, p. 532.

(though he was a prophet). The 'work' of Christ consisted in his obedience to, his unswerving trust in, the silence he called 'Father'. If he 'had time to make his revelation', it was because the revelation that he *was* occurred, definitively, in that act of 'mortal wounding'. Good Friday was not the unfortunate disruption of his preaching. It was the execution of that which his preaching proclaimed: God's transformative fidelity to his creation.

Christians have always been tempted to transform the tragedy of Jesus into comedy by supposing that resurrection gives to his story a 'happy ending'. But no story has an ending until it is fully told. The context that gives meaning (or fails to do so) to the history of each individual (including Jesus) is the history of the human race. And because that history continues, the story has, as yet, *no ending*. The question of the meaning of history (including the question as to whether history has meaning, and the question as to the extent to which such meaning as it has can be mediated into thought and imagination) remains an open question.[97] It is not closed by faith in Jesus' resurrection. Which is why the grammar of the language in which that faith seeks expression is less the language of assertion and prediction than of prayer and trust. The Christian may have grounds for hope, but he has no grounds for 'metaphysical optimism'.

To believe in Christ's resurrection is to believe that Jesus' dying into God, his enactment of his dependence on God was, as dying into *God*, as the enactment of dependence on *God*, the achievement of his freedom, his identity, his eternity. To believe in Christ's resurrection is therefore to believe that, in *that* man's death, 'the *genuine* resolution of the conflict between man and nature, and between man and man',[98] is dramatically, sacramentally realized. If *that* man's death is resurrection, is the 'transcendence' of his mortality, then the outcome of the struggle against all forms of alienation (a struggle that, in certain circumstances, takes the form of endurance) is, in principle, assured. In principle, but not yet in fact. The doctrine of redemption does not afford the Christian any licence to substitute a *theory* of reconciliation, of the 'transcendence' of alienation, for its practice. The doctrine of redemption articulates the form of Christian hope, but that hope has to be *enacted* – in individual and social existence, in marriage, technology, art and politics – in the struggle for the 'true resolution of the conflict between existence and being'.[99]

The Marxian critique stands as a corrective of the Christian tendency to substitute theory for practice, to substitute an *account* of the transcendence of alienation for its achievement. The Christian,

97 Cf. Chapter Six.
98 *EW*, p. 348.
99 Loc. cit.

for his part, may press the Marxist on the adequacy of any expression of hope for the future of man which fails seriously to consider that aspect of our alienation which is most obdurately resistant of attempts to transcend it: namely, our boundedness by mortality, our dependence on death.

15

THEORY AND SYMBOLISM

I suggested, in Chapter Thirteen, that, if we endorse Marx's insistence on the primacy of 'social being' in respect of 'social consciousness', then it is true of a number of elements of the 'superstructure',
and by no means only of religion, that they 'have no content of their
own' in the sense that they 'reflect' more fundamental features of
social reality.[1] But this way of putting the matter, and in particular
the use of the metaphor of 'reflection', is in danger of underestimating the relative autonomy of art, literature and religion. Thus,
for example, when Marx, in a passage that I have quoted more
than once, says that 'The religious *reflections* of the real world can
. . . vanish only when the practical relations of everyday life between
man and man, and man and nature, generally present themselves
to him in a *transparent and rational* form',[2] what presuppositions
concerning the character and functions of human discourse underlie
the metaphors of 'reflection' and rational 'transparency'? In this
chapter I wish to suggest that Marx's account of alienation and its
supersession suffers, as does his treatment of ideology, from a tendency – inherited from Feuerbach, Hegel and the Enlightenment –
to underestimate the cognitive character of modes of discourse other
than the 'scientific' or 'theoretic'. My argument will be extremely
tentative, because the issues are of forbidding complexity, lying, as
they do, at the heart of a number of current debates in aesthetic
theory and in the theory of human rationality. But at least it seems
clear that they are issues which are of some importance for any
consideration of the cognitive status of religious and theological
discourse.

   'It is not true', says E. P. Thompson, 'that Marx passed over in
innocence the need to provide his theory with some "genetics". He
attempted such a provision, first, in his writings on alienation,
commodity fetishism, and reification; and second in his notion of
man, in his history, continuously making over his own nature. . . .
Of the first set of concepts I wish only to say this: they propose to
supply a "genetics" . . . in terms of mystified *rationality* . . . [such

1 Cf. above, pp. 162–3.
2 *Cap. I*, p. 173, my stress.

accounts] are the product of an overly-rational mind; they offer an explanation in terms of mystified rationality for *non*-rational or *ir*-rational behaviour and belief, whose sources may not be educed from reason.'[3] I would prefer to say that the explanation in terms of mystified rationality is the product, not so much of an 'overly-rational' mind, as of a mind too ready to assume that the criteria according to which modes of action and discourse are or are not to be assessed as 'rational' are those provided by a particular conception of theoretic rationality. Judged by this standard, modes of discourse that do not attain that conceptual 'transparency' which is the ideal of theoretic endeavour are deemed to be in some measure defective.

Art and Knowledge

The first chapter in the section on 'Wages' in *Capital* begins: 'On the surface of bourgeois society the worker's wages appear as the price of labour, as a certain quantity of money that is paid for a certain quantity of labour.'[4] At the end of the chapter, we are told that 'what is true of *all* forms of appearance and their hidden background is also true of the form of appearance "value and price of labour", or "wages", as contrasted with the essential relation manifested in it, namely the value and price of labour-power. The forms of appearance are reproduced directly and spontaneously, as current and usual modes of thought; the essential relation must first be discovered by science.'[5] Only two modes of discourse and consciousness feature in this model: on the one hand, how things 'spontaneously' seem to be and are said to be within the capitalist mode of production; on the other hand, how they 'really' are, as discovered by critical, scientific reflection. The distinction between 'practice' and 'theory' is all-embracing and apparently straightforward.

In such passages, Marx has in mind the relationship between a specific mode of industrial production and socio-economic theory. But consider the case of poetry or the novel. The theoretical or 'scientific' correlate of literary production would seem to be the work of the literary critic. Does it follow, then, that the relationship

---

3 E. P. Thompson, *The Poverty of Theory*, p. 357. Anderson's objection that Thompson's account simply omits consideration of 'the thesis that the contradiction between forces of production and relations of production is the deepest spring of long-term historical change', and that it is *this* which serves as an 'explanatory principle of the "genetic" type' in Marx's theory (*Arguments Within English Marxism*, p. 81), seems justified. But it leaves untouched the charge (with which I am concerned in this chapter) that there is, in Marx's thought, a 'rationalist' depreciation of the cognitive import of non-theoretical modes of discourse.

4 *Cap. I*, p. 675.

5 *Cap. I*, p. 682, my stress.

between poetic and literary production, and literary criticism, is similar to that which is said to obtain between industrial production and socio-economic theory? The trouble with this conclusion, which is invited by the generality and comprehensiveness of Marx's use of the distinction between 'practice' and 'theory', is that it reduces the status of poetic and literary discourse to that of expressing 'spontaneously' how things seem to be in contrast with the way in which they really are – for 'the *essential* relation must first be discovered by *science*'. In other words, poetic and literary discourse are, as non-theoretical, implicitly reduced to the status of 'mere ideology'. There seems no room, on Marx's account, for the characterization of poetic and literary discourse as constitutive and expressive of modes of *authentic knowledge*, of how things 'really' are.

We saw, when discussing 'ideology', that Althusser's treatment of the distinction between 'science' and 'ideology', a treatment which implies that only 'scientific' discourse constitutes a mode of *knowledge*, represented the development of a tendency detectable in Marx's own thought.[6] In 1966, asked whether *art* was or was not to be ranked amongst the 'ideologies', Althusser replied: 'Art . . . does not give us a *knowledge* in the *strict sense* . . . the peculiarity of art is to "make us see" something which *alludes* to reality. . . . What art makes us *see* . . . is the *ideology* from which it is born . . . and to which it alludes.'[7] The metaphor of 'allusion' is itself somewhat elusive, but what Althusser seems to be saying is that art, which cannot itself give us true knowledge, does nevertheless serve to give focus or definition to ideological consciousness. It may, therefore, as the 'heightening' or rendering 'visible' ('What art makes us *see* . . .') of ideological consciousness, facilitate or provoke critical (theoretical) awareness of ideological distortion. But what art cannot do, on Althusser's account, is itself constitute a mode of critical awareness, relatively autonomous in respect of scientific consciousness. 'Science' *alone* gives us 'knowledge in the strict sense'.

My suggestion, in this chapter, is that there is, in Marx's thought, a rationalist strand characterized by just this tendency to depreciate the cognitive status and relative autonomy of modes of discourse other than the 'theoretic' or 'scientific'. And the point is of some interest to the theologian because, whatever be the status of the various forms of theological discourse, at least it seems clear that the primary forms of Christian *religious* discourse – in praise, preaching, or proclamation – are poetic or narrative in character. In that sense, at least, religion constitutes a 'form of art'.

If it is true, as Althusser seems to admit,[8] and as Marx frequently recognized, at least in his criticism of 'bourgeois' science, that even

6 Cf. above, pp. 130–1.
7 L. Althusser, *Lenin and Philosophy*, p. 204.
8 Cf. *For Marx*, p. 170, quoted above, p. 130.

'scientific' discourse never, in practice, wholly escapes from the concrete particularity of the 'current and usual modes of thought' in a society, and that it is therefore permanently threatened by ideological distortion, this is *a fortiori* true of other modes of discourse. But the question is: is it in 'scientific' discourse *alone*, and not *also* in poetry and narrative, that the critique of ideology, the quest for knowledge of 'reality' beyond the 'spontaneously' produced 'appearances', is undertaken, and is undertaken in a manner that, as not reducible to, or translateable without remainder into, the language of 'scientific theory', possesses its own relative autonomy? This question raises the whole problem of Marxian aesthetics.

Sense and Thought

According to Mészáros, 'Aesthetic considerations occupy a very important place in Marx's thought.'[9] He therefore devotes a chapter to the 'aesthetic aspects' of alienation and its supersession. In defence of the proposition that 'Realism is the central notion of Marxian aesthetics, as has been made clear in more than one of Lukács' writings',[10] Mészáros polemically contrasts aesthetic 'realism', which aims at the comprehension of the dialectical totality of man by focusing on the *human* significance of the natural objects and artefacts represented by the artist,[11] with both aesthetic 'naturalism' – which contents itself with reproducing the 'deceiving appearances'[12] of reality – and with the plethora of supposedly 'anti-realist' schools of modern art which are, in fact, not anti-*realist* but merely anti-*naturalist*.[13] These schools poignantly illustrate the alienated condition of art and the artist in capitalist society as they 'become more and more entangled in abstract formal preoccupations'.[14]

For art to be 'realistic', in Mészáros' sense, aesthetic production would have to be a contributive factor in the struggle for human emancipation, for the transcending of alienation. Thus the project of 'the complete *emancipation* of all human senses and attributes'[15] is said to sum up 'perhaps better than anything else [Marx's] philosophical programme'.[16] With an eye on Plato and on the Platonic dimension of Hegelian rationalism, Mészáros insists, therefore, that 'Marx strongly opposes the idealist tradition that assigns an inferior place to the sensuous, and consequently also to art'.[17]

9 I. Mészáros, *Marx's Theory of Alienation*, p. 190.
10 Ibid., p. 198.
11 Ibid., p. 195.
12 Ibid., p. 196.
13 Cf. ibid., pp. 196–7.
14 Ibid., p. 197.
15 'Economic and Philosophical Manuscripts', *EW*, p. 352.
16 Mészáros, op. cit., p. 200.
17 Ibid., p. 201.

A vast amount has been written on Marxist aesthetics, and I am unfamiliar with most of this literature. I have confined myself to summarizing Mészáros' account of Marx's aesthetics, for two reasons. Firstly, Mészáros makes persuasive sense of some difficult passages in the Paris Manuscripts in which Marx sketches, in as much detail as anywhere else in his writings, so far as I know, the elements of a theory of aesthetics. Secondly, the drift of these passages, as interpreted by Mészáros, with his insistence on Marx's 'strong opposition' to any assignment of an 'inferior place' to artistic production and appreciation, might seem to run counter to my thesis in this chapter. Or, at least, it might seem to do so on the assumption that *literary* theory and practice are to be regarded as an aspect of the theory and practice of art. In fact, however, one of the most striking features of these passages in the Paris Manuscripts is – as I shall now indicate – the absence of any discussion of poetic and literary production and use.

In a system of social relations characterized by the transformation of everything into *commodities*, the only relationship possible between the human individual and 'objective' reality – whether natural objects that exist prior to human intervention, or the products of human labour, or social relations – is that of actual or possible ownership or loss of ownership, possession or dispossession. Hence 'selling is the practice of alienation.'[18] In the Paris Manuscripts, Marx contrasts this our alienated condition under the capitalist mode of production with a state of affairs in which our 'appropriation' of objective reality would manifest the irreducible richness and variety of our '*human* relations to the world – seeing, hearing, smelling, tasting, feeling, thinking, contemplating, sensing, wanting, acting, loving'.[19] This list appears to embrace the five senses, the intellect ('thinking, contemplating') and the will ('wanting, acting, loving').

Under capitalism, according to Marx, this variety of relations between man and his world has been reduced to the single relationship of actual or potential ownership: '*All* the physical and intellectual senses have been replaced by the single estrangement of *all* these senses – the sense of *having*.'[20] And yet, this impoverishment of humanity (a universal impoverishment, for the rich man is only rich in *possessions*: *humanly* speaking he is as poor as the poor man he exploits) is, historically, a necessary condition for the emergence of human richness, because capitalism has created the material conditions that make a truly *human* existence – an existence in which man could flourish, free from subservience to the domination of untamed natural forces – now possible for the first time: 'So that it

18 Marx, *The Poverty of Philosophy*, p. 28.
19 *EW*, p. 351.
20 *EW*, p. 352.

might give birth to its inner wealth, human nature had to be reduced to this absolute poverty'.[21]

The 'abolition' of capitalism, 'the supersession of private property is therefore the complete *emancipation* of all human senses and attributes'.[22] And it is thus emancipatory because, with the hegemony of 'possession' overthrown, human beings can now relate *humanly* to their world: 'The eye has become a *human* eye'[23] seeing what is there to be seen and not simply what is there to be bought and sold. 'The *senses* have therefore become *theoreticians* in their immediate praxis. They relate to the *thing* for its own sake, but the thing itself is an *objective human* relation to itself and to man . . . nature has lost its mere *utility* in the sense that its use has become *human* use.'[24] (Notice that Marx describes the 'senses' of emancipated humanity as '*theoreticians*' rather than, more generally, as media of knowledge and communication.)

'It is only when objective reality . . . becomes human reality', he continues, 'that all *objects* become for [man] the *objectification of himself*.[25] The ways in which they do so are irreducibly distinct, because our organs or senses are irreducibly distinct: 'An object is different for the *eye* from what it is for the *ear*. . . . The peculiarity of each essential power is precisely its *peculiar essence*. . . . Man is therefore affirmed in the objective world not only in thought but with *all* the senses.' It is by now clear why Mészáros should insist that 'Marx strongly opposes the idealist tradition that assigns an inferior place to the sensuous, and consequently to art.'[26] Nevertheless, it is to be noticed that the framework within which Marx affirms the relative autonomy of the 'senses', and indeed of *each* 'sense', is that of an overall contrast between 'thought' and 'sense'. Moreover, there is no indication of any differentiation, *within the realm of thought*, such as would ascribe a similar irreducible variety, and relative autonomy, to diverse modes of thought, and hence to diverse modes of discourse.

'The *senses* of social man [i.e., emancipated, non-alienated man] are *different* from those of non-social man. Only through the objectively unfolded wealth of human nature can the wealth of subjective *human* sensitivity – a musical ear, an eye for the beauty of form . . . be either cultivated or created. For not only the five senses, but also the so-called spiritual senses, the practical senses (will, love, etc.) . . . all these come into being only through the existence of their objects, through humanized nature. . . . *Sense* which is a pris-

21 Loc. cit.
22 Loc. cit.
23 Loc. cit.
24 Loc. cit.
25 *EW*, pp. 352–3.
26 Mészáros, op. cit., p. 201.

oner of crude practical need has only a *restricted* sense. For a man who is starving the human form of food does not exist . . . it would be hard to say how [his] way of eating differs from that of *animals*. The man who is burdened with worries and needs has no *sense* for the finest of plays; the dealer in minerals sees only the commercial value, and not the beauty and peculiar nature of the minerals; he lacks a mineralogical sense.'[27] I have quoted this passage at some length because, although it does not significantly advance the argument, it admirably illustrates the range and suggestiveness of Marx's treatment.

The section of the Paris Manuscripts on which I have been drawing undoubtedly contains the elements of a theory of aesthetics in the form of a project for the transcending of that condition of alienation which prevents man from realizing, both objectively and subjectively, the richness of the human potential. Throughout the section, however, the disjunction between 'thought' and 'sense' is simply taken for granted. It is, we might say, an outline of a theory of art as non-cognitive. Had Marx included in his outline any consideration of those forms of art, such as poetry and literature, which are essentially *linguistic* (and this, notwithstanding his passing reference to 'the finest of plays', he failed to do), he might have paused to consider the adequacy of that disjunction.

Wealth and Poverty

The theme of this section of the Manuscripts – in relation to which Marx's detailed observations stand as variations (the musical metaphor seems appropriate in view of the subject-matter) – is that of wealth and poverty. This theme reappears in some passages in the *Grundrisse*, the consideration of which will bring us back to the main argument of this chapter. But first, let us look once more at Marx's treatment of the theme in the section we have been discussing.

The rich man, in capitalist society, is the man who 'appears' to be rich because he owns many things. But, because his relationship to the objects of his concern is dominated by commercial considerations – he can only *use* them as objects to be bought, hoarded or sold, and can only *appreciate* them in so far as they have value as commodities – he is, humanly speaking, as poor as the poor man whose human destitution is manifest, not being obscured from view by apparent wealth. In contrast, a society in which alienation has been 'abolished' is a society which 'produces man in all the richness of his being, the *rich* man who is *profoundly and abundantly endowed with all the senses*, as its constant reality'.[28]

27 *EW*, p. 353.
28 *EW*, p. 354.

In such a society, men would know poverty as well as wealth, but 'poverty', like 'wealth', would now take on a wholly new meaning: it would be man's recognition of the depth and permanence of his need, not for possessions, but for 'a totality of vital human expression'.[29] And, where man's relationships with his fellow human beings are concerned, 'poverty' would now refer, not to slavery and dispossession, but to 'the passive bond which makes man experience his greatest wealth – the *other* man – as need'.[30]

In the *Grundrisse*, this theme of wealth and poverty returns in a lyrical sketch of the dialectic of history which must, I think, be heard (to continue my musical metaphor) as counterpointing Hegel's *Phenomenology*. Marx notes that, in antiquity, there was little interest in the production of economic wealth as an 'end in itself': 'The question is always which mode of property creates the best citizens.'[31] This 'old view, in which the human being appears as the aim of production . . . seems to be very lofty when contrasted to the modern world, where production appears as the aim of mankind and wealth as the aim of production.'[32] But appearances are, as always, deceptive – and we are by now alert to the ambivalence, in Marx's dialectical analysis, of the concept of 'wealth'. When the 'limited bourgeois form is stripped away, what is wealth other than the universality of individual needs, capacities, pleasures, productive forces, etc., created through universal exchange?'.[33]

The prospect which classical antiquity entertained was indeed 'loftier', inasmuch as its goal was the production of the *human* and not merely the production of material wealth. But it was a prospect intrinsically limited both by the fact that antiquity lacked the material conditions necessary for the objective realization of the human potential, and also by the fact that, subjectively, it measured the development of human powers 'on a *predetermined* yardstick'.[34] Capitalism accepts no limits, no 'predetermined yardsticks'. It seeks only the creation of unlimited material wealth. Under capitalism, therefore, the 'complete working-out of the human content appears as a complete emptying out, this universal objectification as total alienation, and the tearing-down of all limited, one-sided aims as sacrifice of the human end-in-itself to an entirely external end'.[35] This is why, in comparison with capitalism, 'the childish world of antiquity appears on one side as loftier'.[36] And yet, this 'total alien-

29 *EW*, p. 356.
30 Loc. cit.
31 *G*, p. 487.
32 *G*, pp. 487–8.
33 *G*, p. 488.
34 Loc. cit.
35 Loc. cit.
36 Loc. cit.

ation' is in fact the 'objectification' of wealth. Hence, with the final twist of the dialectic of history, the 'abolition' of capitalism, this 'objective' wealth ceases to be the expression of man's alienation and becomes the possibility condition of unbounded *human* richness.

What has this sweeping panorama of the dialectic of history to do with the theory of art? The clue is contained in that reference to 'the childish world of antiquity'. Armed with this clue, let us now turn to the final section of the Introduction to the *Grundrisse*, a passage in which Marx expresses his puzzlement at the 'eternal charm' exercised by Greek art and epic poetry.

'In the case of the arts', he says, 'it is well known that certain periods of their flowering are out of all proportion to the general development of society, hence also to the material foundation . . . of its organization.'[37] In order to understand this phenomenon, in the case of classical antiquity, we have first to appreciate the relationship between Greek art and Greek mythology: 'It is well known that Greek mythology is not only the arsenal of Greek art but also its foundation.'[38] Greek mythology expressed the human reality, and the reality of man's relationship to nature but, under the existing, exceedingly limited, material conditions, that expression could only be *subjective*, could only occur in the imagination. Or, at least, in so far as *objective* expression was sought, it could only be achieved in the illusory form of the construction of the gods. It follows that Greek mythology, and hence Greek art, cannot fulfil for us the functions which they fulfilled for their original producers: 'All mythology overcomes and dominates and shapes the forces of nature in the imagination and by the imagination; it therefore vanishes with the advent of real mastery over them.' In other words, with the advent of science and technology, mythology is no longer available to us as *a mode of knowledge*. We can tell the tales of the gods only as fairy-tales. For us, demythologization is no longer an option, but a fact. The clear implication is that the only mode of *knowledge* available to us is that which corresponds to our 'real' (i.e. effective, industrial and technological) mastery over nature: namely, science.[39]

And yet, Marx is puzzled: 'the difficulty lies not in understanding that the Greek arts and epic are bound up with certain forms of social development. The difficulty is that they still afford us artistic pleasure and that in a certain respect they count as a norm and as

37 *G*, p. 110.
38 Loc. cit.
39 As Steven Lukes says of this passage, it treats of Greek mythology 'in a way that is closer to Durkheim's . . . account than to the . . . cruder versions of historical materialism' (S. Lukes, *Emile Durkheim. His Life and Work*, p. 234; cf. the Conclusion to E. Durkheim, *The Elementary Forms of the Religious Life*).

an unattainable model.'[40] Notice that he says of Greek art and poetry that they 'afford us pleasure', not that they provide us, in their own way, with knowledge of reality. Thus, on the one hand, we can still detect the presence of that disjunction between 'thought' and 'sense' which we noticed in the Paris Manuscripts – and of the consequent assumption that art operates wholly in the realm of 'sense'. And yet, on the other hand, the Greek arts and epic still 'in a certain respect . . . count as a norm and as an unattainable model'. In *what* respect? Marx does not tell us. One answer – namely, that the differentiation of science and literature, of theoretical 'transparency' and symbolic density, leaves open the possibility that literature may fulfil *cognitive* functions that are not reducible to, or translatable without remainder into, the language of theory – is not available to him because of his assumption that only theoretic discourse can give us knowledge 'in the strict sense'. In fact, he invokes (as he did in the other passage from the *Grundrisse*) the metaphor of infancy: 'A man cannot become a child again, or he becomes childish. But does he not find joy in the child's naiveté, and must he himself not strive to reproduce its truth at a higher state?'[41] The question is left rhetorical, and the possibility is not considered that poetry and literature, narrative and symbolic discourse, might constitute an irreducibly distinct mode for the 'reproduction' of ancient truth and the production of true expression in our own time.

I may seem to have followed an excessively devious route in order to return to the point from which I set out. But it seemed desirable to try to situate my charge that there is a 'rationalist' strand in Marx's thought, a tendency to underestimate or to deny the cognitive character of modes of discourse other than the theoretical, in the context of his general approach to aesthetics and of the location of that approach in his dialectical interpretation of history.

Religion and Theology

Liturgical worship, the focal articulation and expression of Christian faith, is 'dramatic' in character, in the sense that the social celebration of faith is an exercise in interpretative performance. The constitutive elements of liturgy – not only linguistic, but also musical, iconographic and choreographic – are artistic products, works of art. It follows that the problem of the cognitive status of Christian religious discourse is to be considered an instance of the wider problem of the cognitive status of aesthetic expression. However, before we take up the discussion of those epistemological issues

40 *G*, p. 111.
41 Loc. cit.

which are my principal concern in this chapter, it may be helpful
briefly to indicate, more generally, some of the ways in which
Marx's aesthetics, and the theme of wealth and poverty which
provides the framework for that aesthetics, might contribute to
long-standing debates in Christian theology.

Thus, for example, behind some projects for the 'modernization'
of the liturgy it is possible to detect the influence of an aesthetic
'naturalism' (in Mészáros' sense), in so far as attempts are made
to bring liturgical language and symbolism into closer conformity
with the language and symbolism of 'everyday life'. But merely to
bring liturgical forms into closer conformity with how things 'spontaneously' appear to be, in a particular social formation, is to risk
depriving liturgical practice of its prophetic and critical power. This
is not to be taken as an argument against liturgical reform, the
opponents of which are sometimes motivated, on the one hand, by
a politically reactionary separation of 'religion' and 'politics' and,
on the other, by the conviction that Christian believers should be
prepared to serve as the curators of ancient and beautiful artefacts
which nobody else in the society is any longer able or willing to
use. I am merely suggesting that someone persuaded by Marx's
treatment of 'art' in the Paris Manuscripts (as interpreted by Mészáros) might consider the possibility that the goal of liturgical
reform should be liturgical 'realism' rather than liturgical 'naturalism'. To accept this possibility would be to acknowledge the
function of liturgy indirectly to contribute to the liberating transformation of prevailing social conditions and social consciousness.
The question as to what linguistic, musical and dramatic 'styles'
best enable the liturgy to fulfil this function is a practical question,
the answer to which will be different in different social circumstances. But at least it must be insisted that a *Christian* evocation of
the 'sacred' will be an evocation of that which transcends our
present inhumanity.

It is important, however, not to exaggerate the socially transformative potential of liturgical reform. Liturgy, as a form of art or an
assemblage of artistic elements, is – in our culture – both derivative
and marginal. The disappointment experienced by many Christians
in recent decades, who expected great things from carefully thought
out programmes of liturgical reform, arises – in part – from a failure
to perceive the impossibility of reforming the liturgy in abstraction
from the reform of the culture. A 'human' liturgy, in Marx's sense,
would only be possible in a 'human' culture, a culture in which the
'fetishism of commodities' had been 'abolished'.

As a corollary, we might suggest that debates concerning liturgical 'wealth' and 'poverty' could profit from attention to Marx's
dialectical treatment of these concepts. It is sometimes suggested
that, in a drab and impoverished world, the richness of the liturgy

should reflect the glory of God. The 'richness' to which, in such arguments, reference is made, however, is only too often the richness of *commodities*, of artefacts, and not the 'human' richness of the artificers and users of those commodities. If it is true that '*gloria Dei vivens homo*', it is difficult to see how the use of expensive 'things' by impoverished human beings could appropriately reflect the 'richness' of God.

As a further corollary, we might suggest that the theme of 'wealth' and 'poverty', as handled by Marx in the Paris Manuscripts and the *Grundrisse*, might throw fresh light on debates concerning the Christian virtue of poverty. To put it very briefly: I take it that that 'poverty' which is to be accounted virtue is not material destitution but rather that 'passive bond which makes man experience his greatest wealth – the *other* man – as need'.[42] From the earliest days of Christianity, communities have sprung up which sought to give social expression to such poverty, in critical contrast to the *inhumanity* of societies which, obsessed with acquisition and power, alienated human beings from the products of their labour, from each other, and therefore from God. Whether or not such communities are to be described as 'utopian' in character is a question which we shall consider in Chapter Seventeen.

Those last few paragraphs were a detour, but not I think a distraction, from the theme of this chapter. To return to the central problem: if aesthetic expression is confined, as it was by Marx, to the realm of 'sense', 'feeling' or 'imagination' (in the sense in which Feuerbach, for example, contrasts 'imagination' with 'thought'),[43] liturgical expression must be similarly confined. To put it another way: from the standpoint of a non-cognitive theory of art, such as Marx appears to have taken for granted, the fundamental forms of Christian religious discourse must undoubtedly be said to be noncognitive in character. And yet, on the one hand, most Christians seem to suppose that, in giving liturgical expression to their faith, they are not simply expressing their feelings or indulging their emotions, but are using a 'language' which expresses their *knowledge* of God, his presence in history and promise for its future; on the other hand, I cannot see that a non-cognitive theory of aesthetic expression was *demanded* by Marx's general account of man, nature and history – by his historical materialism.

---

42 *EW*, p. 356.
43 Cf. e.g., his chapter on 'The Mystery of the Logos and Divine Image', *The Essence of Christianity*, pp. 74–9. There are some phrases in that chapter, such as the statement that 'Thought expresses itself only in images' (p. 77), which point in a direction in which the contrast between 'thought' and 'imagination' might have been softened. But that is not the direction which he took. The rationalism implicit in his account, in this chapter, of the relation between the first and second persons of the Trinity, becomes explicit in an appendix: cf. pp. 285–7.

Let us consider these two points in reverse order. Frederic Jameson speaks of the influence, on Plekhanov and Lukács, of the Hegelian view that 'the return to symbolic modes is felt to be a historical regression'.[44] But, although Hegel arranged the relationship between art, narrative and philosophy in hierarchic order, and thus exhibited an 'idealist' or 'rationalist' underestimation of the cognitive status of symbolic and narrative modes of expression, he nevertheless regarded all three 'levels' of expression as modes of man's *self-knowledge*. He did not, in other words, suppose that symbolic or 'pictorial' expression, and narrative discourse, were to be accounted *simply* non-cognitive, even though they were deemed to be 'inferior' forms of knowledge, forms to be 'transcended' by pure conceptuality, by philosophy.[45]

Against the background of the Hegelian model, we need to look again at Mészáros' claim that 'Marx strongly opposes the idealist tradition that assigns an inferior place to the sensuous, and consequently to art'.[46] It was a comparatively straightforward matter for Marx to sustain this opposition because, in his discussion of art, the disjunctive contrast between 'sense' and 'thought' facilitated the neglect of those forms of art (namely, poetry and literature) which have the strongest *prima facie* claim to be considered as modes of artistic expression with cognitive import. The only 'location' readily available for poetry and literature, on the Marxian scheme, would seem to be as 'ideological forms'. In view of Marx's handling of the distinction between 'science' and 'ideology', the conclusion seems inescapable that, where poetry and literature are concerned, he stood closer to the 'idealist' tradition than Mészáros indicates, or than he himself was aware.

Both Hegel's hierarchical arrangement of the 'pictorial', the narrative and the conceptual, and Marx's tendency (in his assessment of 'scientific theory' as the only appropriate form of expression of 'thought', and hence of 'real knowledge')[47] to carry over at least one feature of Hegelian rationalism,[48] suppose the supersession of pictorial, symbolic and narrative modes of expression by pure conceptual 'transparency' to be a desirable project. Whether or not this project is completely realizable, to refrain from attempting it would

---

44 F. Jameson, *Marxism and Form*, p. 337.
45 Cf. J. N. Findlay's comment on the passage in the *Phenomenology* in which Hegel says of the 'death' of 'picture-thought' that this 'death is the painful feeling of the Unhappy Consciousness that *God Himself is dead*' (p. 476, Hegel's stress): 'what is really meant by passion and resurrection is the elimination of pictorial particularity and its supersession by the life of thought' (ibid., pp. 588–9).
46 *Marx's Theory of Alienation*, p. 201.
47 Cf. *CW5*, p. 37.
48 As Richard Bernstein has put it: 'Marx's attack in the *Critique of the Philosophy of Right* . . . could only be performed by one who identified himself with the Hegelian project of rational comprehension' (R. J. Bernstein, *Praxis and Action*, p. 38).

be (our discussion of those passages from the *Grundrisse* would suggest) suspect of cultural infantilism and, in that sense, historically regressive.

From the standpoint of one who sought to pursue such a project, whatever truth-content there may be in the 'narrative' which Christian liturgy dramatically enacts, and in the narrative forms which it includes (in the use of Scripture, in preaching, in the creeds and in so many of its prayers), can only, in the last resort, find appropriate expression in 'philosophical' (Hegel) or 'scientific' (Marx) discourse. Concerning this project, however, a number of observations are in order.

In the first place, while there may be subject-matters in respect of which the quest for ever purer conceptual 'transparency' is appropriate, it is by no means obvious that these would include all, or even the more important amongst, the topics that feature on the agenda of the Christian theologian. I have observed, more than once, that there are no expressions of Christian faith – linguistic, pictorial, dramatic or institutional – which can claim immunity from theological criticism. But this is *not* to say that such expressions are 'superseded' by such criticism (any more than a painting or a poem is 'superseded' by the work of the art critic or literary critic). Nor is it to say that the character of such criticism should, in all cases, be 'philosophical' or 'theoretical' (any more than all literary criticism or political analysis is appropriately described as 'philosophical' or 'theoretical').

In the second place, the Hegelian project of rational comprehension, and the Marxian tendency to regard 'scientific theory' as the only appropriate form for the expression of 'real knowledge', both unduly neglect Aristotle's maxim that it is a mark of the educated man that he looks for only so much *akribeia* as the nature of the subject-matter permits.[49] As Professor Copleston puts it: 'Hegel attempted . . . to do what cannot be done, namely to make plain to view what can only be simply apprehended through the use of analogies and symbols.'[50]

In the third place, where Christian theology – considered as critical reflection on Christian practice – is concerned, it may well be that the responsibilities of theology include, in addition to historical, textual and literary-critical tasks, logical and philosophical enquiry and criticism. I would not for one moment wish to deny this. Nevertheless, at the centre of Christian faith there stands, not an absolute idea, but an unsurpassable event, and for that reason alone theology cannot – as Hegel supposed that it must – be reduced to metaphysics.

49 Cf. *The Ethics of Aristotle*, ed. J. A. K. Thomson, Bk. I, Ch. 3, p. 28.
50 F. Copleston, *Philosophers and Philosophies*, p. 115.

In the fourth place (to repeat, for the sake of completeness, a point that I made earlier), from the fact that poetry and literature are (like *all* forms of human discourse) exposed to ideological distortion, it does not follow that they may not function as relatively autonomous instruments contributing to the critique of ideology, to the quest for 'reality' beyond the 'appearances'. And if this is true of poetry and literature, then the same critical potential cannot be denied to the language of Christian belief on the grounds of its formal character as non-theoretical discourse (I put it that way because, clearly, such critical potential could be denied to Christian religious discourse on *other* grounds, such as its inherently illusory or 'mystifying' character).

I have tried, in this chapter, to put my finger on what seems to be an inconsistency in Marx's thought. It is an inconsistency which partly arises, I believe, from the fact that the distinction between 'theory' and 'practice' is simply not flexible enough to accommodate the irreducible variety of forms of human action and reflection. 'Language', said Marx, '*is* practical consciousness.'[51] I have no quarrel with that. But it does not follow that the only *critical* uses of language are those which can appropriately be described as 'theoretical' or 'scientific' in character.

51 *CW5*, p. 44.

16

'SCIENTIFIC' MARXISM: PROBLEMS OF METHOD

Although the sequence of topics selected for comment in this study is by no means arbitrary, there is obviously nothing as conveniently tidy as a 'linear' relationship between them. Therefore, as the necessarily linear sequence of chapters unfolds, certain themes begin (we might say) to make their absence increasingly felt. Thus, for example, the discussion of 'ideology' in Chapter Eleven, and of Marx's aesthetics in Chapter Fifteen, proceeded as if questions concerning what Marx might mean by 'science' and 'scientific theory' were reasonably straightforward. This is, however, far from being the case, as is evident from the voluminous literature on 'Marxism as science'.

My principal concern in this chapter is to try to understand what Marx himself meant by 'science', and hence what it was that he was claiming for his work in declaring it to be 'scientific' in character. I shall therefore discuss in some detail the 1857 Introduction to the *Grundrisse*,[1] a text in which we can follow Marx at work as he seeks to clarify his own methodological strategy in critical contrast to Hegel's method, on the one hand, and to that of the 'bourgeois' political economists, on the other. Before doing so, however, it will be useful to try to 'locate' and specify, in fairly general terms, the problem of Marxism as 'science'. And because assessments of the 'scientific' character of Marxist theory often concentrate on its 'predictive' success or failure, a final section will indicate some of the connections between the questions considered in this chapter and the discussion, in Chapter Seventeen, of Marx's stance in respect of the future.

Senses of 'Science'
Perhaps the best way to approach the question of what Marx means by 'science' is to notice that with which, from time to time, 'science' and the 'scientific' are contrasted in his work. Thus, for example, in the 1844 Manuscripts *'real* science' is contrasted with a science

1 *G*, pp. 83–111, referred to henceforward in the text of this chapter as *1857.*

which is defective on account of being 'abstractly material, or rather idealist'.[2] '*Sense perception* (see Feuerbach) must be the basis of all science. Only when science starts out from sense perception in the dual form of *sensuous* consciousness and *sensuous* need . . . is it *real* science'.[3] 'Real' science, then, sets out from perception, and from a perception of human needs. Hence, 'Feuerbach's great achievement is . . . to have founded *true materialism* and *real science* by making the social relation of "man to man" the basic principle of his theory.'[4] Here, the criteria for distinguishing between the 'scientific' and the 'non-scientific', or between 'real' and defective forms of science, appear to be epistemological and not merely methodological. 'Real' science is that which gives us 'real' knowledge of human beings and their needs: knowledge of social and natural 'reality' and not merely of the forms of its appearance.

Marxists often tend to resist the suggestion that Marx's 'materialism' is appropriately described as 'empiricist', because they associate 'empiricism' with an uncritical acceptance of the appearances of reality, of how things seem to be. Nevertheless, 'critical realism' or 'critical empiricism' do seem suitable epithets to describe Marx's life-long opposition to all forms of 'speculative' theorizing not submitted to empirical control: 'Empirical observation must in each separate instance bring out empirically, and without any mystification and speculation, the connection of the social and political structure with production.'[5]

It is this insistent realism which accounts for the contrasts drawn between 'science' and 'philosophy' (by which he almost invariably means 'idealist' philosophy), and between 'scientific' socialism and all forms of political wishful thinking or mere disapproval of the *status quo*. Thus, in 1874, making notes on Bakunin's *Statism and Anarchy*, in which Bakunin had criticized the concept of 'scientific socialism' which, he said, 'is increasingly found in the works and speeches of the Lasalleans and Marxists',[6] Marx said that the phrase 'was only used in opposition to utopian socialism, which wants to attach the people to new delusions, instead of limiting its science to the knowledge of the social movement made by the people itself.'[7] (We are reminded of the passage in the *German Ideology* in which Marx characterized 'real, positive science' as the exposition of 'the practical activity, of the practical process of development of men'.)[8]

The contrast drawn here is between, on the one hand, a socialism

2 *EW*, p. 355.
3 Loc. cit.
4 *EW*, p. 381.
5 *CW5*, p. 35.
6 Quoted in *FI*, p. 337.
7 *FI*, p. 337.
8 *CW5*, p. 37.

whose criticism of the existing situation gets no further, negatively, than expressing disapproval and, on the other, a socialism which is 'scientific' inasmuch as, by striving to comprehend in knowledge the forces at work in a particular situation, it contributes, as theory, to the effective transformation of that situation. Thus when, six years later, in 1880, Engels claimed that with the 'two great discoveries' that 'we owe to Marx . . . the materialistic conception of history and the revelation of the secret of capitalistic production through surplus value . . . *socialism became a science*',[9] it is clear from the context that 'scientific' socialism is being contrasted with a socialism which confined itself to impotent disapproval: 'The socialism of earlier days certainly criticized the existing capitalist mode of production and its consequences. But it could not explain them, and, therefore, could not get the mastery of them. It could only simply reject them as bad.'[10] In similar vein, in 1894, Lenin said that Marx 'did not confine himself to describing the existing system, to judging it and condemning it; he gave a scientific explanation of it.'[11]

In such passages, two closely related reasons for the Marxist's insistence on the 'scientific' character of Marxism stand out quite clearly. In the first place, to the extent that the 'scientificity' of Marxist theory is presumed to be a necessary and sufficient condition of the truth of its claim to express effective *knowledge* of reality – to have grasped the truth of how things 'really' are – denials of its 'scientific' character will be taken to be tantamount to denials of its truth. In the second place, the denial of the 'scientificity' of Marxism is not only construed as questioning the truth of the theory; it is also taken to be an expression of opposition, in practice, to the political movement whose 'voice' the theory is: 'the social movement made by the people itself'.[12] For the Marxist, someone who denies the 'scientific' character of Marxism is not someone who merely expresses theoretical disagreement; he is also presumed to be a political opponent.

We can put that last point more sharply by saying that, for the Marxist, there is no such thing as 'merely theoretical' or 'merely academic' disagreement. In the natural sciences, the emergence of incompatibility or contradiction between theoretical claims is usually taken to be evidence of the imperfection of our knowledge. Hence theoretical disputes can (at least in principle!) be negotiated in tranquillity, because there is probably an element of truth in both conflicting claims. In the analysis of social formations, how-

9 F. Engels, 'Socialism: Utopian and Scientific', *HM*, p. 180, my stress.
10 Loc. cit.
11 V. I. Lenin, 'What the "Friends of the People" Are and How They Fight the Social-Democrats', *HM*, p. 333.
12 'Conspectus of Bakunin's *Statism and Anarchy*', *FI*, p.337.

ever, theoretical disagreements may also reflect underlying conflicts of interest between social classes. To the extent that this is the case, the resolution of the conflict will necessarily be a practical, political matter. Attempts to resolve it at the theoretical level alone leave the underlying social conflicts unattended to and hence unresolved. In such circumstances, the appeal to the partial and limited nature of all points of view, expressive of the conviction that, if only we *understood* the situation better, disagreement would cease, may unwittingly fulfil an 'ideological' function, strengthening the hands of whatever group at present wields social and political power.[13]

The danger of arguments such as these is that they can also be used, on the other side, ideologically to justify manifold forms of irrationality – of the subordination of the quest for truth to the struggle for power. But it is, I think, impossible to understand Marxist uses of the concept of 'science' unless the force of such arguments is borne in mind.

There are, moreover, significant analogies between Marxist perceptions of the grounds and implications of disagreement concerning the 'scientific' character of Marxism, and hence concerning its truth, and Christian perceptions of the grounds and implications of disagreement concerning the truth of Christianity. Obscurantism, the practical face of which is the repression of dissidence, has too often been a feature of the history both of Marxism and Christianity. But recognition of the obscenity of subordinating the quest for truth to the struggle for power in the name of future freedom does not entail the admission that disagreements concerning the truth either of Marxism or of Christianity are or can ever be *merely* theoretical in character.

Theological disagreement, like all theoretical disagreement, is indeed evidence of the irreducible complexity and variety of patterns of human experience, and hence of the partial and limited nature of all knowledge and all understanding. The insistence on this fact is the strength of theological 'liberalism'. But the weakness of theological, as of political liberalism, lies in the inadequacy of its analysis of the grounds and sources of conflict and contradiction. Jesus' crucifixion was not an excessive expression of disagreement with his views. He posed a threat more fundamental than that, and it was 'necessary' that the attempt be made to dispose of him. And in so far as Christianity succeeds in displaying, in practice, the subversive power of the gospel, Christians should expect to meet, not merely with the attempted refutation of their beliefs, but with more 'practical' forms of resistance.

At this point I would like to return to Engels' suggestion that Marxism is 'scientific' inasmuch as, by 'explaining' the 'capitalist

13 Cf. G. Lukács, *History and Class Consciousness*, p. 10.

mode of production and its consequences', it has made possible the
'mastery' or 'abolition' of capitalism. Does it follow that Marxist
'explanation', as 'scientific' explanation, consists in the discovery of
the 'laws of motion' of capitalism and its supersession? Such interpretations of the claim that Marxist theory is 'scientific' have a
long history in Marxism. They bear witness to the influence on
Marxism, an influence the seeds of which can be detected in Marx's
later writings,[14] and more clearly in the writings of Engels and
Kautsky,[15] of late nineteenth-century 'scientism'. It seems to me
impossible, however, to confine Marx's use of the concept of 'science' within the procrustean bed of any such mechanistic model of
scientific explanation. 'Dialectical materialism', according to Plekhanov, 'has shown that man makes his history not in order to march
along a line of predetermined progress, and not because he must
obey the laws of some abstract evolution. . . . He does so in the
endeavour to satisfy his own needs.'[16] This seems an accurate reflection of Marx's description of 'real science' arising from the
perception of real human need. But, if so, it follows that, in any
reference to the 'laws' of social and economic development, the
concept of 'law' is being used, as E. P. Thompson has suggested,
in a metaphorical sense. 'If', says Thompson, 'we replace the notion
of the *laws* of social change by that of *logic* – a metaphor which may
include the idea of causal relationships while excluding its determinist, predictive connotations – then certain "historicist" features
[in a Popperian sense] of Marx's thought fall away.'[17] Thompson's
suggestion is not, I believe, simply a piece of apologetic generosity.
It is an attempt to recognize that Marx's arguments and analyses
are more complex, more flexible and more interesting than is apparent from the writings of those who take Marx's metaphors at face
value in order to discredit Marxist uses of the concept of 'science'.
'It is clear from the *Introduction* (1857) and many other works', says
Terrell Carver, 'that Marx's scientific research did not aim at the
discovery of universal, or, as he put it, "eternal" laws of political
economy or of human behaviour, though he did not seem to regard
as mutable his presuppositions about the nature of man. . . . Marx
did compare his methods to those of the physicist . . . yet he was

---

14 Cf. *Life*, p. 423.
15 Kolakowski says of Kautsky that 'It was thanks to his interpretative work that
   the stereotype known as scientific socialism – the evolutionist, determinist and
   scientistic form of Marxism – became universally accepted in its main lines
   . . . the scientistic and positivistic version of Marxism developed in Engels' later
   writings was adopted by Kautsky without modification' (*KII*, pp. 32, 36).
16 G. V. Plekhanov, *Fundamental Problems of Marxism*, p. 110.
17 E. P. Thompson, 'An Open Letter to Leszek Kolakowski', *The Poverty of Theory*,
   p. 121.

careful to limit the analogy between his work and that of the natural scientist.'[18]

That late nineteenth-century (and early twentieth-century) 'scientism' to which I referred in the previous paragraph may be seen as a particular development of an ancient tradition according to which 'science', or *'scientia'*, or *'episteme'*, is contrasted – as knowledge – with *mere* 'belief' or 'opinion'. It tended, in two senses, to be reductionist. On the one hand, it tended to exclude from the range of forms of knowledge first-order, prereflexive modes of cognition.[19] On the other hand, it tended to erect as the ideal of 'scientificity' the procedures and techniques characteristic of the so-called 'successful' sciences of nature.

Marx's concept of 'science' was not straightforwardly reductionist in either of these senses. Nevertheless, post-Marxian debates concerning the 'scientific' character of Marxism can hardly be understood except against the background of this twofold tendency. The situation is complicated by the fact that the history of the English word 'science' has been very different from that of the German *'Wissenschaft'* or the French *'science'*. It is perfectly in order to demand, of any academic discipline, that its procedures be *'wissenschaftlich'* or *'scientifique'*. This demand amounts to no more than the stipulation that, in respect of its particular subject-matter, its handling of evidence be appropriately scholarly and its arguments and techniques appropriately rigorous. Thus, whereas it is perfectly possible to describe a piece of historical research, philosophical analysis, or theological enquiry, as *'wissenschaftlich'* or *'scientifique'* (and hence to speak of history, philosophy or theology as *'Wissenschaft'* or as *'science'*) it would be misleading to describe any of these enterprises, in English, as 'scientific'. Marx's own work, and that ideal of the *'wissenschaftlich'* to which he sought to conform, includes historical, philosophical, sociological, economic and political components. To ask whether Marxian theory is *'wissenschaftlich'* or *'scientifique'* is to ask a perfectly intelligible question, even though the answers to it may be both complex and debatable. But either to affirm or to deny that it is 'scientific' in character seems to me to be both confusing and misleading.

With this *caveat* concerning terminology, we can conclude these preliminary remarks on Marx's concept of 'science' (It would be pedantic to refer, from now on, to his concept of *'Wissenschaft'*). The best summary description of Marx's use of the concept that I have come across is that offered by Terrell Carver: 'Marx's conception of science was broad enough to include what appear to be philosophical analyses, assertions, and conclusions. Science for him

18 T. Carver, *Karl Marx: Texts on Method*, p. 41.
19 Cf. above, p. 131.

seems to have represented the active search for, and presentation of, truths and evidence for them, using arguments and data which related not simply to what could be touched or counted, but to what could be stated in more general terms (including moral terms), to be the case with man and his world. The searching process of Marx was essentially active, investigative, critical, and practical; a scientific presentation, in his view, seems to have been one which solved conceptual mysteries and presented the human world accurately, intelligibly, and politically.'[20] There are features of that description, especially the distinction between 'searching' and 'presenting', which are best examined in the context of the 1857 Introduction to the *Grundrisse*, to which we now therefore turn.

Search for a Starting-point

In July 1867, in the Preface to the first edition of *Capital*, Marx remarked that 'Beginnings are always difficult in all sciences'.[21] For over twenty years he had been designing and redesigning his great work on political economy[22] and, for much of the time, the search for a satisfactory starting-point had proved fruitless. The problem had, in fact, two distinct but closely related aspects: on the one hand, there was the question of the overall organization of the work, and hence of where to begin; on the other, there was the problem of appropriately specifying the 'first premises' of his 'scientific' presentation of the critique of political economy. The 'great burst of activity'[23] which began in October 1857 and which produced the *Grundrisse* seems in part to have been due to the fact that, in working on the Introduction, in August and September of that year, he had succeeded in significantly clarifying both aspects of the problem.[24]

The argument of *1857* is 'complex and difficult to follow'.[25] It consists of criticism of the views of others interwoven not only with sketches of his own position but also with historical, philosophical and logical comments – and, as one would expect of one so deeply influenced by Hegel, the 'logic' in question is not only a matter of the relationship between terms and concepts but also of the 'logic of facts'.[26] Drawing heavily on Carver's excellent commentary, I

20 Carver, op. cit., pp. 40–1.
21 *Cap. I*, p. 89.
22 For an account of these successive plans, cf. Carver, op. cit., pp. 11–37.
23 Carver, op. cit., p. 27.
24 Cf. ibid., pp. 27–8; *Life*, p. 290. For a detailed examination of the changes which the design of Marx's project underwent after the autumn of 1857, cf. Rosdolsky, *The Making of Marx's 'Capital'*. pp. 1–55.
25 Carver, op. cit., p. 88.
26 Cf. e.g., the discussion of the 'syllogistic' relationship between production, distribution, exchange and consumption in *G*, p. 89. On the influence of Hegel's *Logic*, cf. Carver, op. cit., pp. 89, 113–20.

intend simply to indicate those features of Marx's argument which throw light on his notion of 'science' and on some of the problems to which that notion gives rise.[27]

Marx announces his 'point of departure' as: 'Individuals producing in society – hence socially determined individual production'.[28] This description of his starting-point – which echoes the account, in *The German Ideology*, of the 'premises' of materialist method: 'real individuals, their activity and the material conditions of their life'[29] – is contrasted with that chosen by Ricardo, Rousseau and Adam Smith, who postulated 'individuals' abstracted from any determining social context and projected these abstractions 'into the past'.[30] They were thus able to treat of 'production' in an entirely abstract, non-historical manner.

'Whenever we speak of production', however, 'what is meant is always production at a definite stage of social development'.[31] Does it follow that, 'in order to talk about production at all', the only options available are *either* to write a history of successive modes of production *or* to declare at the outset that 'we are dealing with a specific historic epoch such as, e.g. modern bourgeois production, which is indeed our particular theme'?[32] The difficulty with either approach is that its results would lack the generality of reference which alone would make it possible to speak, in any sense that would have met Marx's need to establish a *theoretical* critique of political economy, of a 'science' of political economy. He refers ironically to the 'whole profundity' of the bourgeois political economists, whose forgetfulness of the historical specificity of modes of production enables them to 'demonstrate the eternity and harmoniousness of the existing social relations'.[33] And yet, even if '*Production in general* is an abstraction', because modes of production are always historically and culturally specific, it does seem that there are some 'common elements', that 'Some determinations belong to all epochs'.[34] In this sense, the concept of production does not lack all generality of reference. If, then, there are both general, regularly recurring, and particular, culturally specific, aspects of

---

27 *1857* is available in several English translations: in addition to *G*, pp. 83–111, there are those in Carver, op. cit., pp. 46–87, and C. J. Arthur, ed., *The German Ideology*, pp. 124–51. In view of the fact that, unlike the rest of the *Grundrisse*, the text has been available since 1903, and of the detailed attention it has received from the commentators, from Lukács to Althusser, I am at a loss as to why Arthur should say, as recently as 1974, that it 'deserves to be more widely known' (p. 3).

28 *G*, p. 83.

29 *CW5*, p. 31; cf. Carver, op. cit., p. 89.

30 *G*, p. 83.

31 *G*, p. 85.

32 Loc. cit.

33 Loc. cit.

34 Loc. cit.

production, the distinction between the two must be borne in mind and brought out in the analysis. Moreover, it is precisely the variable, culturally specific features of production which account for the *development* of successive modes of production: for the fact that production has a history. This first section of the text concludes with the following summary: 'There are characteristics which all stages of production have in common, and which are established as general ones by the mind; but the so-called *general preconditions* of all production are nothing more than these abstract moments with which no real historical stage of production can be grasped.'[35] It is the fault of the 'idealist' to suppose that, in identifying, by abstraction, these 'general preconditions of all production', he *has* thereby succeeded in grasping the concrete reality of some 'real historical stage of production'.

In *The German Ideology*, Marx claimed that, once philosophy ceases to be regarded as 'self-sufficient', its place can only be taken 'by a summing-up of the most general results, abstractions which are derived from the observation of the historical development of men'.[36] This first section of *1857*, and especially the distinction between the illusory 'eternity' of social relations and modes of production, on the one hand, and the validity, as abstractions, of generalizations on the other, focuses on the same problem. It is, we might say, the problem of the possibility, nature and limits of 'materialist science'. Or, to put it another way, it is the problem of establishing a strategy for the elaboration of modes of *theoretical* discourse (whether scientific or philosophical) which avoid shipwreck either on the Scylla of a relativist historicism or in the Charybdis of an 'idealist' metaphysics. It is a problem to which we shall return.

The thrust of the second section of *1857*, on 'The General Relation of Production to Distribution, Exchange and Consumption', is twofold. On the one hand, Marx argues, against the bourgeois political economists, that all four of these categories have a history; that modes of production, and not only modes of distribution, exchange and consumption, are and have always been subject to historical variation. Hence, for example, his reference, with Ricardo and Mill in mind, to 'the ineptitude of those economists who portray production as an eternal truth while banishing history to the realm of distribution'.[37] On the other hand, although all four categories thus 'form the members of a totality, distinctions within a unity'[38] – a totality the constituent elements of which mutually determine each other – he nevertheless argues for the primacy of production in respect of the other three categories.

35 *G*, p. 88.
36 *CW5*, p. 37.
37 *G*, p. 97.
38 *G*, p. 99.

Thus, in relation to consumption, we are told that 'production is the real point of departure and hence also the predominant moment';[39] in relation to distribution: 'The structure of distribution is completely determined by the structure of production';[40] in relation to exchange: 'Exchange in all its moments thus appears as either directly comprised in production or determined by it'.[41] And his general conclusion is that 'Production predominates not only over itself . . . but over the other moments as well. The process always returns to production to begin anew.'[42]

The method of argument in this second section is – to anticipate a distinction which we shall discuss shortly – 'investigative' rather than 'presentational'.[43] That is to say: Marx is concerned, at this stage, not so much to provide an outline of his own theory, his own 'scientific' account of economic relations, as to come critically to grips with the work of his predecessors. Therefore, the *data* for his enquiry in this section are not this or that specific economic structure, or the history of economic structures, but the standard works on political economy. And the argument is dialectical in the sense that it proceeds by way of critical engagement with the 'appearances' of economic relations in these standard works.[44]

However, his insistence on the primacy of production constitutes an important partial exception to this investigative procedure inasmuch as it not only arises from an internal critique of the textbooks of political economy, but is also expressive of a conviction, derived from elsewhere, that is central to his own distinctive theoretical stance. As a result, there is an element of pure assertion in his manner of arguing for the primacy of production. Thus, for example, in the third section he claims that 'In all forms of society there is one specific kind of production which predominates over the rest, whose relations thus assign rank and influence to the others'.[45] This assertion is illustrated by some exceedingly general historical observations, the last of which is that 'Capital is the all-dominating economic power of bourgeois society'.[46] This may well be the case, and may furthermore be demonstrably the case, thus

39 *G*, p. 94.
40 *G*, p. 95. Carver prefers ' "arrangement", rather than "structure", as a translation of *Gliederung*, in order to avoid begging any question of how distinct or developed an entity Marx had in mind' (p. 65).
41 *G*, p. 99.
42 Loc. cit.
43 Cf. Carver, *Texts on Method*, p. 128.
44 'The English political economists referred to their subject as a science and their work as scientific, since they sought to deal with observed facts' (Carver, p. 5). It is therefore incumbent upon Marx to show himself to be *more* 'scientific' than they were, in coming to grips more thoroughly and more accurately with the 'reality' underlying the 'appearances'.
45 *G*, pp. 106–7.
46 *G*, p. 107.

justifying the decision that the study of capital 'must form the starting-point as well as the finishing point'[47] of his projected work. But where are the warrants for the contention that in *all* forms of society there is one specific kind of production which predominates over the rest? Even if the claim were to the effect that this was one of the 'common elements' which 'belong to all epochs',[48] it would seem that it could only be substantiated by exhaustive and detailed historical investigation such as he never undertook.

Although Marx undoubtedly believed that this claim and, more generally, the assertion that production is ultimately determinative in respect of consumption, distribution and exchange, could be supported by historical argument and theoretical analysis, it does seem to be the case that it also expresses an *anthropological* conviction. It is, says Carver, 'a restatement of the view of man developed in the 1844 *Manuscripts* and the *German Ideology*',[49] a view of man as a being who produces and reproduces his nature and existence through productive labour. Marx's view of 'production as the determining factor seems to follow from the special ontological status assigned to production in the 1844 Manuscripts and the special role it plays in his theory of history'.[50]

I have dwelt on this point at some length because it indicates that there is, in Marx's elaboration of his 'science', an irreducible *philosophical* component. It is, of course, none the worse for that: only a somewhat naive positivist would assume that it is ever possible to construct a large-scale scientific or '*wissenschaftlich*' strategy or viewpoint on which philosophical convictions and presuppositions exerted no influence. It is, nevertheless, a useful reminder to those who, possibly misled by Marx's tendency to restrict the concept of 'philosophy' to metaphysical idealism, suppose themselves entitled to appeal to his work in support of the contention that 'science' and 'philosophy' are mutually exclusive: that they are to be contrasted as 'real knowledge' and 'mere opinion'.

The third section of *1857*, on 'The Method of Political Economy', has been described by Althusser as 'the *Discourse on Method* of the new philosophy founded by Marx'.[51] It is the most difficult and the most important part of the Introduction. The opening argument of the first section amounted, as we have seen, to an endorsement and application of the 'materialist' position on 'premises' which he had announced in *The German Ideology*. In accordance with that position, 'It seems to be correct', he now says, 'to begin with the real and

47 Loc. cit.
48 *G*, p. 85.
49 *Texts on Method*, p. 123.
50 Ibid., p. 151.
51 L. Althusser, *Reading Capital*, p. 86. On Althusser's fondness for this section, see my remarks in Chapter Two, p. 20.

the concrete, with the real precondition, thus to begin, in economics, with e.g. the population, which is the foundation and the subject of the entire social act of production',[52] because the population is the concrete *locus* of 'socially determined individual production'.[53] However, 'on closer examination this proves false.'[54] Why? Because, at the outset, the 'population' does not yet exist *for thought*. As a concrete phenomenon, the population is, in Kolakowski's words, 'the chaotic mass of direct perception',[55] but it is not yet understood. As a concept, 'population' is only an 'abstraction' until I have discovered the elements of which it is composed and the relations that obtain between them.[56]

At this point, therefore, using 'the standard terminology of nineteenth-century logic (derived, in both English and German, from concepts and procedures of ancient and medieval philosophy)',[57] Marx distinguishes two 'journeys' or 'paths' along which the mind in search of knowledge and understanding may travel. In *1857*, these 'paths' are described but not named whereas, as we shall see later on, in the Postface to the second edition of *Capital* they are given their traditional names: the way of 'inquiry' and the way of 'presentation'.[58] 'If', he says, 'I were to begin with the population, this would be a chaotic conception [*Vorstellung*] of the whole, and I would then, by means of further determination, move analytically towards ever more simple concepts [*Begriff*], from the imagined concrete towards ever thinner abstractions until I had arrived at the simplest determinations. From there the journey would have to be retraced until I had finally arrived at the population again, but this time not as the chaotic conception of a whole, but as a rich totality of many determinations and relations.'[59] In other words, only when this twofold process is complete can 'population' exist in thought, no longer as an 'abstraction' (in the sense of an indeter-

52 *G*, p. 100.
53 *G*, p. 83.
54 *G*, p. 100.
55 *KI*, p. 314.
56 *G*, p. 100.
57 Carver, op. cit., p. 129.
58 Cf. *Cap. I*, p. 102. According to Aristotle, someone considering the appropriate means by which a chosen end may be achieved deliberates, 'until they come at last to the cause which, although it is the last in the order of discovery, is the first in the chain of causes' (*The Ethics of Aristotle*, Bk. III, Ch. 3, p. 86). Medieval Aristoteleanism thus spoke of a '*duplex via*': a '*via inventionis*', or 'way of discovery', from the '*prius quoad nos*' to the '*prius quoad se*', and then, having got to the heart of the matter, a return journey, the '*via disciplinae*' or 'way of presentation'. This twofold journey constituted the methodological dialectic of a neo-aristotelean '*scientia*'. For the immediate background to Marx's use of this metaphor, in Kant, Hegel and Feuerbach, cf. Colletti's discussion of this third section of *1857*, in *Marxism and Hegel*, pp. 113–38.
59 *G*, p. 100.

minate general notion) but in the richness and complexity that obtains in concrete reality.

Marx notes that the first journey was 'the path followed historically by economics at the time of its origins',[60] in the seventeenth century. And only when these pioneering investigators had done their work could there emerge, in the eighteenth and early nineteenth centuries, 'the economic systems which ascended from the simple relations, such as labour, division of labour, need, exchange value, to the level of the state, exchange between nations and the world market'.[61] There then follows the crucially important sentence: 'The latter is obviously the scientifically correct method.'[62] Concerning this claim it is sufficient, at this point, to make two comments. In the first place, in declaring that the method which proceeds from simple categories to complex totality and, in *that* sense, from the 'abstract' to the 'concrete',[63] is 'obviously the scientifically correct method', Marx is aligning himself more closely than we would have expected with the method of classical or bourgeois political economy. In the second place, if it is correct to say (with the ancient metaphor of the *duplex via* in mind) that no body of thought has established itself as 'scientific' until *both* paths have been trod, and if both are therefore essential constituents of 'scientific' method, does not the restrictive identification of the 'scientifically correct method' with the method of scientific *presentation* risk unduly depreciating the 'scientific' significance of the way of discovery? To put it another way: any supposition that the investigative moment in the scientific process 'disappears in the result',[64] once the appropriate pattern of theoretical presentation has been arrived at, bears witness to a markedly non-dialectical view of the relationship between the two 'journeys': a view which, in the autonomy it accords to constituted theory, would seem incompatible with historical materialism as Marx understood it. It is considerations such as these which lead E. P. Thompson to say, as we saw in Chapter Two, that 'what we have at the end [in the *Grundrisse*], is not the overthrow of "Political Economy" but *another* "Political Economy" ',[65] and to refer to *1857* as this 'moment of Marx's theoretical . . . immobilism'.[66]

Marx is not, of course, unaware of the danger to which I have

60 Loc. cit.
61 *G*, pp. 100–1.
62 *G*, p. 101.
63 On Marx's two senses of 'abstraction' in this text, as 'mental *generalization*' and as 'an aspect . . . of the particular *object* under consideration', cf. Colletti, *Marxism and Hegel*, pp. 123, 139.
64 L. Althusser, *Reading Capital*, p. 50.
65 E. P. Thompson, *The Poverty of Theory*, p. 252.
66 Ibid., p. 396.

referred.[67] In the movement, along the way of presentation, from simple categories to complex totalities, 'The concrete . . . appears in the process of thinking . . . as a result, not as a point of departure.'[68] But it is therefore only too easy to succumb to Hegel's 'illusion of conceiving the real as the product of thought concentrating itself',[69] of history as the history of the 'idea'. In the following paragraphs, as Marx tries 'to sort out the rational elements in Hegel's method, and put it to use',[70] the complexity, even confusion,[71] of the argument arises from the number of distinct but related issues of which he attempts to treat more or less simultaneously.

'Scientific presentation', along the 'return journey' from cause to effect, from fundamental features to concrete appearances, seeks to reflect the order of things in the order of thought. Thus far, Marx's account of scientific method echoes that offered by both Hegel and Aristotle, with the crucial difference that Hegel, as Marx understands him, had 'inverted' the relationship between the *'ordo essendi'* and the *'ordo cognoscendi'*, attributing the primacy to the latter, with the result that 'the movement of the categories appears as the real act of production'.[72] When, however, the reality under consideration is an historical, changing reality, the concept of 'cause', or determining feature, becomes disturbingly ambiguous. There is no necessary correlation between the structural primacy of the 'simplest determinations' within a particular totality (a primacy which it is the task of 'analysis' to discover, and of 'presentation' to elucidate 'scientifically') and the sequence in which the categories emerge chronologically. Thus, Marx's answer to the question: 'Do not these simpler categories also have an independent historical or natural existence predating the more concrete ones?', is: 'That depends'.[73] And his conclusion is characteristically complex: 'Although the simpler category may have existed historically before the more concrete, it can achieve its full . . . development precisely in a combined form of society, while the more concrete category was more fully developed in a less developed form of society.'[74]

He considers at some length the example of labour, which 'seems

---

67 He had, after all, indicated his awareness of the problem as early as 1844: 'the first criticism of any science is necessarily influenced by the premises of the science it is fighting against . . . Proudhon's treatise *Qu'est-ce que la propriété?* is the criticism of *political economy* from the standpoint of political economy . . . [it] will therefore be scientifically superseded by a criticism of *political economy*, including Proudhon's conception of political economy' (*CW4*, p. 31).

68 *G*, p. 101.

69 Loc. cit.

70 Carver, *Texts on Method*, p. 138.

71 Even Carver's lucid commentary (pp. 140–8) cannot entirely dispel this sense of confusion.

72 *G*, p. 101.

73 *G*, p. 102.

74 *G*, p. 103.

a quite simple category'.[75] But 'the example of labour shows strikingly how even the most abstract categories, despite their validity . . . for all epochs, are nevertheless, in the specific character of this abstraction, themselves likewise a product of historic relations.'[76] It follows, firstly, that they 'can only be *formulated* at a late historical stage',[77] and, secondly, that 'only someone thinking in the context of bourgeois society could hope fully to understand pre-capitalist economics.'[78] As Marx himself puts it: 'Bourgeois economy . . . supplies the key to the ancient.' But he takes care immediately to add: 'not at all in the manner of those economists who smudge over all historical differences and see bourgeois relations in all forms of society'.[79] In spite of this disclaimer, he still seems to be sailing close to the wind of 'political economy'.

What has happened at this stage of the argument, it seems to me, is that Marx, having decided that the method of 'presentation' is 'obviously the scientifically correct method', is attempting, *from the standpoint of political economy*, at one and the same time both to steer clear of Hegel's mistaken identification of the order in which the categories appear in 'scientific' thought with 'the process by which the concrete itself comes into being',[80] and to resist the suggestion that the historical dimension of scientific thought finds adequate expression in a view of history which sees the past as merely leading up to and producing the appearance of the present. Hence his remark that 'The so-called historical presentation of development is founded, as a rule, on the fact that the latest form regards the previous ones as steps leading up to itself, and, since it is only rarely . . . able to criticize itself . . . it always conceives them one-sidedly'.[81]

Historically, capital appears *late* on the scene. It is the product, not the starting-point, of the history of modes of production. Yet, if we bear in mind the structural priority of production in respect of the other constituent elements of the socio-economic totality (a priority on which, as we have seen, he laid considerable emphasis in the previous section), it becomes clear that a 'scientific' treatment of economic reality must *start* with production and hence, when its subject-matter is bourgeois society, with capital. The important conclusion follows that 'It would therefore be unfeasible and wrong to let the economic categories follow one another [in a 'scientific' presentation] in the same sequence in which they were historically decisive'.[82]

75 Loc. cit.
76 *G*, p. 105.
77 Carver, op. cit., pp. 147–8, my stress.
78 *Life*, p. 292.
79 *G*, p. 105.
80 *G*, p. 101.
81 *G*, p. 106.
82 *G*, p. 107.

If my presentation of this Introduction has been somewhat tortuous, this is at least partly due to the fact that any simpler treatment could hardly have indicated the complexity and subtlety of the text. And yet, it is far too central a text to be passed over in silence in any account of Marx's concept of 'science'. Before pulling the threads of the discussion together and indicating the significance of the 1857 Introduction for the theme of this chapter, I propose briefly to turn to two later passages: the 1859 Preface to *A Contribution to the Critique of Political Economy*,[83] and the 1873 Postface to the second edition of *Capital*.[84]

In the 1859 Preface, Marx says that he has 'omitted' a 'general introduction which I had drafted . . . since on further consideration it seems to me confusing to anticipate results which still have to be substantiated'.[85] The editor of the *Early Writings* identifies the suppressed introduction with *1857*,[86] but Carver suggests that the latter is 'best regarded as a rough study towards such an introduction, or even as a compendium of preliminary investigations'.[87] Whichever be the case, the suppression suggests that Marx was not entirely happy with the 1857 text. The only clue, in the 1859 Preface, as to why this may have been the case, is to be found in his statement that, having omitted a general introduction, 'the reader who really wishes to follow me will have to decide to advance from the particular to the general'.[88] What is the significance of this change from the language of *1857*, where the reference was to the movement from the 'abstract' to the 'concrete', or from the 'simple' to the complex totality? Carver tentatively suggests that the change be attributed to a desire to resolve 'what may have been some confusion between relative theoretical simplicity, and the relatively simple *elements* of the process of production in capitalist society'.[89] What is certainly not clear is how movement from the 'particular' to the 'general' could be thought to be an appropriate description of that explanatory method, along the 'way of presentation', which was confidently declared, in *1857*, to be 'obviously the scientifically correct method'.[90] It does not follow that Marx had abandoned the metaphor of the '*duplex via*', but he may have come to see that the sharp distinction between the two 'journeys', and the ascription of scientificity to the 'return journey' *alone*, did not do justice to his own procedures, for 'the two modes (investigation and presentation)' are

83 *EW*, pp. 424–8.
84 *Cap. I*, pp. 94–103.
85 *EW*, p. 424.
86 Cf. *EW*, p. 424.
87 Op. cit., p. 156.
88 *EW*, p. 424.
89 *Texts on Method*, p. 135.
90 *G*, p. 101.

not 'absolutely distinct in his work, since his presentation undoubtedly reproduces some of the investigations'.[91]

In the 1873 Postface to *Capital*, the influence of the metaphor of
the '*duplex via*' is again detectable. 'Of course', says Marx, commenting on reviews of the first edition, 'the method of *presentation*
[*Darstellungsweise*] must differ in form from that of *inquiry* [*Forschung-
sweise*]. The latter has to appropriate the material in detail, to
analyse its different forms of development and to track down their
inner connection. Only after this work has been done can the real
movement be appropriately *presented*. If this is done successfully, if
the life of the subject-matter is now reflected back in the ideas,[92]
then it may appear as if we have before us an *a priori* construction.'[93]
In contrast to *1857*, the indispensability of both aspects of the
'dialectical method'[94] is simply stated, without any suggestion that
'scientificity' is to be attributed to the 'method of presentation' *alone*.
Furthermore, Marx's acknowledgement that the results of the
'method of presentation' cannot fail to have the appearance of an
a priori, idealist construction, prompts us to ask: in what circumstances might this 'appearance' correspond, contrary to intention,
to the 'reality'? That question can perhaps be tentatively answered
as follows.

What Marx needed, in order to establish the 'scientific', or '*wissenschaftlich*' character of his work, was a 'materialist' transposition
of concepts of 'scientificity' inherited from Hegel (and, behind him,
from a tradition reaching back to Aristotle). In order to effect this
transposition, it was of crucial importance that relationships of
mutual, dialectical interaction be sustained between 'inquiry' and
'presentation': between critical empirical and historical investigation and analysis, on the one hand, and the elaboration of theory,
on the other. Once relax the dialectical tension, and all that would
remain would be *either* mere historical description, and elements of
socio-economic analysis, unco-ordinated by theory, by the quest for
explanation, *or* '*a priori* construction', theoretical discourse floating
in illusory autonomy, explaining nothing. My impression is that
although, even in *1857*, and more successfully in his writings as a
whole, he sought to sustain this tension, nevertheless, by apparently
restricting 'scientific' method, in *1857*, to the method of scientific
presentation, he provided subsequent Marxist thinkers with some
warrants for a model of 'scientific' Marxism as a system of knowledge possessed in theoretical form, unrestrained by the need for the

91 Carver, op. cit., p. 136.
92 Carver prefers 'mirrored in ideas', as a translation of '*Spiegelt . . . ideall wieder*',
   so as to avoid linking Marx 'incorrectly . . . with a simple, reflectionist epistemology' (p. 5).
93 *Cap. I*, p. 102, my stress.
94 *Cap. I*, p. 102.

continual submission of its arguments and conclusions to historical enquiry and changing circumstance, which contributed to that shift towards an 'idealist' use of a 'materialist' method which I described in Chapter Nine.

One final comment. Few philosophers are likely to be happy with Marx's characterization of the 'materialist' successor to idealist or 'self-sufficient' philosophy, as 'a summing-up of the most general results, abstractions which are derived from the observation of the historical development of men'.[95] It smacks too much of relativist historicism. But our discussion of *1857* suggests that this description, in *The German Ideology*, is less cavalier than might appear at first sight. Marx was undoubtedly 'deeply suspicious of "eternal" laws and "universal" truths, scorning them as trivial, misleading, or false'.[96] But even if, according to him, all 'abstractions' are historical products, marked by the circumstances of their production, it does not follow that they are merely provisional, wholly determined by their context or entirely revisable. If he is too much of an historian not to be deeply suspicious of abstract generalizations concerning man and society, he is also too much of a philosopher to surrender the quest for theoretical comprehension of those 'common elements' of human life, activity and organization which 'belong to all epochs'.[97]

Science and Prediction

Kolakowski says of Marx's contention, in the third section of *1857*, that correct scientific presentation proceeds on the basis of abstractions reached along the investigative path, that 'In this way Marx attempts to transfer to political economy the basic method of modern science which originated in Galileo's perception that mechanics cannot be an account of actual experience . . . but must presuppose ideal situations that never occur in actual experimental conditions'.[98] In other words, natural-scientific 'laws' are cast in some such form as: if X occurs, Y will occur, other things being equal. Other things never are equal, but the deviations from the norm that take place in empirical circumstances can be taken into account in constructing and interpreting scientific experiments.

'There is, however', Kolakowski continues, 'an essential difference between the use of this method in physics and in political economy',[99] because it follows from the uniqueness, the non-recurrence, of 'complex social phenomena', that there can be 'no instru-

95 *CW5*, p. 37.
96 Carver, op. cit., p. 157.
97 Cf. *G*, p. 85.
98 *KI*, p. 314.
99 *KI*, p. 315.

ments to measure the deviation of reality from the ideal model'.[100] Therefore, we must either admit that Marx's appropriation of the 'basic method of modern science' serves no useful purpose, or attempt to salvage it by interpreting *Capital* 'as relating only to "ideal" capitalism'. This device 'sometimes serves as a means of resisting the empirical evidence that refutes Marx's predictions, which are thus represented as statements of what would happen in a non-existent ideal form of capitalism. But such interpretations protect Marxism against the destructive results of experience only by depriving it of its value as an instrument of real-life social analysis.'[101]

The criticism is a familiar one. What are we to make of it? In the first place, the analogy between the method of natural science and the method of Marx's 'science' as he sketches it in *1857* is a great deal looser than Kolakowski suggests. In the second place, it is important to notice the emphasis which Kolakowski lays on the *predictive* function of scientific 'abstraction'. The model, he says, 'is only of value if it enables us to say: "Capitalism under such and such conditions would undergo such and such changes, but as the conditions are affected in certain ways, the changes will take place somewhat differently, as follows. . . ." But this is precisely what we cannot say.'[102]

Kolakowski is clearly correct in insisting that social-scientific theory, in its attempt to explain historical, as distinct from purely natural phenomena, cannot exhibit the predictive capacity which is a criterion of good theory in the natural sciences (which is not to say that it necessarily lacks *all* predictive capacity). But to suppose that the model of 'scientific method' is therefore simply inappropriate in political and economic studies is unduly to restrict the possible range of differentiated uses of the metaphor of the '*duplex via*'. Natural scientific research and hypothetical explanation is by no means the *only* form of that dialectic of 'enquiry' (from conceptually 'chaotic' experience to 'abstraction') and 'presentation' (from 'abstraction' to the intelligent grasp of concrete totalities) which may be said to characterize *any* form of 'science' or '*Wissenschaft*'.

Moreover, it is a striking feature of the texts which we have considered in this chapter that, throughout, Marx shows little or no interest in assessing the predictive capacity of 'scientific' method as he sought to elaborate it. As he put it in the *Communist Manifesto*: 'The theoretical conclusions of the Communists . . . merely express, in general terms, actual relations springing from an existing class struggle, from a historical movement going on under our very

100 Loc. cit.
101 *KI*, p. 316.
102 *KI*, p. 315.

eyes.'[103] For Marx, it is a sufficient condition of the 'scientificity' of his theoretical work that it succeeds in presenting 'the human world' – what is actually going on and the circumstances which produced the present state of affairs – 'accurately, intelligibly, and politically'.[104]

I am not suggesting, of course, that Marx had no interest in the future, or that he doubted the capacity of a 'scientific' explanation of capitalism's rise and fall to assist our understanding of the direction in which things were moving and could be made to move, thereby contributing to capitalism's 'supersession'. But, for better or for worse, considerations of the predictive capacity of his theory played little part in his attempts to elaborate a method more 'scientific' than that of his predecessors in political economy.

According to Karl Popper, Marx was 'a prophet of the course of history, and his prophecies did not come true . . . he misled scores of intelligent people into believing that historical prophecy is the scientific way of approaching social problems. . . . Marxism is a pure historical theory, a theory which aims at predicting the future course of economic and power-political developments and especially of revolutions.'[105] The situation is, in fact, far more complex and more paradoxical than Popper's polemic indicates. We shall have occasion, in the next two chapters, to consider the possibility that, far from indulging in excessive – and false – 'scientific prediction', it might have been better had Marx considered the problem of the future *more* carefully, rigorously, or – shall we say – 'scientifically'.

As an illustration of some of the problems which we shall shortly be examining (and the examination will enable me to reopen the theological discussion which has been interrupted in this chapter, because my concerns here have been simply exegetical), let me return to Marx's notes on Bakunin's *Statism and Anarchy*. ' "*Scientific socialism*" ', says Bakunin, ' "which [phrase] is unceasingly found in the works and speeches of the Lasalleans and Marxists, itself indicates that the so-called people's state will be nothing else than the very despotic guidance of the mass of the people by a new and numerically very small aristocracy of the genuine or supposedly educated. The people are not scientific, which means that they will be entirely freed from the cares of government, they will be entirely shut up in the stable of the governed. A fine liberation! The Marxists sense this (!) contradiction and, knowing that the government of the educated (*quelle rêverie*) will be the most oppressive, most detestable, most despised in the world, a real dictatorship despite all

103 *R1848*, p. 80.
104 Carver, op. cit., pp. 40–1.
105 K. Popper, *The Open Society and its Enemies, Vol. II*, pp. 82–3; cf. pp. 135–98.

democratic forms, console themselves with the thought that this dictatorship will only be transitional and short." '[106]

Marx comments: '*Non mon cher*! – that the *class rule* of the workers over the strata of the old world whom they have been fighting against can only exist as long as the economic basis of class existence is not destroyed.'[107] This exchange is rich in irony. It is Bakunin who accurately predicts the 'despotic' form which government by an élite who suppose themselves uniquely equipped with 'scientific knowledge' will take. And yet the grounds of Marx's confidence that the future will be less dark, although expressed in 'scientific' form – *when* 'the economic basis of class existence' is destroyed, *then* the 'class rule of the workers' will cease – are quite certainly to be sought elsewhere than in the inappropriate use, in matters of political economy, of the 'basic method of modern science'.

106 Quoted in *FI*, p. 337.
107 *FI*, p. 337.

17

UTOPIA, HOPE AND REVOLUTION

For what did Marx hope, and why? That is to say: what was the character and what were the grounds of Marx's expectations concerning the future, concerning human existence in post-capitalist society? These questions indicate the cluster of problems which we shall consider in this and the following chapter. In view of the fact that Christians have always supposed the movement to which they subscribe to be the vehicle and (in some sense) the embodiment of a 'gospel', a proclamation of hope for mankind, such problems are evidently of some interest to the Christian theologian. In the present chapter I propose, after some introductory remarks, to consider Marx's critique of utopianism and, arising from this, the circumstances in which Christian belief and practice might appropriately be described as 'utopian' in character. I shall then offer some further reflections on the relationship between 'expectation' and 'prediction', and will conclude with a discussion of Marx's concept of 'the last revolution', and of the proletarian class which will be its agent.

Prediction, Persuasion and Preference: Introductory Remarks
In the previous chapter, I was at pains to emphasize the negligible part played, in Marx's attempts to elaborate a method of social analysis that would be, not merely 'scientific', but *more* 'scientific' than that of his predecessors in political economy, by considerations of the *predictive* capacity of the theoretical component of such analysis. This emphasis was necessary as a preliminary indication of why it is that those commentators who suppose the 'scientific' character of Marxian theory to be closely dependent upon its conformity to the methods of the physical sciences do Marx an injustice when they roundly assert that subsequent events 'falsified' his 'predictions'.

There is, nevertheless, a paradox here. Economists, social scientists and meteorologists are not primarily interested in understanding and explaining that which has previously occurred. Unlike the historian, they are interested in the past, not 'for its own sake', but only in so far as comprehension of the past enables them to understand and (in the case of economists and social scientists) to exert some influence on the outcome of the past in the future. To speak of 'the present' is to speak of that which, even as we speak of it, has become the past. To speak of that which is 'going on under our very eyes',[1] is to speak of that which is both past and future. Any description or explanation of 'current' events and processes necessarily contains or entails assertions concerning that which will occur in the future. Thus it is that economists and meteorologists make 'predictions' the characters of which differ, inasmuch as the economist's 'predictions' constitute an 'interference' in the processes described, whereas those of the meteorologist do not (there are usually more economists than meteorologists on panels of government advisors, although the weather exerts at least as significant an influence on the economy as do patterns of human choice). Both the economist and the meteorologist (if they know what they are doing) are far too conscious of the fact that economic and meteorological occurrences are unique instantiations of the confluence of an immense range of variables to suppose that their 'predictions' can be other than abstract expressions of probability. If they are wise, they will say, not that 'X will occur', but that 'X is more likely to occur than Y'. The 'laws' of economics and meteorology are statistical in character.

The paradox to which I referred just now arises from the fact that, although Marx seems to have been well aware of the impossibility of making specific, concrete 'predictions' concerning the future, nevertheless his language usually lacks that note of tentativeness which we might expect to follow from this recognition. A first clue as to why this should be the case is contained in the contrast, mentioned already, between economic and meteorological 'prediction'. When an economist, or a political theorist, speaks of historical 'necessity', of what 'must' happen, he may be incorrectly supposing himself capable of making specific, concrete 'predictions'. But the grammar of the discourse of 'necessity' may simply express the recognition that, in these matters, theoretical pronouncements can, and frequently do, constitute an effective 'interference' in the course of events. The accuracy of the meteorologist's prediction of rain depends not at all upon his success or failure in persuading his audience to carry umbrellas. The accuracy of the economist's predictions, on the other hand, is partially dependent on the reaction of his audience (whose behaviour is the object of his study) to his prognostications. As George Markús puts it: 'the conceptual clarification of some form of "historical necessity" as the form of *prediction* of social events, unlike prediction in the natural sciences, is not merely a theoretical act.'[2] Moreover, as a 'practical' act, the

1 'Manifesto of the Communist Party', *R1848*, p. 80.
2 G. Markús, *Marxism and Anthropology*, p. 53.

social-scientific expression of 'necessity', of what 'must' be done, embodies not only an analytic but also an evaluative judgement. It follows that any assessment of the 'force' of political or economic 'prediction' should include consideration of the evaluative options of the predictor (even when, perhaps especially when, he illusorily supposes his predictions to be 'value-free'). (I am only too well aware that the theological fool is rushing in where social theorists, at least since Max Weber, have trod warily. But I hope that, nevertheless, these remarks may serve to provide a framework for the discussion of Marx's language concerning the future.)

According to Kolakowski, 'It is characteristic of the Hegel-Marx tradition in general to blur the distinction between foreseeing the future and creating it. It is here that prophets and scientists part company.'[3] It is, however, one thing to argue that political and economic discourse can never conform, in practice, to the physical scientist's ideal of 'scientificity' (nor is there any good reason why they should seek to do so). But it is quite another thing to suppose that, where the 'practical' discourses of politics and economics are concerned, the distinction between 'depicting' the future and contributing to its occurrence can ever, in fact, be entirely clear. It would seem moreover, that Christian religious discourse concerning the future is in somewhat similar case. When a Christian confesses his faith that 'God's Kingdom will come', his declaration is by no means 'merely a theoretical act'. It is also an expression of joyful hope, and an acknowledgement of responsibility to work for the realization of that hope. And every theologian is familiar with discussions concerning the extent to which, in the actual order of things, the realization of God's purposes is or is not dependent upon the fact of human hope, of man's co-operation with God's enabling grace.

One thing at least seems clear. In the case of all forms of 'practical' discourse concerning the future, whether Marxist, Christian or other, the appropriate distinction would seem to be not so much that between 'science' and 'prophecy', but rather that between (more or less well founded) expectation and evaluation, expectation and preference. Our preferences may shape our expectations. They may, indeed, contribute to their realization. But reality is by no means wholly plastic to our will: our preferences rarely, if ever, constitute the sufficient conditions of the fulfilment of our expectations. In Marx's case, according to Girardi, human liberty 'in the ethical and economic sense . . . is really the ultimate criterion of value and truth. . . . Reality is structured in such a way that liberty is attainable, and its final triumph possible, through human action, which, for its part, must be organized into a liberating force. The

3 *KIII*, p. 435.

procedure, then, is not from a vision of reality to the affirmation of values, but from the affirmation of values to a vision of reality which renders them attainable.'[4]

The Critique of Utopianism

'Scientific socialism', said Korsch, 'is not at all concerned with the painting of a future state of society. Marx leaves that to the sectarians of the old and new Utopias.'[5] We have already seen, in the previous chapter, that Marx contrasted 'scientific' socialism with 'utopian' socialism's inability to do more, negatively, than to express disapproval concerning the existing state of affairs and, positively, than to construct speculative models of alternative forms of society.[6] It seems appropriate, therefore, to follow my general introductory remarks on the problem of Marx's discourse concerning the future with some consideration of his critique of utopianism.

Marx's references to 'utopianism' are invariably critical, but his criticism is by no means indiscriminate. 'Just as the *economists* are the scientific representatives of the bourgeois class', he wrote in 1847, 'so the *socialists* and *communists* are the theoreticians of the proletarian class. So long as the proletariat is not yet sufficiently developed to constitute itself as a class . . . these theoreticians are merely utopians, who, to meet the wants of the oppressed classes, improvise systems and go in search of a regenerating science.'[7] The 'theoreticians' whom Marx had especially in mind were the members of an earlier generation of French socialist thinkers, such as de Saint-Simon (1760–1825), Fourier (1772–1837) and Cabet (1788–1856). But times and circumstances have changed: 'In the measure that history moves forward, and with it the struggle of the proletariat assumes clearer outlines, socialists and communists no longer need to seek science in their minds; they have only to take note of what is happening before their eyes and to become its mouthpiece. So long as they look for science and merely make systems, so long as they are at the beginning of the struggle, they see in poverty nothing but poverty, without seeing in it the revolutionary, subversive side, which will overthrow the old society. From the moment they see this side, science, which is produced by the historical movement and which associates itself with it with full consciousness, has ceased to be doctrinaire and has become revolutionary.'[8]

It is clear from this passage that Marx is not *blaming* the elaborators of socialist utopias for not having seen the 'revolutionary

4 G. Girardi, *Marxism and Christianity*, pp. 14–15.
5 K. Korsch, *Three Essays on Marxism*, p. 33.
6 Cf. above, pp. 211–2.
7 *The Poverty of Philosophy*, p. 120.
8 Ibid., pp. 120–1.

side' of poverty: it was not yet there to be seen. As Ernst Bloch said, commenting on the same group of writers, 'Social utopias . . . were liable to be abstract, because their designs were not mediated with the existing social tendency and possibility; indeed, they *had to be* abstract, because . . . they came too early.'[9] Whereas, in Marx's judgement, the revolutionary potential of poverty now exists and may be seen to exist.

This assessment of the strengths and weaknesses of utopianism did nót undergo significant change. Thus, in 1873, Marx acknowledged that, in the late eighteenth and early nineteenth centuries, 'social conditions were not sufficiently developed to allow the working class to constitute itself as a militant class'.[10] Therefore, 'Fourier, Owen, Saint-Simon' and others 'were necessarily obliged to limit themselves to dreams about the *model society* of the future.'[11] Or, as he put it in 1871: 'The utopian founders of sects, while in their criticism of present society clearly describing the goal of the social movement . . . found neither in society itself the material conditions of its transformation, nor in the working class the organized power and conscience of the movement.'[12]

That reference to 'sects' reminds us that, in Marx's view, there is a sense in which utopianism, reflecting the ideal in the imagination, is inevitably religious. Lassalle, he wrote in 1868, 'gave his agitation . . . the character of a religious sect, as does every man who claims to have in his pocket a panacea for the suffering masses. In fact, every sect is religious.'[13] In 1872, he spelt out the 'religious' and hence apolitical character of 'sectarianism' in greater detail. 'The first phase in the struggle of the proletariat against the bourgeoisie is marked by sectarianism. This is because the proletariat has not yet reached the stage of being sufficiently developed to act as a class. Individual thinkers provide a critique of social antagonisms, and put forward fantastic solutions. . . . By their very nature, the sects established by these initiators are . . . strangers to all genuine action, to politics, to strikes, to coalitions, in brief, to any unified movement.'[14]

The elements of Marx's critique of utopianism are now clear. At a certain stage, utopianism, reflecting an unattainable ideal in the imagination, expresses the only available form of constructive protest against existing poverty, suffering and injustice. However, once

---

9 E. Bloch, *A Philosophy of the Future*, p. 90. Bloch's contrast between 'utopias', and 'ideologies' which 'vindicate and proclaim the ruling class of their society' (p. 90), owes as much, however, to Mannheim's *Ideology and Utopia* as it does to Marx.
10 'Political Indifferentism', *FI*, p. 329.
11 Loc. cit. Cf. I. Mészáros, *Marx's Theory of Alienation*, pp. 62–3.
12 First draft of 'The Civil War in France', *FI*, p. 262.
13 Letter of 13 October 1868, *FI*, p. 155.
14 'The Alleged Splits in the International', *FI*, p. 298.

'the goal of the social movement' becomes attainable in *reality*, there is no longer any place for utopianism. 'From the moment', says Marx, that 'the working men's class movement became real, the fantastic utopias evanesced.'[15] Or, rather, they *should* have evanesced. Marx's critique of utopianism only becomes outright condemnation when directed at those thinkers who would keep it alive *after* the 'working men's class movement' has become 'real' because, in these circumstances, utopianism – like religion – becomes an 'obstacle', a 'reactionary' distraction from the real movement.[16]

The discussion so far has clearly provided us with materials in the light of which we can consider the question of whether, and in what circumstances, Christian belief and practice are appropriately described as 'utopian' in Marx's sense. Before turning to this question, however, there is one further comment to be made on Marx's own position. His critique of utopianism focuses on the presence or absence of the material conditions necessary for the transformation of social reality. But is there not a streak of unwarranted optimism in his apparent assumption that, once the material conditions are realized, such transformation will occur unhampered by unregenerate human egotism? Is it not unrealistic of Marx to expect the transformation of social structures automatically to generate a corresponding *moral* transformation of attitudes and relationships? We have to be careful here. There is a sober 'realism' which, in order to temper the enthusiasm of those who entertain apparently excessive expectations concerning man's capacity for moral transformation or conversion, issues reminders of the obduracy of egotism. It is not unusual for such down-to-earth common sense to carry the day. But, when it does so, is this, in fact, a victory for 'realism', or for a threatened egotism masquerading as common sense?[17] Such questions are not patent of abstract or theoretical solution. However, even if the basis of the charge that Marx's expectations are unrealistic is not above suspicion, the problem of his optimism, where the transformability of moral attitudes is concerned, remains – and we shall have occasion to return to it.

Utopianism and Christianity

Discussions of the relationship between Christianity and politics, between Church and society, between human history and the reign of God, between the 'world-affirming' and 'world-denying' aspects of Christianity, are frequently conducted on the assumption that to

15 First draft of 'The Civil War in France', *FI*, p. 262.
16 Cf. *FI*, p. 299, and the letter of 1871 quoted in *Life*, pp. 434–5.
17 Cf. Hegel's discussion of the victory of the 'way of the world' over a 'virtue' which 'as yet only *wills* to accomplish the good' (*Phenomenology*, p. 230; cf. pp. 227–35).

recommend one approach or policy in such matters, rather than another, is necessarily to recommend it as appropriate in all situations. This assumption does not only find expression in declarations to the effect that Christianity is 'essentially' world-denying, or world-affirming, political or apolitical in character. Its presence can also be detected in the announcement that Christianity is 'essentially' none of these things, and that therefore the decision as to what 'style' of discipleship is appropriate, in particular circumstances, is always and everywhere simply a matter for individual decision. However, if Marx's analysis of the relationship between social process and the imaginative, symbolic or conceptual expression of the envisaged or desired goal or outcome of that process has anything to commend it, this assumption – whatever the particular form of its expression – becomes highly questionable.

Consider, for example, the theological description of the Church, by the Second Vatican Council, as the 'sacrament of intimate union with God, and of the unity of all mankind'.[18] There may well be circumstances in which the political situation is such that Christians can only give symbolic social expression to their hope of universal brotherhood in God by adopting a stance of 'utopian sectarianism'. And there is a whole range of phenomena in the history of Christianity, from monastic movements in the Roman Empire or mendicant movements in medieval Europe to the Moravians, which might profitably be seen in this light.

But let us suppose that circumstances change, and that Christians find themselves in a situation in which significant steps can in fact be taken towards the realization of the goal of human solidarity, of 'universal brotherhood'; circumstances in which, for example, the revolutionary potential of poverty is a perceptible fact. In such circumstances, would it not be incumbent upon the Church as a social formation, as an historical movement (and not simply incumbent upon individual Christians) to take such steps – which would, inevitably, be 'secular' or 'political' in character? In the measure that the Church refused to take such steps, in the measure that it remained a 'stranger' to 'all genuine action, to politics, to strikes, to coalitions, in brief, to any unified movement'[19] (in the name, perhaps, of the refusal to compromise the purity of its message and its vision); in the measure that the Church's social policy, in other words, was still that of 'standing apart from the contest';[20] would not the Christian confession of hope in a human future for which the Church, *as* a social formation, nevertheless refused to work and struggle, now serve, in practice, as an 'obstacle', helping to perpetuate existing structures of disunity and oppression? (And, once

18 *Dogmatic Constitution on the Church*, para. 1.
19 *FI*, p. 298.
20 'Manifesto of the Communist Party', *R1848*, p. 96,

again, I do not think that it would be difficult to find illustrations, from the history of Christianity, of situations in which this is exactly what has occurred.)

I am really only trying to make one very simple suggestion: namely, that, contrary to the assumption to which I referred at the beginning of this section, there are no timelessly appropriate abstract answers to questions concerning the practical (that is to say, social and political) implications of Christian hope. Christianity is neither 'essentially' utopian, nor 'essentially' non-utopian, nor are decisions as to the appropriate style of discipleship *simply* matters for individual decision. The question as to whether or not fidelity to the gospel demands – as a matter of public, social policy – 'withdrawal' or 'affirmation', the 'sectarian' expression of an unattainable ideal or active engagement in political movements for social change, is a question which can only be decided in the light of particular concrete circumstances. The option for engagement, for a non-utopian stance and policy, is heavy with risk because the purity of the gospel, the universality of Christian hope, *is* threatened by the decision to 'take sides' in social and political struggle. It is not always sufficiently appreciated, however, by Christians in general and church leaders in particular, that the risk is unavoidable.

There are, however, two qualifications which need to be made, but they are *only* qualifications, and not ingenious devices for undermining the general claim made at the beginning of the previous paragraph. In the first place, that transformation of man, and hence of patterns of social relationship, envisaged in the Christian proclamation of the reign of God, is far more radical than that envisaged by any political movement, including Marxism. Whether or not Marxian hope contains eschatological elements (and this is a question we have yet to discuss), Christian hope is irreducibly eschatological in character. That is to say: it envisages the definitive, unsurpassable, liberation of man from all forms of bondage, including the bondage of egotism and death. No 'real movement', political or social, however dramatic the transformation it seeks to achieve and supposes itself in process of achieving, can realize or satisfy the Christian hope. The articulation of Christian hope *always* 'comes too early'.

It follows from this that Christianity, as a social formation, can never identify itself, *without remainder*, with any particular social or political movement. But whereas it is frequently supposed that *therefore* the Church should 'stand apart from the contest' (and I have already indicated my conviction that this 'solution' is, in fact, self-defeating), the inference which I would draw is that even in those circumstances, and perhaps especially in those circumstances, in which engagement in the political struggle for the liberation of man is the appropriate strategic policy for the Christian community, there is *also* need, within Christianity, for 'sects' the 'utopianism' of which serves as a reminder of the partial and provisional nature of all historically realizable achievements of liberty and transformations of social reality. In other words, the eschatological character of Christian hope justifies and demands the presence, within Christianity, of forms of monasticism and of individual 'prophetic utopianism', *not* because 'reality' cannot be changed,[21] but because there are limits to its transformability beyond which it is nevertheless permissible to hope.

In the second place, the tension between historical and eschatological hope is not a tension that only exists between 'utopian' monasticism and non-utopian forms of Christian social strategy. It is a tension which finds expression, not only between different forms of Christian institution, but also at the centre of *every* Christian institution, in the celebration of the Eucharist. As a symbolic, dramatic enactment of Christian hope for 'intimate union with God' and for 'unity for the whole human race', every celebration of the Eucharist contradicts, not only the facts, but also the possibilities, of historically realizable patterns of social relationship. As with all other constituents of Christianity, the Eucharist has often been used to justify and reinforce all manner of human division – by class, race and sex. But the symbol of the Eucharist has its own internal 'logic' which, if it is allowed to 'speak', generates not only a vision of human hope, but also almost insupportable tensions between fact and possibility, between history and the reign of God.

Expectation and Prediction

In the light of our discussion of Marx's critique of utopianism, it is easy to see why he 'very rarely discussed the form of the future communist society',[22] and why he was 'consciously and intentionally *sparing of colour* in depicting the possible future'.[23] Had he done otherwise, he would, on his own terms, have been lapsing into utopian, idealist 'fantasy'. As he 'became more closely acquainted with political realities he took more interest in organizing the revolution than in portraying the ideal society, let alone planning the details of communism in action after the manner of Fourier and others.'[24]

Moreover, however confident Marx may have been that capitalist

21 This is the presupposition underlying Lukács' otherwise penetrating analysis of the 'self-refuting' character of a religion, such as 'the Christianity of the Gospels', which – on his account – sets up the ideal of the 'saint' as one who 'can achieve an inner mastery over the external reality that cannot be eliminated' (cf. *History and Class Consciousness*, pp. 191–4).
22 *Life*, p. 301.
23 E. Bloch, *On Karl Marx*, p. 170.
24 *KI*, p. 174.

society contained contradictions so fundamental as inexorably to lead to its revolutionary 'supersession', the supposition that the details of post-revolutionary society could be 'predicted' before the event would have been inconsistent with his 'materialist' understanding of history. As Mannheim remarked: 'If today we ask a communist, with a Leninist training, what the future society will actually be like, he will answer that the question is an undialectical one, since the future itself will be decided in the practical dialectical process of becoming.'[25] And if there is, nevertheless, in some of Marx's writings, 'a utopian and almost millenial strain',[26] this utopianism consists not in the speculative depiction of future forms of society, but rather in the assurance that, after the revolution, all shall be well and all manner of thing shall be well.

With rare exceptions, therefore, Marx avoided predictive descriptions of 'the essence of *man* . . . the *true community* of man',[27] as it would be realized in a 'society in which the full and free development of every individual forms the ruling principle',[28] and in which the 'universal development of the individual'[29] would thereby be assured. One such exception would be the closing paragraphs of his notes on James Mill's *Elements of Political Economy*,[30] which McLellan describes as 'one of the few passages in which he describes in any detail his picture of the future communist society.'[31] Another would be his description of the Paris Commune,[32] which 'reveals much more about Marx's view of the shape of the future communist society after the revolution than it does about the plans of the Communards.'[33] The model which he then offered (in 1871) was 'noticeably less centralized'[34] than the famous sketch, in the *Communist Manifesto*, of the two stages through which society must pass after the revolution: a first stage in which 'The proletariat will use its political supremacy . . . to centralize all instruments of production in the hands of the state, i.e. of the proletariat organized as the ruling class',[35] and a second stage in which, once 'class distinctions have disappeared, and all production has been concentrated in the hands of a vast association of the whole nation, the public power will lose its political character.'[36]

25 *Ideology and Utopia*, p. 112.
26 *Life*, p. 304, referring to the *Paris Manuscripts* and the *Grundrisse*.
27 'Excerpts from James Mill's *Elements of Political Economy*', EW, p. 265.
28 *Cap. I*, p. 739.
29 *G*, p. 542.
30 Cf. *EW*, pp. 277–8.
31 *Life*, p. 114.
32 Cf. 'The Civil War in France', *FI*, pp. 210–1.
33 *Life*, p. 397.
34 *Life*, p. 396.
35 *R1848*, p. 86.
36 *R1848*, p. 87.

For the most part, the passages in which Marx speaks with confidence concerning that future which will emerge from the over-throw of the capitalist mode of production merely give formal, heuristic expression to the goal of a movement which is (in his view) in *fact* taking place, and to the success of which he seeks to con-tribute. 'Everybody knows', said Lenin in 1894, 'that scientific socialism never painted any prospects for the future as such; it confined itself to . . . studying the trends of development of the capitalist social organization. . . . Everybody knows that *Capital* . . . restricts itself to the most general allusions to the future.'[37] Exaggeration, perhaps, but not significant misrepresentation.

We also need to bear in mind that many of the passages in which Marx is apparently 'predicting' the form of the future occur in political speeches and pamphlets. They are, therefore, exercises in persuasive rhetoric. The language, we might say, is 'homiletic' rather than 'scientific'. Thus, for example, in the *Communist Manifesto* he announces that, 'In place of the old bourgeois society, with its classes and class antagonisms, we shall have an association, in which the free development of each is the condition of the free development of all.'[38] And, in his inaugural address to the First International: 'Like slave labour, like serf labour, hired labour is but a transitory and inferior form, destined to disappear before associated labour plying its toil with a willing hand, a ready mind and a joyous heart.'[39]

Marx confidently believed that the movement he saw going on, the process he sought to understand and assist, would reach fruition in the realization of 'the *true community* of man',[40] in mankind's liberation from servitude and alienation. This confidence may have been unfounded but it was undoubtedly, in his view, a confidence in *human beings* rather than in the predictive capacities of a theory of social history. And because Marx's 'excessive optimism is often mistaken for crude determinism',[41] it must again be insisted – at whatever cost to the tidiness and even the coherence[42] of his thought – that Marx was not an historical determinist. 'He repeated over and over again that men made and had to make their history.'[43] Engels, who was more of a 'determinist' than Marx, claimed, in 1880, that 'Active social forces work exactly like natural forces: blindly, forcibly, destructively.'[44] But he added: 'so long as we do

37 V. I. Lenin, 'What the "Friends of the People" Are', *HM*, p. 355.
38 *R1848*, p. 87.
39 *FI*, p. 80.
40 *EW*, p. 265.
41 B. Ollmann, *Alienation*, p. 239.
42 Cf. C. Taylor, *Hegel*, pp. 556–7.
43 E. Mandel, 'Introduction', *Cap. I*, p. 84.
44 F. Engels, 'Socialism: Utopian and Scientific', *HM*, p. 192.

not understand and reckon with them.'[45] And he went on: 'Once their nature is understood, they *can*, in the hands of producers working together, be transformed from master demons into willing servants.'[46] They can, but perhaps they will not. Because it is *human beings* who make history, and who have it in them to make that history the history of emergent human freedom, they may fail to do so. Hence the condition built into the following passage, which dates from 1872: 'The workers will have to seize political power one day in order to construct the new organization of labour; they will have to overthrow the old politics which bolsters up the old institutions, unless they want to share the fate of the early Christians, who lost their chance of heaven on earth because they rejected and neglected such action.'[47] In practice, of course, Marx was confident that the workers, unlike the early Christians, would rise to the occasion.

Events transpired very differently from the way in which Marx expected that they would. My principal concern in this chapter, so far, has been to suggest that to describe this disappointing turn of events as 'falsifying' Marx's 'predictions' is fundamentally to misrepresent the character of his thought. The dashing of Marx's hopes (though he himself did not live to see them dashed) is an indication, not so much of a flaw in his theoretical analysis, but rather of the extent to which his optimism was unfounded (and we shall consider, later on, the suggestion that non-illusory hope is incompatible with optimism, at least in its nineteenth-century form of subscription to the myth of human 'progress').

I suggested, just now, that Marx's optimism expressed an almost unbounded confidence in human beings. But this suggestion demands some qualification. For all his suspicion of abstract doctrines of 'human nature', is there not a sense in which Marx's confidence in humanity is not so much a confidence in actual human groups and individuals, but rather in a vision of 'man', an anthropology, the components of which are in part historical and in part philosophical? The influence of such a vision in his early writings – in the coupling of the assertion, for example, that 'Human nature is the true community of men'[48] with the assumption that *this* 'nature' will be historically realized – is obvious. Of course, we have to be careful. Gollwitzer, commenting on the passage in the Paris Manuscripts in which Marx declares that communism, 'the true *appropriation* of the *human* essence through and for man . . . is the solution

---

45 Loc. cit.
46 Ibid., p. 193, my stress.
47 'Speech on the Hague Congress', *FI*, p. 324.
48 'Critical Notes on the Article "The King of Prussia and Social Reform. By a Prussian" ', *EW*, pp. 418–9.

of the riddle of history and knows itself to be the solution',[49] advises caution. Although there is no evidence of any 'explicit repudiation of this vision of his youth', with its prognostication of 'an absolute reconciliation within history of the previous contradictions of human existence', it is possible that, 'as his dependence on Hegel lessened . . . the later Marx may have grown less confident about the absolute character of his vision of the last things.'[50] In Gollwitzer's view, the evidence is too fragmentary and uncertain to justify a firm decision one way or the other.

There are two distinct issues here. On the one hand, there is the problem (which we shall discuss in the following chapter) of the extent to which Marx's understanding of human history, as a process the outcome of which will be a state of affairs strikingly different from anything that has hitherto been experienced as 'human history', is shaped by a vision of liberty the appropriate description of which would be that it is 'eschatological' in character. On the other hand, in so far as Marx's definition of *'human* essence' appeals to that of which, because it is not yet realized, we can have no direct experience, there is the problem of the extent to which his vision of the future is empirically based. The road to that future runs through the revolutionary transformation of capitalist society, a transformation which – because of the unique characteristics of that class, the proletariat, which is to be the agent of the revolution – will be quite unlike any other social revolution that the world has ever known. We can therefore focus our discussion of the problem of the relation between the empirical and philosophical components in Marx's anthropology by considering the question: to what extent is Marx's doctrine of the historical role and revolutionary character of the proletariat empirically based?

Proletariat and Revolution

Marx first refers to the proletariat in the closing paragraphs of his Introduction to 'A Contribution to the Critique of Hegel's Philosophy of Right', written between the end of 1843 and the beginning of 1844. With the French Revolution in mind, he contrasts the situation in France with that in Germany: 'In France partial emancipation is the basis of universal emancipation. In Germany universal emancipation is the *conditio sine qua non* of any partial emancipation. In France it is the reality, in Germany the impossibility, of emancipation in stages that must give birth to complete freedom.'[51] Hence the question arises: 'Where is the *positive* possibility of German emancipation? *This is our answer.* In the formation

49 *EW*, p. 348.
50 H. Gollwitzer, *The Christian Faith and the Marxist Criticism of Religion*, pp. 73–4.
51 *EW*, p. 255.

of a class with *radical* chains, a class . . . which is the dissolution of all classes, a sphere which has a universal character because of its universal suffering and which lays claim to no *particular right* because the wrong it suffers is not a *particular wrong* but *wrong in general*; a sphere of society . . . which is, in a word, the *total loss* of humanity and which can therefore redeem itself only through the *total redemption of humanity*. This dissolution of society as a particular class is the *proletariat*.'[52]

(There are two marginal notes that should be attached to this powerful declaration. The first is that it would clearly be impossible to construct a general 'theory of revolution' on the basis of remarks which refer explicitly to the situation in *one* country in contrast with *another*.[53] The second is that the appearance, with the reference to 'redemption', of a soteriological motif, is no accident: the passage ends: 'When all the inner contradictions are met, the *day of the German resurrection* will be heralded by the *crowing of the Gallic cock*.'[54])

'This passage', says McLellan, 'raises an obvious and crucial question as to the reasons for Marx's sudden adherence to the cause of the proletariat.'[55] And he insists on the inadequacy of those interpretations which seek to answer this question in terms of the influence of some one factor alone: Hegel's philosophy, for example, or German Protestant theology. To his list of inadequate, because partial, solutions we could add Tucker's peremptory assertion that 'Marx's image of the proletariat was not of empirical origin.'[56]

According to McLellan, the context shows that 'Marx's account of the role of the proletariat was drawn from his study of the French Revolution, however much his language may be that of Young Hegelian journalism.'[57] But was that study any more than the *occasion* which, together with his 'first-hand contacts with socialist intellectuals in France',[58] stimulated the elaboration of a doctrine the power, and not simply the terminology, of which can only be explained with reference to other sources? Consider the following passage, written only a few months later, in 1844. 'Proletariat and wealth are opposites; as such they form a single whole. They are both creations of the world of private property. The question is exactly what place each occupies in the antithesis. . . . Private property as private property, as wealth, is compelled to maintain *itself*, and thereby its opposite, the proletariat, in *existence*. That is the

52 *EW*, p. 256.
53 In which context, it is worth remembering that, as late as 1880, Marx still
    believed that 'in Britain a peaceful transition to socialism was possible' (*Life*,
    p. 444).
54 *EW*, p. 257.
55 *Life*, p. 96.
56 R. C. Tucker, *Philosophy and Myth in Karl Marx*, p. 113.
57 *Life*, p. 97.
58 Loc. cit.

positive side of the antithesis, self-satisfied private property. The proletariat, on the contrary, is compelled as proletariat to abolish itself and thereby its opposite, private property, which determines its existence, and which makes it proletariat. It is the *negative* side of the antithesis, its restlessness within its very self-dissolved and self-dissolving private property. The propertied class and the class of the proletariat present the same human self-estrangement . . . the proletariat is, to use an expression of Hegel, in its abasement the *indignation* at that abasement. . . . Indeed private property drives itself in its economic movement towards its own dissolution. . . . The proletariat executes the sentence that private property pronounces on itself by producing the proletariat. . . . [The proletariat] cannot emancipate itself without abolishing the conditions of its own life. . . . It is not a question of what this or that proletarian, or even the whole proletariat, at the moments *regards* as its aim. It is a question of *what the proletariat is*, and what, in accordance with this *being*, it will·historically be compelled to do.'[59]

This detailed description of the nature and revolutionary destiny of the proletariat is clearly, at one level, a socio-economic interpretation of Hegel's dialectic of master and slave, of lordship and bondage – a text which, as I suggested earlier, exercised considerable influence on Marx's analysis of 'alienation' and its revolutionary 'supersession.'[60] The 'opposites' of 'private property . . . as wealth' and the poverty of the proletariat may form a 'single whole', but since, to begin with, at the onset of the struggle, 'their reflection into a unity has not yet been achieved, they exist as two opposed shapes of consciousness.'[61] The essential nature of private property is 'to be for itself', to be independent, whereas its opposite is 'the dependent consciousness whose essential nature is simply to live or to be for another.'[62] Private property is lord, proletarian poverty is bondsman.

The consciousness of wealth is the consciousness of unrestricted *desire*. Private property, as wealth, is insatiable: there is no 'thing' which can satisfy wealth's desire to possess all things. The consciousness of poverty is the consciousness of unrestricted *dread*: 'It has been fearful, not of this or that particular thing or just at odd moments, but its whole being has been seized with dread; for it has experienced the fear of death, the absolute Lord.'[63] Desire and dread – since both, in their different ways, are expressive of perceived

---

59 'The Holy Family', *CW4*, pp. 35–7.
60 Cf. above, p. 175. Although I believe this claim to be well-founded, the evidence for it is purely internal, since Marx seems never to have explicitly referred to or quoted from this particular passage in the *Phenomenology*.
61 G. W. F. Hegel, *Phenomenology*, p. 115.
62 Loc. cit.
63 Ibid., p. 117.

'needs': the need to *have* and the need to *be* – are two sides of the same coin. The route to the satisfaction of desire is through the appropriation, the annihilation of the 'otherness' or independence, of the desired object. However, desire is destructive, not only of the object desired, but also of the lordship of the desirer – for he is in thrall to his avarice. The need to have is, in fact, a doomed and distorted expression of the need to be: 'The *truth* of the independent consciousness', of lordship, 'is accordingly the servile consciousness of the bondsman.'[64]

Bondage therefore has the edge over lordship because, in its absolute dread, its experience of the threat and fact of dissolution, its 'pure negativity',[65] it incipiently *knows* this to be its truth: 'the fear of the lord is indeed the beginning of wisdom.'[66] And it is 'through *work* that the bondsman becomes conscious of what he truly is'.[67] Desire seeks merely to appropriate its object, to 'enjoy' or to consume it, and thus to annihilate its independent reality. Work, in contrast, gives to its object '*form* and something *permanent*, because it is precisely for the worker that the object has independence'.[68] In the working out of the dialectical relationship between lordship's desire for all things as its own and slavery's working up of all things into genuine objectivity, 'just as lordship showed that its essential nature is the reverse of what it wants to be, so too servitude in its consummation will really turn into the opposite of what it immediately is.'[69] Lordship is 'real' enough (as the bondsman knows). Yet it is, in fact, for master as well as slave, a form of slavery. Slavery is 'real' enough (as the bondsman also knows). Nevertheless, slavery is, through work, the incipient achievement of a mastery over both self and nature which, once achieved in reality (and no longer only in desire), constitutes at one and the same time the liberation of the slave from his slavery, his 'alienation', and the abolition of the 'lordship' of the lord. To paraphrase Hegel in Marx's language: both master and slave 'present the same human self-estrangement'; lordship 'drives itself . . . towards its own dissolution'; the slave 'executes the sentence that [lordship] pronounces on itself by producing [slavery]',[70] and, in so doing, brings about 'the total redemption of humanity.'[71]

It is impossible, by paraphrase and selective quotation, to indicate the richness of Hegel's text. All that I have tried to do is to

64 Loc. cit.
65 Loc. cit.
66 Ibid., pp. 117–8.
67 Ibid., p. 118.
68 Loc. cit.
69 Ibid., p. 117.
70 Cf. *CW4*, pp. 36–7.
71 *EW*, p. 256.

show how eloquently the two passages which I quoted from Marx illustrate Charles Taylor's contention that 'the underlying idea [in Hegel's text] that servitude prepares the ultimate liberation of the slaves, and indeed general liberation, is recognizably preserved in Marxism.'[72] I am not suggesting that Marx's doctrine of the revolutionary role of the proletariat is devoid of empirical basis. Nevertheless, it is only the Hegelian form of that doctrine which enables Marx to elaborate his vision of a revolution which, unlike all previous social and political revolutions, will achieve, not merely 'partial emancipation', not merely the victory of some particular class or group over other classes and groups in society, but 'universal emancipation', the birth of 'a future society, in which class antagonism will have ceased, in which there will no longer be any classes.'[73]

'An oppressed class', wrote Marx in *The Poverty of Philosophy*, 'is the vital condition for every society founded on the antagonism of classes. The emancipation of the oppressed class implies necessarily the creation of a new society. . . . Does this mean that after the fall of the old society there will be a new class culminating in a new political power? No. The condition for the emancipation of the working class is the abolition of all classes.'[74] And the revolution which effects *this* transformation will be the *last* revolution, because 'it is only in an order of things in which there are no more classes and class antagonisms that *social evolutions* will cease to be *political revolutions*.'[75] Therefore he can refer, some years later, to 'the last form of servitude assumed by human activity, that of wage labour on the one side, capital on the other.'[76]

It is, I believe, abundantly clear that an anthropology, a conception of the 'essence' or 'nature' of humanity, occupies a central place in Marx's thought. According to this conception, 'the "essence" of man is to be found in work, sociality and consciousness, and in that universality which embraces these three moments and expresses itself in each of them.'[77] His suspicion of abstract, or 'philosophical' doctrines of 'human nature' arises from his conviction that the *meaning* of 'work, sociality and consciousness' may not be construed in abstract or timeless terms, as if they referred, in the concrete, to transculturally invariant, immutable features of human existence. This cannot be the case, not least because the recorded history of mankind is a history of the *non*-existence – or, at most, of the partial and transient existence – of these features in a *human*

---

72 C. Taylor, *Hegel*, pp. 154–5.
73 *The Poverty of Philosophy*, p. 58.
74 Ibid., p. 169.
75 Ibid., p. 170.
76 *G*, p. 749.
77 Markús, *Marxism and Anthropology*, p. 36.

form: that is to say, in circumstances such that, for all human beings, their work, their relationships and their consciousness were, in reality (and not merely in appearance or in aspiration) aspects of freedom, of man's unconstrained self-disposal. In large part, the history of work has been a history of subservience either to the forces of nature or to human 'alien powers'; the history of social relationships has been a history of self-deception and illusion. That is why, on Marx's account, the 'essence' or 'nature' of man has to be conceived and enacted historically, as a movement or process of becoming, a struggle for freedom, for the realization of the 'essence' of man. That this struggle would eventually be successful was the substance of his hope, his confident expectation.

Kolakowski would therefore seem to be justified in saying that 'Marx constantly regarded the historical process from the point of view of the future liberation of mankind.'[78] Concerning such a doctrine of man, and of man's emergent freedom – a doctrine which is set in sharpest focus in his account of the role of the proletariat as agent of the last revolution – a number of questions need to be considered, and these will form the agenda for our final chapter.

In the first place, Marx may well have been correct in supposing – as a matter of practical, political judgement – that the structures of lordship and bondage which existed in his day (in Germany, and perhaps elsewhere), could only be 'superseded' by the revolutionary transformation, rather than by the gradual adaptation, of social formations. Nevertheless, the idea of the *last* revolution, as expounded by him, is quite certainly mythological or symbolic in character, rather than descriptive of any historical revolution that would or could occur. It is mythological because, central and indispensable to its construction is the concept of a proletariat defined, in Hegelian terms, as existing in 'pure negativity'. But, as Calvez has said: 'On ne peut manquer de se demander si l'agent idéal de cette révolution, le prolétariat, défini à priori comme la véritable sociéte universelle en négatif, existe vraiment ou peut exister dans les conditions de l'histoire.'[79]

In describing Marx's concept of the proletariat as 'mythological' or 'symbolic', I am not suggesting that it is incoherent or lightly to be dismissed. I am only suggesting that, in so far as 'the last revolution' is descriptive of an event which is historically unrealizable, we need to consider the implications of the presence, in Marx's thought, of an eschatological (rather than 'utopian') element. (And, in doing so, it will be useful to bear in mind that there is a sense in which Christian faith in Christ's resurrection 'constantly regards

---

78 *KI*, p. 348. As Rosdolsky puts it: 'Human history is . . . seen in terms of its most basic final outcome; as a necessary process of the elaboration and development of the human personality and its freedom' (*The Making of Marx's 'Capital'*, p. 415).
79 *La Pensée de Karl Marx*, p. 270.

the historical process from the point of view of the future liberation of mankind'.)

In the second place, because no social class has ever existed, or could ever exist, in 'pure negativity', it would seem impossible for there ever to occur, within human history, a social revolution the agent or agents of which were devoid of *all* 'particular' interest. Some of the questions which arise here concern the morality of revolutionary strategy, and it will be appropriate to consider them under the rubric of the relationship between divine mercy and the execution of divine judgement.

According to Edward Thompson, 'The recognition of man's dual role, as victim and as agent, in the making of his own history is crucial to Marx's thought.'[80] It seems that Marx prospected a future, be it near or far, in which all 'victimhood', all servitude, would have been definitively superseded. Does it follow that he envisaged a future in which human beings would exist, as it were, in a condition of 'pure agency'? Whatever be the answer to this question, it suggests that we should consider, in the third place, the relationship between 'freedom' and 'necessity', between man's self-disposal and the unsurmountable limits within which his existence is set. Under this heading, we shall have to consider the relationship between 'hope' and 'optimism'.

In the fourth place, I have suggested that Marx had good reasons for refusing to indulge in specific predictions concerning the form of a future which had not yet been constructed. Nevertheless, any student of Christian history knows that the longer the 'delay' between an event construed as decisive for the achievement of human liberation and the 'appearance' or *parousia* of the anticipated 'realm of freedom', the more urgent become questions concerning the *organization* of freedom.

---

80 E. P. Thompson, 'An Open Letter to Leszek Kolakowski', *The Poverty of Theory*, p. 152.

18

OPTIMISM, ESCHATOLOGY AND THE FORM OF THE FUTURE

The 'Birth' of History

'There is no trace of utopianism in Marx, in the sense that he made up or invented a "new" society. No, he studied the birth of the new society *out of* the old, and the forms of transition from the latter to the former, as a natural-historical process.'[1] Thus Lenin, in 1917. Biological analogies for historical process abound in Marx's work, as in that of so many nineteenth-century writers. And one image in particular occurs, again and again, in his statements concerning the emergence of that human future which – he hoped and confidently expected – would eventually succeed modern capitalism: it is the image, picked up there by Lenin, of *birth*.

This image occurs as early as 1843: 'The more time history allows thinking mankind to reflect and suffering mankind to collect its strength the more perfect will be the fruit which the present now bears within its womb.'[2] And the following year: 'The entire movement of history is therefore both the *actual* act of creation of communism – the birth of its empirical existence – and, for its thinking consciousness, the *comprehended* and *known* movement of its becoming.'[3] In another passage in the Paris Manuscripts, a passage which we have come across more than once, the use of the image reminds us that *human* wealth, the wealth of human being, is the antithesis of private property's obsession with wealth as possession: in the realm of private property, '*all* the physical and intellectual senses have been replaced by the simple estrangement of *all* these senses – the sense of *having*. So that it might give birth to its inner wealth, human nature had to be reduced to this absolute poverty.'[4]

By 1871, Marx's language may have lost some of its exuberance, but his confidence is undiminished that a new order of things is in process of gestation: 'The working class . . . know that in order to work out their own emancipation, and along with that higher form to which present society is irresistibly tending by its own economical

---

1 V. I. Lenin, 'The State and Revolution', Ch. 3, *HM*, p. 557.
2 Letter to Ruge of May 1843, *EW*, p. 206.
3 *EW*, p. 348.
4 *EW* p. 352. Cf. above, pp. 89, 199–202.

agencies, they will have to pass through long struggles, through a series of historic processes, transforming circumstances and men. They have no ideals to realize, but to set free the elements of the new society with which old collapsing bourgeois society itself is pregnant.'[5] In 1875, he warns that 'We are dealing here with a communist society, not as it has *developed* on its own foundations, but on the contrary, just as it *emerges* from capitalist society. In every respect, economically, morally, intellectually, it is still stamped with the birth-marks of the old society from whose womb it has emerged.'[6] Of these 'birth-marks', amongst which he lists the economic inequality consequent upon the application of the (bourgeois) principle of 'equal rights' to 'unequal individuals (and they would not be different individuals if they were not unequal)',[7] he says: 'Such defects . . . are inevitable in the first phase of communist society, given the specific form in which it has emerged after prolonged birth-pangs from capitalist society.'[8]

What is it to which the present is painfully giving birth? It is variously described as 'communism', human nature's 'inner wealth', a 'new' and 'higher' form of society, and 'communist society'. Is the image of 'birth', then, merely a metaphor for the production of the future from the past? Although some of the later passages could be read this way, there is undoubtedly more to Marx's use of the image than this. In his early writings, we remember, 'the essence of *man*' was defined as 'the *true community* of man.'[9] Although, in his later work, the language becomes less 'philosophical', there is no evidence that he ever ceased to define the human in terms of that which he confidently believed human society would become in the future. It therefore follows that the 'birth' to which he looked forward would be not simply the beginning of a new social formation but would, in some sense, be the *birth of man*. To put it another way: Marx's use of the image of 'birth' invites us to see the entire process of human existence, past and present, not as the history of man, but as a prolonged and often agonizing process of gestation: as the process of man's *pre*history. And he says precisely this: 'The bourgeois mode of production is the last antagonistic form of the social process of production. . . . The prehistory of human society accordingly closes with this social formation.'[10] To accept this description is to take the image of 'birth' very seriously indeed. As Markús puts it: 'The concept of "prehistory", which traverses Marx's whole life work, is not to be understood as a simple metaphor. The process

5 'The Civil War in France', *FI*, p. 213.
6 'Critique of the Gotha Programme', *FI*, p. 346.
7 *FI*, p. 347.
8 Loc. cit.
9 *EW*, p. 265.
10 'Preface to "A Contribution to the Critique of Political Economy",' *EW*, p. 426.

of human genesis is, according to Marx, not completed with the formation of *homo sapiens* as a biological species.'[11] All 'history', between the emergence of *homo sapiens* and the appearance of communist society, is 'prehistory' because it is not as yet (to use the language of the Paris Manuscripts) the *human* history of man.

How are we to characterize language which appears to prospect a state of affairs in relation to which all previous history is declared to be – as the history of *in*humanity, of conditions in which human beings have been prevented by circumstances from enjoying a truly human existence – merely the *pre*history of man? I propose to suggest that there is, in Marx's thought, an element of eschatological prophecy.

For a number of reasons, this suggestion is likely to be misunderstood. For example, where prophecy is concerned, it bears a *prima facie* resemblance to Kolakowski's claim that 'Marx's faith in the "end of prehistory" is not a scientist's theory but the exhortation of a prophet.'[12] However, Kolakowski, like Popper,[13] seems to assume that it is characteristic of prophecy to issue unwarranted predictions concerning the future. As I understand the language of prophecy, however, its reference to the future is usually *mediated* by that criticism of the present which is its immediate concern.

A theological illustration may help. Those Christians who accept the theological description of the Church as the 'sacrament of intimate union with God, and of the unity of all mankind', see in the celebration of the Eucharist the symbolic expression of their hope. In the Eucharist there is symbolically enacted a sharing of human life and love, in the life of God, which forms the substance of Christian hope but which – in the present conditions of human existence – can only be articulated indirectly. Christians, if they are wise (and not all Christians are, or have been, wise in this respect) will not suppose that there are *direct* connections to be made between the symbolic, prophetic language of the Eucharist, and specific projects for the construction of a less inhuman future. The connections – between the eucharistic sharing of food and the feeding of mankind, between the eucharistic celebration of brotherhood and the resolution of political conflict – are never direct. They have always to be *mediated*, as do all non-idealistic policies and programmes, through critical reflection on social and political fact, and through the practical labour of transforming that fact.

The extent to which there is, in the celebration of the Eucharist interpreted as an act of prophetic criticism, an element of 'utopian' protest (in Marx's sense) will largely depend upon the circum-

11 G. Markús, *Marxism and Anthropology*, p. 48.
12 *KI*, p. 375. Cf. above, p. 233.
13 Cf. above, p. 229.

stances in which a particular celebration occurs.[14] But whether such prophetic criticism is, in a specific situation, primarily 'utopian' in character, or whether it serves to shape the imagination of Christians practically engaged in the transformation of circumstances, what Christian hope in general, and its eucharistic expression in particular, can *never* do is to furnish us directly, immediately, with 'blueprints' for a future social order.

Marx once remarked that, 'just as ancient peoples lived their previous history in the imagination, in *mythology*, so we Germans have lived our future history in thought, in *philosophy*.'[15] To 'live the future in thought', rather than to work for the construction of a future whose lineaments cannot be directly discerned before the event, would be symptomatic of that 'idealism' to which Marx was implacably opposed. The purpose of my remarks on prophetic criticism has been to suggest that although – in his use of the concept of 'prehistory', of the metaphor of the 'birth' of humanity from the last revolution, and in his occasional lyrical descriptions of communist society[16] – Marx tended to 'live the future in imagination' (and in *that* sense to use 'mythological' language), it does not necessarily follow that he was thereby collapsing into speculative fantasy or issuing unwarranted predictions. His unswerving confidence that the present was pregnant with a less inhuman future undoubtedly introduced a certain ambiguity into his language. There are passages which suggest that his confidence in the outcome of the historical process took him dangerously near to attempting the impossible: to lifting what Newman called 'the curtain hung over [our] futurity.'[17] But attempts to iron out these ambiguities, whether on the part of critics such as Kolakowski, or disciples such as Mészáros,[18] achieve their clarity at the cost of suppressing elements of his rich, evocative, and in some ways very *un*systematic language concerning his hopes for the post-revolutionary future.

Let us now turn to the question of eschatology. Kolakowski says of Cieszkowski's 'idea of the future identification (and not merely reconciliation) of intellectual activity and social practice', that 'it was out of this seed that Marx's eschatology grew.'[19] And, summarizing Marx's thought up to 1846, he claims that 'Marx's point

---

14 Cf. above, pp. 236–9.
15 'A Contribution to the Critique of Hegel's Philosophy of Right. Introduction', *EW*, p. 249.
16 I have in mind, for example, the famous passage in *The German Ideology* quoted above, pp. 46–7.
17 J. H. Newman, *Apologia Pro Vita Sua*, ed. M. J. Svaglic, p. 217.
18 Cf. I. Mészáros, *Marx's Theory of Alienation*, pp. 241–53.
19 *KI*, p. 88. There have been many studies of the eschatological features of Marxist thought, but perhaps few as intemperate and bizarre as a massive (1200–page) treatise by a South African Calvinist: F. N. Lee, *Communist Eschatology*.

of departure is the eschatological question derived from Hegel: how is man to be reconciled with himself and with the world?'.[20]

It is not, however, the mere fact that Marx's language concerning the 'birth' of humanity from the revolutionary overthrow of capitalism announces a state of affairs in which human existence will be 'redeemed' or 'reconciled', in which man's fourfold alienation will be healed, that justifies the description of such language as 'eschatological'. What renders the description appropriate, in my view, is Marx's apparent conviction (which Kolakowski presumably has in mind) that this state of affairs, once achieved, will be *irreversibly* achieved.

Whatever changes and modifications individual existence and social organization may undergo after the post-revolutionary 'birth' of man from his 'prehistory', these changes will not be such as any longer to carry with them the risk of disaster, or reversal, of the re-emergence of conflict and oppression. One way of putting this would be to say that it is Marx's conviction, that the 'labour' which gives birth to mankind's *human* existence thereby marks the irreversible end of his conflictual 'prehistory', which indicates the presence of an eschatological element in his thought.

Some Marxist commentators are at pains to play down this element. Thus Mészáros claims that 'In Marx's vision . . . there can be no place for a utopian golden age, neither "around the corner" nor astronomical distances away. Such a golden age would be the end of history, and thus the end of man himself.'[21] But this is to offer, in defence of Marx, an account of his 'vision' which simply suppresses the paradoxical features of the language in which that 'vision' was expressed. There is clearly a qualitative difference, on Marx's account, between human existence before and after the last revolution. According to Mészáros (whose silence on the question of revolution we have noted already),[22] 'What gives sense to human enterprise in socialism is not the fictitious promise of a fictitious absolute (a world from which all possible contradiction is eliminated for ever) but the *real* possibility of turning a menacingly *increasing* trend of alienation into a reassuringly *decreasing* one.'[23] As a reading of Marx, even as an attempt to 'work out' answers to questions on which Marx himself was not wholly explicit,[24] this sober (if still optimistic) expression of hope in a gradual improvement in the 'humanity' of man's condition is, quite simply, unconvincing. And it is unconvincing because of its suppression of just those paradoxical aspects of Marx's language to which I have referred.

20 *KI*, p. 177; cf. pp. 77, 174.
21 Mészáros, op. cit., p. 241.
22 Cf. above, p. 191.
23 Mészáros, op. cit., p. 249.
24 Cf. ibid., p. 242.

If there is a qualitative difference between human existence before and after the last revolution, and if that difference consists in the 'abolition' or 'supersession' of just those features which led Marx to speak of all history before this revolution as 'prehistory', then, indeed, there is a sense in which, with the 'birth' of man, history – as we have hitherto known, experienced, suffered and enacted it – ends. And the usual term for discourse concerning the 'end' of history is: eschatology.

In order for the term 'eschatological' to be appropriate as a description of at least one strand of Marx's language concerning the future, it is not necessary to suppose that, after the last revolution, *nothing further happens*. Christian eschatology, in referring to a life 'after' death, a life 'after' the abolition of the vicissitudes of history, often does so in terms which seem to suppose the 'continuing existence' of human beings in God's eternity. (Whether it is wise to do so without adverting to the implications of the metaphorical status of such language,[25] or whether and to what extent the 'coming of the Kingdom', or the irreversible 'birth' of man from his conflictual 'prehistory', can intelligibly be conceived as intrahistorical projects, are questions we have yet to consider.) Nor is it necessary, in order for the description 'eschatological' to be appropriate, to claim that Marx supposed that, after the last revolution, 'all possible contradiction is eliminated for ever'[26] from human existence. There may well be 'limits', or 'constraints', within which even 'redeemed' human existence must continue to operate if it is still to be, in any intelligible sense, *human* existence. We have yet to discuss the extent to which Marx took this possibility seriously into account.

Marx's use of the metaphor of 'birth', and of the concept of 'prehistory', bear out Kolakowski's contention that he 'constantly regarded the historical process from the point of view of the future liberation of mankind.'[27] If, as a result, he was driven to speak in paradox concerning those events which both precede and follow that revolutionary process which irreversibly 'abolishes' man's four-fold alienation, it would be surprising if there were not analogies between some of the more puzzling features of his language concerning the future and attempts, in Christian theology, similarly to ascribe unique and unsurpassable redemptive significance to particular historical events.

Some forms of Christian theology, though not all, confront similar difficulties concerning the notion of the 'end' of history. These difficulties are (at least apparently) avoided by interpretations of Jesus which construe his significance in purely 'exemplary' terms, thereby seeking to avoid describing his person, work and fate, in

25 Cf. N. L. A. Lash, *Theology on Dover Beach*, pp. 164–82.
26 Mészáros, op. cit., p. 249.
27 *KI*, p. 348.

terms of an historically particular, irreversibly effective, liberating act of God. In the judgement of some Christians, however (including myself), the price paid for such intelligibility, such diminution of paradox, is too heavy. It seems to me that no description of that which Jesus exemplified, and of the manner in which he exemplified it, is adequate unless it includes some account of what it was that was uniquely and irreversibly achieved in him by the action of God.

However, thus to attribute irreversible redemptive significance to that which was done in Jesus is to claim eschatological significance for the events of his history. It is thereby to claim that, in some sense, the history of man's redemption *ends* with the end of his history. And this claim, even if unavoidable, is exceedingly dangerous. It is dangerous because it too easily encourages Christians, forgetful of the fact that the history of Jesus has not ended,[28] to suppose that all that is necessary, after his death, is the administration of an achievement. This supposition, I suggest, throws some light on the insensitivity which Christians have often shown (both in practice, and in the absence of any perceptible *theoretical* pain or puzzlement) in face of the indubitable fact that human history, after the death of Jesus, continues to be a history of conflict, suffering and oppression – a history, in other words, of *un*redeemed humanity. As I hinted in Chapter Fourteen, Christians have too often been led, by the manner in which they ascribe irreversible redemptive significance to the obedience and death of Jesus, to substitute a theory of reconciliation for its practice.

For Christians, there is a straightforward sense in which that event, for which irreversible, eschatological redemptive significance is claimed, is a *past* event. It is possible approximately to date the death of Jesus. For Marx, the last revolution to which he looked forward was – be it near or far, immensely protracted or a more or less 'overnight' affair – a *future* event. But some Marxists have interpreted a particular past event (the October Revolution, for example) as, if not the complete realization, at least the unsurpassable inception, of the irreversible achievement. They have therefore been tempted to suppose that all that is necessary, since 1917, is the administration of an achievement. And the consequences have been painful for the victims of the Marxist, as of the Christian, illusion.

Just as Marx spoke of the end of prehistory, of the 'supersession' of mankind's fourfold alienation, of the 'birth' of authentically *human* existence, so Christians have spoken of the birth of a 'new man', of human existence freed from the bondage of sin, freed from a condition of alienation from God and from fellow human beings. If, as I suggested in the previous paragraphs, attempts to locate this

28 Cf. above, p. 193.

'birth' *simply* in the past are dangerous and illusory, it is also true that attempts to locate it *simply* in the future risk reducing both Christian and Marxist hope to 'utopian fantasy'. In order for either Christian or Marxist hope to retain an element of 'realism', it is essential that the language in which that hope is expressed be such as to stimulate, and not to distract from, the permanently particular labour of contributing, in practice, to the actualization of that hope. For the Christian, the 'work of our redemption' refers not merely to a deed once done, or to the substance of hope for the future, but also to tasks to be performed, in hope, in virtue of that deed. In the remaining sections of this chapter, I shall try to give to these exceedingly general observations somewhat less formal and abstract expression.

Judgement and Mercy

According to David Fernbach, 'throughout his life Marx always held that a new class, including the working class, could only come to power and transform society to its design if it represented, not merely its own particular interest, but a universal interest of historical development, so that only those with a vested interest in the old order would stand in its way.'[29] This statement is surely misleading. Marx seems never to have abandoned his conviction that that revolution of which the industrial proletariat was to be the agent would be the *last* revolution. And it would be the last revolution because the proletariat, the bondsman existing in 'pure negativity', is that 'sphere which has a universal character because of its universal suffering ... which is, in a word, the *total loss* of humanity'.[30] In other words, the proletariat's *only* 'particular' interest is the 'universal' interest of humanity. Deprive the proletariat of this unique characteristic, and there would be no grounds whatsoever for supposing that the revolutionary triumph of *this* class would lead to the abolition of 'classes and class antagonisms'.[31]

Any interpretation of Marx's doctrine of the proletariat, and of the extent to which the prophetic clarity of some of his earlier expressions needs to be modified by later, somewhat more sober, descriptions of the course and character of the revolution,[32] is bound to be both tentative and controversial. Thus, for example, from the theoretical standpoint, it is not easy to see why it should be the

29 'Introduction', *FI*, p. 37.
30 *EW*, p. 256. Cf. above, pp. 243–8.
31 *The Poverty of Philosophy*, p. 170.
32 Cf. eg, McLellan's remarks on the Preface to the 1872 edition of the *Communist Manifesto* (*Life*, pp. 187–8). The section of the Preface on which he comments was quoted again, by Engels, in the Preface to the English edition of 1888: cf. *R1848*, p. 66.

industrial proletariat, rather than the 'lumpenproletariat', whose
condition is such as to constitute 'the total loss of humanity'. Yet
Marx, who refers to the latter as 'the social scum, that passively
rotting mass thrown off by the lowest layers of old society', says
that 'its conditions of life' prepare it 'for the part of a bribed tool
of reactionary intrigue', rather than for a revolutionary role.[33] As a
political judgement, that may well have been sound, and yet the
lumpenproletariat's 'conditions of existence' would seem to approximate, more closely than those of the industrial proletariat, to the
bondsman's condition of 'pure negativity'.

Be that as it may, the problem that I now want to discuss arises
from the claim that that revolution of which the proletariat is the
agent will be the *last* revolution precisely because the proletariat, as
a class, has no 'particular interest' to defend. There is an ethical
dimension to the problem: to the extent that the proletariat exists
in a condition of pure 'victimhood', its execution of its revolutionary
destiny will be 'pure' in the sense that it will not be contaminated
by group egotism, by 'particular interest'. I wish to suggest that
any revolutionary movement which supposes its agency to be thus
'pure' is the victim of an exceedingly dangerous illusion. Perhaps
(with an eye to the theological reflections with which I shall conclude this section) we can call this the illusion of 'social messianism'.

It could be objected, of course, that although Marx did not
consider the ethical dimension of the problem, he was well aware
of its political dimension, in the sense that he acknowledged the
inevitability that, until the abolition of 'class and class antagonisms'
is achieved, the proletariat is a particular class, representing its own
'particular' interests, interests that cannot yet appear as the 'universal' interests which, in reality, they are. Hence the distinction, in
the *Communist Manifesto*, between that stage in which 'the proletariat
organized as the ruling class' will 'use its political supremacy',[34]
and that later stage at which, class distinctions having disappeared,
'public power will lose its political character'.[35] Hence, too, the
references, in the *Critique of the Gotha Programme*, to those 'birth-
marks of the old society' by which communist society 'as it *emerges*
from capitalist society' will inevitably be 'stamped'.[36]

In a key passage in the *Critique of the Gotha Programme*, in answer
to the question: 'What transformation will the state undergo in a
communist society?', Marx says that 'Between capitalist and communist society lies a period of revolutionary transformation from
one to the other. There is a corresponding period of transition in
the political sphere and in this period the state can only take the

33 'Manifesto of the Communist Party', *R1848*, p. 77.
34 *R1848*, p. 86.
35 *R1848*, p. 87.
36 *FI*, p. 346.

form of a *revolutionary dictatorship of the proletariat*.'[37] It may well be a mistake to fasten too rapidly, as critics of Marxism are apt to do, on the term 'dictatorship'. For Marx, says Fernbach, 'the proletarian dictatorship means simply the unrestrained political power of the working class.'[38] Nevertheless, the absence of any consideration of the criteria on the basis of which the exercise of such power could be shown to be in the 'real' interests of the whole of humanity, and not merely of the class which had won such power, betrays the enduring influence of the unquestioned assumption that the proletariat, by its very nature, its 'being',[39] represents and can only represent the 'universal' interest.

In 1918, commenting on the *Critique of the Gotha Programme*, Lenin said that the 'transition' from capitalism to communism would 'obviously be a lengthy process',[40] and insisted that questions concerning 'the time required for, or the concrete form of, the withering away of'[41] the state had to be left 'quite open, because there is *no* material for answering these questions'.[42] It is not, however, the refusal to indulge in speculative prediction concerning the duration or specific characteristics of that '*class dictatorship* of the proletariat' which Marx had described, in 1850, as 'a necessary intermediate point on the path towards the *abolition of class differences in general*',[43] which is disturbing. Nor am I concerned, at this point, with the problem of the warrants for the assumption (shared by both Marx and Lenin) that the 'dictatorship of the proletariat' would necessarily constitute a merely 'transitional' or 'intermediate' phenomenon. When, in the same year (1918), Lenin defined 'dictatorship' as 'rule based directly upon force and unrestricted by any laws',[44] we are confronted, once again, by the problem of the grounds on which it can be assumed that such unconstrained force will in fact be used, and will only be used, in the 'real' interests of humanity. These grounds, I suggest, can only be sought in the further assumption that the agency of the new 'ruling class' would be 'pure' in the sense of being uncontaminated by group or sectional interest. And this is the assumption which I have described as the illusion of social messianism.

Marx's doctrine of the revolutionary role and redemptive capacity of the proletariat is, says Calvez, 'd'une extrême richesse, en particulier dans son signification théologique, et on peut y voir une

---

37 *FI*, p. 355.
38 'Introduction', *FI*, p.62.
39 Cf. *CW4*, p. 37.
40 'The State and Revolution', Ch. 5, *HM*, p. 564.
41 Ibid., p. 573.
42 Loc. cit.
43 'The Class Struggles in France', *SE*, p. 123.
44 'The Proletarian Revolution and the Renegade Kautsky', *HM*, p. 607.

sort de figuration athée de ce qu'est l'Incarnation de Dieu pour les chrétiens'.[45] That Jesus, in his passion and crucifixion, was 'victim', is historically indisputable, even if it can be argued that there is a sense in which he brought his death upon himself. But that, *as* victim, he was also 'agent', transcribing historically the agency of God, is central to Christian belief in the possibility of imperishable human freedom. Thus to interpret Jesus' suffering and death is to acknowledge, with Hegel, the one-sidedness of all concepts of 'lordship' (including, especially, all concepts of the lordship of God) which have not been transformed by recognition of the fact that that which 'lordship' seeks is only realizable through dispossession.

To speak of Jesus as the historical transcription of the 'agency' of God, and to leave the matter there, would, however, be wholly unsatisfactory. It is necessary to give some material content to the exceedingly formal and abstract concept of 'agency'. What is it which God is declared here to work: death, or life? Or, to put it another way: without attempting to slacken the paradox indispensable in all our attempts to do the impossible, and to speak truthfully of the being and action of God, how are we to relate the death-dealing and life-giving aspects of God's activity?

In an earlier chapter, I spoke of Good Friday as the execution of that which Jesus' preaching proclaimed: God's transformative fidelity to his creation.[46] Thus to speak of Good Friday is to interpret the death of Jesus, in the light of resurrection, as the manifestation of divine 'mercy' or 'lovingkindness'. But such language needs to be set in counterpoint with another register of discourse – equally ancient and equally central in Christian theology – which interprets the death of Jesus as a 'judicial' act, as the execution of divine judgement. And, in order not to lose sight of the analogies between Christian interpretations of the passion and death of Jesus, and the Marxian interpretation of the redemptive role of the proletariat, let us remember Marx's claim that 'The proletariat executes the sentence that private property pronounces on itself by producing the proletariat'.[47]

The death of Jesus, interpreted in the light of resurrection, is declared to be the manifestation, not only of divine mercy, but also of divine judgement. That is to say: in Jesus' 'servitude', his submission to 'alien power', the sentence of judgement is seen to have been executed. Upon whom? The 'alien power' to which Jesus submitted was not the 'Father' with whose purpose he identified himself, even at the cost of his life, but was rather the force of 'historical necessity', in the sense that the message which he proclaimed and embodied could not but be resisted by those who,

45 *La Pensée de Karl Marx*, p. 328.
46 Cf. above, p. 193.
47 *CW4*, p. 36.

identifying 'freedom' with *retention* – whether of material, political or conceptual possessions – 'necessarily' sought to abolish, to destroy, one whose freedom threatened and undermined the foundations of egotism.

It can therefore be said that the obedience unto death of the 'suffering servant' executes the sentence which egotism pronounces on itself by producing servitude. And if that obedience results in the imperishable freedom, not only of the servant, but also of those who produced his and all servitude; if, that is to say, the 'total loss' of his humanity has as its result 'the total redemption of humanity'; this can only be because his 'agency' was wholly 'pure', sinless, uncontaminated by 'particular' individual or group interest and egotism.

The ascription of 'sinlessness' to one who was, as all men are – at least as long as the 'prehistory' of man endures – the product of an inherently 'sinful' situation is, of course, highly problematic. If sense is to be made of this ascription, it can only be made by remembering, firstly, that it expresses a theological and not merely a moral judgement and, secondly, that – as with all christological concepts – it contains an eschatological and, specifically, a future dimension. Therefore, as with all such concepts, the fundamental context in which its use is appropriate is that of prayer and expectation, of hope rather than assertion.

One thing at least is certain: of no individual or group, other than him who uniquely personifies the mystery of God, can any such claim be made. Christian forms of the Marxian illusion of social messianism all stem from the mistaken belief that the agency of the Church, or of the individual Christian, exhibits or can exhibit that 'purity', that absence of particular interest, which is uniquely characteristic of the incarnation of the mystery of God.

Sometimes, in this quest for purity of action, and conscious of the fact that 'Mercy and gentleness . . . are absolute imperatives for all Christians, and at all times',[48] Christians have sought to abstain from all exercise of political power and all use of political force. There is thus a tradition of Christian pacifism as there is not, nor is there likely to be, a tradition of Marxist pacifism. And if this tradition may be said frequently to have been an important exercise in 'utopian' prophetic criticism, it is nevertheless threatened by abstractness in the measure that it fails to take account of the extent to which the pacifist is inevitably caught, as the inhabitant of a social context, in the play of forces and structures of social and political power.

Sometimes, the quest for purity of action has taken the form of

---

48 W. Stein, 'Mercy and Revolution', *From Culture to Revolution*, ed. T. Eagleton and B. Wicker, p. 232.

the elaboration of doctrines of 'just war' or, in our times, of 'just revolution'. The strength of this tradition lies in its recognition – wholly absent, it seems to me, from the Marxian treatment of revolution – that 'whilst violence remains a crucial constituent of our world . . .justice and mercy require a framework of minimum moral restraints'.[49] One way of putting this would be to say, with Lenin's definition of 'dictatorship' in mind, that 'rule based directly upon force', while it cannot be restricted by existing laws (because the legal system is, as are all aspects of the social 'superstructure', subject to revolutionary transformation), must nevertheless be subject to certain 'moral restraints', and in that sense to *moral* 'law', if it is in fact to be constitutive rather than destructive of the 'authentically human'. The weakness of the tradition of 'just war', or 'just revolution', lies partly in its tendency to facilitate the complacent habituation to force and violence as 'a simply fated permanent presence in history',[50] and partly in its tendency to foster the illusion that the exercise of force can *ever* lack moral ambiguity.

For Marx, the 'bondsman' redeems by taking control of the situation in the fullness of time. The Christian, as I understand the matter, is constrained – both by his remembrance that the 'agency' of Jesus, which he acknowledges to have been supremely effective in the work of our redemption, was an agency of submission, and not of force, and by his recognition that he is not Jesus – not to lose sight of the fact that the 'negativity' of the bondsman is never 'pure' enough to ensure that the victory of the dispossessed will not turn out, after the event, to have been, in reality, yet another victory for the 'lordship' or 'dictatorship' of particular interest. 'Absolute ends justify total means – or so the messianic revolutionary is convinced.'[51] But revolutionary messianism is, on a Christian understanding of these matters, a form of blasphemy.

Freedom and Necessity

During the late eighteen-seventies, Engels triumphantly announced that 'The possibility of securing for every member of society, through social production, an existence which is not only perfectly adequate materially and which daily becomes richer, but also guarantees him the completely free development and exercise of his physical and mental faculties – this possibility is now present for the first time, but it is *present*.'[52] And he described the realization of

---

49 Stein, art. cit., p. 231.
50 Loc. cit.
51 Ibid., p. 241.
52 *Anti-Dühring*, p. 366.

this satisfactory state of affairs as 'humanity's leap from the realm of necessity into the realm of freedom'.[53]

This is, admittedly, the voice not of Marx but of Engels, even though Marx collaborated with Engels in the production of *Anti-Dühring*.[54] I have quoted it because it illustrates the links between the cluster of topics on which I propose to comment in this section: namely, the relationships between freedom and necessity, progress and optimism, optimism and hope.

Two connected themes run through Marx's lifelong reflections on the problem of freedom. In the first place, there is the conviction that, in social formations in which human beings are still alienated from each other, and in which the development of the individual can therefore only be 'partial',[55] such 'particular' freedoms as are secured in appearance – through constitutional arrangements, for example – also represent, in reality, an aspect of enduring 'universal' *un*freedom and, as such, invite their own dialectical reversal. Thus, in 1843, commenting on the assertion, in the French 'Declaration of the Rights of Man and of the Citizen' of 1791, that 'Liberty consists in being able to do anything which does not harm others', he says: 'the right of man to freedom is [here] not based on the association of man with man but rather on the separation of man from man.'[56] This is expressed more concretely in the *Communist Manifesto*: 'By freedom is meant, under the present bourgeois conditions of production, free trade, free selling and buying.'[57] It is not however, 'individuals who are set free by free competition; it is rather, capital which is set free'.[58] Or, as he puts it with heavy irony: 'If one grows impoverished and the other grows wealthier, then this is of their own free will and does not in any way arise from the economic relations.'[59] Hence his suspicion of those 'pompous catalogues of the "inalienable rights of man" ',[60] whose function it is to protect 'such sacred things as the rights of property, freedom and the self-determing "genius" of the individual capitalist'.[61]

In the second place, if theoretical criticism of bourgeois concepts of freedom is to get to the heart of the matter, it will have to deal with the 'unresolved antinomy', in Hegel's thought, between 'external necessity' and 'immanent end'.[62] Given 'the *universal* relation-

---

53 Ibid., p. 367.
54 Cf. *Life*, p. 423.
55 Cf. *Cap. I*, p. 618.
56 'On the Jewish Question', *EW*, p. 229.
57 *R1848*, p. 81.
58 *G*, p. 650.
59 *G*, p. 247.
60 *Cap. I*, p. 416.
61 *Cap. II*, p. 477.
62 Cf. 'Critique of Hegel's Doctrine of the State', *EW*, pp. 58–60.

ship of *freedom* and *necessity*',[63] that antinomy will not be resolved by the abolition of necessity, but rather by its appropriation as immanent end. This seems to be the sense, for example, of the contrast drawn between animals who 'produce only when immediate physical needs compel them to do so', and man, who 'produces even when he is free from physical need and truly [i.e. humanly] produces only in freedom from such need'.[64] In other words, if communism is 'the true resolution of the conflict . . . between freedom and necessity',[65] this is because, under communism, the 'totally developed individual'[66] will be free from external constraint – whether imposed by other individuals, by social structures, or by the forces of nature. Thus it is that communism represents 'a higher form of society . . . in which the full and free development of every individual forms the ruling principle',[67] an 'association, in which the free development of each is the condition of the free development of all'.[68] In a word: in circumstances in which man's fourfold alienation – from that which he produces, from the process of production, from himself and from his fellow-men[69] – has been healed, human beings will no longer be subject to *external* necessity. In Engels' formulation: 'Men, at last masters of their own mode of social organization, consequently become at the same time masters of nature, masters of themselves – free. To accomplish this world-emancipatory act is the historical mission of the modern proletariat.'[70]

At first sight, this expression of the Promethean dream, this vision of freedom unconstrained by external necessity, seems to prospect a freedom which is *absolute*. But a spectre haunts all expectation of 'absolute freedom': the spectre of Hegel's analysis of the totalitarianism of the French Revolution. In the realm of 'absolute freedom', of the 'universal will', nothing can 'break loose to become a *free object* standing over against it'.[71] Absolute or universal freedom can therefore 'produce neither a positive work nor a deed; there is left for it only *negative* action; it is merely the *fury* of destruction.'[72] For that fury, death is deprived of significance: 'It is thus the coldest and meanest of all deaths, with no more significance than cutting off a head of cabbage or swallowing a mouthful of water.'[73] The

63 *EW*, p. 64.
64 'Economic and Philosophical Manuscripts', *EW*, p. 329.
65 *EW*, p. 348.
66 *Cap. I*, p. 618.
67 *Cap. I*, p. 739.
68 'Manifesto of the Communist Party', *R1848*, p. 87.
69 Cf. above, pp. 170–1.
70 *Anti-Dühring*, p. 369.
71 *Phenomenology*, p. 358.
72 Ibid., p. 359.
73 Ibid., p. 360.

realm of absolute freedom thus reveals itself to be no more than the dictatorship of particular interest: by 'excluding all other individuals from its act . . . it is absolutely impossible for it to exhibit itself as anything but a *faction*. What is called government is merely a *victorious* faction.'[74]

According to Hegel, there is no way *back* from this 'sheer terror of the negative'[75] to 'the ethical and the real world of culture'[76] (i.e. eighteenth-century France as he had analysed it in earlier sections of the *Phenomenology*) because all specific, individual, social and cultural determinations have been annihilated. But there is a way *forward*. The 'essential being' of the 'universal will' is 'nothing else but pure knowing'.[77] Absolute freedom, nihilistic totalitarianism, thus brings about its own reversal, leaving 'its self-destroying reality and [passing] over into another land of self-conscious Spirit where, in this unreal world, freedom has the value of truth'.[78] Thus it is that, 'in the last section of the chapter on spirit we go from Revolutionary France to the awakening moral spirit of German philosophy'.[79]

According to Charles Taylor, 'Marx's variant of [Hegel's notion of] "absolute freedom" is at the basis of Bolshevik voluntarism which, strong with the final justification of history, has crushed all obstacles in its path with extraordinary ruthlessness, and has spawned again that Terror which Hegel described with uncanny insight.'[80] But is this not to attribute to Marx, by implication, a very 'idealist' vision of the 'realm of freedom' as the realization or 'incarnation' of the *idea* of freedom? 'Absolute freedom', on Hegel's account, is unconstrained because it is indeterminate. For Marx, however, 'the real issue is *human* freedom, not an abstract principle called "freedom".'[81]

Human freedom, on Marx's account, is not and cannot be 'absolute' because it consists, not in transcending 'the limitations (specific character) of human nature but a *coincidence* with them'.[82] But in what do these specifying limitations consist? From where we stand, within the 'prehistory' of human freedom, any answers that we give to this question will, admittedly, be provisional and heuristic in character. We cannot foretell a future we have not yet constructed and, when we try to do so, we usually get it wrong. Thus, for example, the possibility of securing 'for every member of

74 Loc. cit.
75 Ibid., p. 362.
76 Ibid., p. 361.
77 Ibid., p. 363.
78 Loc. cit.
79 C. Taylor, *Hegel*, p. 188.
80 Ibid., p. 558.
81 Mészáros, *Marx's Theory of Alienation*, p. 163.
82 Loc. cit.

society' economic conditions such as would guarantee him 'the completely free development and exercise of his physical and mental faculties' appears a far more distant (and manifestly utopian) dream today than it did to Engels (and to many others) in the late nineteenth century.

Nevertheless, the question must be pressed. If, in characterizing human freedom as coincident with natural necessity, we construe 'necessity' *simply* in terms (for example) of the need for man to produce his existence through labour, and to do so in society,[83] the aspects of 'necessity' thus selected for consideration may render the goal of 'freedom', coincident with *such* 'necessity', an attractive prospect. But there are other aspects of 'necessity' less readily assimilable as 'immanent ends' of human action. Can death cease to be experienced as 'external' necessity? And what grounds do we have for supposing that human beings will undergo that *moral* transformation which would abolish the 'externality' of one man's egotism to the needs of another? Only if the 'mastery of nature' included the mastery of death, and 'self-mastery' the moral transformation of mankind, would the prospect of the coincidence of freedom and necessity be a cheerful one. Until death and sin are conquered, it is difficult to see why the prospect of the coincidence of freedom with necessity should generate optimism rather than despair. Marx ignored death, and took it for granted that the necessary moral transformation would occur. Yet there is nothing in his analysis of man's 'prehistory', or of that 'essence' of humanity which this 'prehistory' will eventually produce, which would either justify the neglect or furnish him with warrants for the assumption.

We shall consider the question of 'self-mastery', of the relationship between freedom and 'social' necessity, in the following section. For the remainder of the present section, I shall take the question of the 'mastery of nature' as the basis for some general reflections on forms of hope.

Engels' casual reference to free human beings as 'masters of nature' is more reminiscent of the early Marx's exuberant description of the eventual 'identity of man and nature'[84] than of his later, more sober, appreciation of the fact that 'Man cannot in the last resort be emancipated from the necessities imposed by nature'.[85] Thus, for example, in a famous passage in the third volume of *Capital* he says that 'The realm of freedom actually begins only where labour which is determined by necessity and mundane considerations ceases'.[86] In 'all social formations and under all possible

---

83 Mészáros' sketch of seven 'elements and stages of a possible definition' of 'non-alienated man' gets no further than this: cf. ibid., pp. 173–4.
84 Cf. A. Schmidt, *The Concept of Nature in Marx*, p. 137.
85 Ibid., p. 139.
86 *Cap. III*, p. 820.

modes of production,' man 'must wrestle with Nature to satisfy his wants, to maintain and reproduce life'.[87] 'Freedom in this field can only consist in socialized man, the associated producers, rationally regulating their interchange with Nature, bringing it under their common control, instead of being ruled by it as by the blind forces of Nature. . . . But it nonetheless still remains a realm of necessity. Beyond it begins that development of human energy which is an end in itself, the true realm of freedom, which, however, can blossom forth only with this realm of necessity as its basis.'[88]

The first thing to be said about this passage is that it does not envisage (as Engels' version appeared to do) the relationship between the 'realm of necessity' and the 'realm of freedom' in terms of *chronological succession*. The 'realm of necessity' is not left behind: it remains the permanent 'basis' of the 'realm of freedom'.

Nevertheless, the second thing that needs to be said is that Marx's concentration on the *economic* dimension of the resolution of the conflict between freedom and necessity gives to his grandiose talk of the 'birth' of man, of the realization of the 'essence' of man, an air of curious unreality. As Kolakowski says: 'Man is wholly defined in purely social terms; the physical limitations of his being are scarcely noticed. Marxism takes little or no account of the fact that people are born and die, that they are men or women, young or old, healthy or sick; that they are genetically unequal, and that all these circumstances affect social development irrespective of the class division, and set bounds to human plans for perfecting the world. . . . Evil and suffering, in [Marx's] eyes, had no meaning except as instruments for liberation; they were purely social facts, not an essential part of the human condition.'[89]

I suggested, in an earlier chapter, that any expression of hope for the future of man which fails to take seriously the most 'absolute' of all 'natural limitations': namely, the determination of freedom by mortality – both individual and social, is seriously inadequate.[90] To the question of death, says Calvez, 'Marx, dans son optimisme, n'a consacré qu'une phrase'.[91] That 'phrase' occurs in the Paris Manuscripts: '*Death* appears as the harsh victory of the species over the particular individual, and seemingly contradicts their unity; but the particular individual is only a particular *species-being*, and as such mortal.'[92] A remark which seems curiously to imply the immortality of the species.

It must, moreover, be insisted that mortality is not simply a

87 Loc. cit.
88 Loc. cit.
89 *KI*, p. 413.
90 Cf. above, pp. 191–4.
91 *La Pensée de Karl Marx*, p. 284.
92 *EW*, p. 351.

terminal condition. To say that we are subject to mortality is not simply to say that, at a certain point in time, our individual and social histories *end*. It is also to say that the story of human existence, and of every moment and phase of that existence, is a story of corruption and decay. 'Living' and 'dying' are – for the individual and for the race – not simply successive processes, but permanent dimensions of one single historical process.[93] Nor is this merely a biological truism: it is a reminder that any anthropology, any account of the 'essence' of man, which is (as Marx's was) neglectful of mortality is intolerably abstract.

There are two ways of telling the story of man: as tragedy or as comedy.[94] To tell it as comedy is to give the story a 'happy ending' in which all conflict is resolved and the needs of all participants are met. To tell it as tragedy is to refuse to provide the story with such an ending. This distinction is, however, too neat. There are, as Walter Stein has argued, *two* forms of the tragic vision: that which finds expression in 'a cry of protest or despair', and that (of which, he suggests, *Lear* would be an example) in which 'desperation is somehow transcended from within, through the tragic experience itself'.[95] He goes so far as to speak of *Lear*'s 'tragic joy',[96] while insisting that this is not a joy which can find expression in the depiction of a satisfactory outcome.

Adopting (and somewhat adapting) Stein's distinction, I would like to suggest that the possibility of the second form of the tragic vision arises partly from the fact that we who tell the story live *within* the historical process. For us, therefore, the future is open. This 'openness' of the future cannot, of itself, furnish grounds for hope (these, if they exist, are to be sought elsewhere). Nevertheless, it is the characteristic weakness of both optimism (the voice of comedy) and of despair that, forgetful of the fact that the story has not ended, they suppose the future to be 'closed'. In other words, both optimism and despair take it upon themselves to provide the unfinished narrative with the ending which it has not yet, in fact, achieved.

According to George Steiner, 'the Marxist world view, even more explicitly than the Christian, admits of error, anguish and temporary defeat, but not of ultimate tragedy.'[97] This reading of Marx contrasts rather sharply with that offered by Raymond Williams. 'I see revolution,' says Williams, 'as the inevitable working through

---

93 Cf. Lash, *Theology on Dover Beach*, pp. 174–5.
94 It is, of course, also possible to tell it as farce (cf. *SE*, p. 146). But since this option is not usually taken up either by Marx or by Christian theologians, I shall not give it further consideration.
95 W. Stein, *Criticism as Dialogue*, p. 92.
96 Ibid., p. 110.
97 G. Steiner, *The Death of Tragedy*, p. 342.

of a deep and tragic disorder, to which we can respond in varying ways but which will in any case, in one way or another, work its way through our world, as a consequence of any of our actions. I see revolution, that is to say, in a tragic perspective . . . [and] Marx's early idea of revolution seems to me to be tragic in this sense.'[98]

I suggested earlier that there is a qualitative difference, on Marx's account, between human existence before and after the 'last revolution', between the process of 'prehistory' and that to which this process eventually 'gives birth'. There *is* a tragic dimension to the Marxian vision, and it is this dimension, underestimated by Steiner, which Williams seeks to recover.[99] To acknowledge the presence of this dimension is, therefore, to reject Steiner's claim that 'Marx repudiated the entire concept of tragedy'.[100] Nevertheless, I believe that Steiner is justified in asserting that 'the Marxist creed is immensely, perhaps naively optimistic.'[101] The source of the incoherence at the heart of Marx's vision is to be sought in what I have described as the abstract character of his account of the 'essence' of man, an account unduly neglectful of the mortality both of the individual *and* of the species, and in the unreality and the unrealizability of the prospected 'last revolution'. The 'tragic perspective' within which he viewed the 'prehistory' of man is thus, as it were, overridden by his optimistic vision of that which will be born as the irreversible 'fruit' of this prehistory. In *this* sense, Steiner seems to me justified in describing 'the Marxist conception of history' as 'a secular *commedia*.'[102]

I would now like to return to my distinction between optimism and the two forms of the tragic vision – one of which finds expression in the voice of despair and the other in that 'tragic joy' which is, or can be, a form of hope. If such hope is not to 'topple over' into optimism, it must retain the *reticence* which reflects the fact that it is only 'through the tragic experience itself' that 'desperation is somehow transcended.'[103] Hope, unlike optimism, does not 'leave behind' the tragic experience which is its enduring context. Both optimism and despair 'know the answer', whereas it is characteristic of hope (as one form of expression of the tragic vision) that it is

---

98 R. Williams, *Modern Tragedy*, p. 75. In illustration, he quotes from *EW*, p. 256. Cf. Stein, op. cit., p. 199.

99 On the confusions inscribed in this attempt, cf. Stein, op. cit., pp. 199–202. It is, however, important to add that Stein's criticisms occur in the course of a discussion of Williams' book which is not only penetrating but deeply appreciative: cf. 'Humanism and Tragic Redemption', *Criticism as Dialogue*, pp. 183–246.

100 Steiner, op. cit., p. 4.

101 Ibid., p. 342.

102 Ibid., p. 343.

103 Cf. Stein, op. cit., p. 92.

articulated in the interrogative mood. Hope may, indeed, be questionable but, if it is to remain hope, it can only take the form of a question. For the Christian, that question is cast as request: 'Thy kingdom come.' And whether such hope alienates or liberates depends, firstly on whether or not there is God and, secondly, on whether or not God is 'objectified' as 'alien power' – whose 'intervention' is passively awaited – or as that mystery which creates both the grounds of human hope and the conditions of its fulfilment. In the latter case, the hope is not that human beings be absolved from responsibility for the production of their humanity, but that they be enabled to contribute to the eschatological 'birth' of man from his conflictual and enigmatic 'prehistory'.

I have suggested that hope consists in the refusal to succumb to either of the twin temptations of optimism and despair. Perhaps we could say that hope is inherently unstable, precarious, because the 'focal length' of its vision is to the middle distance. The eyes of the mind, and of the heart, tend to wander to the far horizon – which, to the optimist, appears attractive because it is, in fact, invisible – or to the foreground, where the sharp and painful edges of existing fact obliterate from view the possibilities inherent in the present situation.

According to Lukács, 'when theory and practice are united it becomes possible to change reality.'[104] That is the voice of optimism, overlooking the possibility that there are insurmountable limits to the mutability of reality, whereas for despair 'reality' is admitted to be *simply* immutable.

It is in the interests of those who, in any given situation, operate the levers of power, to ensure that the despair of the powerless is dulled, rendered endurable by 'utopian' visions of a future which does not lie within their grasp. Marx's optimism is, at one level, an expression of his practical resistance to the ideological exploitation of pessimism. But his vision of the future was infected with abstractness and unreality. It remained optimistic, prematurely transcending desperation in the imagination, and did not, therefore, mature into hope.

All this is easily, perhaps too easily, said. But it is more difficult coherently to articulate the standpoint from which it is said. Many Christians have been, and continue to be, optimists. But far from such optimism being (as Steiner supposes) integral to Christian faith, it arises from a forgetfulness of the eschatological character of the language of resurrection. Such forgetfulness transposes the interrogative language of faith, of prayerful trust in man's future in God, into predictive assertion: it prematurely 'closes', in the imagination, the question of the future.

104 G. Lukács, *History and Class Consciousness*, p. 189.

Moreover, many Christians, in modern times, have cast their optimism into the form of a subscription to the myth of human 'progress'. Belief in 'progress', as a general framework within which to set the narrative of human history, is mythical because it ignores both the fact of social mortality – the fact that the story of the race, and not merely that of the individual, comes to an *end* (and possibly a most unpleasant end), and the implications of that fact, and also because (in its theological uses) it illusorily supposes that the happiness, the achieved 'humanity', of future generations could be thought to 'justify' the misery of those who suffered and died in the course of mankind's dark 'prehistory'.

The Marxist has no need to 'justify' the horrors of the past: it is sufficient for his purposes if he can provide them with some plausible explanation. But the question of theodicy, of the justification of past and present misery, cannot be evaded by a Christian who wishes to claim that all that occurs, in nature and history, is the contingent expression of a God to whom the *moral* quality of 'goodness' is ascribed.

And yet, all theodicies – in the sense of theoretical attempts to demonstrate the compatibility of the 'tragic disorder' with the goodness of God – are, however indispensable in principle, suspect in practice as ideological rationalizations of other people's meaningless suffering. Armed with a satisfactory theodicy, the need to ameliorate suffering, to contribute, in practice, to the redemptive liberation of mankind, is sometimes less sharply felt.

I suggested earlier that only if the 'mastery of nature' included the mastery of death could the prospect of the coincidence of freedom and necessity be a cheerful one. The object of Christian hope is indeed the mastery of death: of all men's deaths and of all their lifelong dying. To speak of 'resurrection' is to speak of imperishable human freedom as the conquest of death's 'external' hegemony. But, for reasons that I indicated earlier when attempting to delineate 'hope' as a form of the tragic response, there is a sense in which it must necessarily be impossible, *within* a history bounded and determined by mortality, appropriately to speak of resurrection. Or, at least, the only way in which it is possible to speak of resurrection without lapsing into optimism is by a use of a language whose dominant mood – whatever its semantic form – is interrogative. The language of resurrection requests the 'coincidence' of 'appearance' and 'reality': it requests the 'actualization', in the future, of that which it confesses, in darkness, to be 'ultimately' the case in virtue of its interpretative experience of a particular past event. In this sense, the discourse of resurrection is, or should be, for the Christian, more fundamentally the discourse of prayer than of assertion. Christianity remains a matter of hope.

Both optimism and despair, I have suggested, purport to 'know the answer', whereas hope finds expression in the interrogative mood. Does it follow that hope – precarious, unstable, construct in tragedy – is *simply* nescient: that it 'only' hopes and in no sense 'knows'? Or is it possible that, just as – on the one hand – the 'knowledge' to which both optimism and despair lay claim may lack adequate warrant and be, in fact, illusory, so also – on the other – the 'tragic joy' which suffuses hope may spring from a form of knowledge? To put it another way: when Christian hope finds expression in the declaration that we 'know' that 'our redeemer liveth', of what 'knowledge', if any, are we speaking?

If 'knowledge' is and can only be the name of a 'commodity' which either is or is not 'possessed',[105] then such a declaration *either* lays claim to such possession (and thereby 'topples over' from hope into optimism) *or* gives grossly misleading expression to our nescience. If, however, 'knowledge' is to be construed as conformity with truth, as relationship, rather than as possession, then it would seem possible for hope to be, in practice, thus related to its object, and hence to be in some sense an instance of knowledge. For this to be the case, it is not necessary that it should, or even could, be *demonstrated* to be the case. It is not, in all circumstances, a necessary condition of our knowledge that we can 'show that we know'.

Thus summarily to touch on issues of forbidding complexity in the philosophy of 'knowledge' and 'belief'[106] is, for all its inadequacy, by no means a distraction from the themes with which this section is concerned. Whether or not the grammar of the concept of 'knowledge' is or should be flexible enough to accommodate the suggestion at which I have hinted, at least it seems to be the case that both Christian hope and Marxist optimism, in so far as they are prudently fearful of irrationality and illusion, will be suspicious of any supposed *understanding* of the future which precedes, in the imagination, the labour of its construction. Marx's overriding optimism concerning the satisfactory outcome of the tragic 'prehistory' of man is quite compatible with his reluctance (on which I have insisted) to attempt the depiction, before the event, of the form of that outcome. In this sense Marxian optimism is to be construed as a form of faith, and the Marxist historian Lucien Goldmann would seem to be correct in saying that 'the phrase *Credo ut intelligam* provides a common basis for Augustinian, Pascalian and Marxist epistemology'[107] – a claim likely to be resisted by both Marxist and Christian rationalists and idealists.[108]

105 Cf. above, pp. 105–8, 149–50.
106 Issues explored with some subtlety by Newman in the *University Sermons* and the *Grammar of Assent.*
107 L. Goldmann, *The Hidden God,* p. 94.
108 An interesting example of such resistance is Francis Barker's (Althusserian)

It has been the purpose of these scattered reflections to suggest that even if, from the standpoint of a particular form and interpretation of Christian belief, Marxian optimism seems devoid of adequate warrants, this is no way entitles the Christian to suppose that he has at his disposal some set of either practical or theoretical 'solutions' to the question of human freedom and its coincidence with necessity. The interpretation of Jesus' passion and death as resurrection, as the conquest of the 'lordship' or 'externality' of death, may or may not furnish grounds for hope – that is a practical question – but it cannot provide grounds for optimism. Whether or not the story of man should turn out, after all, to have been a comedy – a tale with a satisfactory resolution – it most certainly cannot be demonstrated to be such, this side of death. Mindful of our boundedness by mortality, the coincidence of freedom and necessity may perhaps constitute a promise, but it also indubitably constitutes a threat.

The Organization of Freedom
The 'series of historic processes', the 'long struggles', through which humanity has to pass before there can emerge that 'higher form to which present society is irrestibly tending', must – and will, according to Marx – be such as to transform not only 'circumstances', but 'men'.[109] For that higher form of society to be realized, it is essential that not only our alienation from the process and products of our labour be 'superseded', but also our alienation from ourselves and from our fellow human beings. It is, in other words, a necessary condition of the emancipation of the world, of the birth of *human* 'freedom', that human beings achieve 'self-mastery'.[110] And such self-mastery is not, of course, to be construed in purely individualistic terms: it must refer to the emergence of a society in which social self-mastery is achieved through the abolition of 'external' necessity, of domination, whether the agent of domination be a 'victorious faction', the state or the individual tyrant.

In the previous section, we considered the question of mankind's achievement of freedom from external domination by 'natural' necessity. We saw that Marx's inattention to the problem of mortality led him to be unduly optimistic concerning the prospects for such freedom. If, however, there is a *'universal* relationship of *freedom*

---

contention that 'If Marxism admits "belief" as an epistemological category it will turn into its opposite, not a revolutionary praxis but an ideology of protest' ('The Morality of Knowledge and the Disappearance of God', *New Blackfriars*, Vol. 57 [1976], p. 410; cf. the same author's 'Science and Ideology', *New Blackfriars*, Vol. 58 [1977], pp. 473–82).
109 'The Civil War in France', *FI*, p. 213.
110 Cf. Engels, *Anti-Dühring*, p. 369.

and *necessity*',[111] and if the 'true resolution of the conflict . . . between freedom and necessity'[112] consists, not in the abolition of necessity, but in the abolition of its externality, its subsumption as 'immanent end', we need to ask: is it also the case, where '*social*' necessity is concerned, that there are insurmountable limits to the abolition of its 'externality'?[113]

There are at least two ways in which that question can be rendered less abstract. In the first place, it is a question concerning the plausibility of the expectation that the first phase of the revolutionary process – the phase characterized by the 'dictatorship of the proletariat' – will give way to the second. In the second place, it is a question concerning the plausibility of the expectation that the transformation of structures and circumstances will lead, not simply to a corresponding transformation of *consciousness* (i.e. of language and mental attitudes), but to a *moral* transformation – a transformation of patterns of behaviour and relationship – such that human egotism will have been irreversibly uprooted and 'abolished'. Only if the expectation can plausibly be entertained that attainable 'self-mastery' will include the moral transformation of mankind, that the lordship and bondage of sin will be abolished, is the prospect of the 'coincidence' of freedom and necessity a cheerful one. We shall consider these two issues in turn, and then conclude by reflecting on the problem of the 'location' of those models of humanity which form the substance of Marxian and Christian hopes for the future freedom of man.

'The changes in the economic foundations', wrote Marx in 1859, 'lead sooner or later to the transformation of the whole immense superstructure.'[114] From 1884 onwards, he went through 'alternative phases of expecting an early European revolution and reconciling himself to a longer wait':[115] sometimes it seemed that it would come 'sooner', sometimes 'later'. But he never doubted that it would come. Similarly, although his descriptions of the relationship between the initial phase of the revolution and the emergence of that classless society from which all oppression will have vanished for ever, and in which the 'free development' of each will be the effective

---

111 *EW*, p. 64.
112 *EW*, p. 348.
113 The distinction between 'nature' and 'society' is not, of course, as sharp in Marx's thought as the arrangement of these two sections might suggest (cf. above, pp. 99–103). Thus, in criticism of Lukács' claim that 'Nature is a [purely] social category' (*History and Class Consciousness*, p. 234), Schmidt points out that 'If nature', for Marx, 'is a social category, the inverted statement that society is a category of nature is equally valid' (Schmidt, *The Concept of Nature in Marx*, p. 70). In other words, the topics I am considering in these two sections could be considered, from one point of view, as aspects of 'natural necessity'.
114 'Preface to *A Contribution to the Critique of Political Economy*', *EW*, p. 426.
115 *KI*, p. 309.

condition for the 'free development of all',[116] may have varied, he never appears to have doubted that the 'more advanced phase of communist society'[117] would eventually be realized. It may be that, unlike 'Bourgeois revolutions such as those of the eighteenth century', which 'storm quickly from success to success . . . Proletarian revolutions . . . such as those of the nineteenth century, constantly engage in self-criticism, and in repeated interruptions of their own course.'[118] But he did not doubt that this course would, eventually, be run.

As we suggested earlier, however, the prospect of the definitive obliteration of the 'birth-marks of the old society'[119] presupposes a revolutionary agent lacking all 'particular interest' and, in that sense, 'free from sin'.[120] Therefore, not only is it the case that 'Rien ne *garantit* le passage de la dictature du prolétariat à cette seconde étape',[121] but that there is no reason to suppose this transition to be *possible* within the limits of history. Or, at least, the abolition of egotism – which we shall consider shortly – would be a necessary condition of the realization of such a possibility.

Mészáros correctly insists that 'the total abolition of human institutions would amount . . . not [to] the abolition of alienation but its *maximization* in the form of total anarchy . . . *order* . . . in human society, is inseparable from some *organization*'.[122] I am not suggesting that Marx's descriptions of the stages through which the revolutionary process would pass are, explicitly, descriptions of a movement towards a social 'formation' without form – without organization, without determination, without limits – but that the absence of any discussion of what such limits might be infects his vision. In saying this, I have in mind, for example, Alvin Gouldner's suggestion that the expectation that all limits, all social necessity, *can* be surmounted, while not an explicit theme in Marxian or Marxist thought, is yet a 'fugitive fantasy to which [Marxism] was open and from which it drew a hidden, extra strength'.[123] Lukács seems to have admitted as much when, in 1922, he acknowledged that 'It is precisely the problem of organization which has languished longest in the half-light of utopianism'.[124]

The problem of the organization of freedom is the problem of its structuring limits or determinations: a freedom *without* determinations would be a freedom that was 'absolute'. Marx's optimism 'led

116 'Manifesto of the Communist Party', *R1848*, p. 87.
117 'Critique of the Gotha Programme', *FI*, p. 347.
118 'The Eighteenth Brumaire', *SE*, p. 150.
119 *FI*, p. 346.
120 Cf. above, pp. 257–62.
121 Calvez, *La Pensée de Karl Marx*, p. 271, my stress.
122 *Marx's Theory of Alienation*, p. 245.
123 A. Gouldner, *The Dialectic of Ideology and Technology*, p. 76.
124 *History and Class Consciousness*, p. 297.

to a gross oversimplification of process, a very serious underestimation of the difficulties of socialist institution-making'.[125] We are
now, therefore, in a position to acknowledge that although Charles
Taylor's reference to 'Marx's' variant of [Hegel's] notion of "absolute freedom" '[126] is unhelpfully and misleadingly imprecise, he is
putting his finger onto a very real problem: that of the legacy which
Marx's optimism concerning the form of human self-mastery be-
queathed to those who followed him.

This is a problem with which any Christian theologian has good
reason to feel some sympathy, for it is not unlike that which was of
particular concern to the second generation of Christians. 'Jesus',
said Alfred Loisy, 'foretold the kingdom, and it was the Church
that came.'[127] As the expectation of the imminent arrival of the
parousia faded, the problem of the organization of Christian freedom
loomed large.

I do not believe, however, that it is the time-factor which is of
crucial significance for either Christianity or Marxism (There is,
after all, no suggestion that Marx expected the 'imminent' achievement of the second phase of the communist revolution). The heart
of the matter, I suggest, is contained in Lukács' claim that 'Only
when the revolution has entered into quotidian reality will the
question of *revolutionary* organization demand imperiously to be admitted to the consciousness of the masses and their theoreticians'.[128]

'Revolution' speaks of change, of transformation. 'Organization'
speaks of order, structure and stability. If we accept Lukács' definition of 'organization' as 'the form of mediation between theory
and practice',[129] we can say that the problem of 'revolutionary
organization' is that of achieving and sustaining such mediations,
such structuring determinations of freedom, as can give to a revolutionary movement its necessary form without betraying its vision
of that future to which it has not yet attained and without slackening
its energy in the construction of that future. What tends to happen
is that the movement either 'accommodates' its vision to the con-
tours of existing possibility or attempts to anticipate the fulfilment
of the vision by riding roughshod over the limits within which such
possibilities should, in fact, constrain it if it is not to suppress that
very freedom which it exists to enhance.

Christianity has succumbed, frequently enough, to both temptations. It has sometimes so accommodated its vision to existing social
reality as either to render the proclamation of the gospel of freedom

125 E. P. Thompson, 'An Open Letter to Leszek Kolakowski', *The Poverty of Theory*,
     p. 157.
126 *Hegel*, p. 558.
127 A. Loisy, *The Gospel and the Church*, tr. C. Home, p. 166.
128 Lukács, op. cit., p. 297.
129 Ibid., p. 299.

impossible or, as and when that gospel is nevertheless proclaimed, to dismiss the message and to silence the messenger as a dangerous and 'unrealistic' purveyor of subversion (Dostoevsky's 'legend of the Grand Inquisitor' would be a parable of this tendency). On the other hand, it has sometimes, in its concern for the maintained purity of the vision, been theocratically impatient of all complexity, oppressive of all 'free objects standing over against it'.[130] (And such knowledge as I have of the history of Marxism would suggest that this movement has been similarly prone to both temptations.)

One device to which Christian theology often has recourse, and by means of which it unwittingly obscures from view the abyss which yawns between theory and practice, is to employ, as purported descriptions of the Church – the organizational 'medium' between theory and practice – language which should rather function as critical, stipulative definition: as expression of what 'ought' to be, as distinct from what is in *fact*, the case. This is true, for example, of much use, in textbooks of Christian theology, of statements such as 'the Church is one' or 'the Church is holy'. And it is instructive to come across an instance of it in Lukács' statement that 'The Communist Party *is* an autonomous form of proletarian consciousness serving the interests of the revolution'.[131]

The time factor may not be the heart of the matter, where problems of the organization of freedom are concerned, but it is certainly not unimportant. Lukács speaks of the 'renunciation of individual freedom' as a 'step' towards the post-revolutionary 'realm of freedom'.[132] And it does seem appropriate to ask: for *how long* is the freedom of how many to be renounced in the name of a future freedom the realization of which cannot be guaranteed? In the measure that the 'realm of freedom' is envisaged in eschatological terms, in terms which render its complete achievement within the historical process impossible, this question acquires particular urgency.

Optimism, we suggested in the previous section, is the voice of comedy. And 'realism', the 'sensible' recognition that 'reality' is immutable, is often the voice of resignation and despair. To this we must now add that optimism, with its sights set on the far horizon, is only too often destructive of that very freedom whose eventual fulfilment it so confidently announces. Whereas hope only *remains* hope in the measure that it refuses either to resign itself to the insurmountability of existing 'limits' or to trample on those limits in the name of the future. Despair surrenders the future; optimism sacrifices the present. The precariousness of hope arises from its refusal to tolerate either of these destructive 'renunciations'.

130 Cf. Hegel, *Phenomenology*, p. 358.
131 *History and Class Consciousness*, p. 330, my stress. Cf. above, pp. 109–10.
132 Ibid., p. 315.

In order for the organization of freedom to be expressive, not of optimism but of hope, it would – I suggest – be necessary for the 'shape' of freedom, thus organized, to be that of a love which attributed to each individual human being a signifiance that cannot simply be cancelled in the name of 'humanity'. 'Love' is a word which it is almost impossible to use with appropriate precision. And it is a word which is only introduced with considerable difficulty, if at all, into political discussion. Yet I cannot see how Christian reflection on these problems could eschew its use. From a Christian standpoint the question *must* be asked: 'What are the implications – moral, social, ecclesial – of a politics defined and transcended by a kingdom whose laws of mercy and sacrificial redemption are already in some sense absolutely in force?'.[133]

I am suggesting that the theological form of 'the question of *revolutionary* organization' is the question of *redemptive* organization, of the 'form' or 'determination' of redemptive love. And this brings us to our second problem – that of moral transformation – because the concept of redemption refers to the 'transcending' of human egotism by the transformative, liberating grace of God. It refers to the 'abolition' of that illusory 'autonomy' of man, in respect of God and of his fellow men, which is, in fact, dependence as bondage, and to the establishment of that *genuine* human autonomy which grows in proportion to our dependence on a God who is not 'lord' but life-giver, and which finds social expression in our ability to experience our greatest wealth, our fellow human beings, as transformed need.[134]

Christianity, like Marxism, looks forward to the 'total redemption' of humanity. Both Christianity and Marxism refuse to accept the insurmountability of human egotism. But whereas Marx's writings exhibit an 'undue optimism as to the revolutionary transformation of human nature',[135] the Christian theologian is tempted (as Marx well knew) indefinitely to postpone his expectation. And yet, to surrender the struggle for the transformation of patterns of human behaviour and relationship, to cease to grapple with the practical problems – at once moral, social and ecclesial – of the organization of redemptive love, would be to surrender hope. Both egotism and disease are aspects of 'necessity' which resists all attempts at definitive 'supersession'. The healing of man remains a permanent task, but nonetheless a task concerning which those who purport to be its executants cannot expect to be taken seriously if they do not show results. If it could be shown, therefore, that Christianity had not, in fact, effectively contributed to the liberating transformation of human structures and relationships, the legitimacy of Christian

133 W. Stein, 'Mercy and Revolution', p. 225.
134 Cf. above, pp. 181–2.
135 E. P. Thompson, *The Poverty of Theory*, p.157.

hope would already have been deprived of one of its necessary conditions.

Our final question concerns the 'location' of that model of humanity which forms, differently in each case, the substance of both Marxian and Christian hopes for the future freedom of man. Mészáros, insisting that 'there can be no other *measure of humanness* than *man himself*', adds: 'it would be no use to try to answer the question that arises at this point, namely: "which man", by saying: "non-alienated man". Such an answer would amount to reasoning in a circle.'[136] Mészáros, like Marx, locates his model of humanity in the future – not in a future speculatively delineated in 'utopian' fashion, but in that future the outlines of which are supposedly discernible on the basis of a study of the past.

The Christian locates his model of humanity in the past. (This is the first thing that needs to be said even if, as we shall see in a moment, it demands qualification.) Not in some mythical 'golden age', but in a particular individual who lived, worked, spoke, suffered and died. It does not follow that Christianity is characterized by nostalgia, rather than by hope, because that for which this one man worked, and for which he died, was that imperishable reconciliation of man with man, of time with eternity, of all particular existence with the mystery of God, for which he hoped. To be a Christian is to seek to conform the practice and substance of one's hope to the hope of Jesus.

At this point, we must introduce the qualification mentioned just now, because it is clear that no models for the organization of freedom, for mediations between theory and practice which would contribute to the production rather than the destruction of freedom, can be directly deduced from the fact and significance of a single individual. But if, in that individual existence, God's transformative fidelity to his creation is enacted, then – even if we could not have similarly supposed this before the event – it must be the case that *all* events can be hoped to be enactments of that fidelity. Christians have no internal criteria, other than the history of Jesus, in the light of which to contribute – either in practice or in theory – to the common quest and struggle for human existence. But, in seeking to conform the practice and substance of their hope to the hope of Jesus, that quest and struggle are sustained by the expectation that the whole of human history, and each moment and event in that history, are contingent expressions of the action of God. In other words, a Christology which lacks a doctrine of the creative and redemptive Spirit is internally incoherent.

One of the reasons why, for a Marxist, there is a sense in which Marx's life and thought are now of no more than 'archeological'

136 *Marx's Theory of Alienation*, p. 173.

interest is that, as Edward Thompson puts it: 'Marx is on our side: we are not on the side of Marx'.[137] The christological focus of Christian hope, its curious location of the model of humanity, may be indicated by suggesting that, in the case of Jesus, and *only* of Jesus, the Christian hopes both that he is on our side and that we are on his.

'At this moment of historical time, neither despair nor optimism appear to me to be founded upon rationally compelling arguments. It remains for men to act and choose.'[138] I have tried to indicate some reasons for supposing that action and choice might take less inappropriate forms than they often do if we were able – both as individuals and in terms of social policy – to eschew both optimism and despair. I confess that, in the light of our present experience of limited resources, of appalling and deepening world-wide economic misery, of particular revolutions whose dawning is swiftly eclipsed by new forms of oppression, of powerful structures of exploitative egotism self-described as oases of freedom, I see no rational grounds for optimism concerning the future of mankind. But there does exist, with whatever fragility and ambivalence, a form of hope, focused in the death of one man interpreted as resurrection, for which the struggle for humanity is deemed to be worthwhile because not just that one man's death but the entire wilderness of the world's Gethsemane is trusted to be the expression of that mystery whose truth will be all men's freedom.

137 *The Poverty of Theory*, p. 384.
138 Ibid., p. 172.

PART III   POSTFACE

19

IN PLACE OF CONCLUSION

Why not, more simply, 'Conclusion'? Because that might imply that I supposed the contents of Part Two to constitute a single (even if complex) argument. They do not. Not that the order in which topics were treated was arbitrary: it was, for instance, no accident that whereas the concepts of 'revelation' and 'providence' entered the discussion at the beginning of Part Two, questions of hope and eschatology were only considered in the last two chapters. However, if I was to be faithful to my stated intention of 'taking Marx seriously', the structure of the book had to reflect, not what I wished to find in Marx's texts, but what I found there. To construct a linear argument, it would probably have been necessary to present Marx's thought as a unified theoretical system, 'a self-sufficient body of doctrine, complete, internally-consistent'.[1] I do not believe that it has this character, and I share E. P. Thompson's suspicions of such versions of 'Marxism', and of the uses to which they have been put.[2]

Calvez describes his final, critical chapter as 'un bilan critique de la pensée de Marx, soumise d'ailleurs au seul test de sa cohé-rence'.[3] But the only sort of coherence that he seems to have in mind, one by the standards of which Marx is found seriously want-ing, is a systematic, theoretical coherence. There *is*, I believe, a fundamental coherence, an internal consistency, to Marx's thought, but it is not of this order. It would, I think, be better (even if imprecisely) described as a developing unity of method, of concern, of understanding, of expectation – even, perhaps, of 'vision'.

A 'reading' of Marx such as that which I have tried to present is unavoidably eclectic, at least in the sense that it selects and emphasizes only those aspects of Marx's thought which provoke critical reflection on the practice of Christianity and on the forms and contents of its self-understanding. Nevertheless, such eclecti-cism risks allowing the interpreter to 'domesticate' Marx's thought,

---

1 E. P. Thompson, *The Poverty of Theory*, p. 110.
2 Cf. my discussion of Thompson's 'Marxism (1)' in Chapter Three. In what follows, it will be useful to keep Thompson's fourfold classification of meanings of 'Marxism' in mind.
3 J.-Y. Calvez, *La Pensée de Karl Marx*, p. 313.

to appropriate it to his own prior structure of experience and understanding, and thereby to evade the Marxian challenge:[4] a challenge which is inscribed in the 'political' character of almost all his writings. If, however, Marx's thought has the kind of unity which I indicated in the previous paragraph, this challenge may not be thus evaded. To what extent do I, as a particular individual who is, by conviction and profession, a Christian and a theologian, find myself able to endorse his method and to share his concern, his understanding, his expectation and his vision? I have tried to indicate my answers to such questions as I have gone along. But because, in respect of particular themes and topics, the complexity of the problems was such as rarely to permit a straightforward, unqualified 'Yea' or 'Nay', and also as a reminder that it is not merely 'theoretical' agreement or disagreement that is at issue,[5] it may now be helpful to pull these questions together into their simplest form and to ask: do I or do I not see myself as standing somewhere in the Marxist tradition?

And the simple answer is: No. Although (as I shall indicate again in a moment) I find myself, in many respects, far closer to 'Marx's side' than many Christians would regard as proper or many Marxists as possible, it is precisely the *unity* of his thought which prevents me from identifying with any form of Marxism whose self-perception and strategy remains in discernible continuity (or identity through historical change) with his own thought.

Thus, for example, I do not believe that it is possible, without doing violence to the unity of Marx's thought, to *separate* the economic theory and political strategy from the philosophy, and to endorse the former while rejecting the latter.[6] Marx's understanding of the process of history (and hence his 'political economy') is far too tightly interwoven with his anthropology – his conception of the 'nature' or 'essence' of man – for any such separation to be feasible. It follows that an individual or a group which judges the anthropology to be unacceptable because it is insufficiently recognizant of the limits within which the natural and social production of authentically 'human' existence, as an intra-historical project, is unsurpassably bounded, will be unable to endorse without qualification that political strategy to which Marx's understanding of the historical process (and, specifically, the 'necessity' of the revolutionary 'supersession' of capitalism) gives rise.

That compressed statement does no more than pull together a number of points made in more detail in the previous two chapters. However, inasmuch as it appears to constitute an argument against the coherence of the concept of 'Christian Marxism', it demands

4 Cf. above, pp. 30–2.
5 Cf. above, pp. 212–3.
6 Cf. above, pp. 16–7.

further expansion, the outlines of which can be indicated by three questions. Firstly, in view of the fact that the statement makes no mention of the concept of 'materialism', am I suggesting that, if the concept of 'Christian Marxism' is judged to be incoherent, the grounds of this judgement do not include the incompatibility of Christianity with Marxian materialism? Secondly, in view of the fact that I made no mention of Marx's 'atheism', am I suggesting that, if the concept of 'Christian Marxism' is judged to be incoherent, the grounds of this judgement do not include the incompatibility of Christianity with Marxian atheism? Thirdly, in view of my reference to the impossibility of endorsing, 'without qualification', Marx's political strategy, am I suggesting that, if the concept of 'Christian Marxism' is judged to be incoherent, the grounds of this judgement do include the incompatibility of Christianity with whole-hearted commitment to revolutionary struggle?

The first of these questions is the easiest to answer. I have argued that although Marx's 'naturalistic' assumption, that the very *question* of God can only arise as an expression of human alienation, is incompatible with Christian belief,[7] nevertheless the character of Christianity is, in principle, and should be, in fact, 'materialist' in Marx's sense. I presented this argument formally in Chapter Twelve, but it is implied by my recurring insistence both that the 'premise' of Christianity is not an 'idea', but an event, a life lived, a deed done, a death undergone, and that the practice of Christianity – the 'following of Christ' in action, prayer and suffering – is prior to attempts critically and theoretically to 'reflect' that practice in Christian theology.

Christianity is more adequately defined as a tradition of action and interpretation than as a system of ideas or beliefs. But the same may be said, and has often been said by Marxists, of Marxism. In so far as either Marxism or Christianity is thus defined, the goal of the movement, and the criteria of speech and action appropriate to the pursuit of that goal, can be described in terms of 'truthfulness': of the identity of 'appearance' and 'reality'. But the quest for 'truthfulness' *includes*, and is not a substitute for or alternative to, the quest for 'truth' more formally or 'theoretically' conceived: 'correctness' *does* matter.[8] The 'materialist' insistence upon the primacy of the practical affords no licence to that intellectual sloth which disdains concern for theoretical rigour and adequacy.

To insist that Christianity is, or should be, in the sense just indicated, 'materialist' in character, is not to deny that Marx was correct in supposing that Christianity has often been, both in practice and in self-description, thoroughly 'idealist'. It does not, how-

7 Cf. above, p. 136.
8 Cf. above, pp. 77–87.

ever, follow from this (as Marx supposed that it did) that Christianity is 'necessarily' or 'essentially' idealist, but only that those Christians who reject its idealist forms are committed to struggle for its transformation. But this internal struggle, I have suggested, is – in one form or another – as old as Christianity. The histories of both Marxism and Christianity suggest that a movement or tradition which seeks to secure its identity either by declaring its truth to be already possessed, or by the sheer exercise of power, will be corrupted, in practice, by the very 'idealism' it supposes itself to reject in principle.[9]

The short answer to my first question, therefore, is: if the concept of 'Christian Marxism' is judged to be incoherent, the grounds of this judgement do not (with the exception noted concerning Marx's 'naturalism') include the incompatibility of Christianity with Marxian materialism. (And the title of this book is intended, in part, to echo this conviction.)

My second question, being somewhat more difficult to answer, is best approached indirectly. There are many good reasons – practical and theoretical, political and historical, ethical and metaphysical – for being an atheist in today's world. But the assumption that Marx's criticisms of religious belief and practice, and the philosophical 'naturalism' on which they in part depend, may be taken to have disposed of the question of God, is not among such good reasons. Or, at least, the historical superficiality and theoretical insouciance of his treatment of the matter render this assumption distinctly fragile.

However, the inadequacy of the grounds on which Marx refused seriously to entertain the question of God cannot be sufficiently indicated by making an historical and philosophical case for the claim that the God whose reality and fidelity are confessed in Christian faith and hope is the antithesis of that 'alien' and alienating 'power' of which Marx supposed all concepts and models of God to be but variant expressions.

It may, indeed, be exceedingly important for Christians both to insist that it is possible to conceive of God as other than a power alien to the freedom and flourishing of man, and also to acknowledge that all attempted 'objectifications' of the mystery of God, in concept, metaphor, and social structure, are liable to contribute to our alienation in the measure that they are taken to be direct and adequate descriptions or exemplifications of that mystery. Nevertheless, the question of God is more fundamentally a practical than a theoretical matter. That is to say: unless the question is appropriately kept open by the quality of Christian practice, theoretical

9 Cf. above, pp. 105–11, 149–51.

reflection upon its character and content is 'a purely *scholastic*'[10] affair.

The character of the question of God is (I would say) only appropriately exhibited by strenuous engagement – in action, prayer and suffering – in the work of transforming the circumstances of human existence. To put it in more traditional theological terms: the character of the Christian form of the question of God is displayed in the work of Christ and in Christian participation in that redemptive work. And the content of the question of God is only appropriately exhibited when it is seen to be, not peripheral or alien to, but the heart and centre of, the question of man. Religion, we agreed with Marx, 'has no content of its own'.[11] But it does not follow that it has no content. The 'content' of religion is, or should be, the 'content' of politics, ethics and art; of law, economics, and physics. It is the 'content' of whatever it is that constitutes the 'project' of human existence in the world of nature. But the 'content' of this project (or of any particular aspect of this project) is only apprehended as identical with the 'content' of religion in so far as questions of human and natural existence are apprehended as aspects of the question of God. For such questions to be thus apprehended, it is not necessary that they be given categorical, 'objective' expression in explicitly religious or theistic terms. In other words, the question of man may, concretely, take the form of the question of God without 'God' being *named* in the formulation of the question.

It does not follow that it is of little or no consequence whether or not the question of man is expressed – somewhere, by somebody – in explicitly religious and theistic terms. It may be that the survival of such expressions (for all their ambivalence – their bias towards 'idealism' and idolatry) is indispensable if the project of human existence in the world of nature is to be appropriately – that is to say, 'humanly' – executed.

By 'appropriately', in this context, I intend to refer to our discussion of the distinction between 'hope' and 'optimism' in Chapter Eighteen. There I suggested that, whereas it is characteristic of both optimism and despair to suppose that they 'know the answer' to the question of man, it is characteristic of hope never to relinquish the interrogative mood. And that mood is never sustained with more difficulty than in circumstances in which the 'limits' of human existence are so tightly drawn as to render interrogation almost unendurable. In such circumstances, the conviction that the answer is known provides an apparent way through otherwise insurmountable limits. If there is a way through, there is only *this* way through:

10 Cf. *EW*, p. 422.
11 Cf. above, pp. 167–8.

those who possess the answer to the question of man are exceedingly single-minded. Hope, as I have tried to characterize it, neither succumbs in the face of resistant facticity nor seeks simply to sweep aside the obstacles in its path, whereas optimism, when married to power, only too often displays that impatience with particularity which Hegel described.[12]

To sum up: it is the manner in which the question of God is *correlated* with the question of man which renders Marx's thought incompatible with Christian belief as I understand it. Marx regards these questions as necessarily antithetical, whereas I would see the first as implied by the second. If the concept of 'Christian Marxism' is judged to be incoherent, therefore, the grounds of this judgement (so far as my second question is concerned) lie *directly* in what seem to me to be irreconcilable differences between Marxian and Christian anthropology and only *in*directly in the incompatiblity of Christianity with Marxian atheism.

My third question concerned the incompatibility of Christianity with whole-hearted commitment to revolutionary struggle. I have suggested that, although Christian faith and hope cannot directly furnish blueprints for a future social order,[13] and although there are no timelessly appropriate abstract answers to questions concerning the social and political implications of Christian hope,[14] nevertheless, not only is that hope inherently political – inasmuch as its object is the transformation of man – but, in so far as it remains recognizant of God's radical transcendence, it embodies an implicit or explicit critique of all absolutizations of historically particular forms of social organization, and hence of all structures of alienation and domination.[15]

It follows that, in circumstances in which the transformation of competing egotism into fraternity, of lordship and bondage into the organization of freedom, was, in some measure, a real possibility, those working to effect such transformation would be entitled to expect the Christian movement to be 'on their side' in the common struggle (and the fact that this expectation will often be disappointed does not render it less legitimate). It also follows, therefore, that this expectation is in order in circumstances in which the transformation, if it is to be effected, has to be 'revolutionary', rather than 'gradual' or 'evolutionary' in character.

There is no doubt, in other words, but that Christianity is, in principle, compatible with commitment to revolutionary struggle. For a number of reasons, however, Christian participation in that struggle will, or should be, ambiguous. In the first place, the Christ-

12 Cf. above, pp. 264–5.
13 Cf. above, pp. 252–3.
14 Cf. above, p. 238.
15 Cf. above, p. 183.

ian community will, or should, always include elements which insist on 'standing aside' from the struggle to bear witness both to the partial and provisional nature of all historically realizable transformations of social reality,[16] and to the antithetical relationship between divine power and human force.[17] In the second place, in the course of the revolution, Christian participation should include the reminder that 'social messianism' is a dangerous illusion: that no political movement is lacking in 'particular interest',[18] that the use of force is always morally ambigous and infected with impurity (killing is not, and can never be, an act of love), and that not all means are appropriate in pursuit of even the most admirable of ends.[19] In other words, Christian participation in revolutionary struggle is, or should be, 'complicated' by the fact that the language of Christian hope, and hence the practice which the use of that language expresses, is a language the grammar of which admits no exceptions to the imperatives of mercy, gentleness and compassion.[20]

It is, however, 'after' the revolution, when the locus of power has shifted, that the peculiarity of the Christian contribution to political process should become most evident. Because every revolution that has occurred, or that *can* ever occur, within the historical process, represents the victory of particular interest, therefore there will always be those, after the revolution, whose needs and interests do not coincide with the interests of the group newly in power. To say this is not cynically to suggest that no revolution is, in fact, any more than a glorified *coup d'état*. It is merely to insist that no revolution can be such as to ensure that new forms of oppression and alienation do not emerge in its aftermath. That same eschatological hope, that same trust in the transformative fidelity of a transcendent God, which led the Christian community to participate in the revolutionary process, now, on the same grounds, obliges it, or should oblige it, to 'change sides'. The only 'permanent allies' of Christianity are, or should be, the weak and dispossessed: and their identity changes.

The expectation that the Church will thus 'change sides' may be unrealistic, even 'utopian' in character. But, before dismissing the possiblity out of hand, it is worth bearing in mind that there does exist, as a 'fact in the world's history', a diverse movement many of the constituent elements of which have shown themselves, in recent years, newly sensitive to the need not to repeat the 'Constantinian error' of allowing the recognition of the political impli-

16 Cf. above, pp. 238–9.
17 Cf. above, p. 182.
18 Cf. above, p. 258.
19 Cf. above, p. 262.
20 Cf. above, pp. 262, 278.

cations of Christian hope to lead Christian communities to identify their interests with those of political power.

To suggest that, if the concept of 'Christian Marxism' is judged to be incoherent, the grounds of this judgement include the incompatibility of Christianity with whole-hearted commitment to revolutionary struggle, would be misleading because the concept of 'whole-heartedness' is unhelpfully imprecise. In answer to my third question, therefore, I have issued reminders concerning why and in what sense it is the case that Christianity, as a social formation, may never identify itself, without remainder, with any particular social or political movement,[21] even with (perhaps especially with) a movement which, like itself, purports to represent only the universal interest of humanity.

It will not have escaped the reader's attention that I have been hedging my bets on the matter of the coherence of the concept of 'Christian Marxism'. There is a simple explanation for this. As I remarked in the Introduction, this is a study not of Marxisms but of Marx. Therefore, my questions concerned the compatibility of Christianity with Marx's thought, and with those patterns of action expressed in and implied by that thought. However, the 'meanings of Marxism' are by no means reducible to the content of Marx's thought. Marxism, as a 'fact in the world's history', is a movement, or tradition, subject to conditional change and of increasing internal diversity. Nor is there anything in the 'logic' of Marxism which would oblige the movement to cease describing itself as 'Marxist' if the modifications introduced into either its practice or its theory rendered it barely recognizable as an 'interpretation', in changed circumstances, of Marx's thought. Although any Marxist would presumably wish to endorse the broad outlines of Marx's method, and of the content of his thought, agreement with Marx is not a necessary condition of Marxist integrity.[22] This I take to be implied, for example, by Thompson's remark that 'Marx is on our side; we are not on the side of Marx'.[23] (Whereas, if we describe Christianity as a movement which seeks, in both its practice and its theory, faithfully to 'interpret', in changing circumstances, the fact and significance of Jesus, there *is* a sense in which 'agreement' with him – conformity to his hope, and to the patterns of action in which that hope was expressed – is a necessary condition of Christian integrity. The complexity of hermeneutical problems should not be allowed to obscure the simple fact that Christianity seeks its criterion of authenticity in Jesus, whereas Marxism does not seek its criterion of authenticity in Marx.)

21 Cf. above, pp. 238–9.
22 Some forms of 'Marxism (1)' would appear to constitute an exception to this: cf. above, pp. 26–9.
23 *The Poverty of Theory*, p. 384.

It follows that it may not be asumed, *a priori*, that forms of Marxism could not emerge which were no longer incompatible with Christianity on any of the grounds that I have indicated. And the fact that there are many people today who call themselves 'Christian Marxists' is an indication that this may perhaps already be the case. If, notwithstanding this fact, I persist in affirming that I do not see myself as standing in the Marxist tradition, this affirmation reflects, in part, my insufficient familiarity with the literature on 'Christian Marxism', and with the contexts of experience which have given rise to this literature, and, in part, my impression that those forms of 'Christian Marxism' with which I *am* familiar have not successfully overcome the obstacles that I have indicated. In a word: while I am unable to describe myself as a 'Christian Marxist', I regard the question of the coherence of the concept as an open one, although I must admit that I doubt whether a form of Marxism sufficiently modified to render the concept coherent would be recognizable, *as* a form of Marxism, by other forms of the Marxist tradition.

That point can, of course, be made the other way round: I doubt whether a form of Christianity suffcently modified to render the concept coherent would be recognizable, *as* a form of Christianity, by other forms of the Christian tradition. This way of putting it reminds us that it is incumbent upon Christians to take very seriously the question of the meanings that may be attached, without evasion or 'mystification', to the notion of a common Christian tradition.[24] This is a question which, for all its practical urgency and theoretical interest, cannot be considered here and now: its adequate exploration would demand another and very different book. Concerning it, therefore, I shall simply make three commonplace observations. Firstly, it is increasingly evident that there are, and have long been, within Christianity, fundamental differences in *ways of believing*, of perceiving the connections between human experience and Christian belief, and that these differences cut deeper than, and cut across, historically inherited denominational divisions. Secondly, that the most serious and intractable divisions within Christianity are increasingly perceived to be social, cultural, and even political in character. Thirdly, that in circumstances in which disagreement and conflict have hardened to the point at which Christians find it necessary to acknowledge that the notion of a 'common tradition' has become, in practice, meaningless, simply to *accept* this fact would be to have surrendered hope.

The phenomenon of 'Christian-Marxist dialogue' is, in part, a reflection of newly emerging patterns of consciousness (and hence, implicitly, of unity and division). The difficulty that I have with

24 Cf. above, p. 34.

this concept, however, is that it too easily suggests that, if the relationship between Marxism and Christianity (or between certain forms of Marxism and certain forms of Christianity) is to be other than one of mutual ignorance, misrepresentation and hostility, the appropriate catalyst for such a transformation would be an academic seminar. And this would surely be a very 'idealist' suggestion. In so far as Christians and Marxists are in fact engaged in the work of the liberation of mankind, engaged in the work of our redemption, it will be in the shared prosecution of particular tasks that both the scope and the limits of common understanding and common hope will emerge. This is not to suggest that the grounds on which such co-operation occurs either are or should be merely pragmatic or opportunistic: it is, after all, (differently) axiomatic for both Marxism and Christianity that it is truth which sets us free.

I said, in the Introduction, that this is not, in any straightforward sense, a work of Christian theology. According to Bernard Lonergan, however, 'a theology mediates between a cultural matrix and the significance and role of a religion in that matrix'.[25] In so far as this book contributes to the achievement of such mediation, it may perhaps be said to have fulfilled a theological function.

25 B. J. F. Lonergan, *Method in Theology*, p. xi.

LIST OF WORKS CITED

(Except where otherwise indicated, place of publication is London)

Karl Marx
Marx, Karl. *Capital. I.* Introd. E. Mandel. Penguin, 1976.
  Capital. II. Introd. E. Mandel. Penguin, 1978.
  Capital. III. Lawrence and Wishart, 1959.
  Early Writings. Introd. L. Colletti. Penguin, 1975.
  Grundrisse. Introd. M. Nicolaus. Penguin, 1973.
  Karl Marx. Early Texts. Ed. D. McLellan. Oxford, Basil Blackwell, 1979.
  Political Writings. I. The Revolutions of 1848. Introd. D. Fernbach. Penguin, 1973.
  Political Writings. II. Surveys From Exile. Introd. D. Fernbach. Penguin, 1973.
  Political Writings. III. The First International and After. Introd. D. Fernbach. Penguin, 1974.
  The Poverty of Philosophy. Peking Foreign Languages Press, 1978.
  Theories of Surplus Value. Part III. Tr. J. Cohen and S. W. Ryazanskaya. Moscow, Progress Publishers, 1971.
Marx, Karl, Frederick Engels. *Collected Works. IV.* Lawrence and Wishart, 1975. (Principal contents: *The Holy Family; The Condition of the Working-Class in England.*)
  Collected Works. V. Lawrence and Wishart, 1976 (*Theses on Feuerbach; The German Ideology*).
  The German Ideology. Part One. Ed. C. J. Arthur. Lawrence and Wishart, 1974.
Marx, Karl, Frederick Engels, V. I. Lenin. *On Historical Materialism.* Moscow, Progress Publishers, 1972 (Extracts from their writings).

Others
Abbot, W. M., ed., *The Documents of Vatican II.* Geoffrey Chapman, 1966.
Althusser, Louis, *Essays in Self-Criticism.* New Left, 1976.
—, *For Marx.* New Left, 1977.
—, *Lenin and Philosophy and Other Essays.* New Left, 1971.
—, E. Balibar, *Reading Capital.* New Left, 1970.
Anderson, Perry. *Arguments Within English Marxism.* New Left, 1980.
Aristotle. *The Ethics of Aristotle,* ed. J. A. K. Thompson. Penguin, 1955.
Bachelard, Gaston, *La Formation de l'Esprit Scientifique: Contribution à une Psychanalyse de la Connaissance Objective.* Paris, J. Vrin, 1947.

Bakunin, Michael, *God and the State*. Introd. P. Avrich. New York, Dover, 1970.

Barker, Francis, 'The Morality of Knowledge and the Disappearance of God', *New Blackfriars*, lvii (1976), 403–14.

—, 'Science and Ideology', *New Blackfriars*, lviii (1978), 473–82.

Bernstein, Richard J., *Praxis and Action*. Philadelphia, University of Pennsylvania Press, 1971.

Bloch, Ernst, *A Philosophy of the Future*. New York, Seabury, 1970 (First German edn 1963).

—, *On Karl Marx*. New York, Seabury, 1971 (Extracts from *Das Prinzip Hoffnung* 1959).

Calvez, J.-Y., *La Pensée de Karl Marx*. Rev. edn Paris, Seuil, 1970.

Carver, Terrell, *Karl Marx. Texts on Method*. Oxford, Basil Blackwell, 1975.

Chambre, H., *De Karl Marx à Lenine et Mao Tsé-Toung*. Paris, Aubier, 1976.

Chrétiens Devant Marx et Les Marxismes. Les Quatre Fleuves. Cahier 8. Paris, Seuil, 1978.

Clarkson, K. L., D. J. Hawkin, 'Marx on Religion: The Influence of Bruno Bauer and Ludwig Feuerbach on His Thought and its Implications for the Christian-Marxist Dialogue', *Scottish Journal of Theology*, xxxi (1978), 533–55.

Colletti, Lucio, *Marxism and Hegel*. New Left, 1973.

Cooper, Rebecca, *The Logical Influence of Hegel on Marx*. Seattle, University of Washington, 1925.

Copleston, Frederick, *Philosophers and Philosophies*. Search Press, 1976.

Coste, René, *Analyse Marxiste et Foi Chrétienne*. Paris, Ouvrières, 1976.

Cottier, Georges M.-M., *L'Athéisme du Jeune Marx. Ses Origines Hégeliennes*. Paris, Vrin, 1969.

Davis, Charles, *Theology and Political Society*. C.U.P., 1980.

Durkheim, Emile, *The Elementary Forms of the Religious Life*. Allen and Unwin, 1915.

Eagleton, Terence, B. Wicker, ed., *From Culture to Revolution*. Sheed and Ward, 1968.

Engels, Frederick, *Anti-Dühring*. Peking, Foreign Languages Press, 1976.

—, V. I. Lenin, K. Marx, *On Historical Materialism*. Moscow, Progress Publishers, 1972.

Evans, Donald, *Communist Faith and Christian Faith*. S.C.M. Press, 1965.

Feuerbach, Ludwig, *The Essence of Christianity*, tr. George Eliot, introd. Karl Barth. New York, Harper and Row, 1957.

Fierro, Alfredo, *The Militant Gospel*. S.C.M. Press, 1977.

Flew, Antony, *An Introduction to Western Philosophy. Ideas and Argument From Plato to Sartre*. Thames and Hudson, 1971.

Foster, M. B., 'Historical Materialism', *Christian Faith and Communist Faith*, 85–97, ed. D. M. MacKinnon. Macmillan, 1953.

Frankfurt Institute for Social Research, *Aspects of Sociology*. Pref. M. Horkheimer and T. W. Adorno. Heinemann, 1973.

Garaudy, Roger, *From Anathema to Dialogue*. Collins, 1967.

—, *Marxism in the Twentieth Century*. Collins, 1970.

Giddens, Anthony, *Capitalism and Modern Social Theory*. C.U.P., 1971.

—, *Central Problems in Social Theory*. Macmillan, 1979.

Girardi, Giulio, *Marxism and Christianity*. Dublin, Gill and Son, 1968.

Goldmann, Lucien, *The Hidden God*. Routledge and Kegan Paul, 1964.

Gollwitzer, Helmut, *The Christian Faith and the Marxist Criticism of Religion*. Edinburgh, St Andrew Press, 1970.

Gouldner, Alvin W., *The Dialectic of Ideology and Technology*. Macmillan, 1976.

Gutierrez, Gustavo, *A Theology of Liberation*. S.C.M. Press, 1974.

Hebblethwaite, Brian, S. Sutherland, ed., *The Philosophical Frontiers of Christian Theology. Essays Presented to D. M. MacKinnon*. C.U.P., 1981.

Hebblethwaite, Peter, *The Christian-Marxist Dialogue and Beyond*. Darton, Longman and Todd, 1977.

Hegel, G. W. F., *Lectures on the Philosophy of World-History. Introduction: Reason in History*, tr. H. R. Nisbet. C.U.P., 1975.

—, *Phenomenology of Spirit*, tr. A. V. Miller. Foreword and analysis of text J. N. Findlay. O.U.P., 1977.

—, *Philosophy of Right*, tr. T. M. Knox. O.U.P., 1942.

—, *Science of Logic*, tr. A. V. Miller. Allen and Unwin, 1969.

Held, David, *Introduction to Critical Theory: Horkheimer to Habermas*. Hutchinson, 1980.

Horkheimer, Max., *Critical Theory*. New York, Seabury, 1972.

—, *The Eclipse of Reason*. O.U.P., 1947.

Hyppolite, Jean, *Etudes sur Marx et Hegel*. Paris, Marcel Rivière, 1955.

Jameson, Frederic, *Marxism and Form*. Princeton University Press, 1971.

Jay, Martin, *The Dialectical Imagination*. Heinemann, 1973.

Kautsky, Karl, *Foundations of Christianity*, tr. H. F. Mins. New York, Russell, 1953.

Kolakowski, Leszek, *Main Currents of Marxism. I. The Founders; II, The Golden Age; III. The Breakdown*. 3 vols. O.U.P., 1978.

—, *Marxism and Beyond*. Paladin, 1971.

Korsch, Karl, *Marxism and Philosophy*. New Left, 1970.

—, *Three Essays on Marxism*. Pluto, 1971.

Lash, N. L. A., *Change in Focus*. Sheed and Ward, 1973.

—, 'Ideology, Metaphor and Analogy', *The Philosophical Frontiers of Christian Theology*, ed. B. Hebblethwaite, S. Sutherland. C.U.P., 1981.

—, 'Introduction' to *An Essay in Aid of a Grammar of Assent*, by J. H. Newman. University of Notre Dame Press, 1979.

—, 'Second Thoughts on Walgrave's "Newman" ', *Downside Review*, lxxxvii (1969), 339–50.

—, *Theology on Dover Beach*. Darton, Longman and Todd, 1979.

—, 'Theory, Theology and Ideology', *The Sciences and Theology in the Twentieth Century*, ed. A. R. Peacocke (Oriel Press, 1981), 209–28.

—, *Voices of Authority*. Sheed and Ward, 1976.

Lecompte, Denis, 'Marx Selon Althusser: La "Coupure Epistémologique" ', *Chrétiens Devant Marx et Les Marxismes, Les Quatre Fleuves*. Cahier 8, 90–5. Paris, Seuil, 1978.

Lee, Francis Nigel, *Communist Eschatology: A Christian Philosophical Analysis of the Post-Capitalist Views of Marx, Engels and Lenin*. Nutley, New Jersey, Craig Press, 1974.

Lenin, V. I. *Materialism and Empirio-Criticism*. Peking Foreign Languages Press, 1976.

—, F. Engels, K. Marx, *On Historical Materialism*. Moscow, Progress Publishers, 1972.

Lewis, John, Karl Polanyi, Donald K. Kitchin, ed., *Christianity and the Social Revolution*. Gollancz, 1935.

Lobkowicz, Nicholas, 'Karl Marx's Attitude Toward Religion', *The Review of Politics*, xxvi (1974), 319–52.

—, *Theory and Practice: History of a Concept from Aristotle to Marx*. University of Notre Dame Press, 1967.

Lochman, Jan Milič, *Encountering Marx*. Philadelphia, Fortress, 1977.

Loisy, Alfred, *The Gospel and the Church*, tr. C. Home. Isaac Pitman, 1903.

Lonergan, B. J. F., *Method in Theology*. Darton, Longman and Todd, 1972.

Luijpen, William A., *Phenomenology and Atheism*. Pittsburgh, Duquesne University Press, 1964.

Lukács, Georg, *History and Class Consciousness*. Merlin, 1971.

—, *Political Writings, 1919-1929*. New Left, 1972.

Lukes, Steven, *Emile Durkheim. His Life and Work: A Historical and Critical Study*. Penguin, 1975.

McCarthy, Thomas, *The Critical Theory of Jürgen Habermas*. Hutchinson, 1978.

McGovern, A. F., *Marxism: an American Christian Perspective*. New York, Orbis, 1980.

MacKinnon, D. M., ed., *Christian Faith and Communist Faith*. Macmillan, 1953.

—, *Explorations in Theology. 5*. S.C.M. Press, 1979.

McKown, Delos B., *The Classical Marxist Critiques of Religion: Marx, Engels, Lenin, Kautsky*. The Hague, Martinus Nijhoff, 1975.

McLellan, David, ed., *Karl Marx. Early Texts*. Oxford, Basil Blackwell, 1979.

—, *Karl Marx: His Life and Thought*. Macmillan, 1973.

—, *Marx*. Collins, Fontana, 1975.

—, *Marx Before Marxism*. Penguin, 1972.

—, *Marxism After Marx*. Macmillan, 1979.

Machoveĉ, Milan, *A Marxist Looks At Jesus*. Darton, Longman and Todd, 1976.

Mannheim, Karl, *Ideology and Utopia*. Routledge and Kegan Paul, 1936.

Markús, George, *Marxism and Anthropology: The Concept of 'Human Essence' in the Philosophy of Marx*. Assen, Van Gorcum, 1978.

Mészáros, István, *Marx's Theory of Alienation*. [4]Merlin, 1975.

Miller, Alexander, *The Christian Significance of Marx*. S.C.M. Press, 1946.

Miranda, José P., *Marx Against the Marxists: The Christian Humanism of Karl Marx*. S.C.M. Press, 1980.

—, *Marx and the Bible: A Critique of the Philosophy of Oppression*. S.C.M. Press, 1977.

Newman, John Henry, *Apologia Pro Vita Sua*, ed. M. J. Svaglic. O.U.P., 1967.

—, *An Essay in Aid of a Grammar of Assent*. University of Notre Dame Press, 1979.

—, *An Essay on the Development of Christian Doctrine*. [3]Pickering, 1878.

—, *Newman's University Sermons*. Introd. D. M. MacKinnon, J. D. Holmes. S.P.C.K., 1970.

Ollmann, Bertell, *Alienation: Marx's Conception of Man in Capitalist Society.* ²C.U.P., 1976.

Pannenberg, Wolfhart, *Theology and the Philosophy of Science.* Darton, Longman and Todd, 1976.

Peacocke, A. R., ed., *The Sciences and Theology in the Twentieth Century.* Oriel Press, 1981.

Plamenatz, John, *Ideology.* Pall Mall, 1970.

—, *Karl Marx's Philosophy of Man.* O.U.P., 1975.

Plekhanov, G. V., *Fundamental Problems of Marxism.* Lawrence and Wishart, 1969.

Popper, Karl, *The Open Society and Its Enemies. II. The High Tide of Prophecy: Hegel, Marx and the Aftermath.* ⁵Routledge and Kegan Paul, 1966.

Rahner, Karl, 'Thoughts on the Possibility of Belief Today', *Theological Investigations,* v, 3–22, tr. K.-H. Kruger. Darton, Longman and Todd, 1966.

Raines, J. C., Thomas Dean, ed., *Marxism and Radical Religion: Essays Toward a Revolutionary Humanism.* Philadelphia, Temple University Press, 1970.

Reding, Marcel, *Thomas von Aquin und Karl Marx.* Graz, Akademische Durk und Verlagsanstalt, 1953.

Romeyer, B., 'L'Athéisme Marxiste' *Archives de Philosophie,* xv (1939), 293–353.

Rosdolsky, Roman, *The Making of Marx's 'Capital'.* Pluto, 1980.

Rosen, Zvi, *Bruno Bauer and Karl Marx.* The Hague, Martinus Nijhoff, 1977.

Rotenstreich, Nathan, *Basic Problems of Marx's Philosophy.* Indianapolis, Bobbs-Merrill, 1965.

Sartre, Jean-Paul, *Search for a Method.* New York, Vintage Books, 1968. (First published 1960 as a prefatory essay to *Critique de la Raison Dialectique*).

Scheler, Max, *Problems of a Sociology of Knowledge.* Routledge and Kegan Paul, 1980.

Schmidt, Alfred, *The Concept of Nature in Marx.* New Left, 1971.

Segundo, Juan Luis, *The Liberation of Theology.* Dublin, Gill and Macmillan, 1976.

Seliger, Martin, *The Marxist Conception of Ideology.* C.U.P., 1977.

Stein, Walter, *Criticism as Dialogue.* C.U.P., 1969.

—, 'Mercy and Revolution', *From Culture to Revolution,* ed. T. Eagleton and B. Wicker. Sheed and Ward, 1968.

Steiner, George, *The Death of Tragedy.* ²Faber and Faber, 1963.

Sweezy, Paul, *The Theory of Capitalist Development.* New York, O.U.P., 1942.

Taylor, Charles, *Hegel.* C.U.P., 1975.

Thompson, E. P., *The Poverty of Theory and Other Essays.* Merlin, 1978.

Tucker, R. C., *Philosophy and Myth in Karl Marx.* ²C.U.P., 1972.

West, Charles C., *Communism and the Theologians: Study of an Encounter.* S.C.M. Press, 1958.

Wetter, Gustav A., *Dialectical Materialism: A Historical and Systematic Survey of Philosophy in the Soviet Union.* Routledge and Kegan Paul, 1958.

Wicker, Brian, 'Marxist Science and Christian Theology', *New Blackfriars,* lviii (1977), 85–100.

—, T. Eagleton, ed., *From Culture to Revolution.* Sheed and Ward, 1968.

Williams, Raymond, 'Base and Superstructure in Marxist Cultural Theory', *New Left Review,* lxxxii (1973), 3–16.

—, *Marxism and Literature*. O.U.P., 1977.
—, *Modern Tragedy*. Chatto and Windus, 1966.

INDEX OF MARX REFERENCES

'Alleged Splits in the
  International', *FI* 176n, 235
'British Constitution, The', *SE* 53
Capital 11–13, 15–16, 18–20, 40,
  169, 228, 241; Preface to First
  edition 101–2, 216; Postface to
  Second edition 95–6, 98, 221,
  225–6; I 54, 59–60, 78, 91–2,
  100n, 127–8, 157–8, 171, 174–9,
  181, 195–6, 240, 263–4; II 263;
  III 266–7
'Civil War in France, The', *FI* 53,
  190n, 240, 251, 273
'Class Struggles in France: 1848 to
  1850, The', *SE* 52–3, 128, 259
Communist Manifesto, The, see
  'Manifesto of the Communist
  Party'
'Concerning Feuerbach', ('Theses
  on Feuerbach'), *EW* 11, 60,
  64–5; First Thesis 99, 100n, 102,
  146n; Second 73, 79–80; Third
  95, 146, 148; Fifth 146n;
  Eleventh 36
'Conspectus of Bakunin's *Statism
  and Anarchy*', *FI* 211–2, 229–30
'Contribution to the Critique of
  Hegel's Philosophy of Right:
  Introduction', *EW* 92, 153–4,
  156–8, 160–1, 168, 180, 190,
  243–4, 246, 253, 257
*'Contribution to the Critique of Political
  Economy, A:* Preface', *EW* 12,
  115–6, 120, 122–3, 125, 127, 134,
  225, 251, 274
'Critical Notes on the Article "The
  King of Prussia and Social
  Reform. By a Prussian" ', *EW*
  52, 164, 242

'Critique of the Gotha
  Programme', *FI* 15, 43, 54, 165,
  251, 258–9, 275
'Critique of Hegel's Doctrine of the
  State', *EW* 56–8, 176n, 178,
  263–4, 274
'Economic and Philosophical
  Manuscripts (1844)', (the 'Paris
  Manuscripts'), *EW*
  10–11, 13, 19, 36, 40, 56, 75–84,
  89, 98–9, 100–2, 120, 143, 149,
  169–72, 175–8, 180, 182, 191–3,
  198–201, 204–6, 210–11, 220,
  242–3, 250–1, 264, 267, 274
'Eighteenth Brumaire of Louis
  Bonaparte, The', *SE* 51, 66, 73,
  114, 116, 136, 268n, 275
'Excerpts from James Mill's
  Elements of Political Economy', *EW*
  177, 240–1
'First Draft of "The Civil War in
  France" ', *FI* 53, 128, 190n
  235–6
German Ideology, The 9–13, 19–20,
  36–47, 64–5, 70, 77, 94–5, 100n,
  106, 112, 114n, 126–8, 130–2,
  165–7, 173, 189, 192, 207, 209,
  211, 217–8, 220, 227, 253;
  Preface 37–8, 118, 126–7
Grundrisse 10, 13, 15, 18–20, 37, 44,
  53–4, 90, 92, 95, 177, 201–4,
  240, 247, 263; Introduction
  (1857) 13, 20–2, 203–4, 206–8,
  210, 214, 216–8, 227–8; 'The
  General Relation of Production
  to Distribution, Exchange and
  Consumption' 218–26; 'The
  Method of Political Economy'
  20, 220–1

'Holy Family, The', *CW4* 53, 73, 96–7, 99, 137n, 176, 245–6, 259–60

'Inaugural Address of the International Working Men's Association', *FI* 190, 241

'Manifesto of the Communist Party', *R1848* 9, 11, 52, 109, 113–4, 164, 190, 228–9, 232, 237, 240–1, 257–8, 263–4, 275

'On the Jewish Question', *EW* 59, 90–1, 171, 176, 263

Paris Manuscripts, see 'Economic and Philosophical Manuscripts'

'Political Indifferentism', *FI* 176n, 235

Poverty of Philosophy, The 20, 21n, 59, 103–4, 164, 171, 199, 234, 247, 257

'Speech on the Hague Congress', *FI* 242

Theories of Surplus Value 140

Theses on Feuerbach, see 'Concerning Feuerbach'

INDEX OF NAMES

The more important discussions are indicated in bold type

Adorno, T. W., 4
Althusser, L., 11, **14–23**, 34, 55, **60–3**, 64, 71, 78, 96, 102, 105f, 117n, 122, 130f, 163, 197, 217n, 220, 222
Anderson, P., 26n, 196n
Annenkov, P., 78
Aquinas, T., 18, 28
Aristotle, 18, 28n, 208, 221n, 223, 226
Arthur, C. J., 10f, 40, 173, 217n
Avenarius, R., 135

Bachelard, G., 15
Bacon, F., 99
Bakunin, M., 167n, 211, 229f
Balibar, E., 16n
Barker, F., 272n
Bauer, B., 53, 73, 97, 154, 162, 176
Benton, G., 186
Bernstein, R., 207n
Bloch, E., 4, 84, 95, 98, 235
Bloch, J., 121f, 235, 239

Cabet, E., 234
Calvez, J.-Y., 5, 36n, 54, 56, 96, 169, 179, 248, 259f, 267, 275, 283
Carver, T., 214–30
Chambre, H., 5n
Cieszkowski, A. von 253
Clarkson, K. L., 154n
Colletti, L., 13f, 27, 79f, 103, **105–7**, 109, **139–40**, 142f, 149, 172, 221f
Cooper, R., 19n
Copleston, F., 208

Coste, R., 5n
Cottier, G. M.-M, 178n

Darwin, C., 102n
Davis, C., 4n
Dean, T., 6n
Dietzgen, J., 103
Dostoevsky, F., 277
Durkheim, E., 184, 203n

Engels, F., 10–3, 52, 80f, 103, 106, 109f, 113, 119, 121f, 125, 154, 156, 163, 165ff, 212ff, 241, 262ff, 266f, 273n
Evans, D., 4n

Fernbach, D., 11, 14n, 257, 259
Fierro, A., 5, 17
Feuerbach, L., 10f, 36, 39, 55, 57f, 60, 62, 88, **93–104**, 119, 139, **141**, 145ff, 153, **154–6**, 160f, 166, 168, 177f, 181, 184, 195, 206, 211, 221
Findlay, J. N., 146, 207n
Flew, A., 88–9, 93, 101, 136
Foster, M. B., 151
Fourier, C., 234f, 239
Frankfurt School 4, 110

Garaudy, R., 4, 30, 88, 186
Giddens, A., 17, 19, 60, 112n, 126, 129, 153
Girardi, G., 5, 233f
Goldmann, L., 272
Gollwitzer, H., 243
Gouldner, A. W., 129, 134, 275
Gramsci, A., 105

Gutierrez, G., 4n, 16

Habermas, J., 4
Hawkin, D. J., 154n
Hebblethwaite, P., 4n, 17n, 35
Hegel, G. W. F., 12, 19, 22, 36, **38f**, 44, 52, **55–60**, 63ff, **68–71**, 73, 79, 88, **93–104**, 106f, 115, 120, 126, 139f, 143, 146f, 155, 158, 166, 169–72, 175, 177, 181, 195, 202, 207f, 210, 216, 221, 223f, 226, 236n, **244–7**, 254, 263ff, 276, 277n, 288
Held, D., 4n
Hess, M., 11, 91
Holmes, J. D., 14
Horkheimer, M., 4, 18, 183
Hromadka, J., 5f
Hyppolite, J., 170n

James, W., 81
Jameson, F., 207
Jay, M., 4n

Kant, I., 18, 221n
Kautsky, K., 3, 13, 159, 161, 214
Kitchin, D. K., 4n
Knox, T. M., 39
Kolakowski, L., 6, 7n, 12f, 15f, 18f, 28, **30–1**, 36f, 39, 64, 77, **80–4**, 90f, **108–9**, 116n, 121f, 135, 142, 146, 185, 214n, 221, **227f**, 233, 248, 252ff, 255, 267, 274
Korsch, K., 12, 27, 64, 84n, 106, 234
Kruschev, N., 14

Lassalle, F., 54, 235
Leavis, F. R., 26
Lecompte, D., 22n
Lee, F. N., 253n
Lenin, V. I., 10, 13, 22, 28, 55, 77, 80f, 84n, 101f, 105f, 109, 127, 129, 135, 139, **159f**, 163, 212, 241, 250, 259, 262
Levisky, I., 4n
Lewis, J., 4n
Lobkowicz, N., 100n, 154, 156, 166
Lochman, J. M., 6
Loisy, A. F., 276

Lonergan, B. J. F., 292
Luijpen, W. A., 4n
Lukács, G., 13, 17f, 20, 29, 90, 100, 103n, 105ff, **109f, 172**, 181, 198, 207, 213n, 217n, 239n, 270, 274n, 275, 277
Lukes, S., 203n

McCarthy, T., 4n
MacKinnon, D. M., 14, 108, 146
McKown, D. B., 91, 153n, 154, 165, 166f
McLellan, D., 9, 12f, 15n, 17ff, 22, 36ff, 47, 66, 78, 90f, 94, 103, 114f, 122, 135, 153, 162f, 214, 224, 239f, 244, 257n, 263
Mach, E., 135
Machoveč, M., 3
Mandel, E., 241
Mannheim, K., 125n, 131, 235n, 240
Markús, G., 82n, 232, 247, 252
Mehring, F., 121n
Mészáros, I., 8n, 12n, 19n, 25n, 98n, 101n, **169–73**, 176, **187f**, **190f**, 192, **198ff**, 205, 207, 235n, 253ff, 265, 275, 279
Metz, J.-B., 4
Mill, J., 177, 240
Miller, A., 4n
Miranda, J. P., 4n
Moltmann, J., 4

Newman, J. H., 3, 14, **93–4**, 253, 272n
Nicolaus, M., 13n, 18
Niebuhr, R., 4n

Ollman, B., 170n, 241
Owen, R., 235

Pannenberg, W., 4, 101n
Pius X 28
Plamenatz, J., 19n, 36, 59, 89, 112n, 125f
Plato 198
Plekhanov, G. V., 13, 28, 29, 106, 121, 207, 214
Plotinus 171n
Polanyi, K., 4n

Popper, K., **65–71**, 229, 252
Proudhon, P., 21, 53, 103f, 223n

Rahner, K., 143, 182n
Raines, J. C., 6n
Raven, C., 4n
Reagan, R., 6
Reding, M., 28n
Ricardo, D., 217
Richards, I. A., 26
Romeyer, B., 154n
Rosdolsky, R., 19n, 248n
Rosen, Z., 154n, 158n
Rotenstreich, N., 171n
Ruge, A., 154, 162

Saint-Simon, H., 234f
Sartre, J.-P., 27f, 94, **105–8**, 151, 180
Scheler, M., 110
Schillebeeckx, E., 4
Schleiermacher, F. D. E., 142

Schmidt, A., 70, 77, 100–3, 165f, 180, 266n, 274
Segundo, J.-L., 4n
Seliger, M., 112n, 125f, 130

Sharratt, B., 19n
Smith, A., 217
Stalin, J., 13, 27, 105
Stein, W., 261f, 268, 278
Steiner, G., 268ff
Stirner, M., 38
Strauss, D. F., 38
Sweezy, P. 12n

Taylor, C., 39, 55f, 65, 70, 80, 98, 241, 247, 265
Thompson, E. P., 11, **20f**, 25, **26–35**, 62, 102, 105, **117**, 122, 131n, 141f, 145, 149, 195f, 214, 222, 249, 276, 278, 280, 283, 290
Tillich, P., 4n
Tucker, R., 7f, 12, 244

Valéry, P., 108
Vatican II 75, 237

Weber, M., 233
West, C., 4n
Wetter, G. A., 3n, 166n
Wicker, B., 126
Williams, R., 26, 112n, **113–20**, 129, 268f

INDEX OF SUBJECTS

'Abolition' *see* Transcendence

Aesthetic theory *see* Art; Literature; Rationalism

Alienation 14, 18–9, 22, 44–6, 169–94; economic 18, 90–1, 176–7, 179; and estrangement 171–3, 175, 189, 191, 245–6; four aspects of 170–1, 191; from God 177–8, 180, 182–3, 187–9, 256, 285; history of concept of 171–2; 'human' 176, 178; from human beings 36, 89–90, 171, 175, 178–80, 187–8, 191, 273; and the 'human condition' 171, 175, 186–91, 187–8, 191; Marx's terminology concerning 173; from nature 36, 170, 174–5, 179–80, 187–8, 191, 273; political 57, 166, 176, 178; religious 18, 57, 90–2, 157, 163, 166, 176–86; from self 170, 173–5, 275; and sin 188–91; *see also* Atheism; Capitalism; Dependence; God; Money; Objectification; Redemption; Transcendence

Anthropomorphism 84; and alienation 181, 183f, 186; critique of 161, 183; and idolatry 119, 158; and iconoclasm 158; and objectifications of God 183

Apologetics and ideology 21, 128; and theology 5

Appearance: of freedom 132, 271; and necessity 271; and reality 73–7, 129, 211, 271, dialectic of 51–63, 64–8, 73–7, 108, 198, identity of 77, 120–1, 157, 285; and truth 55, 73–8, 84, 158,

coincidence of in Jesus Christ 76f, identity of in Jesus Christ 76

Art 162–3; and ideology 197, 201, 207, 209; and knowledge 196–8, 203–4; and literature 201, 204, 207; *see also* Autonomy; Liturgy

Atheism 6, 17, 146, 154–5, 162, 285–6, 288; and alienation 57, 84; and materialism 88, 90, 96, 136; 'practical atheism' and deism 137, 156

Atonement, theories of 146

Autonomy 182, 278; of art 163, 195, 197–8, 200, 209; of literature 163, 195, 198, 200, 209; of religion 163, 195, 200; of theology 5, 134, 197; of theory 43, 78, 86, 95, 112, 120, 123, 222, 226; *see also* Dependence

Bondage *see* Freedom

Calvary 161, 178; and 'determination' 119, 138; and self-destruction of God's image 119

Capitalism 224, 228; and alienation 19, 45–6, 89–92, 169–72, 174–5, 179, 187–8, 190–1, 199–200; and Christianity 140–1, 159; and the 'fetishism of commodities' 195, 205; and ideology 120, 127–9; and the objectification of wealth 90, 202–3; *see also* Transcendence

Christian Marxism 284–6, 288–91

Christian-Marxist dialogue 4–5, 283–4, 291–2

Christianity: as iconoclastic 132,

158; and idealism 61, 105, 111, 132, 135–6, 139–45, 147–9, 151–2, 153, 160, 285–6; as interpretative 29, 61, 71, 146–8, 185, 285; and materialism 88, 104, 135–44, 146, 148–52, 285–6; and the organization of freedom 276–7; and politics 6, 31, 160–1, 166, 181, 236–9, 261–2, 288–90; as tradition 32–3, 291; as transformative 123, 146–8, 278–9; truthfulness of 29, 55, 85–6, 132–4, 151, 213, 285; see also Capitalism; Ideology; Judaism; Religion; Utopianism

Christology 177; and eschatology 77, 143–4; and the problem of God 186; and redemptive Spirit 279; see also Incarnation; Jesus Christ

Church 132 and kingdom 75, 158; as organisation 277; as sacrament 75, 237, 252; social policy of 237–8, 289–90

Class: conflict of 128–9, 159, 190, 213, 257, abolition of 164, 243, 247, 258; consciousness 109–10, 113–14; rule 43–6, 114, 132, 229–30, 234–5, 240, 258–9; see also Proletariat

Comedy see Optimism and Tragedy

Consciousness: ambivalence of 116; and being 57–8, 160, 162, 195; as 'determined' 95, 118, 141–2, 146, 160; and language 44, 82; and life 38, 41–3, 95, 97, 112–117, 120–3, 129, 141, 146; modes of 125, 147, 196; see also Class; Ideology; Redemption

Contemplativity 5, 60, 62, 103

Conversion 138; and moral transformation 148

Correctness see Truth

Cross, doctrine of 67, 119, 182, 192

Death: and dependence on God 193; and freedom 192, 238, 264, 267–8, 271; of God 119, 178; as insurmountable barrier 84, 192; and resurrection 85–6, 192–4,

280; see also Jesus Christ; Mortality; Necessity

Dependence 116; and autonomy 178–9, 182; on death 194; on God 143, 182, 193, 278; and need; 182–3; see also Alienation

Despair 150; and hope 161, 269–70, 277–8; and optimism 266, 268–72, 277, 280, 286–7; and tragedy 268–9; see also Transcendence

Determination 117–19, 121, 141, 146, 188, 241–2 see also Calvary; Consciousness; Freedom

Dialectic 28–9; and epistemology 77; and explanation 70; Hegel's compared with Marx's 70, 95–8, 100–1; and interpretation 70; and science 17, 222–8; theology as 144, 156; see also Appearance; History; Materialism; Revelation

Dogmatism: and critical thought 15, 27–9, 34, 106, 109; and idealism 106

Egotism 236, 258; and the freedom of Christ 260–1; 'necessity' of 274; and the organization of freedom 278, 280; and self-mastery 266, 273–4, 276; see also Transcendence

Empiricism: and materialism 41–2, 99, 106, 211, 243, 247; and positivism 61–3, 99; and religion 61–2, 190; see also Realism

Epistemology see Knowledge

Eschatology 46, 77, 277; and the 'birth' of humanity 251, 253–7, 267, 270; and the end of history 243, 255–6; and hope 72, 143–4, 170, 231, 238–9, 254, 257, 261, 270, 289; and redemption 254–7, 261, 270; and utopianism 238–9, 257; see also Jesus Christ; Kingdom of God; Revolution

Estrangement see Alienation

Ethics, Christian 189

Eucharist 132; and hope 239, 251–3; and prophecy 252–3; and

social action 239; symbolism of 239

Faith 131, 208; confession of 184, 286, as self-involving 86–7; and hope 69, 71, 85–6, 143, 150, 161, 252–3, 270, 272, 288; and prediction 71, 233; and reason 14–15, 155–6, 272–3; and social criticism 183; and trust 71, 86, 193, 270; see also Knowledge; Narrative; Prayer; Quietism
Fetishism 168, 177, 179, 185, 195, 205
Freedom 14, 248; 'absolute' 132, 264–5, 275–6; and bondage 59, 148, 157, 238, 245–8, 256–8, 260–2; determination of 267; 275–6; organization of 249, 273, 275–9, 288; and redemptive love 278; realm of 265; and the rights of man 263; of thought 58–9; and truth 39–40, 280; see also Appearance; Death; Egotism; Necessity
Future: expectation concerning 137–8, 165, 194, 231, 237, 239–43, 250–1, 256–7, 267, 274, 279; openness of 261, 268, 270; predictions of 46, 69, 71, 76–7, 228–30, 232–3, 248–9, 251, 253–6; unpredictability of 188

Gethsemane 62, 119, 138, 161
God: agency of 186, as alternative to human and natural 136–8, and natural explanation 136–8, and passion of Christ 178, 260, 262; as 'alien being' 37, 57, 160, 177, 181–2, 184, 260, 270, 286; appearance of: in Christ 76, 144, 183–5, 189, in human language 138, 141, 185; experience of 133, 142, as never unmediated 138; fidelity of 149, 192–3, 260, 279, 286, 289; images of 119, 155–6, 160–1, 166, 180–1, 183–5; impoverishment of, and human enrichment 178; incomprehensibility of 156, 167–

8, 183; knowledge of 17, 133, as given, not possessed 149–50, liturgical expression of 206; and Logos 61, 139, 143; 'mercy' and 'judgement' of 249, 260–2; names of 145, 168; power of 177, 181–2, 289; as projection 141, 168; the question of 83–4, 180–6, 285–8; as referring expression 141; Spirit of 137, 139, 145, 147, 279; as symbol of alienation 83, 160, transcendence of 31, 178, 183, 288–9; as ultimate object of trust 136; Word of 145, become flesh 143–4; see also Calvary; Dependence; Grace; Kingdom of God, Incarnation; Liturgy; Money; Objectification; State, the; Theodicy
Gospel 123, 151; fidelity to 148, 238, 276–7; of hope 231; of Jesus Christ 31; purity of 238; subversive power of 158, 213, 276–7
Grace: conversion by 148; cooperation with 233; and dependence 182; and human action 138; and transcendence of sin 188–9; as transformative 123, 150, 188, 278

Hermeneutics see Interpretation
Historicism 71, 122; and providence 65–7; and science 68, 105–6, 214, 227; two senses of 64–8, 70, 188; see also Theodicy
History: 'birth' of 250–7, 275; as dialectic 16–17, 51, 55–7, 60–1, 63, 70, 96–8, 101–3, 106–7, 202–4, 240; and eschatology 243, 251, 253–6, 268–9; meaning of 61, 65–71, 193, 271; natural 40, 101; see also Jesus Christ; Kingdom of God; Materialism; Metaphysics; Nature; Necessity; Philosophy; Providence; Revelation
Hope 77, 149, 161, 190, 193–4, 248, 267, 271, 274, 279, 289–90; and certainty 67–9, 71; and the

interrogative mood 271–2, 287; of Jesus Christ 279–80; and optimism 193, 241–2, 249, 254, 263, 269–73, 277–8, 287–8; rationality of 69; and tragedy 268–72; universality of Christian 238; *see also* Despair; Eschatology; Eucharist; Faith; Knowledge; Prediction; Utopianism

Human existence 180, 186–91, 199, 251, 256, 266–7, 279; limits of 284, 287; as the meeting of needs 82–3; as natural existence 79–80, 82, 100–1, 274, 287; as 'victimhood' and 'agency' 249; *see also* Jesus Christ

Human nature *see* Human existence *and* Man

Humanity 14, 82, 89–90, 143–4, 279–80; 'true' humanity 76–7; *see also* Human existence; Jesus Christ; Man; Work

Humanism 11, 20, 99, 187

Idealism 207, 253; absolute 62–3, 101; Hegelian 10–13, 15–16, 19–20, 22, 36, 37–9, 55–8, 60, 64–5, 88, 95–7, 102–4, 138, 172, 265; and idolatry 150; left-hegelian 38–40, 96–7, 99; and materialism 18, 21, 34, 38, 55, 88, 94–100, 102–3, 105–8, 110, 112–13, 135, 148, 227; and natural science 100–1; and power 110, 149–51; and religion 38, 55, 60, 123–4, 135–6; speculative 42, 97; structuralist 21; and theology 62, 103–4, 105, 108, 118, 135–6, 139–45, 147–52, 285–6 *see also* Dogmatism; Ideology; Interpretation; Metaphysics; Philosophy; Rationalism; Realism; Tragedy

Ideology: Christian discourse as 125–7, 131–2; and class conflict 128–9; critique of 37–42, 129, 132–3, 198, 209; and error 125–6, 130; as explanation 16, 128; and false consciousness 125; and

idealism 126–7; 'ideological forms' 31, 118, 123, 127, 163, 166, 207, post-revolutionary correlates of 154, 163, 166; and science 16–17, 125, 130–1, 133, 197–8, 207; as socially integrative 39, 128–32; and 'superstructure' 113–21, 123, 127, 131, 142, 154, 162–3, 195; and theology 5, 123–4, 132–3, 150–1; and utopia 270; *see also* Apologetics; Art; Capitalism; Knowledge; Literature; Philosophy

Incarnation: and christology 143–4, 186; and the negation of the finite 143; and the realization of God 261; redemptive, as transformative of circumstances 147–8, as transformative of consciousness 147–8; *see also* God, Word of

Interest: common 45; general 45, 128, 132; particular 45, 128, 132, 157, 257–9, 261–2, 265, 270, 289; universal, 257–9, 290, of Christianity 261, of proletariat 116, 258–9

Interpretation 25, 61; and explanation 25, 69–70; and idealism 70, 145, 147–8; as production 62–3; redemptive 29, 146–8, 271; religious 61, 123, 138, 290; and theology 5, 29, 138, 146–7; and transformation 146–8; *see also* Christianity; Dialectic; Theology

Jesus Christ: agency of 260–2; birth of 144; death of 31, 62, 178, 192–3, 256, 259–61, 273, 280; eschatological significance of 143, 255–6, 261; following of 189–90, 285; history of as not yet ended 193, 256; as image of humanity 279–80; as mediator 177; self-conception of 76; as social construct 76; sinlessness of 261; as 'true individual' 76; as 'truly God and truly man' 144,

177, 185–6; work of 192–3, 287; as 'victim' and 'agent' 260; see also Calvary; Christology; Egotism; Gethsemane; God, appearance of; Gospel; Hope; Incarnation; Resurrection; Revelation
Judaism and Christianity 91

Kingdom of God 31, 158, 233; and eschatology 255; and history 75, 239; see also Religion
Knowledge: and belief 215, 271–2; and construction 149–50; and discovery 106; as donation 61, 106–7, 149; and faith 150, 155; first-order 131, 215; and hope 69, 150, 272; and ideology 15–16, 36, 37–8, 60–1, 130–1, 133; interpretative and explanatory 69; and literature 197; modes of 42, 69, 130–1, 196–7, 206–7; mythology as mode of 203; and opinion 79, 130, 215, 220; as possession 107, 149–50, 272; and production 62–3; as relationship 56–7, 82; scientific 15–18, 42, 69, 78, 130–1, 133, 155, 197–8, 203, 207–8, 211–12; as task and responsibility 107; and theory 79, 197, 226–7; and vision 61–2; see also Art; Dialectic; God; Reality

Labour: division of 41–3, 45–7, 115–16, 175; and labour-power 54, 174–5, 196; see also Work
Liberalism, theological and political 213
Literature: and ideology 197–8, 207, 209; literary criticism 26, 162–3, 196–7; literary expression as cognitive 204, 207; literary production 196–7, 199; see also Autonomy; Knowledge; Theory
Liturgy: as art 204–6, 208–9; reform of 205, and social transformation 205; and the 'richness' of God 205–6; see also God, knowledge of

Logos see God
Love 155, 157, 289
crucifixion as cost of 192; redemptive 189, 278

Man 14, 287; 'essence' of 266–9, as 'true community' 240–2, 251; as image of God 184–5; and nature 40, 80, 82–3, 99–103, 195, 266–7; 'true' 76–7; see also Human existence; Humanity
Marxism: as doctrine 26–30, 33–4; and existentialism 27, 108, 190; as heritage 26, 30–3; as heuristic 94, 107–8, 122, 241; meanings of 16, 24–35, 290; as method 17, 26, 29–30, 32–3; orthodox 13, 18, 29–30, 105, 122, 145, 186; scientific 7, 10, 15–16, 71, 210–22, 226–9, 231; as system 28, 283; as theory 3, 5, 10, 14, 16–18, 20, 27, 42 , 195–6, 210, 229, 283; as tradition, 8, 26, 30, 32–4; as Weltanschauung 94; see also Christian Marxism; Christian-Marxist dialogue
Materialism 88–104; absolute 101, 136; contemplative 146; dialectical 13, 16, 101, 103, 106, 139; as explanation 70, 102; historical 11, 27, 40–1, 97–8, 101–3, 115, 117, 121–3, 162, 222, 240; and humanism 99; Marx's compared with Feuerbach's 10, 39, 88, 95, 98–100, 102–3, 139, 146; as mechanistic reductionism 93, 113, 116; metaphysical 88, 93–4, 101, 103, 106–7, 136; methodological 41, 94, 104, 110, 217; monistic 101–2, 121–2, 136; as obsession with possession 89–90, 92; ontological 104, 106–7; and the primacy of the spiritual 92–3; see also Atheism; Christianity; Empiricism; Idealism; Naturalism; Realism; Science
Meaning: creation of 83; mediation of 63; and truth 61, 83; see also History

Mediation 56–7, 177, 182; solution of theoretical problems mediated through practice 252, 276–7, 279; structures of 157–8; *see also* Meaning

Metaphysics 193; and history 70, 122; and idealism 106; and theology 208; *see also* Materialism

Monasticism 239

Money: as 'alien mediator' 177; as expression of alienation 45, 89–91, 93, 136; as God 90–2

Mortality: freedom as coincident with 192, 267, 271, 273; individual and social 84, 192, 268–9, 271; *see also* Death; Resurrection; Transcendence

Narrative 206–7; credal confession as 67, 144; discourse of faith as 55, 63, 197, autobiographical 68–9, 133, incomplete 71, provisional 69; liturgy as dramatic enactment of 208; and theology 147; *see also* Theory

Naturalism 5, and materialism 99–103, 104, 136, 181, 285–6; *see also* Realism

Nature 266, 271; and humanity 19, 100, 120, 191–2, 200; as product of man 40, 80, 82–3, 195; as resistance 82, 137; and society 100, 274; *see also* Alienation; History; Necessity

Necessity: 'external', abolition of 264, 273–4, 278, death as 266, 269; and freedom, 191–2, 249, 262–4, 267, 273–4, coincidence of 265–6, 271, 273–4; historical 188, 232–3, 260–1; natural 266–7; realm of 263, 265–7; social 188, 266; *see also* Egotism

Objectification 75, 157–8, 200; and alienation 98, 172–3, 180–5, 200, 202–3; of God 180–5, 270, 286; and production 202

Optimism: and belief in progress 241–2, 271, 275–6, 278; and

comedy 268, 273, 277; and tragedy 268–9; and utopianism 240–3, 250, 270; *see also* Despair; Hope

Pacifism 261–2

Philosophy: and history 36–8, 60, 102; and idealism 11–14, 36–42, 70, 105–6, 126, 139–40, 143, 220; and ideology 11, 15–16, 35–44, 126, 219; and science 20, 42, 78–9, 211, 218, 220, 227; and theology 28–9, 38, 55, 208

Political economy 21, 53, 128, 160, 216–30, 231, 284

Positivism *see* Empiricism

Poverty: 'absolute' 200, 250; consciousness of 245; and dispossession 201–2; human 199, 202; liturgical 205–6; and the religious life 206; revolutionary side of 234–5, 237; virtue of 206; *see also* God, impoverishment of

Pragmatism 292; and truth 79–81, 83–4, 87; *see also* Prometheanism

Prayer 287; discourse of resurrection as 86, 193, 271; language of faith as 193, 270; and the openness of the future 261, 270

Prediction 68, 70; and expectation 46, 231–3, 240–2, 248–9; and hope 69, 233; *see also* Faith; Prophecy; Science

Production: as aim of mankind 201–2; forces of 116, 120, 196; modes of 40–1, 43, 45, 54, 59–60, 62–3, 90–2, 112–13, 115, 120, 170, 173–4, 187, 190, 196, 199, 214, 224, 241; primacy of 218–20; relations of 90, 103, 112, 115–21, 123, 174, 199–200, 217–18; 'scientific' treatment of 196–7, 217–23; *see also* Interpretation; Knowledge; Literature; Objectification; Wealth; Work

Proletariat: and the abolition of 'external necessity' 274–5; dictatorship of 259, 274; as instrument of redemption 190,

244, 246, 257–60, 262, 264;
mythological character of
concept of 248–9; revolutionary
role and destiny of 46, 52–3,
109–10, 243–5, 247–8; as ruling
class 45–6, 234–5, 240; and
wealth 244–5; see also Interest,
universal
Prometheanism 180, 182, 264; and
pragmatism 80–1, 83, 87
Prophecy 151, 261; and prediction
71–2, 228–30, 233, 251–3, 257
Providence, and the meaning of
history 38, 65–7, 68, 71, 138

Quietism: historical 118–19; and
faith 137–8; see also
Determination

Rationalism 156; and aesthetic
theory 195–204, 207; and
idealism 145
Rationality 64–5, 69, 165; and
actuality 39; criteria of 121, 134;
see also Hope
Realism 257, 277; and empiricism
211; and idealism 37–8, 39, 62,
198; and materialism 40–2, 107;
and naturalism 198, 205
Reality 37–40, 211, 233–4; and
actuality 39–40; and knowledge
15–16, 55–6, 203–4; mutability
of 223, 270, 277; as
preconstituted 60; as process 38,
51; and truth 38, 73–8, 82, 84;
see also Appearance
Redemption 7; and alienation 22,
170, 188–9, 192–3, 254–6, 264; of
consciousness 147; 'first
premises' of doctrine of 189–90;
and liberation 271; 'total
redemption of humanity' 157,
246, 261, 278; as transformation
123, 146–7, 188, 278, 292; work
of 287; of the world 147–8; see
also Eschatology; Incarnation;
Interpretation; Love; Proletariat;
Spirit
Reification 89–90, 165, 169, 172,
195

Relations see Production
Religion: abolition of 156–8, 164,
165–7; 'absolute' 147, 166;
artificial 59; content of 155–6,
162–3, 166, 167–8, 195, 287; as
error 166–7; as form of art 197;
as human construct 44, 155, 157,
168; as illusion 156, 158–9, 162,
176; and the kingdom of God
158; natural 165, 167; as 'opium'
158–62; post-revolutionary
correlate of 154; as protest 161–
2; 'social' 165, 167; see also
Alienation; Autonomy;
Christianity; Empiricism;
Idealism; Interpretation;
Theology
Resurrection 270; and human
liberation 248–9, 271; of Jesus
Christ, 260, 273, 280, truth-
conditions of 85–7; and the
meaning of history 193, 271; as
transcendence of mortality 192–
3, 271; see also Prayer
Revelation: and history 29, 66–7;
as occurring in death of Christ
193; and Marxian dialectic 51–3,
55, 63
Revolution 12, 52; and education
191; and evolution 164, 288; and
justice 260, 261–2; 'last' 231,
247–9, 253–8, 269; and mercy
249, 262; 'revolutionary
organization' 275–8; two phases
of 274–6, 289; see also Poverty;
Proletariat
Richness see Wealth

Sacrament 167, 183; as symbol of
hope 157, 252; see also Church
Salvation 123
Sanctity 123
Science: and belief 215; criteria of
210–11; and explanation 212,
214; as 'investigation' and
'presentation' 219, 221–8; laws
of 214–15, 227; materialist 11,
42, 105–6, 218, 226; and the
method of political economy
216–30, 232; natural and human

100–1, 228; and opinion 215;
and prediction 228–30, 231–3;
and scientism 81, 110, 214–15;
and truth 78, 212–13, 216; unity
of 218; and *Wissenschaft* 42, 215,
220, 226, 228; *see also* Dialectic;
Historicism; Idealism;
Knowledge; Philosophy;
Socialism; Theory; Utopianism
Self-mastery *see* Egotism; Ideology
Sense: emancipation of 198; of
'having' 199, 250; and thought
198–201, 204, 206–7
Social messianism 258–9, 261–2,
289
Socialism: scientific 10, 211–12,
228–30, 234, 241; utopian 211–
12, 234–5
Spirit 97; and reason 139;
redemptive 147, 279; *see also* God
State, the 45, 52; 'abolition' of
163–5, 166–7; and God 56–8,
166
Subject: and object 102, 141–2,
172, 179; and predicate 57–8, 60,
99–100, 104, 107, 119, 139, 141,
144, 149, 162, 168; *see also*
Theology
Supersession *see* Transcendence

Theodicy: and historicism 65; and
the justification of misery 271
Theology: apophatic 156, 168; and
'broken' logic 144; as critical
reflection on Christian practice
6, 133–4, 153–4, 208, 251–2,
286–7; and the critique of
ideology 132–3; 'determination'
of 118–19; 'grammar' of 146,
193; as instrument of power
150–1; interrogative character of
5; 'liberation theology' 4; and
the primacy of experience 99–
100, 142, 149, 285; and religion
133–4, 156–7, 292;
responsibilities of 5–6, 208; and
social criticism 161, 177, 183;
'subject' and 'object' of 104,
141–2, 144, 149, 179; and theory
133–4, 277; *see also* Apologetics;

Autonomy; Dialectic; Idealism;
Ideology; Interpretation;
Metaphysics; Narrative;
Philosophy
Theory: and art 196–201, 203–4,
206–9; and literature 196–8, 199,
201, 204, 207; and narrative 133;
and practice 78–9, 84–5, 99,
106–8, 110, 133–4, 141, 150,
153–4, 170, 193, 196–7, 209, 256,
270, 276–7, 279; and science
207, 212–13, 226–7, 231; and
symbolism 195–209; *see also*
Autonomy; Knowledge;
Theology
Thought *see* Consciousness
Tragedy 271; and comedy 193,
268, 273; and idealism 108; and
the openness of the future 268;
transcendence of 269; *see also*
Despair; Hope; Optimism
Transcendence: of alienation 5, 71,
98, 157, 169–70, 172, 176, 180,
182–3, 187–94, 195, 198, 201,
241, 245, 249, 254–6, 273, 288;
of capitalism 17, 170, 172, 191,
200, 214, 229, 240–1, 243, 254;
'necessity' of 187–8, 284; of
despair 278; of egotism 238, 275,
278, 288; of mortality 192–4,
271; as process 170; of sin 188–
90; *see also* Class; God; Necessity;
Tragedy
Truth 61–2; as commodity 107–8,
149–50; 'correctness' and 84–6,
105, 285; as created 83; criteria
of, 80, 'objectivity' and
'subjectivity' of 73, 79–80, 82,
98; as possession 5, 107–8, 149–
50; and reality 38, 73–8, 82, 84,
158; as relationship 73, 84, 87,
272; the 'true individual' 74, 75–
7, 98; the 'true society' 74–7;
two theories of 80–1, 84; *see also*
Appearance; Freedom; Meaning;
Pragmatism; Science

Utopianism 18–19, 46, 275, 279;
and Christianity 206, 231, 236–
9, 289; as constructive protest

235–6, 252–3; and hope 72, 143, 231, 238–9, 270; 'prophetic' 239, 251–3, 261; and science 211–12, 234–5; sectarian 235, 237–9; *see also* Eschatology; Idealism; Optimism

Wealth: as aim of production 90, 175, 201; appearance of 201; consciousness of 245; 'human' 199–200, 202, 250–1, 278; liturgical 205–6; objective 175, 200; and poverty 46, 182, 200–2, 206, 245; *see also* Capitalism: Proletariat

Work: as constitutive of humanity 40–1, 83, 98, 108, 119, 173, 220, 247–8, 262; and desire 246; as dialogue between need and object 83; as productive 173; as transformative 103; *see also* Jesus Christ, work of